D1808606

NMAA COOKS

Compiled by
NURSING MOTHERS' ASSOCIATION OF AUSTRALIA

5 Glendale Street,
Nunawading, Vic. 3131
Phone: 878 3304—Counselling
877 5011—Enquiries

First printed 1975
Reprinted June 1976
Second edition October 1976
Revised September 1977
Reprinted 1978
Reprinted 1979
Reprinted 1980
Reprinted 1982
Reprinted twice 1983
Reprinted 1985
Reprinted 1986
Reprinted 1988
Reprinted 1989
© 1975 Nursing Mothers' Association of Australia

ISBN 0 9597108 1 7

Printed by The Book Printer, Victoria

 NMAA Cooks is published by the
NURSING MOTHERS' ASSOCIATION OF AUSTRALIA

- Nursing Mothers' is a Self-Help organisation
- We encourage and support women who wish to breastfeed
- We have Groups of mothers throughout Australia
- Breastfeeding Counselling is available throughout Australia to all mothers at all times.

Would you like to support Nursing Mothers' by:

☐ Becoming a member

☐ Buying a product from our large Mail Order range of goods for Mother and Babies

☐ Making a donation

Information will be sent on request

Latest Mail Order Catalogue will be sent on request

Thank you

Please tick one or more boxes and forward to:

**NURSING MOTHERS' ASSOCIATION OF AUSTRALIA
PO BOX 231
NUNAWADING VIC 3131**

NAME ....

ADDRESS ....

.... POST CODE: ....

TELEPHONE: ....

Enclosed is my cheque $ .... (payable to NMAA)
OR please charge my—

☐ Bankcard   ☐ Visa Card   ☐ Master Card
☐ American Express with $........

☐☐☐☐☐ ☐☐☐☐☐ ☐☐☐☐☐ ☐☐☐☐☐

Exp Date .... Signature ....

CONTENTS

ABOUT THIS BOOK

AT LAST THE NMAA RECIPE BOOK . . . *NMAA Cooks* has been "in the works" for the past 11 years, in fact it was mentioned in the minutes of an early meeting of the Founding Members. Like so many other aspects of our Association's development and success, it stems back to the initial inspiration and encouragement of Founder Mary Paton. Over the years there have been bursts of enthusiasm to complete it, but always something more important came along and the sheets of recipes already collected went back into their box under someone's bed.

When I retired as NMAA President in 1973, I undertook to fill my "spare" time completing the book. Founding Member Jan Barry with Jenny Jordan, Jennie Meares and Myra Sawyer formed a sub-committee to help me. Little did we realize what we had undertaken! The few months of work we envisaged stretched to over a year, and the past weeks have seen frantic activity as the recipes were typed, checked, re-typed and placed in order. We hope you enjoy the results!

ABOUT THE BOOK . . . This is a book for busy people. There are quick and easy recipes, and some more exotic ones if you have the urge to spend extra time in preparation and presentation.

Our system of numbering recipes consecutively through the book is designed to make referring to a recipe easier; for example (R 432) indicates the reference is to Recipe number 432.

This is a metric book; however, as few of us can re-equip our kitchen entirely, we have included standard imperial measures in brackets. Conversions are not exact, but approximate—cooking is more an art than a science! Conversions are based on the recommendations of the Australian Metric Conversion Board. Wherever possible, measures are in cups, tablespoons and teaspoons. All measures are level. Can sizes are approximate because of discrepancies in sizes and labelling and also because some manufacturers are in the process of changing to the metric system.

We suggest that first you read carefully the definitions of cooking terms included at the end.

In writing this book we have been mindful of the importance of good family nutrition, while purposely avoiding adherence to any particular school of thought. We believe that it is a balanced diet which is important, and endorse the statement by Margaret Corden that if emphasis is placed on the five essential food groups the desire for less nutritious foods containing sugar and refined and processed foods will diminish.

We have not included a special section for recipes for young children. NMAA's policy is to encourage children of all ages to partake of the family fare. If it's not acceptable to the family, why feed it to your toddler!

THOSE WHO MADE IT POSSIBLE. . .

As with all projects undertaken by Nursing Mothers' Association of Australia, *NMAA Cooks* has been made possible by the efforts and enthusiasm of many members working in a voluntary capacity.

To the many who typed and re-typed sheets of recipes, our sincere appeciation. We would never have done it without you!

We acknowledge the early work on the book of Jenny Jordan, Founding Member Glenise Francis and Joyce Culpan.

We thank NMAA's dietetic advisor, Margaret Corden, for her preface on nutrition.

Margaret Power is responsible for the cover and the delightful illustrations which help make this book different; the explanatory sketches are the work of Margaret Mitsikas. We also thank Ailsa Jacques for her assistance with the art work. Beverley Rae, as Executive Editor, has provided the expertise and encouragement at the time we most needed it.

Without the help of Rosemary Balmford, I doubt that you could have found your way through this book! Its continuity and clarity is a result of her eye for detail and her command of English, aided and abetted by her editing pencil!!

To the members all over Australia who contributed recipes, our thanks. It was our intention to include contributors' names at the end of each recipe but what do you do when you get 28 recipes for oat biscuits and 52 for ice-cream . . .? As we combined many recipes and altered others, we have listed all contributors together.

Finally, cooking is fun. We have tried to provide not just a collection of recipes but a lively companion. We hope *NMAA Cooks* gives you new ideas, reminds you of some old ones and takes pride of place on your kitchen shelf.

Judith Laird,
November 1975.

SECOND EDITION
Jennie Meares was responsible for the revision for this second edition, first published in 1976, which incorporated some further recipes and ideas.

LET'S LOOK AT FAMILY NUTRITION

Nutritious meals need never be dull. Even the busiest mother, with a little thought and care, can serve attractive meals varying in colour, flavour and texture. The majority of recipes in this book should be suitable for all members of the family although some of the strongly flavoured, very salty or heavily spiced dishes may offend the sensitive taste buds of the under three year olds. In such cases an alternative more simple dish may be served for them, but should a child request the adult dish, small amounts, to taste, should not be harmful.

Important components of foods are called nutrients. Proteins, fats and carbohydrates provide energy which is now measured in kilojoules (kJ). One gram of fat provides 37 kJ; 1g protein 17 kJ; 1g carbohydrates 16 kJ and 1g alcohol yields 29 kJ. Protein is also necessary for growth and tissue repair.

A child up to about the age of 9 years needs approximately 35-40 grams protein per day. This amount can be achieved with 600ml milk, 2 slices of bread, ⅓ cup cooked oatmeal or ½-¾ cup of other cereal, 1 egg or 20g cheese plus the amount of meat present in a small lamb chop, together with small amounts of vegetables. I'm sure that the vast majority of Australan children over five years have a lot more than that. At periods of rapid growth, appetite also increases so the extra protein required is normally taken, unless hunger is completely satisfied with sweets and confectionery.

The protein needs of adults are not that much higher than a child's relative to their size. Generally they need about half the quantity of milk and the other 15-20 grams of protein required can be obtained by doubling the above quantities of bread, cereal and meat.

People do not realise, I think, that every slice of bread provides 2g protein and each average sized serving of potato or peas a further 2 or 3 grams. Although animal protein is recommended because the amino acid patterns are nearer human needs, there is no need for large quantities of animal food. Even small amounts will supply reasonable supplementary amounts of the amino acids "limiting" (not lacking) in cereals and vegetable foods. A pregnant or lactating woman can obtain her additional protein needs by having 600ml milk daily or the equivalent in cheese, plus the small amounts of protein in the slightly larger helpings of food she takes because of increased appetite.

There are many essential mineral nutrients—iron, calcium, sodium, potassium and magnesium to name but a few. Generally speaking if one has milk for calcium, and red meat, eggs, wholegrain cereals, vegetables and fruits for iron, the other minerals will also be consumed in adequate amounts. Each mineral has specific functions and is an essential component of body cells and body fluids.

Vitamins are needed in quite tiny amounts but are nevertheless essential (or vital) for health. The fat soluble vitamins are A, D and E. Vitamin A is needed for healthy skin and eyes and protects the mucous membranes of the body. Vitamin D is essential for strong bones and teeth and Vitamin E has many important chemical roles at cell level.

Fat soluble vitamins are obtained from fat containing foods so that the best sources of vitamins A and D are fish liver oils, animal and bird livers, butter or margarine, and of E, again liver, vegetable oils and the small amount of fat of whole grain cereals, wheatgerm etc. It is possible for fat soluble vitamins A and D to accumulate in the body and thus become toxic and dangerous. So far, no ill effects have been noted as a result of the habitual ingestion of large amounts of vitamin E, but I would be very wary about pronouncing this practice as harmless, because the vitamin can accumulate in body fat tissues.

The B group vitamins are water soluble. They are needed for the proper digestion of carbohydrates and proteins, and are necessary for growth and for the prevention of skin and nervous disorders. Vitamin C is also soluble in water and is easily destroyed on exposure to air and heat. It is found in most fruits and vegetables, the richest sources being the berry and citrus fruits, tomatoes and tropical fruits like paw paw. This vitamin is necessary for healthy gums and body tissues. Until very recently it was thought that it was not harmful to have very large doses of the water soluble vitamins, because the kidneys daily excrete the amounts not required by the body. It is now thought that people can become habituated to large doses and that their continued health is dependent upon these large amounts. Thus a pregnant woman taking massive doses of vitamin C conditions her child to require considerably more of this vitamin than is normally recommended and adequate for other children not so conditioned.

In order to obtain all these nutrients, and also fibre, the bulk factor, it is best to choose a variety of foods each day from each of the basic five food groups, namely:—
1. Milk, yoghurt, cheese and other milk products.
2. Meat, fish, poultry, eggs, cheese, nuts, dried peas and beans
3. Vegetables and fruits
5. Wholegrain cereals including bread
5. Butter and table margarine

If these basic foods are consumed, the appetite for less nutritious foods containing sugar, refined and highly processed foods, alcohol and large amounts of fat will diminish.

Margaret W. Corden BSc.Cert.Dietetics, M.I.D. (NSW)
Senior Nutritionist
Australian Department of Health

METRIC CONVERSION TABLES

All quantities and temperatures in this book are given in both imperial and metric measures. However, you will have other recipe books which are not metric, and for which the following tables may be useful.

AUSTRALIAN STANDARD MEASURES

Measure	Old [Imperial]	New [Metric]
Cup	8 fl. oz (227ml)	250ml
Tablespoon	½ fl. oz (14.2ml)	20ml
Teaspoon	1/8 fl. oz (3.6ml)	5ml

Note: There is no Australian standard dessertspoon.

METRIC CONVERSION

Direct conversion from imperial to metric measurements is totally unrealistic, since there is no simple relationship between the two, e.g. 1 ounce = 28.3 grams, 1 cup = 227.3 millilitres, 1 pint = 568 millilitres. The most satisfactory basis for converting recipes is as shown below, although the metric equivalents are about 10% more than the imperial measurements.

CONVERSION OF LIQUIDS AND CUP MEASURES

Imperial Fluid Ounces	Imperial and Metric Cup	Metric Millilitres
1 fl oz		30ml
2 fl oz	¼ cup	
3 fl oz		100ml
4 fl oz	½ cup	
5 fl oz (¼ pint)		150ml
6 fl oz	¾ cup	
8 fl oz	1 cup	250ml
10 fl oz (½ pint)	1¼ cups	
12 fl oz	1½ cups	
14 fl oz	1¾ cups	
16 fl oz	2 cups	500ml
20 fl oz (1 pint)	2½ cups	
35 fl oz	4 cups	1 litre
40 fl oz (2 pints)	5 cups	1.25 litres

CONVERSION OF MASSES

Ounces	Grams
½ oz	15g
1 oz	30g
2 oz	60g
3 oz	90g
4 oz (¼ lb)	125g
5 oz	155g
6 oz	185g
7 oz	220g
8 oz (½ lb)	250g
9 oz	280g
10 oz	315g
11 oz	345g
12 oz (¾ lb)	375g
13 oz	410g
14 oz	440g
15 oz	470g
16 oz (1 lb)	500g
24 oz (1½ lb)	750g
32 oz (2 lb)	1000g (1kg)
3 lb	1500g (1.5kg)
4 lb	2000g (2kg)

OVEN TEMPERATURE CONVERSION

Note: In the range given below, the number of degrees Celsius is approximately half the number of degrees Fahrenheit.

Usual Description	Thermostat Setting ° Fahrenheit	Thermostat Setting ° Celsius
Cool	200	100
	225	110
Very slow	250	120
	275	140
Slow	300	150
Moderately slow	325	160
Moderate	350	180
Moderately hot	375	190
	400	200
Hot	425	220
	450	230
Very hot	475	250
	500	260

In the Beginning

In the Beginning

100 APPETIZERS

This section contains ideas for pre-dinner "eats" and includes pates which can also be used as entrees or main courses. See R2400 for other recipes.

101 ONION DIP

Basic ingredients:
1 packet French onion soup
300 ml [½ pint] or more yoghurt or sour cream, or 250g [8 oz] cottage or cream cheese

For variety, add any of the following:

1. *2 teaspoons curry powder and 1 teaspoon chili powder*
2. *2-3 tablespoons crumbled blue or other matured cheese*
3. *¼ teaspoon tabasco or other strong sauce*
4. *1 teaspoon paprika, or cayenne pepper to taste*
5. *1-2 cans smoked oysters, drained and chopped*
6. *60g [2 oz] salted almonds or walnuts, roughly chopped*
7. *2 tablespoons chopped pickled onions or chives and stuffed olives*
8. *2 tablespoons chopped dill cucumbers or gherkins*
9. *90g [3 oz] chopped cooked bacon*

Mix all ingredients together well. Chill and use as dip for savoury biscuits, (R 1540), potato chips, raw vegetables (e.g. carrots, celery, cauliflower) etc.

102 TROPICAL DIP

125g [4 oz] cream or cottage cheese
1 425g [15 oz] can crushed pineapple, drained, but juice reserved
2 teaspoons pineapple juice
salt
cayenne pepper

Beat cream cheese and pineapple juice to smooth consistency. Add other ingredients and chill well.
Variations:

1. *Gherkin: Add 125g [4 oz] grated tasty cheese and 4 chopped gherkins.*
2. *Smoked oyster: Omit pineapple and juice and substitute 1 small [100g] can smoked oysters, drained and chopped, 2 teaspoons cream, 1 teaspoon lemon juice and 2 teaspoons chopped chives or parsley.*

2

103 AVOCADO DIP

2 medium avocados
2 tablespoons lemon juice
1 tablespoon finely grated onion or chopped chives

185g [6 oz] cream cheese
¼ teaspoon tabasco sauce
salt and pepper

Stone avocados, mash or sieve flesh until smooth. Add remaining ingredients and mix well. Chill.

104 AVOCADO DIP OR SPREAD (GUACAMOLE)

3 avocados, mashed
1 large ripe tomato, finely chopped
1 cup chopped celery
½ teaspoon salt

1 teaspoon chili powder
1 tablespoon finely chopped onion
1 teaspoon lemon juice
little crushed garlic [optional]

Combine all ingredients and chill.

105 CURRIED EGG DIP

1 cup mayonnaise [R 1001, 1002, 1003]
3 hard boiled eggs, finely chopped

1 teaspoon curry powder

Combine all ingredients and chill.

106 CHEESE STACK-UPS

6 thin slices cheese
6 thin slices ham or other cold meat

softened cream cheese or flavoured butter [R 1044]

Spread slices of cheese and meat with cream cheese or flavoured butter. Stack alternate slices of cheese and meat using three slices of each to a stack. Wrap in greaseproof paper or plastic and press with a weight. Chill. Cut into bite-sized squares or triangles. Insert a toothpick in each and stick into an apple or orange to serve.

107 HAM "SANDWICHES"

6 slices ham
250g [8 oz] creamed cottage cheese
2 hard boiled eggs, finely chopped

½ teaspoon curry powder [optional]

Combine cheese, eggs and curry powder together. Spread over ham slices and sandwich together. Chill, then cut each sandwich into 6 fingers or triangles. Garnish with parsley. Yields 18.

3

108 SALAMI "PIZZAS"

125g [4 oz] sliced salami [skin left on]

2 medium tomatoes, sliced

2 fresh or drained canned mushrooms, sliced

125g [4 oz] matured cheddar cheese, sliced

30g [1 oz] grated parmesan cheese

¼ cup tomato soup

1 tablespoon worcestershire sauce

¼ teaspoon mustard

Place salami flat on grill pan. Top each with a slice of tomato and mushroom. Cover with sliced cheddar and sprinkle with grated parmesan. Grill until salami curls into cups and cheese is golden. Combine soup, worcestershire sauce and mustard. Heat and spoon over "pizzas".

109 CHEESE AND WALNUT BALLS

250g [8 oz] grated cheese

½ teaspoon worcestershire sauce

top of milk or cream to mix

finely chopped walnuts

Mix cheese with worcestershire sauce and sufficient top of milk to make firm consistency. Shape into about 16 bite sized balls. Roll in finely chopped walnuts. Chill.

110 CHEESE BALL

125g [4 oz] tasty cheese, grated

60g [2 oz] ham, chopped

1-2 gherkins, chopped

1 tablespoon snipped chives

1 teaspoon lemon juice

salt and pepper

250g [8 oz] cream cheese, softened

60g [2 oz] walnuts, finely chopped

Mix cheese, ham, gherkins, chives, lemon juice, salt and pepper. Refrigerate until firm. Roll into a ball, cover with cream cheese, then walnuts.

111 DEVILLED PARTY NIBBLES

60g [2 oz] butter

2 tablespoons oil

1 teaspoon curry powder

salt

½ teaspoon paprika

125g [4 oz] assorted nuts [brazil nuts, almonds, cashews, etc.]

2 cups rice cereal squares

Melt butter and oil in large heavy frying pan. Stir in curry powder, salt and paprika and fry gently for a few minutes. Add nuts and cereal and fry until well coated and browned for about 10-15 mins. Drain on absorbent paper and allow to cool.

4

112 DEVILS ON HORSEBACK

prunes　　　　　　　　　　　　　*bacon*
almonds or cream cheese,
*　[optional]*

Remove stones from prunes and replace with almonds or cream cheese if desired. Wrap each prune right around with a slice of bacon, and secure with a toothpick. Grill or bake until bacon is cooked. Both adults and children enjoy these!
Variation: Substitute chicken livers for prunes.

113 SAVOURY FINGERS

Butter bread, spread with one of the following, cut into fingers and bake in a moderate oven 10-15 mins. Serve hot or cold. Can be stored in airtight jar.

1. *Yeast extract and grated cheese*
2. *Parmesan cheese and garlic salt*
3. *Sesame or poppy seeds*

114 HAM AND CHEESE SLICES

5 layers thin streudel pastry　　*125g [4 oz] ham, sliced*
*　[available from continental*　　*125g [4 oz] cheese, sliced*
*　delicatessens]*
2 tablespoons [approx]
*　melted butter*

Brush each layer of pastry with melted butter, put ham and cheese up one end of the top layer and roll as for a Swiss roll. Brush with butter and bake in hot oven 400°-425°F, (200°-220°C) for 20 mins. Cut in slices immediately.

Variation: Cut each sheet of pastry into four strips lengthwise and roll up like a parcel.

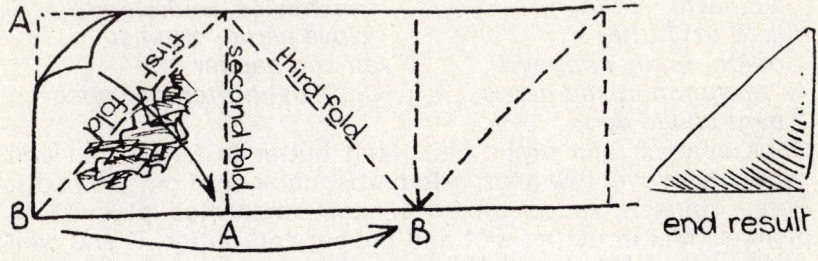

Ham and Cheese slices.

115 MUSHROOM AND BACON SLICE

250g [8 oz] short crust pastry [R 1301]
3 rashers bacon, chopped

250g [8 oz] field mushrooms cooked in butter or canned mushrooms, drained

Roll pastry thinly and place on greased lamington tray. Spread with thin layer of mushrooms and then bacon. Bake at 400°F (200°C) for 10 mins.

116 CHEESE SLICE

Onion Dip [R 101] made with cottage or cream cheese

2 layers puff pastry [R 1310]

Sandwich dip between pastry, cut in squares and bake in hot oven 425°F (220°C) for 15-20 mins.

117 MEATBALLS WITH BARBECUE DIP

Meatballs:

500g [1 lb] finely minced steak or ½ pork and ½ veal
125g [4 oz] grated mature cheese

2 teaspoons worcestershire sauce
salt
cayenne pepper

Combine all ingredients together and shape into small balls. Grill 10 mins. or until meatballs are cooked through. Serve hot with toothpicks and allow guests to "dip" into Barbecue Dip or tomato sauce.

Barbecue Dip

1 cup tomato soup
¼ cup worcestershire sauce

½ teaspoon mustard

Combine all ingredients together in a saucepan. Stir over low heat until hot but not boiling. Serve immediately.

MEAT PIES (R 2113)

118 SPINACH PATE

1 packet 300g [10 oz] frozen spinach
60g [2 oz] butter
1 onion, finely chopped
¼ teaspoon mixed herbs
3 hard boiled eggs

1 50g [1¾ oz] can flat anchovies, undrained
1 clove garlic, crushed
salt and pepper
60g [2 oz] butter, softened

Cook spinach and drain well. Melt butter in frying pan and saute onion over low heat. Add herbs, cook until onion is soft. Puree spinach, onion mixture, eggs, anchovies plus oil in blender. Mix in garlic, salt and pepper and butter. Blend well and leave to set in small covered containers. Keeps three days in refrigerator.

119 CHICKEN LIVER PATE (1)

250g [8 oz] chicken livers
125g [4 oz] butter, melted
2 tablespoons cream cheese
1 tablespoon brandy

1 tablespoon snipped chives
1/4 teaspoon mixed herbs
nutmeg, salt and pepper

Chop livers and cook slowly in a quarter of the butter. *Do not brown.* Remove from pan. Puree in blender livers, cheese, brandy and seasonings, rest of butter melted and mix well together. Keeps in refrigerator up to two weeks if placed in containers and sealed with melted butter.

120 CHICKEN LIVER PATE (2)

Use 9" earthenware dish with either a lid with a hole or aluminium foil.

15g [1/2 oz] stale bread
2 tablespoons brandy
2 teaspoons salt
1/2 teaspoon pepper
1 egg
60g [2 oz] white onions,
    chopped

500g [1 lb] chicken livers
500g [1 lb] pork and veal,
    minced finely
3 small bay leaves
2 teaspoons gelatine
    dissolved in 1/2 cup water

Mix together bread, brandy, salt and pepper. Add egg, onion and meat. Alternatively, puree all in blender. Pour into earthenware dish and place bay leaves on top. Cover and cook at 450°F (230°C) for 35 mins. When juice is no longer pink, remove lid and pour gelatine mixture over meat. Bake further 5 mins with lid off until top is brown. Will keep in refrigerator for approximately two weeks. Serve two slices per person with buttered toast, gherkins and French salad.

FISH PATE (R 2416)

It's a very strange thing,
As strange as can be,
That whatever Miss T. eats
Turns into Miss T.

Walter de la Mare

121 LIVER PATE (1)

500g [1 lb] calf or pig livers, chopped
125g [4 oz] very lean ham or bacon, chopped
1 small onion, chopped
90g [3 oz] butter
salt and pepper

¼ teaspoon mixed herbs
1 tablespoon [approx.] extra melted butter
Optional: 2-3 gherkins, chopped; 1-2 hard boiled eggs; 1 tablespoon cream

Saute liver, ham and onion for no longer than 10 mins. Mince finely twice to give a very smooth texture. Add salt and pepper, herbs, gherkins and eggs if desired. For a very soft pate add cream. Put into dish and stand in another dish of cold water to prevent mixture becoming dry. Cover with buttered paper and bake at 350°F (180°C) for about 30 mins. When cooked cover with a layer of melted butter. Serve in slices on a bed of crisp lettuce, accompanied by hot, buttered toast.

LIVER PATE (2) (R 1803)

PIROZHKI (Sour cream pastries with filling) (R 2411)

BLINI (Yeast pancakes with caviar and sour cream) (R 2410)

122 SAVOURY PUFFS

As (R 1405) but fill with bechamel sauce (R 1018) flavoured with oysters, asparagus, white bait, cheese or anything else you like.

SMOKED OYSTERS IN VOL-AU-VENT CASES (R 319)

EGG AND BACON TARTLETS (R 416)

MELON CHEESE BITS (R 2109)

From the Tureen.

From the Tureen

Soup of the evening, beautiful Soup!

Lewis Carroll, Alice in Wonderland

200 SOUP

With a little imagination soup can be not only nutritious but also quite exciting. It is an excellent means of providing children with a variety of good foods, of the kinds which they often refuse to eat if served separately. Even the child under a year can enjoy the experience. With the availability of a wide choice of canned and packet soups many of us have lost the art of making our own. It is an art worth reviving as many recipes are simple and economical.

Interesting results can be obtained by combining two varieties of canned or packet soup. They can be enhanced by the addition of varied ingredients e.g. tiny button mushrooms (or larger ones sliced) sauteed and added to mushroom soup, asparagus tips in asparagus soup, shellfish in lobster bisque, scallop chowder, or oyster soup etc. Grated parmesan cheese is delicious in minestrone or other vegetable soups. If you are pureeing a homemade soup reserve a few of the ingredients to garnish.

Besides parsley, chopped chives or watercress make an excellent garnish, or alternatively place a spoonful of sour cream or yoghourt in each soup bowl—do not stir.

Use a soup to suit the occasion—a lighter consomme as a first course, a more filling vegetable type such as minestrone can provide a meal, and what about trying a cold soup as a delightfully refreshing hot weather dish?

STOCK

Stock is the basis for many soups—it can be made at the same time as the soup, but it is often more convenient to keep a supply frozen which can be added to canned soups or casseroles as well as providing the source for your own soups. Try freezing small amounts in ice cube trays or plastic cream bottles. The contents can then be added to gravies or made into small portions of soup for young children. In an emergency a stock cube and water can be substituted for home-prepared stock.

201 BEEF STOCK

1.25kg [2½ lb] beef bones
  [some gravy beef can be
  included]
margarine [optional]
2 onions, chopped
2 carrots, chopped
1 turnip, chopped
1 large leek, chopped
water or vegetable water to
  cover, approx. 3 litres
  [5 pints]

2 celery stalks with leaves,
  chopped
1 clove garlic, crushed
2 teaspoons cooking salt
6-8 peppercorns
2 cloves
bouquet garni

Brown bones in stockpot or very large pan over medium heat. If using gravy beef add a little margarine and brown meat and bones well. Add onions, carrots and turnip and brown until almost burnt. Alternatively put meat, bones and these vegetables into hot oven 450°F (230°C) for about 30 mins, turning them after 15 mins, then place in stockpot. Cover by at least 1" with water. Add other ingredients. Washed leftover vegetable peelings, eg. from pumpkins and parsnips can also be added. Preferably simmer 6-9 hours or alternatively boil 4 hours. Strain through colander, allow to settle, skim off fat. Strain through fine sieve.

202 CHICKEN STOCK

The nicest way to prepare chicken to eat cold is to cook the chicken in a saucepan with water to cover, an onion, a stick of celery, a piece of carrot, parsley, thyme, a bay leaf, pepper and salt. Simmer for about an hour, then strain off the juice and when it cools, you have a very pleasant moist cold chicken and a bowl full of good stock.

Another way of making the stock is, after you have used most of the chicken, to put the bones, neck and liver in a saucepan with the same additives as above and simmer for 1 hour. You will have a less concentrated but nevertheless very useful stock. When it is cold, skim off all the fat before storing in the refrigerator or freezer.

---

*Freeze soup, stock or other liquids in milk cartons. These are easy to stack in the freezer and the carton can be peeled off and thrown away.

203 CHICKEN SOUP

1 boiling fowl
1 onion, diced
2 small carrots, diced
2 sticks celery, diced
giblets [except liver]
salt and pepper

Cut chicken into portions. Place in saucepan and cover with cold water. Bring to boil, skim, and simmer for 30 mins. Add diced vegetables and seasonings. Simmer for further 2 hours. Remove chicken pieces—which can be used in another recipe. May be served with noodles, cooked lima beans or small dumplings.

204 EGG AND LEMON SOUP

7-8 cups chicken stock
90g [3 oz] uncooked rice
2 eggs
juice of large lemon

Bring stock to boil and add rice. Cook 15 minutes or until rice is just tender. Beat eggs and gradually add lemon juice. Add two cups of stock, stirring continually. Add lemon mixture to rest of stock, simmer for 2 mins. Allow soup to stand for a minute before serving.

205 EGG FLOWER SOUP

4-5 cups strong chicken stock
1 tablespoon light soya sauce
2 tablespoons sherry
1 tablespoon cornflour
3 eggs, beaten
2 spring onions, chopped

Place chicken stock in saucepan and bring to boil. Add soya sauce and sherry. Mix cornflour with little water and add to stock. Cook for 2 minutes and remove from heat. Add beaten eggs, stirring vigorously to form threads. Garnish with spring onions.

206 ARTICHOKE SOUP

2 large onions, sliced in rings
30g [1 oz] butter
1kg [2 lb] Jerusalem
   artichokes, chopped
2 large potatoes, chopped
1 chicken stock cube and
   2½ cups water or 2½ cups
   chicken stock
1 leek
cloves
1¼ cups milk
salt and pepper
1 egg, beaten
cream
chopped parsley

Gently fry onion rings in butter. Add artichokes and potatoes. Cover with chicken stock. Add leek stuck with cloves. Boil for 30 mins, remove cloves then vitamize. Add milk, salt and pepper, gradually stir in beaten egg. Reheat, add a little cream and chopped parsley before serving. Add more stock if thinner soup is required.

207 CREAM OF ASPARAGUS SOUP

60g [2 oz] butter
60g [2 oz] flour
2 cups hot chicken stock

1 can green asparagus, undrained
1¼ cups milk or cream

Melt butter, add flour, cook a few mins without browning. Blend in hot stock, stir until smooth, simmer 15 minutes. Retain a few choice cuts of asparagus and puree or sieve the remainder. Add to the soup together with liquid from can. Add cream or milk and reheat (do not boil). Check seasoning before garnishing with reserved asparagus and croutons if desired.
Variation: Substitute 1-3 cups cooked diced or sieved vegetables for asparagus, eg. carrots, peas, cauliflower, onions, spinach, pumpkin, tomato and if desired, appropriate vegetable water for stock.

RASSOLNIK (Kidney and Dill Cucumber Soup) (R 2412)

208 TOMATO SOUP

1 tablespoon butter
1-2 onions, chopped
1kg [2 lb] fresh tomatoes, peeled and roughly chopped
1 cup chicken stock
1 tablespoon chopped fresh herbs, eg. parsley, chives, basil, chervil, OR

¼ teaspoon dried mixed herbs
1 bay leaf
2 teaspoons sugar
salt and pepper
3 tablespoons cream
1 tablespoon chopped chives

Lightly fry onions in butter. Add tomatoes, stock, herbs, bay leaf and sugar. Bring to the boil and simmer 10-15 mins. Season. Remove bay leaf. Sieve or puree in blender. Reheat until boiling. Just before serving, add cream. Sprinkle with chives.
Variations:
1. Lightly fry 1-2 rashers chopped bacon with onion.
2. Fry 1 chopped green pepper with onions.
3. Add extra 2 cups stock. After sieving, thicken with 1 tablespoon cornflour blended with a little stock, water or milk, and stir into soup.
4. Substitute canned tomatoes, and use tomato liquid to replace some of stock.

209 MUSHROOM SOUP

250g [8 oz] mushrooms
salt and pepper
1 425g [15 oz] can beef
  consomme

1½ cups water or stock
½ cup dry sherry
juice of ½ lemon
2 teaspoons grated lemon rind

Slice mushrooms finely, sprinkle with salt and cook gently over low heat. Remove a few slices for garnish and press those remaining into juices in the pan. Push mushrooms through sieve into consomme, add water or stock, sherry and lemon juice. Heat and serve garnished with mushrooms and sprinkled with lemon rind. It is also very tasty chilled.

210 FRESH PEA SOUP

60g [2 oz] butter
1 leek or large onion, sliced
6 shredded lettuce leaves [use
  outside dark green leaves]
500g [1 lb] peas, shelled

3 cups water
6 pea pods
1 teaspoon salt
½ teaspoon sugar
cream, [optional]

Melt 40g (1½ oz) butter over a low heat in saucepan and add sliced leek, lettuce, peas, salt and sugar. Cook gently for 5 minutes. Add water and pods (these improve colour and flavour). Cover and simmer 15-20 minutes. Sieve or puree soup. Reheat, remove from heat and stir in remaining butter. If desired, add some cream too.

211 DRIED PEA SOUP

250g [½ lb] split peas
250g [½ lb] bacon bones
and/or bacon pieces
6½ cups water
1 onion, chopped
1 carrot, chopped

1 stick celery, chopped
1 potato, chopped
1 teaspoon sugar
salt and pepper
2 tablespoons finely chopped
  mint

Soak peas overnight in water. Drain and place in large saucepan with measured water. Add vegetables, bacon, salt, pepper and sugar. Simmer 3 hours. (Can be done for 1 hour in pressure cooker). Remove bones and push through a coarse sieve or puree in blender. Add mint and reheat, diluting with milk if desired. Improves if made a day in advance.

Old Noah he had an ostrich farm and fowls on the largest scale,
He ate his egg with a ladle in an egg-cup as big as a pail,
And the soup he took was Elephant Soup and the fish he took was Whale.
                                                    G. K. Chesterton.

212 BEAN SOUP

60g [2 oz] cannellini beans
60g [2 oz] lima beans
60g [2 oz] sallugia beans
15g [½ oz] butter
2 teaspoons oil
2 small tomatoes, skinned
   and pulped
2 small potatoes, diced
60g [2 oz] white onion, sliced
155g [5 oz] French beans,
   sliced

8 cups stock
2 cloves garlic, crushed
1 teaspoon basil
2 teaspoons salt
pepper
60g [2 oz] shell noodles
½ green pepper, chopped
   [optional]
black olives [optional]

Soak dried beans in water overnight, drain well. In a large saucepan melt butter and oil and add onion to soften. Add tomatoes, potatoes, French beans, then lastly dried beans. Stir well, add stock and other seasonings. Cook slowly 2 hours. Add noodles and green pepper during last 30 mins of cooking. This soup is better made 24 hours before using and will keep well in the refrigerator. For a change it can be pureed in blender or stoned black olives can be added.

213 PUMPKIN SOUP

15g [½ oz] butter
2 tablespoons chopped onion
500g [1 lb] pumpkin, cubed
2½ cups chicken stock
   [or chicken stock cube and
   2½ cups water]
1/8 teaspoon ground cloves

½ teaspoon sugar
1 teaspoon salt
2-3 drops tabasco sauce
2½ cups milk
1 teaspoon lemon juice
4 tablespoons cream
croutons [optional]

Melt butter and fry onion 2-3 mins. Add pumpkin, stock, cloves, sugar, salt and tabasco. Cook until pumpkin is quite soft, adding milk as liquid evaporates. Puree in blender or push through a sieve. Add lemon juice and reheat. Stir in cream and serve with croutons if desired.

*To make croutons — cut stale bread into 2" dice and fry in butter. For flavoured croutons sprinkle with garlic, onion or celery salt. Use to garnish soup.

214 PUMPKIN SOUP FRENCH STYLE

1 hard-skinned pumpkin
   which will fit your oven
500g [1 lb] thinly sliced
   French bread, toasted
750g [1½ lb] gruyere cheese

salt and pepper
1½ cups thick cream
nutmeg

Remove top of pumpkin and set aside — remove seeds and stringy pulp — dry and season inside with salt and pepper. Fill to ¾ with alternate layers of toast and thin strips of gruyere, seasoning with salt and lots of pepper. Replace top, and place in a slow to moderate oven till cooked — approx. 2-3 hours. When coloured and soft add cream and nutmeg. The pumpkin serves as a soup bowl and each guest is served with soup and pumpkin. It is very filling, so accompany with just a salad, and follow up with fruit.

215 ONION SOUP

750g [1½ lb] onions, thinly
   sliced
2 tablespoons butter
1 tablespoon oil
1 teaspoon salt
¼ teaspoon sugar
2 tablespoons flour
¼ cup dry white wine or
   vermouth

7-8 cups boiling beef stock
   [R 201]
salt and pepper
3 tablespoons cognac
1 French stick
125-250g [¼-½ lb] Swiss,
   parmesan or gruyere cheese,
   grated

Cook onions slowly in butter and oil in large, heavy-based covered saucepan for 15 mins. Stir in salt and sugar, cook uncovered, stirring frequently over moderate heat for 30-40 mins, until onions are golden brown. Sprinkle in flour and stir, gradually blend in wine then boiling stock. Simmer partially covered 40 mins or more, stirring occasionally. Add salt and pepper. Just before serving add cognac. Slice French bread into thick rounds and toast lightly or bake in 325°F (160°C) oven for 30 mins until thoroughly dried and lightly browned. If desired butter lightly. Put bread into soup tureen, pour soup over, and serve with cheese. Alternatively pour soup into individual heatproof bowls, float toast on top, spread with cheese, bake for 20 mins in 350°F (180°C) oven and/or put under preheated grill for few mins to brown top lightly.

He may live without love — what is passion but pining?
But where is the man that can live without dining?

Owen Meredith

216 POTAGE BONNE FEMME

60g [2 oz] butter
2 large leeks, finely sliced
2 large carrots, sliced
1 stick celery, sliced
500g [1 lb] potatoes, diced

4 cups water
salt and pepper
½ teaspoon sugar
3 tablespoons cream
parsley, finely chopped

Clean leeks very well and discard the dark green leaves before finely slicing the remainder. Melt butter in a large saucepan and add leeks and carrots. Stir over a low heat until butter is absorbed. Add celery, potatoes, water and seasonings. Bring to the boil and simmer covered for 30 mins. Sieve or puree in blender. Use a small quantity of vegetables for garnish if you like. Stir in cream and parsley just before serving.

217 MINESTRONE

The vegetables can be varied according to season and availability.

7 cups beef (R201) or veal
   stock
60g [2 oz] lean bacon or ham
1 cup celery, sliced
½ cup fresh or frozen peas
1 cup spinach or silver beet,
   chopped [include stalks]
¼ cup finely diced onion
1 carrot, diced
1 small zucchini, sliced
1 small leek, sliced thinly
3 medium tomatoes, skinned
   and diced

½ cup cauliflower and/or
   broccoli
½ cup dried lima or kidney
   beans soaked for several
   hours before cooking, or
   pre-cooked canned beans
2 tablespoons oil
125g [4 oz] macaroni or
   spaghetti
1 clove garlic, crushed
2 teaspoons minced fresh sage
1 tablespoon chopped parsley
½ cup grated tasty cheese

Place stock and bacon in large saucepan, and bring to boil. Add beans. Saute fresh vegetables lightly in oil and add to stock. While stock is boiling, add macaroni and simmer for 20 minutes. Add garlic and sage. Garnish with parsley and cheese and serve with chunks of Italian bread.

218 ZUCCHINI SOUP

500g [1 lb] zucchini
2½ cups milk

1 teaspoon butter
salt and pepper

Cook zucchini in boiling water until tender. Drain and put through sieve or puree in blender. Combine with milk, butter, salt and pepper. Reheat slowly before serving.

219 FISH SOUP

This traditional Christmas fish soup comes from Czechoslovakia. However, the fish available in Australia are far superior to those indigenous to Czechoslovakia and thus a better result will be obtained. The recipe yields about 4-5 litres of soup.

Fish:
*1 large schnapper head—
   about 1500g [3 lb],cleaned,
   washed, scaled*
*roe, cleaned, washed,
   sectioned*
*sperm, cleaned, washed,
   sectioned*
Vegetables:
*4-5 stalks and tops celery,
   sliced*

1 medium carrot, diced
*1 bunch parsley, half
   chopped, half retained in
   bunch*
1 onion, sliced
Other optional ingredients:
1 egg white, whipped
salt and pepper
60g [2 oz] butter
3 tablespoons flour

Place the head in about 5 litres salted water together with the retained half bunch of parsley. Boil gently for about 1 hour, until the head starts to disintegrate. Strain the liquid from the head. Strip all the meat from the head, including eyes and skin, but discard fins, scales, bones and parsley. If a clear, thin soup is desired, clarify the opaque liquid by adding egg white. Stir in thoroughly, cool and allow egg to surface. Skim egg layer and discard. Reheat stock, add fish, roe, sperm and vegetables and simmer until vegetables are tender. Season if desired and serve garnished with chopped parsley. If a thicker soup is required, omit the clarifying procedure. Further thickening can be effected by the addition of "jiska" after the vegetables. (Jiska: Gently brown butter in frying pan. Add flour and stir continuously until a light brown mass of sandy consistency results.)

220 SMOKED OYSTER SOUP

1 can [100g] smoked oysters
*1 large can [454g] cream of
   oyster soup, undiluted*
1¾ cups milk

*2 tablespoons dry sherry or
   white wine*
150 ml [5 oz] cream
salt and pepper

Chop oysters coarsely and add to soup and milk. Heat gently, (do not boil). Stir in cream and wine and reheat gently. Season.

18

221 TUNA AND TOMATO BISQUE

50g [1½ oz] butter
1 tablespoon oil
1 medium onion, sliced thinly
1 clove garlic, crushed
5 tomatoes, skinned and
   sliced [or use canned
   tomatoes]
½ teaspoon salt
pepper

1 tablespoon tomato paste
2 tablespoons flour
2½ cups chicken stock or
   water
200g [6½ oz] can tuna
   chunks, drained
½ cup cream
parsley, chopped

Melt butter and oil in saucepan, add onion and garlic, fry until golden brown. Add tomatoes, salt and pepper and cook slowly 5 mins. Stir in tomato paste and flour. gradually add chicken stock and bring to boil, stirring constantly. Add tuna and cream, heat but do not boil. Serve garnished with parsley.

Cold Soup

222 CHERRY SOUP

Any dried or fresh fruits, cooked until they are easily pureed may be used, and while cherries are the most popular, plums and damsons are interesting. Fruit soup may be served hot or cold. Cold fruit soup makes a delicious and unusual start to a summer meal.

500g [1 lb] stoned cherries or
   canned morella cherries
5 cups water and/or juice
   from fruit
½ cinnamon stick
¼ cup sugar, more if you like
   it sweeter

1 teaspoon grated lemon rind
½ cup red or white wine
2 teaspoons arrowroot
cream, whipped but not
   flavoured

Combine fruit, water, lemon rind and sugar in saucepan. Add cinnamon stick and simmer for 20 mins or until fruit is soft. Remove cinnamon and puree fruit in blender or push through a fine sieve. Mix arrowroot with a little water and add to soup, reheat stirring constantly. Add wine and simmer for a few mins but do not boil. Serve with a dob of whipped cream.

223 GAZPACHO

1-2 slices bread
1-2 cloves garlic
1kg [2 lb] tomatoes
1 green pepper
1 cucumber, peeled
3 tablespoons olive oil

2 tablespoons vinegar
salt and pepper
2½ cups water
3 hard boiled eggs, chopped
[for garnish]

Place bread, garlic, tomatoes (keep one), half the pepper and half the cucumber into blender. Add oil, vinegar, salt and pepper and blend until smooth. Strain, add water and mix well. Add more vinegar if required. Chill and serve very cold with ice cubes floating in each bowl. Garnish with finely chopped pepper, cucumber, tomato and egg. Tiny bread cubes and chopped onion may also be added.

224 VICHYSSOISE

3 leeks, finely chopped
1 onion, finely chopped
30g [1 oz] butter
3 potatoes, peeled and diced
4 cups chicken stock

salt and pepper
1 cup cream
¼ teaspoon mace
2 tablespoons finely chopped
  chives

Wash leeks very well, discard green leaves and mince white parts together with onion. Melt butter and saute leeks and onion for 3 mins—do not brown. Place stock and vegetables in saucepan and bring to boil. Simmer covered for 30 mins. Puree in blender or push through sieve. Add cream, mace, seasoning and reheat but do not boil. Garnish with chives. Delicious served cold in summer.

225 AVOCADO SOUP

2 ripe medium avocados,
  peeled and stoned
2 teaspoons chopped onion
  or chives

2 teaspoons lemon juice
2½ cups chicken stock
1¼ cups cream
salt and pepper

Puree avocados and onion with lemon juice in blender or rub through a sieve. Gently heat avocado mixture and stock, preferably in a double saucepan. Simmer gently 10 mins, then add cream, salt and pepper, stirring continually. Cook for further 5 mins but do not boil. Strain and chill well before serving.

Gift from the Sea

Gift from the Sea

This dish of meat is too good for any but Anglers or honest men; and, I trust, you will prove both, and therefore I have trusted you with this Secret.
Izaak Walton, The Compleat Angler, 1653

300 FISH

Fish is a very nourishing, easily digested source of protein and vitamins and deserves a regular place on the menu of every household. It is important to remember that all varieties are equal in nutritional value, so whenever possible, use local fish which is normally cheaper.

The tail end is the most suitable for children as it has the least bones.

Try to garnish well with parsley, lemon, sliced blanched almonds (for adults) or a sauce. Some unusual accompaniments are fried parsley and chipped pumpkin.

For very young children and invalids, steaming is the best method of cooking. Place the fillet of fish on an enamel plate with a nob of butter, cover with another plate or saucepan lid and simmer over boiling water until cooked. Make sure it is not overcooked as it then becomes very dry and unpalatable. Remember that fish is cooked when it has lost its opaque look. Delicate fish such as whiting and garfish can be easily and appetizingly cooked by dipping first in seasoned flour then in beaten egg and breadcrumbs and gently fried in butter until golden brown. Coarser fish such as flake, flathead and schnapper is delicious fried in butter (R 1200) which keeps it moist during the longer cooking time required. Coat fish lightly with flour, dip in batter, and either deep or shallow fry in hot oil. For serving suggestions see also sauces, marinades and flavoured butters (R 1000).

301 TROUT IN CREAM

1 trout [rainbow or brown]	30ml [1 oz] brandy
60g [2 oz] butter	salt and pepper
2 tablespoons chopped almonds	½-1 cup cream [depending on size of fish]

Melt butter, brown almonds, saute trout, remove from pan and keep warm. Pour in brandy and ignite. Add salt, pepper and cream. Bring to boil, pour over trout and sprinkle with almonds.

302 STUFFED CARP

1-1.5kg [2-3 lb] carp
5 cups milk approx.
250g [8 oz] black olives,
    stoned and finely chopped
2 cloves garlic, crushed
juice one lemon

1 tablespoon snipped chives
2 sprigs parsley, chopped
salt and cayenne pepper
1 tablespoon olive oil
1 tablespoon breadcrumbs
½ cup hot water

Scale, clean and wash carp and soak in milk for 24 hours. Remove fish, wash well and rub with salt. Throw away milk or give to dog or cat! Mix olives, garlic, lemon juice, chives, parsley, salt, cayenne pepper and oil. Stuff carp with this mixture and put in a greased baking dish. Sprinkle with breadcrumbs and bake in a moderate oven for about 20 mins. About half way through cooking, add hot water and then baste occasionally with the pan juices. Serve hot or cold.

303 SQUID AND OCTOPUS

To prepare: Place in a large bowl of cold water and pull tentacles away from hood. Rinse ink away and feel for the transparent spine bone in hood. This slides out very easily. Slice hood into rings. Leave tentacles whole for squid, but slice into rings for octopus.

Fried Squid: Toss sliced squid in seasoned flour and fry in hot oil (preferably olive) for 3-4 mins only.

Squid in Batter: Dip pieces of squid into batter (R 1203) and shallow fry in hot oil for 4-6 mins. Serve with tartare sauce (R 1009).

Greek Octopus: Octopus requires a longer cooking time than squid as it is not so tender. Place sliced octopus into a pan and add cold water just to cover. Add ½ cup white vinegar, bring to boil and simmer 20-30 mins. Octopus should turn pink when cooked. Add salt to taste and serve with lemon wedges.

Octopus in Tomato Sauce: Shallow fry the sliced octopus quickly in hot olive soil to which a crushed clove of garlic has been added. Add enough fresh tomato sauce (R 1013) to cover octopus, cover pan and simmer for 1 hour.

*To scale fish easily dip them in hot water for a few minutes.

CRAYFISH CREOLE (R 2423)

MARINARA SAUCE (R 513)

SEAFOOD SAUCE (R 1014)

304 GARFISH

Preparation: Clean and scale the fish and remove the head. Slit right along the underside, remove the inside and rub with salt to remove any black lining. Open the fish out laying it flat with the opening underneath. Press all along the backbone to flatten, or roll with a small glass. Turn the fish and ease away the main bone with a sharp knife, leaving the tail on.

Cooking: Dust garfish with seasoned flour. Heat equal proportions of butter and oil, and just before frying, dip fish briefly in water. Fry until tender. Alternatively deep fry in very hot oil as the smaller bones then tend to disintegrate. Serve with lemon wedges and tartare sauce (R 1009) or a homemade spicy tomato sauce.

305 BARBECUED FISH

Freshly caught fish gutted, salted and cooked over the coals is a taste sensation.

There is no need to scale the fish as the outside becomes charred and can easily be lifted off after cooking.

As soon as the fish stops wriggling, slit the underside and remove the inside. If you have a lemon, squeeze the juice into the cavity, sprinkle with salt and place the whole fish on a grid or flat sheet of metal, over the glowing coals.

When cooked, the flesh will be moist and succulent and beautifully flavoured. Do not overcook.

First they ate the sturgeon, Nahma,
And the pike, the Maskenozha,
Caught and cooked by old Nokomis;
Then on pemican they feasted,
Pemican and buffalo marrow,
Haunch of deer and hump of bison,
Yellow cakes of the Mondamin,
And the wild rice of the river.
H. W. Longfellow, Hiawatha's Wedding Feast.

306 SCHNAPPER BAKED IN WINE

1 schnapper approx. 1.25 kg
[2½ lb] [or any other large
fish e.g. tailor, tuna, king
fish, trevalley]
2 slices bread with crusts
removed
juice 1½ lemons
approx. 30 bottled or canned
oysters, undrained

1 onion, peeled and finely
chopped
1 clove garlic, crushed
1 tomato, skinned and
chopped
salt and pepper
1 cup white wine
½ cup olive oil
parsley to garnish

Scale and clean schnapper leaving whole. Soak bread in lemon juice and half the oyster liquid. Add onion, garlic, tomato, half the oysters, salt and pepper. Stuff fish and sew up cavity or skewer together. Slash fish diagonally through to the bone two or three times on each side to allow heat to penetrate. Arrange fish in a buttered baking dish. Pour wine and oil over and cover with foil. Bake in moderate oven for 30 mins or until fish is cooked and flakes easily. Drain off liquid, reduce over high heat to approx. one cup and puree in blender with remaining oysters. Garnish fish with parsley and serve with sauce.

307 SCHNAPPER BAKED IN CHEESE SAUCE

4 pieces schnapper [or other
fresh or frozen fish
e.g. bream, whiting, hake]
300ml [½ pint] white sauce
[R 1010]
3 tablespoons grated cheese
2 teaspoons chopped spring
onions [or white onions]

2 tablespoons chopped
parsley
3 tablespoons breadcrumbs
1 tablespoon butter
extra parsley [optional]

Add ½ tablespoon cheese to the white sauce. Butter a fireproof dish well, sprinkle with half the chopped parsley and onion. Place fish in dish. Sprinkle with remaining onion and parsley and 1½ tablespoons cheese. Pour over the sauce. Sprinkle with remaining tablespoon cheese and breadcrumbs. Dot with butter. Cook in moderate oven for 15-20 mins. Sprinkle with extra parsley if you like.

The Whale that wanders round the Pole
Is not a table fish.
You cannot bake or boil him whole
Nor serve him in a dish.

Hilaire Belloc, The Bad Child's Book of Beasts

308 FISH CUTLETS IN PRAWN SAUCE

6-7 fish cutlets, e.g. flake,
  flounder, hake, halibut,
  schnapper
pepper
60g [2 oz] butter or margarine
2 cups milk
1 tablespoon cornflour

125g [4 oz] canned or frozen
  prawns
1 teaspoon anchovy essence
1 tablespoon tomato sauce
fresh prawns to garnish
  [optional]

Wash and dry fish and place in a buttered fireproof dish. Sprinkle with pepper and dot with butter. Add one cup milk. Cover and bake for 30 mins 375°F (190°C) then cook uncovered for 15 mins to brown fish. Mix cornflour to a smooth paste in a little milk. Strain liquid from fish and add to remaining milk and bring to boil. Add cornflour mixture to boiling milk and fish stock, stirring constantly. Simmer over low heat for 2-3 mins. Add prawns, anchovy essence and tomato sauce. Mix well over low heat until boiling again, then pour over fish. Garnish with fresh prawns.

309 FISH INDONESIAN STYLE

2 whole fish [schnapper, flathead or bream]
4 teaspoons curry powder
2 cloves garlic, crushed
2 tablespoons white vinegar
  or lemon juice

1 teaspoon salt
¼ teaspoon ground ginger
1 egg, beaten
oil for frying

Gash fish deeply in a diamond pattern on both sides (about 6 cuts each side, depending on size of fish). Combine curry, garlic, vinegar, salt, ginger and egg. Spread over fish. Allow to stand at least 30 mins. Heat a little oil in a large baking dish and brown fish on both sides. Transfer to moderate oven and cook 25 mins or until tender. Serve with Island Rice (R 832).

*If not used at once, cover freshly-caught fish with water in suitable container and freeze. Stops fillets drying out.

310 FISH DISHES (Quick and easy)

1. Place fillets of fresh fish in casserole dish and dot with butter. Add a little chopped bacon, milk to barely cover and a bayleaf. Cook in 250°F (130°C) oven for ½-¾ hour.
2. Place fillets of fresh fish on well greased foil. Dot with butter. Squeeze over a little lemon juice, place a thin slice of lemon on each fillet and sprinkle very lightly with fennel seeds. Put another piece of foil on top. Roll the edges tightly and bake in a hot oven 400°F (200°C) for 7-10 mins.
3. Place fillets of fresh or frozen fish in shallow ovenproof dish in single layer. Sprinkle with chopped parsley, lemon juice, thyme, salt and pepper, and dot with butter. Cover and bake in a moderate oven until cooked, about 20 mins. Sprinkle with dried breadcrumbs, grated cheese, melted butter and paprika. Return to oven until topping is lightly browned.

311 FISH QUICHE

1 large [454g, 1 lb] can
  salmon, flaked, OR
4 fillets fresh fish, e.g.
  mullet, bream, steamed in
  oven with
1 tablespoon butter, juice of
1 lemon, and 1 tablespoon
  chopped parsley
250g [8 oz] short crust pastry
  case, [R 1301] pre-cooked

1 tablespoon tomato paste
2-3 tomatoes, sliced
1 red pepper, sliced in rings
  and blanched, if desired
½ cup [approx.] cream
2 eggs, beaten
60g [2 oz] cheese, grated
salt and pepper

Spread base of pastry case with tomato paste, tomatoes and peppers and add fish. Measure juice from fish and add cream up to ¾ cup. Mix with eggs, cheese, salt and pepper and pour over mixture in pastry case. Bake at 425°F, (220°C) for 15 mins. Reduce heat to 400°F (200°C) for a further 15 mins. Cover with foil if necessary. Let stand for a while before cutting.

312 FISH PIE

1kg [2 lb] good flaking fish,
  e.g. flathead, salmon, trout
2 tomatoes, skinned and
  chopped
3 hard boiled eggs, chopped
1 onion, finely chopped
2 bananas, sliced
1 cup grated cheese
¼ cup chopped parsley
600ml [1 pint] bechamel
  sauce [not too thick] [R 1018]
salt and pepper
3-4 tablespoons tomato sauce
3 tablespoons breadcrumbs
1 tablespoon butter

Poach fish in water until cooked, skin and flake and mix with tomatoes, eggs, onion, bananas, cheese and parsley. Stir all into sauce. Season with salt and pepper, put in casserole lined with tomato sauce. Top with breadcrumbs, dot with butter. Cook in moderate oven 30 mins.

FISH BALLS (R 1811)

313 SEAFOOD PIE

Pie shell:

250g [8 oz] savoury biscuits,
  crushed
90g [3 oz] butter, melted
¼ cup water

Mix all ingredients well. Press mixture on to base and sides of 9" pie plate. Chill at least one hour.

Filling:

1 onion, finely chopped
1 tablespoon chopped green
  pepper
1 tablespoon oil
1 284g [10 oz] can oyster soup
3 eggs
¼ cup milk
125g [4 oz] small shelled
  prawns
salt and pepper

Heat oil, saute onion and green pepper for a few mins, stir in soup, remove from heat. Beat eggs with milk, add to soup mixture, stir in prawns. Add salt and pepper and stir into prepared pie case. Bake in moderately slow oven 40-50 mins.

We may live without poetry, music and art;
We may live without conscience, and live without heart;
We may live without friends; we may live without books;
But civilised man cannot live without cooks.
He may live without books — what is knowledge but grieving?
He may live without hope — what is hope but deceiving?

Owen Meredith

314 PRAWNS WITH CURRIED RICE

250g [8 oz] shelled prawns [or
    canned prawns or shrimps]
125g [4 oz] butter
2 ripe tomatoes, peeled and
    chopped
1 clove garlic, crushed
3 drops tabasco sauce
1 teaspoon worcestershire
    sauce
salt and pepper
4 tablespoons flour
1 cup milk

Melt butter in saucepan, add tomatoes, garlic and sauces, then add salt and pepper. Cover and simmer 5 mins. Add flour and blend thoroughly. Add milk gradually, stirring well until thickened and smooth. Add prawns, cover and simmer 5-10 mins.

Curried Rice

60g [2 oz] butter
½-1 cup almonds, blanched
    and slivered
1 teaspoon curry powder
3 cups hot rice, drained and
    salted

Melt butter in pan, add almonds and curry powder, saute until golden, tossing constantly. Add hot rice and toss lightly to mix. Arrange rice in a circle on a platter and pour prawn mixture into centre.

315 WHITING FILLETS WITH SALMON

6 fillets whiting, approx. 750g
    [1½ lb]
1 220g [7½ oz] can red
    salmon
juice ½ lemon
salt and pepper
lemon wedges and parsley to
    garnish

Sauce
60g [2 oz] butter
2 tablespoons finely chopped
    onion
1 tablespoon flour
½ teaspoon salt
¼ teaspoon tabasco sauce
1 cup white wine
½ cup cream

Sauce
Melt butter, saute onion until clear. Stir in flour until smooth. Sprinkle with salt and tabasco sauce. Slowly pour in wine and stir until thick and smooth. Add cream.

Fish
Dry fillets, place on board and season. Drain and mash salmon and season with lemon juice. Roll each fillet around handle of wooden spoon. Secure with toothpicks. Stuff with salmon. Place in buttered dish, spoon sauce over and bake in 350°F (180°C) oven 15-20 mins. Garnish with parsley and lemon wedges.

316 SCALLOPS SUPREME

scallops
salt and pepper
lemon juice
flour

butter
chopped parsley
crushed garlic [optional]

Cut red coral off scallops and set aside. Season remainder of scallops with salt, pepper and lemon juice to taste, dust with flour. Fry in butter for a few mins only. Add coral, chopped parsley and garlic. Heat through and serve immediately with juice from pan poured over them. Allow 125g (4 oz) per person as entree.

317 SMOKED COD CASSEROLE

500g [1 lb] smoked cod
1 tablespoon butter
2 tablespoons flour
1¼ cups milk
salt and pepper
3 hard boiled eggs, chopped
1 298g [10½ oz] can creamed
    sweetcorn

1 tablespoon chopped parsley
2 teaspoons lemon juice
2 cups cornflakes
3 tablespoons grated cheese
2 tablespoons coconut

Soak cod in cold water for 1-2 hours. Drain and place in fresh cold water to cover, then simmer about 10 mins or until tender. Drain. Remove skin and bones and flake flesh.
Melt butter, add flour, then gradually add milk and stir until boiling. Add salt and pepper, fish, eggs, sweetcorn, parsley and lemon juice. Pour into greased casserole dish. Mix together cornflakes, cheese and coconut and pile on casserole. Bake in moderate oven about 20 mins until cheese melts.

318 CREAMED WHITEBAIT

1 can [105g, 3½ oz] whitebait
1 tablespoon butter
1 tablespoon flour
1 cup milk
1 tablespoon whipped cream

squeeze lemon juice
few drops tabasco sauce
salt and pepper
chopped parsley

Melt butter and stir in flour. Add milk very gradually. Simmer for a few mins. Add cream, lemon juice, tabasco, salt and pepper, and whitebait. Sprinkle with parsley. Goes well with fingers of hot buttered toast, or in small vol-au-vent cases which are available in most supermarkets.

319 SMOKED OYSTERS IN VOL-AU-VENT CASES

6 four inch vol-au-vent cases
2 rashers bacon, chopped
30g [1 oz] butter
2 tablespoons flour
1 439g [15½ oz] can oyster
   soup
3 tablespoons sour cream
1 tablespoon dry sherry
2 100g [3 oz] cans smoked
   oysters, drained, and
   chopped
1 tablespoon chopped parsley

Cook bacon gently until lightly brown. Melt butter in saucepan, remove from heat, add flour, and stir until smooth. Add soup, cream and sherry. Stir until well blended. Return to heat and bring to boil, stirring constantly. Add oysters, parsley and bacon.
Warm vol-au-vent cases on a baking tray in a moderate oven for 10 mins. Fill with warm filling and serve immediately.

320 INDIAN "OYSTERS"

1½-2 cups cooked rice
1 can [92g, 3¼ oz] sardines,
   mashed
1 egg, beaten
1 small onion, grated
salt and pepper
fat for frying

Mix all together and drop by spoonfuls into very hot shallow fat. They will cook in 3-4 mins each side.

321 SALMON STUFFED AVOCADOS

3 ripe avocados
1 small [225g, 7½ oz] can red
   salmon or crabmeat
½ cup mayonnaise [R 1001]
2 tablespoons lemon juice
⅓ cup chopped onion
2 tablespoons chopped green
   pepper
2 tablespoons butter or margarine
sour cream

Split avocados in half, remove stones. Drain and flake salmon, remove bones. Combine salmon with mayonnaise and lemon juice. Saute onion and green pepper in butter. Add to salmon. Spoon mixture into avocado halves. Bake at 350°F (180°C) for 20-25 mins. Top each avocado half with a dollop of sour cream.
Variation: Replace avocados with aubergine but hollow out the halves.

322 SALMON BAKE

1 454g [1 lb] can salmon or
   tuna
1 tablespoon butter
2 tablespoons finely chopped
   onion
2 tablespoon flour
2 cups milk and salmon liquid
salt and pepper

1 teaspoon dry mustard
1 tablespoon mayonnaise
1 tablespoon chopped parsley
3 hard boiled eggs, sliced
1 283g [10 oz] can asparagus,
   drained
lemon wedges and parsley to
   garnish

Topping [optional]: breadcrumbs, grated cheese

Drain salmon and reserve liquid. Remove skin and bones. Melt butter and saute onion gently, then blend in flour and cook 2 mins. Add liquid and stir until sauce boils and thickens. Season with salt and pepper, mustard, mayonnaise and parsley. Put a layer of sauce in buttered casserole and add a layer each of sliced eggs, salmon and asparagus. Cover with sauce. Repeat layers finishing with sauce. Add topping if desired. Bake in moderate oven 30 mins. Garnish with lemon and parsley.

Variations:

1. Add 125g (4 oz) grated cheddar cheese to sauce.
2. Omit eggs and mayonnaise and include 3 tablespoons currants, 3 tablespoons sultanas, ¼ teaspoon nutmeg and 2 teaspoons lemon juice.
3. Omit asparagus and subsitute small can sweetcorn or pineapple pieces drained, or 1 cup cooked green vegetables.

On the rocks and grass the diligent ants were crossing miniature Saharas of dry sand, jungles of seeding grass, in the never ending task of collecting and storing food. Here, scattered about amongst the mountainous human shapes were Heaven-sent crumbs, carroway seeds, a shread of crystallized ginger—strange, exotic but recognizably edible loot. A battalion of sugar ants, almost bent in half with the effort, were laboriously dragging a piece of icing off the cake towards some subterranean larder dangerously situated within inches of Blanche's yellow head, pillowed on a rock.

Joan Lindsay, Picnic at Hanging Rock. 1970.

323 FISH AND POTATO DISH

1 large [454g, 1 lb] can tuna
  or salmon
1½ tablespoons margarine
2 tablespoons flour
1½ cups [approx.] milk
salt and pepper
1 teaspoon worcestershire
  sauce or dry mustard

squeeze lemon juice
1 tablespoon chopped
  parsley
1 tablespoon grated onion
3 cups mashed potato
125g [4 oz] cheese, grated

Drain fish and add milk to the liquid to make up to 1¾ cups. Mash fish. Melt margarine and add flour and cook gently 2 mins. Stir in milk and fish liquid and stir until boiling. Add fish, salt and pepper, sauce, lemon juice, parsley and onion. Line dish with half the potato then sprinkle in half the cheese. Put in fish mixture. Top with remaining potato and then remaining cheese. Heat through in moderate oven.

Variation: Add half cup each of cooked peas and diced cooked carrot or quarter cup chopped celery to fish mixture.

324 FISH CASSEROLE

Filling

1 large [454g, 1 lb] can tuna or
  fresh or frozen fillets or
  smoked fish
1 454g [16 oz] can soup
  [oyster, celery, asparagus,
  tomato], undiluted
1½ cups cooked rice

squeeze lemon juice
salt and pepper
Topping
¾ cup cornflake crumbs or
  breadcrumbs
30g [1 oz] butter, melted
125g [4 oz] cheese, grated

Combine filling ingredients, pour into shallow greased casserole. Mix topping ingredients and cover filling. Bake in moderate oven 30 mins.

Variations:
1. Substitute 2 cups cooked mixed vegetables for rice.
2. Use spaghetti or macaroni instead of rice.
3. Replace soup with white sauce and add some sliced tomatoes and celery.
4. Add sauteed onion and green pepper or sliced hard boiled eggs.
5. Substitute 10 fish sticks for tuna and omit rice.
6. Add 2-3 chopped gherkins.
7. Use potato chips and paprika (optional) as an alternative topping.

325 TUNA AND PINEAPPLE
(Quick to prepare)
1 large [454g, 1 lb] can tuna
1 cup milk
2 teaspoons cornflour
1 small [425g, 15 oz] can pineapple pieces

juice of one lemon
1 teaspoon butter
2 teaspoons curry powder
1 tablespoon chutney
salt and pepper

Warm milk in saucepan, then thicken with cornflour. Combine all other ingredients and cook for 8 mins. Serve with boiled rice.

326 TUNA SWEET AND SOUR
A quick dish prepared while rice is cooking.

1 small [425g, 15 oz] can pineapple pieces
1 large [454g, 1 lb] can tuna
¼ cup sugar
½ teaspoon salt
2 tablespoons cornflour

1 chicken cube dissolved in 1
  cup water or 1 cup chicken
  stock
2 tablespoons vinegar
2 teaspoons soya sauce
1 green pepper, cut in strips

Pre-heat electric frypan to 250°F. Drain pineapple and reserve syrup. Combine sugar, salt, cornflour. Stir in chicken stock, vinegar, soya sauce and pineapple syrup. Pour into pan and stir until mixture boils. Cook 1 min. Add tuna and pepper. Cover and simmer 10 mins. Serve with hot rice.

327 TUNA AND CASHEWS
1 large [454g, 1 lb] can tuna
2 tablespoons butter
1 small onion, chopped or
  1 tablespoon snipped
  chives
2 tablespoons flour
1¼ cups milk and tuna liquid

salt and pepper
¾ cup chopped celery
½ cup cashew nuts [or
  almonds]
1 cup grated cheese
1 cup cooked rice
1 large tomato, sliced

Drain tuna and add enough milk to tuna liquid to make 1¼ cups. Remove bones and flake. Melt butter, saute onion gently until cooked, but not brown. Remove from heat, add flour, then milk and tuna liquid and return to heat. Stir until sauce boils and thickens. Add tuna, salt and pepper, celery and cashews. Put half cheese on base of greased casserole then add rice and finally tuna mixture. Cover with tomato slices and rest of cheese. Bake in moderate oven for 30 mins or until heated through and cheese browned.

328 TUNA CAULIFLOWER CHEESE

1 large [454g, 1 lb] can tuna
1 small cauliflower
125g [4 oz] green beans
45g [1½ oz] butter
1 onion, chopped
3 tablespoons flour
450ml [¾ pint] milk
2 teaspoons lemon juice
salt and pepper
125g [4 oz] tasty cheese
1 tablespoon breadcrumbs
paprika [optional]

Cut cauliflower into small flowerets. Top, tail and string beans and cut into 2" pieces. Cook cauliflower and beans in boiling salted water until just tender. Drain. Melt butter, fry onion until transparent. Remove from heat and add flour and gradually add milk. Return to heat. Stir until sauce boils and thickens. Add lemon juice, salt and pepper, beans, tuna and three-quarters of the cheese. Arrange cauliflower on base of greased ovenproof dish. Pour in tuna mixture. Sprinkle with breadcrumbs and remaining cheese. Add a little paprika if desired. Bake in moderate oven for 30 mins.

329 CURRIED TUNA

1 large [454g, 1 lb] can tuna
1 tablespoon margarine
2 onions, sliced
1 small apple, peeled and
  diced
1 tablespoon flour
2 teaspoons sugar
2 teaspoons curry powder
1 250g [8 oz] can button
  mushrooms
salt and pepper
2 cups stock or water
2 teaspoons chutney
2 teaspoons sultanas

Melt margarine over low heat, add onions and apple and fry until lightly browned. Stir in flour, sugar, curry powder, mushrooms, salt and pepper and cook 1 min. Add stock or water and stir until mixture boils. Add tuna, chutney and sultanas. Reheat. Serve with boiled rice.

Variation: Put tuna mixture into greased casserole dish, top with parsley scone whirls and bake in hot oven 10 mins then reduce to moderate and bake further 5 mins.

Parsley Scone Whirls

250g [8 oz] scone dough
  [R1439]
milk for glazing
2 tablespoons chopped parsley

Roll dough into thin oblong sheets, sprinkle with parsley and roll up. Cut into 1" slices and place on top of tuna. Glaze with milk.

35

Cold Fish

330 SALMON MOUSSE

1 large [454g, 1 lb] can red
    salmon
¼ cup vinegar
¼ cup sour cream
1 tablespoon horseradish
3 teaspoons gelatine
¼ cup lemon juice

½ teaspoon garlic salt
½ teaspoon salt
½ tablespoon prepared
    mustard
½ cup whipped cream
1 125g [4 oz] jar red caviar,
    [optional]

Drain, bone and skin salmon. Mix in vinegar. Fold in sour cream and horseradish. Dissolve gelatine in lemon juice and stir into salmon mixture. Add salt, mustard and cream. Pour into mould and refrigerate. Delicious served with red caviar.

331 TAHITIAN FISH

1.5kg [3 lb] firm, white fish
    fillets
juice of 3 lemons
2 medium onions, finely
    sliced

1 tomato, chopped
½ cup chopped parsley
salt and pepper
¼ cup [approx.] French
    dressing [R 1004]

Skin and bone fish, cut flesh into ½" dice. Place in glass or earthenware bowl and pour lemon juice over. Cover and chill at least overnight or until fish is white, turning occasionally with a spatula or wooden spoon. Avoid using anything metal.
When fish is white and looks like cooked fish, squeeze out all liquid by placing fish in a colander or strainer and pressing with spatula or wooden spoon. Put into a clear bowl and add other ingredients. Toss to coat well. Serve cold. Excellent as an entree.

332 CURRIED FISH

1-1.5kg [2-3 lb] fish
2 large onions, chopped
few peppercorns
4 teaspoons curry powder

2 teaspoons sugar
2 cups brown vinegar
1 cup water

Place all ingredients except fish in a saucepan and bring to boil. Simmer for at least 20 mins. Fry fish in usual way (in batter if you like). Cool and place in a dish. Pour sauce over fish and stand until required. Will keep well in refrigerator. Can be eaten cold with salad or reheated and served hot with rice.

Sustaining Savouries

Savouries to Sustain

Being kissed by a man who didn't wax his moustache was — like eating an egg without salt.

Rudyard Kipling. The Gatsbys.

400 SAVOURY DISHES

Try some of these for unusual breakfasts, lunches, suppers or entrees!

401 SAVOURY SNACKS

Six slices bread or crumpets lightly toasted and buttered.
Cover with one of the following combinations, and grill or bake in moderate oven until cheese melts and browns.
1. Mustard, sliced ham, sliced pineapple, sliced cheese.
2. Sliced tomato, sliced cheese, chopped bacon (optional).
3. 1½ cups grated cheese, 1 tablespoon chopped chives or grated onion, ½ cup chutney, 1 tablespoon tomato sauce, 2 teaspoons worcestershire sauce.
4. 250g (½ lb) grated cheese combined and melted in saucepan with 1 egg, salt and pepper, 150ml (¼ pint) milk. Top with grilled slice of apple and grilled bacon.
5. Mayonnaise (instead of butter), sliced onions, sliced cheese or chopped cooked bacon.

Cut into fingers and serve hot or cold. They can be frozen if desired.

402 OPEN SANDWICHES

Open sandwiches are quick and easy to assemble. Wholemeal or rye bread makes a tasty base; French sticks or large cracker biscuits can also be used for variation. Open sandwiches may be as dainty or "man size" as required.
Butter the bread and top with any of the following:
  sliced tomato
  grated cheese
  sliced cold meat e.g. roast beef with horseradish sauce
  cold grilled sausages
  flaked cooked fish
  pickled rollmops
  lettuce, cucumber, beetroot
  celery
  grated apple
  pineapple rings
  cottage, cheese, dill cucumber and olives

SANDWICH FILLINGS (R 1801, 1802, 1803, 1804)

403 SAVOURY FRENCH BREAD

French stick
2 tablespoons prepared French
  mustard
4 large slices cheese cut in
  halves

125g [4 oz] salami, sliced
90g [3 oz] butter
1 clove garlic, crushed
1 tablespoon chopped
  parsley

Cut stick lengthwise, three-quarters the way through and open out carefully. Spread one side with mustard, place cheese on top of mustard. Arrange salami on top, and close loaf. Cream butter and garlic, add chopped parsley, and mix well. Spread butter mixture evenly over top and sides of loaf, wrap in aluminium foil, and place in moderate oven until heated through, approx. 15 mins. Serve cut in slices.

404 CREAM CHEESE LOAF

It is essential to prepare this the day before it is required.

500g [1 lb] square white
  sandwich loaf
butter
1 hard boiled egg
mayonnaise or cream
1 teaspoon curry powder or
  mustard
1 220g [7½ oz] can red salmon
salt and pepper
125g [4 oz] chicken, finely
  minced
125g [4 oz] ham, finely
  chopped

mustard
125-250g [4-8 oz] cream cheese
300ml [½ pint] cream
garlic salt [optional]
finely chopped chives
  [optional]
stuffed olives, parsley,
  cayenne pepper, shredded
  lettuce or chopped gherkins
  for garnishing

Slice crusts off all six sides of loaf. Cut loaf lengthwise into five. Butter inside slices of bread. Spread each layer with a different filling.
(a) hard boiled egg, finely mashed with mayonnaise and curry.
(b) drained, boned and finely flaked salmon, salt and pepper.
(c) minced chicken, mayonnaise, salt and pepper.
(d) ham and mustard.
Assemble loaf, wrap in foil, place bread board and a weight (e.g. a can of fruit) on top and refrigerate overnight. Next day allow cream cheese to come to room temperature, beat to soft consistency and add cream, salt and pepper. If desired add garlic salt and chives. An hour prior to serving unwrap foil, spread cheese mixture on outside of loaf and garnish centre or edges with finely sliced olives, parsley, cayenne pepper, lettuce or gherkins. Chill again before cutting.

39

405 TOMATO RAREBIT

1 cup tomato soup
1/4 teaspoon dry mustard
1/4 teaspoon worcestershire
  sauce
185g [6 oz] cheddar cheese,
  grated

1 egg, beaten
hot buttered toast
parsley

Heat soup, mustard and worcestershire sauce in saucepan. Add cheese and stir until it melts. Add egg and cook, stirring until slightly thickened. Serve over hot buttered toast and garnish with parsley.

406 CHEESE FONDUE

1 clove garlic
1 1/2 cups dry white wine
1 teaspoon lemon juice
315g [10 oz] emmenthal
  cheese, grated
315g [10 oz] gruyere cheese,
  grated

3 tablespoons kirsch
1 tablespoon cornflour
white pepper, grated nutmeg
  and paprika
French bread for serving

Rub inside of fondue pot with garlic. Heat wine and lemon juice carefully and add cheese gradually, stirring in a figure-of-eight motion. Blend kirsch and cornflour and add to the bubbling mixture. Cook for 2-3 mins. and season to taste with pepper, nutmeg and paprika.
Cut French bread into 1" cubes. Impale cubes on fondue forks and dip into cheese mixture.
Always use an earthenware pot and stir mixture with a wooden spoon—cheese, wine and metal just don't mix.

*Kitchen scissors are invaluable. Here are some uses you can put them to:
Cutting up cooked meat or sausages for a toddler.
Chopping parsley—place parsley in a glass, insert scissor points and snip while revolving the glass. The chopped parsley can be stored in the glass covered with plastic wrap.
Trimming pastry.
Chopping spring onions, chives, celery and rhubarb.
Trimming bacon rinds.

407 OMELETTE

2 eggs
salt and pepper
2 tablespoons water

15g [½ oz] butter
parsley to garnish

Beat eggs thoroughly. Add salt and pepper. Just before cooking add water. Heat butter in frying pan and pour in egg mixture. Quickly tilt pan to spread mixture all around. Cook quickly—about 1 or 2 mins. Do not over-cook. The omelette should be creamy and moist in centre. Using egg slice, fold in half and garnish with parsley.

Variations:
1. Cheese—add 2-3 tablespoons cheese either combined with eggs or sprinkled on top of omelette before folding.
2. Herbs—add 1 tablespoon chopped fresh herbs e.g. parsley, chives, tarragon etc.
3. Onion—add 1 small onion, finely sliced and sauteed in the butter.
4. Mushroom—add 2 or 3 medium mushrooms, sliced.
5. Chicken—add 2-3 tablespoons chopped chicken.
6. Bacon—fry 2 rashers of chopped bacon in the butter.
7. Ham—add 2 tablespoons chopped ham.
8. Tomato—peel and chop 1 tomato and add to butter before eggs.
9. Asparagus—add 2 stalks chopped fresh (cooked) or canned asparagus to butter.
10. Apple—saute half a peeled, thinly sliced apple in the butter until soft and golden brown.
11. Potato—saute hot or cold boiled, sliced potato in the butter until brown.

408 POACHED EGGS WITH CHEESE SAUCE

1 cup milk
salt and pepper
4 eggs

4 slices hot buttered toast
60g [2 oz] cheese, grated

Heat milk to boiling point in a frying pan. Add salt and pepper. Break eggs into milk and poach gently until set, spooning milk over eggs. Remove eggs with slotted spoon and place on hot buttered toast. Keep warm. Add cheese to milk in pan and stir until melted. Spoon sauce over eggs and serve.

EGG FLUFFS (R 1705)
EGG IN THE HOLE (R 1706)
EGG IN A NEST (R 1807)

409 SPECIAL SCRAMBLED EGGS

For each person you will need:—

1 slice bacon, chopped	2 eggs
1 small onion, finely chopped	salt and pepper
mushrooms as desired, chopped	butter for frying
1 small tomato, skinned and chopped	other ingredients as well as or instead of these, to taste
30g [1 oz] or more cheese, diced	

Melt butter, add bacon and fry gently until just beginning to crisp. Add onion, mushrooms and cook 5-10 mins. Next add tomatoes, cook few mins and then add cheese. Just as the cheese begins to melt, add eggs, salt and pepper. Mix well and scramble until eggs are just cooked.

PETER'S SCRAMBLED EGG VARIATIONS (R 1707)

410 EGGS FOO YEUNG

5 eggs, well beaten	1 cup bean shoots
½ cup finely diced, cooked ham, chicken or bacon	½ cup diced celery
1 cup minced onion	1 large green pepper, chopped
	oil for frying

Combine all ingredients, divide into 6 portions and fry one at a time in hot oil. Serve with soya sauce.

411 GLAMORGAN "SAUSAGES"

2 eggs, separated	¼ teaspoons each salt, mustard, mixed herbs
1 small onion, finely chopped [optional]	flour
90g [3 oz] cheese, grated	extra breadcrumbs
125g [4 oz] soft breadcrumbs	fat or oil for frying

Mix egg yolks, onion, cheese, breadcrumbs and seasonings. Make into sausage shapes and roll in flour. Beat egg whites until frothy, dip "sausages" into whites and then roll in breadcrumbs. Fry in hot fat or oil.

SWEETCORN CASSEROLE (R 809)

412 SWEETCORN FRITTERS

1 large [454g, 1 lb] can cream
    style sweetcorn
2 tablespoons cornflour
    blended with
2 tablespoons milk

4 eggs, beaten
salt
1 tablespoon melted butter

Mix all ingredients except butter. Just before cooking add butter. Drop half tablespoonfuls of mixture into frypan and fry until golden brown on both sides. Delicious served hot with tomato wedges, celery and carrot sticks or with soya sauce.

413 CHEESE PIZZA

1 cup S.R. flour
water or milk

¼ teaspoon salt
1 tablespoon butter or oil

Sift flour and salt, rub in butter and mix into a scone dough with liquid. Put aside while preparing topping:

1 cup grated cheddar cheese
1 or 2 rashers bacon, chopped
½ egg, lightly beaten
parmesan cheese

1 teaspoon dried onion
1 tablespoon chopped parsley
¼ teaspoon paprika

Grease pizza tray. Roll out dough thinly and place on tray. Cover with egg, sprinkle with other ingredients. Bake in hot 400°F (200°C) oven for 10-15 mins. Serve hot, or cold for barbecues with salads etc.

Alternative fillings:

1. 60g [2 oz] melted butter
    1 onion, grated
    4 tomatoes, fresh or
        preserved, peeled and
        chopped
    1 cup diced polony or salami

    2 tablespoons tomato paste
        [or sauce]
    1 cup grated cheese
    ¼ teaspoon mixed herbs
    salt and pepper

Brush dough with melted butter. Mix half cheese with other ingredients and spread on dough, top with remaining cheese.

2. 1 onion sliced and sauteed in
    15g [½ oz] butter
    1 cup mozzarella cheese
    60g [2 oz] stuffed olives,
        sliced

    60g [2 oz] can anchovies
        or small can sardines or
        smoked oysters, drained
        and chopped
    1 teaspoon oregano

Variations:

1. Individual pizzas can be made using the scone dough as above.
2. Yeast pizza dough (R 1613).

414 MINCED STEAK PIZZA

Pastry

2½ cups S.R. flour, sifted 1 egg, beaten
¼ cup oil ¾ cup milk

Mix oil with sifted flour, add egg and milk and make a stiff dough. Roll out to ¼" thickness. Place in a large, greased lamington tin or pizza pan. Make edges 1" high to contain filling. Do not stretch pastry. Refrigerate while making filling.

Meat sauce

500g [1 lb] minced steak 1 cup red wine or beef stock
1 large onion, chopped ¼ teaspoon oregano
oil salt and pepper
1 clove garlic, crushed 2 tomatoes, sliced
1 small [142g, 5 oz] can 1 cup grated cheese
  tomato paste olives if desired

Fry meat and onion in a little oil for 10 mins until browned. Add garlic and stir in tomato paste, wine or stock, oregano, salt and pepper. Simmer 10-15 mins. Fill pastry case, cover with tomato slices, cheese and olives. Bake in hot 400°F (200°C) oven for 15-25 mins until browned. Serve with tossed salad.

*White sauce too thin? Cream an extra tablespoon of flour with one table-spoon of butter and stir into the hot sauce. It will melt and thicken the sauce without any lumps. Casseroles and gravies can be thickened in the same way.

415 QUICHE

Pastry

125g [4 oz] flour
60g [2 oz] butter
salt

1½ tablespoons [approx]
water

Work together with enough water to make a firm dough. Roll out and line a tart plate, making a pastry case.

Basic filling

125g [4 oz] white onions,
finely sliced
15g [½ oz] butter
2 eggs

salt and pepper
¾ cup cream
60g [2 oz] cheese

Cook onions slowly in butter for 5-6 mins. Allow to cool. Beat eggs, salt and pepper, add cream and cheese and one of the following:

1. **Lorraine**—60g (2 oz) bacon softened in butter or 60g (2 oz) chopped ham.
2. **Leek**—1 leek cut in thin rings and cooked in butter.
3. **Spinach**—155g (5 oz) chopped spinach and ¼ teaspoon grated nutmeg.
4. **Asparagus**—1 small (285g, 10 oz) can asparagus tips, well drained.
5. **Crab**—1 can crab meat, flaked, ¼ teaspoon nutmeg, 2 teaspoons finely chopped parsley and 1 tablespoon dry sherry.

Pour into uncooked pastry case and bake at 425°F (220°C) for 10 mins, then 375°F (190°C) for 20 mins.

416 EGG AND BACON TART

250g [8 oz] short crust pastry
[R 1301]
3 rashers bacon
1 medium onion chopped or
1 tablespoon chopped chives
3 eggs

1½ cups milk or cream
2 teaspoons chopped parsley
salt and cayenne pepper
125g [4 oz] cheese,
grated

Line a 9" pie plate with the pastry and bake blind in 375°F (190°C) oven for 10 mins. Chop bacon and fry lightly with onion. Beat eggs and add all other ingredients. Pour into pastry shell. Bake in 350°F (180°C) oven for 35-45 mins or until set.

Egg and Bacon Tartlets: Line greased patty tins (about 36) with 1/8" thick rounds of pastry. Put a tablespoonful of mixture into each one and bake at 375°F (190°C) for 15 mins.

45

417 EGG AND BACON PIE

250g [8 oz] puff pastry
  [R 1310]
90g [3 oz] bacon
4-6 eggs

1 teaspoon chopped parsley
1 teaspoon snipped chives
salt and pepper
egg yolk or milk for glazing

Remove rind from bacon and cut into 2" lengths. Line a pie plate with two-thirds of the pastry. Place bacon in pie and break in eggs. Sprinkle with parsley, chives, salt and pepper. Glaze edges and cover with remaining pastry which has been rolled to fit the top. Glaze top with egg yolk or milk and bake in a hot oven for 10 mins. Reduce heat to moderate and cook a further 20 mins.

Variation: 2-3 sliced tomatoes can be added.

418 ONION TART

125g [4 oz] puff pastry
  [R 1310]
4 white onions, very finely
  sliced
2 tablespoons melted butter
salt and pepper

3 eggs, beaten
1 cup cream
½ cup grated parmesan
  cheese
butter
1 tablespoon chopped parsley

Roll pastry and line pie plate. Refrigerate. Put onions in saucepan with butter, salt and pepper. Cover with lid and saute for a few mins until soft, do not brown. Add beaten eggs and cream and pour into pastry shell. Sprinkle with cheese and dot with small pieces of butter. Bake in 400-425°F (200-220°C) oven for about 30 mins and serve at once sprinkled with parsley. Good for lunch or supper served with a tossed salad.

Variation: Add a few black olives.

419 SWEETCORN AND HAM FLAN

375g [12 oz] short crust pastry
  [R 1301]
30g [1 oz] butter
2 tablespoons chopped onion
1 298g [10½ oz] can
  kernel sweetcorn
2 teaspoons chopped parsley

3 eggs, beaten
salt and pepper
1 cup lukewarm evaporated
  milk
60g [2 oz] ham, sliced
90g [3 oz] cheese, sliced

Line an 8" flan tin with pastry and bake blind at 375°F (190°C) for 10 mins. Melt butter and saute onion without browning. Add corn and parsley and fill pastry case. Mix eggs, salt, pepper and milk and pour over corn. Top with slices of ham and then cheese. Bake at 375°F (190°C) for 30-35 mins until filling is set.

420 CHOUX CHEESE RING

45g [1½ oz] butter, melted
¾ cup water
salt and freshly ground
   pepper

75g [2½ oz] flour
125g [4 oz] Swiss cheese, cut
   in small pieces
2 eggs [125g, 4 oz in weight]

Add water to melted butter, salt and pepper. Bring to boil and add flour immediately. Stir over heat until dough is completely detached from saucepan. Add cheese and work it in until it has melted. Add 1 egg and beat in well, then add other egg.
Have oven tray well buttered and floured. Place mixture on it in a ring (either pipe or place in spoonfuls). Bake in a moderate oven for 50 mins. Prick it and serve hot or cold. Nice served with champignons in mustard or spinach filling the centre of the ring.

421 CHEESE AND BACON SAVOURY

6 rashers bacon
4 large slices cold toast
3 eggs

1¼ cups milk
salt
2 cups grated cheese

Halve bacon rashers and remove rind. Place on oven tray. Cut toast in halves and arrange in shallow greased casserole. Beat eggs well, add milk, salt and cheese. Pour over toast, bake in moderate oven until puffed and brown. Place bacon in oven 5 mins after cheese dish and bake until crisp. Arrange on top of dish before serving.

422 CHEESE AND BACON CUSTARDS

2 rashers bacon, cooked and
   crumbled
125g [4 oz] cheddar cheese
   grated

¾ cup milk
2 eggs, beaten

Combine bacon and cheese. Stir milk gradually into eggs. Pour over bacon and cheese mixture. Mix well, pour into four buttered ramekin dishes. Place in pan of hot water and bake in moderate oven for 30-35 mins or until a knife inserted in the middle comes out clean. These custards may also be gently steamed on top of the stove by placing them in a pan of hot water and covering well.
Variation: Place 1 tablespoon milk each in 2 ramekins, break in eggs whole, add cheese and bacon.

CHEESE SOUFFLE PUDDING (R 1809)

423 EGG AND CHEESE PIE

6-8 hard boiled eggs
300ml [½ pint] well seasoned
   cheese sauce
500g [1 lb] potatoes, cooked
   and mashed

3-4 tablespoons grated
   cheese

Halve eggs and put into ovenproof dish and cover with cheese sauce. Pipe a border of mashed potato. Cover with cheese and brown under grill or in oven.

424 TOMATO MACARONI CHEESE

250g [8 oz] uncooked
   macaroni
4 rashers bacon, chopped
30g [1 oz] butter
1 onion, chopped
1 green pepper, chopped
   [optional]

2 tablespoons flour
1 454g [1 lb] can tomato soup
½ cup milk or water
250g [8 oz] cheese, grated
salt and pepper

Cook macaroni in boiling salted water until tender, about 10 mins, and then drain well. Fry bacon until crisp, remove from pan, add butter and saute onion and green pepper. Add flour, then soup and milk, stirring until mixture boils and thickens. Add three quarters of the cheese and stir until it melts. Combine with cooked macaroni, pour into buttered ovenproof dish, top with remaining cheese and bake in a moderate oven about 20 mins until heated through.

425 CHEESE FONDANT

1¼ cups milk
1 cup soft breadcrumbs
1 cup grated cheese

60g [2 oz] butter
salt, pepper, cayenne, chives
2 eggs, separated

Boil milk and pour over breadcrumbs. Add cheese, butter, seasoning, chives and egg yolks. Just prior to baking in a moderate oven for 30 mins, beat egg whites and fold in. Cook in small well buttered moulds or pie dish.

Many's the long night I've dreamed of cheese — toasted mostly.
Ben Gunn, the marooned sailor,
in Treasure Island by R. L. Stevenson

426 CHEESE SOUFFLE

30g [1 oz] butter
30g [1 oz] flour
150ml [¼ pint] milk

3-4 eggs separated
125-185g [4-6 oz] cheese
salt and pepper

Make a thick white sauce from butter, flour and milk. Add egg yolks. Whisk egg whites in electric mixer and while they are getting stiff, grate cheese into sauce. Fold sauce into beaten whites and pile into a well greased souffle dish. Place in 350°F (180°C) oven in pan of cold water and bake about 15-25 mins until high and golden. Avoid opening oven door. Serve immediately.

427 EGG AND ASPARAGUS CASSEROLE

2 tablespoons butter
2 tablespoons flour
450ml [¾ pint] milk
salt and cayenne pepper
½ cup grated cheese
1 large [425g, 15 oz] can
  asparagus, drained

2 hard boiled eggs, chopped
125g [¼ lb] luncheon meat or
  ham, chopped
soft breadcrumbs
grated cheese, butter
parsley and hard boiled
  eggs for decoration

Make white sauce with butter, flour, milk and seasoning, and add grated cheese. Fold in asparagus, eggs, and meat. Spoon into greased casserole dish. Sprinkle with breadcrumbs, cheese and dot with butter. Bake in moderate oven 20 mins. Garnish with eggs and parsley.

Variations:
1. Substitute 298g (10½ oz) can creamed sweetcorn for meat.
2. Increase eggs to four and ham to 250g (½ lb), omit asparagus and substitute 2 cups cooked sliced potatoes.

428 ASPARAGUS HAM ROLLS

18 cooked fresh or canned
  asparagus spears
6 thin slices ham
4 teaspoons butter
4 teaspoons flour

1 cup milk
½ cup grated cheese
salt and pepper
toast triangles and parsley for
  serving

Place 3 asparagus spears on each ham slice and roll up. Arrange in a single layer in a lightly greased, shallow oven-proof dish. Melt butter and stir in flour until smooth. Cook one minute without browning. Stir in milk and cook, stirring until sauce boils and thickens. Simmer two mins. Add cheese, salt and pepper. Pour over ham rolls and place in moderate oven until heated through and the top lightly browned. Garnish with toast triangles and parsley.

429 HAM AND CELERY

1 cup chopped ham	½ teaspoon mustard
1 cup chopped, cooked celery	3-4 tablespoons breadcrumbs
1 cup white sauce [R 1010]	1 tablespoon butter
salt and pepper	2 tablespoons grated cheese

Mix ham, celery, white sauce, salt, pepper and mustard. Place in casserole dish. Cover with thick layer of breadcrumbs, dot with butter and sprinkle with cheese. Bake in moderate oven until heated through and browned on top, about 20 mins.

Variation:
Substitute sliced cooked green beans for celery and add ¾ cup grated cheese and ¼ teaspoon nutmeg to white sauce. Stir over low heat until cheese has melted, then proceed as above.

OTHER HAM RECIPES (R 658-660)

430 BROCCOLI SAVOURY

1 bunch broccoli or 3 packets frozen broccoli	2 tablespoons parmesan cheese
125g [4 oz] bacon, chopped	salt and pepper
1 small onion, chopped	2 tablespoons fresh bread-
60g [2 oz] butter	crumbs
2 tablespoons flour	extra butter
1¼ cups milk	

Fry bacon and onion gently in bacon fat. Cook broccoli, drain, mash gently with 30g (1 oz) butter. Make thick white sauce with remaining butter, flour, milk, salt, pepper and half the cheese. Combine with bacon and onion. Put broccoli in greased ramekin dishes, pour sauce on top. Add breadcrumbs, cheese and dot with butter. Brown in top of moderate oven about 20 mins.

431 TOMATOES IN CHEESE SAUCE

6 small firm tomatoes or well-drained canned tomatoes, halved	2½ cups cheese sauce
	60g [2 oz] grated cheddar cheese
12 rashers streaky bacon	2 cups white breadcrumbs
salt and pepper	

Wrap each tomato half in a rasher of bacon. Sprinkle with salt and pepper. Place in buttered fire-proof dish and pour cheese sauce around. Mix cheese and breadcrumbs and sprinkle on top. Brown in moderately hot oven for 15 mins.

*Why not cook the whole packet of brown rice? It keeps well in a covered container in the fridge and is a great time-saver.

432 BARBECUED BEANS

1/4 cup sliced onion
1 tablespoon butter
2 cups cooked or canned soya
  beans
1/2 cup tomato puree
1 tablespoon brown sugar or
  molasses

salt and pepper
1/2 teaspoon sage, thyme or
  other herbs
1/2 cup breadcrumbs or wheatgerm
1/2 cup grated cheese

Fry onion in butter until light brown. Mix with all other ingredients except cheese; place in greased casserole, sprinkle with cheese, cover and bake in moderate oven for 30 mins. Remove cover and allow to brown.

Variations:
1. Substitute 454g (16 oz) can baked beans for soya beans and tomato puree, omit breadcrumbs and add 125g (4 oz) bacon fried with the onion, or chopped ham.
2. Add 1 finely chopped green pepper and 1 tablespoon worcestershire sauce.

433 CARROT RICE CASSEROLE

This dish is enjoyable freshly made as a main course, reheated for breakfast or cold as part of a salad meal.

2 1/2 cups finely grated carrot
250g [8 oz] cheese, grated
2 cups cooked brown rice
2 eggs, well beaten
1 1/4 cups milk

2 teaspoons melted butter
2 teaspoons finely chopped
  onion
salt and pepper

Mix carrot, cheese and rice in a greased casserole dish. Combine other ingredients and add to carrot mixture. Cover and bake in a moderate oven for 40 mins. Serves 8.

*One cup of raw rice equals three cups cooked rice.

*Brown rice needs to be cooked at least 30 mins. To make it a little lighter add some raw white rice during the last 10-15 mins. of cooking.

434 BACON RATATOUILLE

This dish is delightful served hot with cooked rice or cold as an unusual summer appetiser or as an accompaniment to steak or chops.

1 large aubergine, diced
salt
125g [4 oz] bacon, diced
1 tablespoon oil
1 clove garlic, crushed
2 onions, sliced
2 green peppers, sliced

4 or 5 tomatoes, skinned and quartered
2 zucchini, sliced
125g [4 oz] mushrooms sliced
chopped parsley to garnish

Sprinkle aubergine with salt and set aside. Saute bacon in pan until transparent and remove. Add oil to pan and heat, add garlic and onions, and cook gently until onions are transparent. Add peppers and drained aubergine. Cover pan, cook gently 15 mins. Add tomatoes, zucchini and mushrooms. Season and cook uncovered for 15 mins. Gently stir in bacon. Sprinkle with parsley.

RATATOUILLE (R826)

435 PANCAKES WITH SAVOURY FILLING

300ml [½ pint] pancake batter [R 1205]
60g [2 oz] butter
90g [3 oz] mushrooms, finely chopped
salt and pepper
1 rounded tablespoon flour

150ml [¼ pint] chicken stock
250g [8 oz] ham or cold cooked chicken, diced
1 teaspoon chopped parsley
2 hard boiled eggs, chopped
1 tablespoon cream
1 tablespoon grated cheese

Melt half butter. Add mushrooms, salt and pepper. Cover and cook slowly 3-5 mins. Stir in flour then stock. Bring to boil. Add chicken, eggs, parsley and cream. Keep warm. Prepare and cook the pancakes. Put a spoonful of the filling in the middle of each pancake, fold over and arrange in ovenproof dish. Melt remaining butter. Sprinkle pancakes well with butter and grated cheese and brown under the griller.

Variations:

1. Omit mushrooms, substitute half a small (298g, 10½ oz) can creamed sweetcorn or a 300g can asparagus tips, drained.
2. Salmon filling: Combine 1 small (220g, 7¾ oz) can red salmon, drained and flaked, (125g,) 4 oz cream cheese, 1 tablespoon chopped mint, 1 tablespoon lemon juice, 2 teaspoons grated onion, salt and pepper.

52

The Italian Touch

The Italian Touch

500 PASTA

Pasta is an Italian word which describes all types of noodles—spaghetti, macaroni, lasagne and dozens of other shapes. Some have spinach juice added, giving them a green colour and a wholemeal pasta is also available from health food shops.

How to Cook

Use plenty of boiling, salted water (about 8 cups to 250g [8 oz] pasta) and add pasta gradually so that water does not go off the boil. A teaspoon of oil in the water prevents boiling over. Commercial pasta takes anything from 10-20 mins to cook—it should be tender but still firm, i.e. "al dente", meaning with a little "bite" left in it. When cooked, drain in a sieve or colander and add a teaspoon of butter or oil to prevent sticking. Homemade pasta cooks in a few mins, particularly if freshly made—slightly longer if it has been allowed to dry.

501 PASTA

3 eggs   *flour—approx. 3-4 cups*
1 teaspoon salt

Break eggs into bowl, add salt and enough flour to make a non-sticky dough. Knead well and roll out as for pastry as thinly as possible on a lightly floured board, then cut into desired shape.

If you have a pasta machine (obtainable from Italian grocers or gourmet cookware shops), kneading is not necessary. Put small handfuls of the mixture through the roller of the machine several times, flouring dough as required so that it does not stick to the roller. When the dough has reached a firm, non-sticky consistency, adjust the roller each time the dough is passed through, until the pasta is of the desired thickness. After a little experience you should be able to estimate the thickness you like.

Then lay out the long flat pieces on tea towels until the batch is completed. It can then be used as it is for lasagne or ravioli (see later) or passed through the tagliatelli or spaghetti cutters of the machine. If the pasta is not to be used immediately allow to dry on tea towels overnight and store in a large flat box (a large chocolate box or shirt box is ideal) to prevent breaking. Sprinkle a little polenta (cornmeal) between layers of pasta to prevent sticking. Polenta is used in preference to flour as it is easily brushed off before cooking.

Wholemeal pasta is made in exactly the same way substituting wholemeal flour for plain flour. It is a little more difficult to handle and breaks more easily but with a little practice can be very successful. One tablespoon of oil added to the dough makes it easier to work with.

---

*To crush garlic, sprinkle the peeled clove liberally with salt and flatten it with the flat side of your chopping knife. Mash it thoroughly with the salt. (Remember to allow for this when adding salt to whatever the garlic goes into). Keep a small tile especially for garlic to avoid contaminating your chopping board.

502 LASAGNE

250g [8 oz] lasagne [try the green lasagne for a change]
Meat sauce

1 tablespoon oil	½ teaspoon sugar
1 onion, finely chopped	**Cheese sauce**
1 clove garlic, crushed	60g [2 oz] butter or margarine
500g [1 lb] minced steak	3 tablespoons flour
2 x 425g [15 oz] cans tomatoes,	2½ cups milk
undrained or 1kg [2 lb] fresh	125g [4 oz] tasty cheese
tomatoes, chopped	**Topping**
1 150g [5 oz] can tomato paste	60-90g [2-3 oz] mozzarella or
1 teaspoon oregano	cheddar cheese, sliced
½ teaspoon basil	½ cup grated parmesan
½ teaspoon rosemary	cheese
1 teaspoon salt	½ cup cream

Heat oil, saute onion and garlic for a few mins, add meat and cook, stirring, until brown. Add chopped tomatoes with their liquid, tomato paste and remaining ingredients. Cook until tender.

Cook lasagne in boiling, salted water until tender but take care not to overcook (15 mins). Meanwhile, make cheese sauce. Melt butter, stir in flour and cook 1-2 mins. Gradually add milk and stir over low heat until boiling. Stir in grated cheese and cook until melted.

In an oblong baking dish place alternate layers of lasagne and meat sauce, lasagne and cheese sauce, repeating until all are used up. Lay slices of mozzarella cheese on top and cook in a moderate oven for 15 mins. Five mins before end of cooking time pour over the combined parmesan cheese and cream.

503 RAVIOLI WITH RICOTTA CHEESE AND SPINACH FILLING

250g [8 oz] ricotta cheese	1 egg
1 250g [8 oz] packet frozen	nutmeg
spinach, thawed and well	salt and pepper
drained OR 315g [10 oz]	home-made pasta [R 501].
can spinach, drained	

Mix well ingredients for filling. Take a long wide strip of pasta, (R 501), and put teaspoonfuls of the mixture 1" apart on the strip. Cover with another strip of the same size and cut in between fillings with a sharp knife or pastry wheel to make individual parcels of filling. Cook in boiling, salted water 5-10 mins, drain well and serve with Tomato and Sour Cream Sauce (R 510), Pesta (R 509) or Bolognese Sauce (R 507).

504 FARFALLE ALLA CARBONARA

(Farfalle are butterfly-shaped noodles)

12 rashers steaky bacon
4 eggs
2 tablespoons chopped
   parsley

90g [3 oz] grated parmesan
   cheese
freshly ground black pepper
250g [8 oz] farfalle

Remove bacon rind and cut into julienne strips. Fry gently until crisp and pour off fat.

Beat the eggs well and add parsley, cheese and a liberal amount of freshly ground black pepper. Mix well and add 2 tablespoons of cooked bacon.

Cook the farfalle in boiling salted water until tender but not soft. Drain well and immediately add the egg mixture to the hot pasta (this will thicken and partially cook the sauce). Sprinkle with the remaining bacon.

505 SPAGHETTI ALLA SICILIANA

Pasta

500g [1 lb] spaghetti
2 tablespoons butter, melted
4 tablespoons grated
   parmesan cheese

Sauce

2 tablespoons olive oil
1 large onion, grated
1 clove garlic, crushed
3 cups peeled and diced
   aubergine
1 cup finely chopped green
   pepper

3 cups peeled and diced
   tomatoes
½ teaspoon dried basil or
   1 teaspoon fresh
1 45g [1½ oz] can anchovies,
   drained
1 tablespoon capers
½ cup black olives, stoned
salt and pepper
2 tablespoons finely chopped
   parsley

Heat oil in large frying pan or saucepan and saute onion for 10 mins. Add garlic, aubergine and green pepper. Saute for 5 mins. Add tomatoes and basil, cover and cook over low heat 30 mins, stirring frequently. Chop 6 anchovies finely and mix in. Add capers, olives, salt and pepper. Cook over low heat for 10 mins. Mix in parsley.

Cook spaghetti, drain and toss in melted butter and parmesan cheese. Pour sauce over spaghetti and garnish with remaining anchovy fillets.

506 SPAGHETTI VONGOLE

8-12 oz uncooked spaghetti
90g [3 oz] oil
2 cloves garlic, chopped
1 425g [15 oz] can tomatoes or
500g [1 lb] fresh tomatoes,
  skinned and chopped
1 tablespoon tomato paste

salt
freshly ground black pepper
1 315g [10 oz] can baby clams,
  undrained
1 tablespoon finely chopped
  parsley

Heat oil and add garlic, saute 1-2 mins. Add chopped tomatoes with juice and tomato paste. Add salt and pepper and simmer gently for 15 mins until sauce has thickened. Cook spaghetti. Add clams and as much of their liquid as necessary to give sauce the required consistency. Add chopped parsley and simmer 1 min longer.
Serve over cooked spaghetti.

507 BOLOGNESE SAUCE

15g [½ oz] butter
1 medium onion, finely
  chopped
1 medium carrot, finely
  chopped
1 stick celery, finely chopped
60g [2 oz] bacon, finely
  chopped
250g [8 oz] minced steak
4 tablespoons white wine or
  sherry

1¼ cups stock
1 150g [5 oz] can tomato paste
salt and freshly ground black
  pepper
1 teaspoon mixed herbs,
  [parsley, basil, thyme, rosemary, etc.]
grated nutmeg
2 tablespoons cream or
  30g [1 oz] butter

Melt butter and gently fry the onion, carrot, celery and bacon until soft—about 10 mins.
Add meat and raise heat until it is brown, stirring continuously. Add wine or sherry and cook briskly until almost evaporated. Stir in stock and tomato paste, add salt, pepper, herbs and nutmeg to taste. Cover and simmer gently 1-1½ hours. Stir in cream or butter. This quantity will be sufficient for 375-500g (12-16 oz) uncooked spaghetti.

*Garlic and onion odours can be removed from your chopping board with a paste made by mixing baking soda with a little water. Apply liberally, leave to dry then rinse off.

508 RIGATONI WITH MEAT SAUCE

1 tablespoon oil or butter
1 clove garlic, minced
1 small onion, chopped
1 90g [3 oz] can mushrooms, drained
500g [1 lb] minced steak
1 cup tomato puree [or juice]
250g [8 oz] can tomato paste
½ teaspoon salt
¼ teaspoon cayenne pepper
250g [8 oz] rigatoni, cooked and drained
grated parmesan cheese

Heat shortening, cook garlic, onion and mushrooms for 5 mins. Add meat and cook just until red colour disappears and meat is crumbly. Add tomato puree, tomato paste, salt and pepper. Cover and simmer gently 30-45 mins. Spoon over hot rigatoni. Serve with grated parmesan cheese.

509 PESTA

Pesta can be served over plain spaghetti or any other noodles, or used as extra flavouring for meat sauce.

60g [2 oz] fresh basil [or a mixture of parsley and basil]
30g [1 oz] pine nuts
2 cloves garlic
¼ teaspoon salt
3-4 tablespoons oil
45g [1½ oz] parmesan cheese, grated

Roughly chop basil and nuts. Place garlic in a mortar with salt and pound with the basil and nuts to a thick paste. Add oil gradually, beating well to a creamy consistency. Alternatively, place basil, nuts, garlic and salt in blender with 2 tablespoons oil and blend at slow speed, adding remaining oil gradually Stir in cheese.

510 TOMATO AND SOUR CREAM SAUCE

2 cloves garlic, crushed
2 tablespoons olive oil
1 425g [15 oz] can tomatoes
2 tablespoons tomato paste
1 chicken or beef stock cube
½-¾ cup sour cream
salt and pepper
2 teaspoons fresh herbs [parsley, basil, thyme, rosemary or a mixture of any of them] OR
2 teaspoons pesta [R 509] OR
1 teaspoon mixed dried herbs

Fry garlic in oil, add tomatoes and their liquid, mashing the tomatoes finely as they cook. Add tomato paste, stock cube and herbs and simmer for 30 mins. Stir in sour cream and reheat without boiling. Season.
Serve over any type of cooked pasta (especially good with ravioli).

511 GREEN ALMOND SAUCE

1 bunch young spinach cooked and drained or 250g [8 oz] frozen spinach, thawed and drained
½ cup chopped parsley
60g [2 oz] blanched almonds
60g [2 oz] butter or margarine
1 clove garlic, crushed
2 tablespoons oil
½ cup grated parmesan cheese
3 tablespoons boiling water

Blend all ingredients except boiling water to a smooth paste. Add boiling water and blend again. Serve on cooked spaghetti, vermicelli or other noodles with extra parmesan cheese if desired.

512 MUSHROOM/ANCHOVY SAUCE

125g [4 oz] butter or margarine
2 shallots, chopped [or 1 small onion, chopped]
250g [8 oz] mushrooms, chopped
2 tablespoons flour
300ml [½ pint] milk
1 cup cream
salt and pepper
2 tablespoons tomato paste
60g [2 oz] anchovy fillets, drained and chopped
1 220g [7 oz] can tuna, drained and flaked

Melt butter and saute shallots for 2 mins. Add chopped mushrooms, saute 5 mins longer. Stir in flour and cook 2 mins stirring well. Remove from heat and gradually add milk, blending well. Return to heat and cook until thickened and boiling. Add cream, tomato paste, anchovies and tuna and season to taste. Simmer 10 mins.
Serve over pasta and sprinkle with parmesan cheese.

513 MARINARA SAUCE

30g [1 oz] butter
1 clove garlic, crushed
1 425g [15 oz] can tomatoes, undrained or 500g [1 lb] fresh tomatoes, skinned and chopped
2 tablespoons tomato paste
½ cup water
1 chicken stock cube
750g [1½ lb] scallops
salt and freshly ground black pepper
3 tablespoons chopped parsley

Saute garlic in butter for a few mins. Add chopped tomatoes and their liquid, tomato paste, water and stock cube. Bring to the boil and simmer gently uncovered for 15 mins. Add scallops, salt and pepper and cook for a further 5 mins then add parsley. This quantity will be sufficient for 375-500g (12-16 oz) uncooked spaghetti.
Variation: Use a combination of either fresh, canned or frozen shellfish, e.g. lobster, crab, oysters, prawns, mussels.

60

The Butcher's Hook.

The Butcher's Hook

600 MEAT

Included in this section are recipes for beef, lamb, pork, ham, veal, savoury meats and minced steak. For other ideas see sauces, marinades and flavoured butters (R 1000).

MAKING A CASSEROLE

There are six steps involved in making a casserole.

1. Browning of meat (and usually of onion too) in oil, margarine, butter, or dripping. Oil gives very satisfactory results but a combination of butter or margarine and oil also works well and gives a more subtle flavour. Use butter if the dish is to be a creamy one, eg. Veal with Herbs and Cream (R 669) or with chicken. Olive oil goes well with a tomato or zucchini dish. Allow approximately 1.25kg (2½ lb) meat for six people. Trim excess fat and cut meat into large cubes, about 1½". For this quantity about 60g (2 oz) margarine or 5-6 tablespoons oil will be required. Fry and seal the meat well on all sides, remove and fry onion. Sometimes this step can be omitted and the meat simply mixed with the thickening in the casserole dish. If your casserole dish can also be used on the stove, you can use it for the browning too (instead of a frying pan) and so save washing up!

2. Thickening: Usually with flour either plain or seasoned, or packet soups etc. Sometimes the thickening can be added towards the end of the cooking time, eg. rice, potatoes, noodles. Allow about 1 heaped tablespoon flour for 1.25kg (2½ lb) meat and stir into remaining oil or equivalent in frying pan.

3. Adding liquid: Stir gradually into flour mixture about 2½ cups of one or a combination of stock (either home-made or prepared with cubes); water; vegetable water; red or white wine; beer; liquid from cans, eg. tomatoes or sweetcorn; juicy tomatoes; tomato paste or sauce or soup; other canned soups; gravy; worcestershire sauce; vinegar, soya sauce, etc. Return meat to pan.

4. Flavouring: Adding one or a combination of salt and pepper, chopped herbs (eg parsley, thyme, oreano, basil, chives, mint), bouquet garni, spices (eg. cloves, nutmeg, ginger), shallots, garlic, green pepper, mustard, curry powder, paprika, sugar, stock cubes, etc.

5. Simmering: Long slow cooking in a covered saucepan or casserole dish on either cooktop or in a slow oven gives a tastier result than fast cooking but many people have to use a pressure cooker or equivalent at times. For 1.25kg (2½ lb) beef, allow approximately 2-2½ hours, depending on the cut, for pork 1¾ hours, for lamb and veal 1½ hours, and for chicken 1 hour.

6. Garnishing: When the meat is partially or completely cooked, add any of the following: diced or small whole mushrooms, quartered tomatoes, diced carrots or parsnips, chopped celery, shredded cabbage, cauliflower or broccoli flowerets, peas, beans, bean shoots, sweetcorn, stoned prunes, chopped bacon, stoned olives, walnuts, pineapple pieces, sultanas, parsley, noodles, rice, etc. Sometimes these can be added with the other flavouring. However they tend to disintegrate and their flavour becomes dulled during the long cooking time required for the meat.

Beef

601 BEEF'N BURGUNDY

1kg [2 lb] bladebone steak
1 cup burgundy
30g [1 oz] butter
1 packet mushroom soup

1½ cups water
salt and pepper
1 tablespoon red currant jelly
125g [4 oz] maraschino cherries

Cut steak into 1" cubes and marinate in burgundy for 1 hour, turning frequently. Melt butter in pan, add drained meat, fry until browned. Place meat in casserole. Pour contents of soup packet into pan, add water gradually and cook until thickened, then add burgundy, salt, pepper and red currant jelly. Pour over the meat, cover and cook at 325°F (160°C) for 1½ hours. Add cherries and cook further 30 mins.

BEEF CASSEROLE (R2417)

602 BEEF AND BEAN CASSEROLE

2 tablespoons butter
750g [1½ lb] topside steak,
  cut in strips
2 rashers bacon, chopped
1 medium onion, chopped
1 454g [16 oz] can tomatoes
¼ cup water
¼ cup chopped green pepper
1 284g [10 oz] can lima beans,
  drained
salt and cayenne pepper

Pre-heat oven to 350°F (180°C). Melt butter and fry meat quickly until sealed. Remove and place in a casserole. Fry bacon and onion together for 5 mins. Add tomatoes, water, green pepper, lima beans, salt and cayenne. Bring to the boil, pour over meat, stir and place lid on casserole. Bake for 1 hour.

603 BEEF, NOODLES AND VEGETABLES

750g [1½ lb] oysterblade or
  topside steak
3 cups water
60g [2 oz] egg noodles
1 packet chicken noodle soup
1 tablespoon soya sauce
1 tablespoon oil
1 clove garlic, crushed
  [optional]
2-3½ cups chopped
  vegetables

Use mixtures of any of the following: peas, beans, celery, onion [brown or spring], cabbage, bean sprouts, sweet corn, broccoli, cauliflower, fresh mushrooms, parsley, carrot, green pepper, celery.

Cook noodles in boiling water for 3 mins and add contents of soup packet. Cook for further 3 mins. Remove from heat. Slice beef very thinly and mix with soya sauce. Heat oil and brown beef with garlic for about 5 mins. Add vegetables and noodle mixture. Cook until vegetables are just soft.

604 BEEF AND RICE SWISS STYLE

125g [4 oz] bacon, chopped
1 onion, finely chopped
500g [1 lb] bladebone steak,
  cubed
3 cups beef stock [R201]
salt and pepper
1 cup rice
1 tablespoon chopped parsley

Fry bacon and onion in large saucepan until transparent. Add meat and fry until browned. Add 1 cup stock, salt and pepper and simmer until meat is cooked, about 1 hour. Add remaining 2 cups stock, bring to boil, add rice and simmer further 15-20 mins, until rice absorbs liquid. Add parsley.

605 BEEF OR CHOPS IN SPICY SAUCE

500g-1kg [1-2 lb] stewing
  steak or chops
2 tablespoons flour
1 teaspoon mustard [or ¼
  teaspoon each of ginger,
  mustard, curry and mixed
  spice]
1 carrot, sliced
1 onion, sliced

2 tablespoons worcestershire
  sauce
1 tablespoon vinegar
1¼ cups water
1 teaspoon sugar
1 teaspoon salt
4 tablespoons tomato sauce
  or 1 tablespoon tomato
  paste

Mix flour and mustard. Chop meat, roll in flour and place in casserole, cover with carrot and onion. Combine all other ingredients, pour over meat. Cover and cook in moderate oven 1½-2 hours.

Variations:
1. Add 2 tablespoons plum jam and 1 tablespoon lemon juice.
2. Add ½ cup sultanas.

606 BEEF IN TOMATO SAUCE

750g [1½ lb] round steak
2 tablespoons flour
oil
½ cup tomato sauce
¼ cup chopped onion
1 very small clove garlic,
  crushed

¼ teaspoon oregano
thyme
½ teaspoon salt
black pepper
¾ cup stock

Cut meat into 3-4 pieces. Roll in flour. Heat a little oil in saucepan, brown meat. Mix tomato sauce, onion, garlic, oregano, thyme, salt, pepper and stock and pour over meat. Cook slowly until tender, about 1¼ hours. Skim any fat from sauce before serving.

Variations:
1. Add 2 tablespoons vinegar, 1½ teaspoons prepared mustard, 1 teaspoon horseradish.
2. Omit tomato sauce, substitute 500g (1 lb) chopped fresh or canned tomatoes and 2 large chopped green peppers.
3. Add 125g (4 oz) chopped cooked bacon, 1 cup chopped celery, 2 tablespoons sherry, 1 tablespoon soya sauce, 1 teaspoon worcestershire sauce and use only ½ cup stock. Substitute 3-4 fresh sliced tomatoes for tomato sauce.

607 BEEF AND APRICOTS

1/2 cup dried apricots
boiling water to cover
1kg [2 lb] bladebone steak, cubed
2 tablespoons flour
1 onion, sliced
2 tablespoons oil
1 1/4 cups stock
2 tablespoons brandy
1 tablespoon brown sugar
salt and pepper
2 teaspoons lemon juice
2 tablespoons cream

Soak apricots in boiling water for several hours or overnight. Coat meat in flour. Fry onion in hot oil, remove from pan. Brown meat thoroughly and remove. Add stock, brandy, sugar, salt and pepper and bring to boil. Add meat, onion and drained apricots. Cover tightly and simmer 1 1/2 hours or until meat is tender. Add a little water if necessary. Just before serving stir in lemon juice and cream.

608 PICKLED WALNUT STEW

750g [1 1/2 lb] oysterblade steak,
   cubed
2 tablespoons oil
1 large onion, sliced
1 cup stock or water
6 pickled walnuts, quartered
   [obtainable from most
   supermarkets]
2 teaspoons of the pickle juice
1 teaspoon vinegar
1/2 teaspoon ground ginger
12 peppercorns
1 bay leaf
1 clove
salt
1 clove garlic, crushed
1/2 cup breadcrumbs

Brown meat in oil, place in casserole. Fry onion until lightly browned and add to meat. Add liquid ingredients to pan, scraping off all browned pieces and blending well. Pour into casserole with all other ingredients except crumbs. Cook 1 hour at 350°F (180°C), then stir in breadcrumbs and bake further 30 mins. Serve with extra pickled walnuts.

*When ravenous children keep asking "Is dinner ready yet?" offer them an hors d'oevre by placing a plate of chopped or sliced raw vegetables on the table. Some suggestions: carrot sticks, celery spread with cream cheese, cauliflower, tomatoes, cucumber, lettuce or green pepper.

609 BEEF RAGOUT AU GRATIN

4 large potatoes
1.5kg [2½ lb] bladebone steak
2 tablespoons butter
500g [1 lb] green peas
salt and pepper

2 egg yolks
½ cup cream
½ cup dry white wine
grated cheese

Boil and mash potatoes. Cut meat in small cubes, fry in hot butter. Reduce heat, cover and simmer for 1 hour, adding, if necessary, a little water. Add peas, season and cook for another 10 mins. Line deep ovenproof dish with mashed potatoes and fill with meat mixture. Beat egg yolks, slowly add cream, then wine. Pour over meat. Sprinkle with grated cheese and put in oven to heat and brown top. Can be prepared the day before required.

610 BEEF AND ONION CASSEROLES

1. 750g [1½ lb] oysterblade
steak
1 425g [15 oz] can crushed
pineapple, undrained

1 packet French onion soup
½-1 cup stock or water

Dice meat, place in casserole, add pineapple, sprinkle with contents of soup packet. Add stock and simmer or cook in moderate oven 1½ hours.

2. 750g [1½ lb] oysterblade
steak

1 cup claret
1 packet French onion soup

Marinate chopped steak in claret for approx 2 hours. Line baking dish with enough foil to fold over and cover steak. Place steak on foil, sprinkle with soup and claret, cover with foil. Bake in moderate oven 1½ hours.

611 BEEF, MUSHROOMS AND TOMATOES

750g [1½ lb] bladebone steak
seasoned flour
1 large onion, sliced
250g [8 oz] can mushrooms
in sauce

500g [16 oz] can tomatoes,
drained but liquid reserved
½ cup water
½ cup claret [optional]

Cube steak, roll in flour and place in casserole. Cover with layers of sliced onion, mushrooms in sauce, chopped tomatoes, tomato juice, water and claret. Cover and cook at 325°F (160°C) for 2 hours.

612 BEEF STROGANOFF

A Russian dish, nice enough for a special dinner, yet quickly and easily made.

500-750g [1-1½ lb] bladebone steak
1 tablespoon flour or cornflour
1 small onion, chopped
1 clove garlic, finely chopped
1 teaspoon sugar
250g [½ lb] tomatoes, skinned and chopped, or 1 large can tomatoes
1 packet mushroom soup
1¼ cups water [if you use tinned tomatoes, use juice plus enough water to make 1¼ cups]
½ cup plain yoghurt or sour cream

Cut meat into finger lengths and toss in flour. Put meat, onion, garlic, sugar, tomatoes and mushroom soup blended with water into a casserole. Bake in a moderate oven 350°F (180°C) for 2-2½ hours. Add yoghurt just before serving. Very good served with jacket potatoes.

613 BEEF SATAY

This is a very simplified method of preparing beef satay.

1kg [2 lb] bladebone steak
1 tablespoon ground cummin seed
1 tablespoon ground coriander
1 tablespoon brown or white sugar
3 teaspoons ground ginger
3 teaspoons ground pepper
½ teaspoon ground saffron [optional]
1 teaspoon salt
3 cloves garlic, crushed
melted butter

Cut meat into ½" cubes. Mix with all other ingredients and marinate for two hours or longer (preferably leave overnight in refrigerator). Thread meat on to metal skewers and brush with melted butter. Grill, turning frequently until brown and tender. Alternately fry meat in butter. Serve with salads and sauce.

Sauce

4 tablespoons crunchy peanut butter
1½ tablespoons tomato sauce
1 teaspoon brown sugar
1-2 teaspoons vinegar or lemon juice
1½ tablespoons boiling water
salt

Mix all ingredients well, adding more water if a thinner sauce is desired.

614 BEEF ROLLS

1kg [2 lb] bladebone or round
  steak, sliced thinly
flour
oil
1½ cups beef stock

Flatten beef pieces, place a portion of filling on each piece, roll up, fasten with toothpicks and then dredge with flour and brown in hot oil. Simmer in 1½ cups stock until tender.

Fillings

1. *60g [2 oz] butter*
¼ cup chopped onion
½ cup chopped celery
1 cup fresh breadcrumbs
½ teaspoon salt
¼ teaspoon sage
pepper

Saute onion in butter, add celery and cook until soft. Place in basin with breadcrumbs and seasonings, moisten with a little water if necessary.

2. *1 cup cooked spinach, pureed*
1 cup ricotta cheese
¼ cup chopped spring onions
1 tablespoon chopped parsley
salt and pepper
cream or milk

Blend well together, moisten with a little cream or milk if necessary.

615 CURRIED BEEF AND BANANA ROLLS

4 bananas
8 thin slices of topside or
  round steak 4" square
2 tablespoons seasoned flour
30g [1 oz] butter
1 tablespoon oil
2 rashers finely chopped
  bacon
1 tablespoon chopped onion
1 tablespoon chopped
  green pepper
1½ teaspoons curry powder
1 cup water
1 small [113g] can tomato
  paste

Peel and slice bananas in half, crossways. Roll steak in seasoned flour and tie around banana halves. Melt butter and oil and fry steak quickly on all sides to seal. Remove and place in a casserole. Fry bacon until crisp, add onion and green pepper, saute 2 mins, add curry powder and fry for a further 5 mins. Add water and tomato paste. Pour sauce over the rolls. Place lid on casserole and cook for 1½ hours in moderate oven.

An army marches on its stomach.
                    Napoleon

616 STEAK IN FOIL

500g [1 lb] rump or oysterblade
   steak
butter
1 packet brown onion sauce
   mix

1 tablespoon each chopped
   onion and green pepper
125g [4 oz] mushrooms,
   chopped [optional]
salt and pepper

Grease foil with butter. Sprinkle half the sauce mix over. Place
the steaks on foil. Chop green pepper and onion and put on
top. Add mushrooms and rest of sauce mix. Put dob of butter
on each steak. Sprinkle with pepper and salt. Fold up into
parcel and cook in moderate oven for approx. 40 mins.

617 BEEF CURRY

750g [1½ lb] bladebone steak
1-2 tablespoons curry powder
   [Vencatachellum]
1 tablespoon flour
salt and pepper
oil for frying
1 onion, chopped
2 cups stock or water

1 apple, peeled and chopped
1 banana, chopped
1 tomato or 2 tablespoons
   tomato sauce
1 tablespoon sultanas
1 tablespoon coconut
1 tablespoon chutney or plum
   jam

Cut meat into neat pieces, roll in mixture of curry powder,
flour, salt and pepper. Brown meat in oil, then remove from
pan. Fry onion until brown, gradually add stock and when
boiling, add meat and remaining ingredients. Simmer for 1½
hours, adding more water if necessary. Even nicer if made the
day before required. Serve with boiled rice through which
finely chopped parsley has been folded, lemon wedges and
side dishes e.g.:

1. Sliced banana, dipped in lemon juice, then rolled in
   coconut.
2. Chopped tomato and green pepper.
3. Chutney (Mango is tasty).
4. Peanuts or cashew nuts.
5. Diced hard boiled egg and dill cucumber.
6. Sultanas.
7. Sliced, peeled cucumber coated with sour cream or yoghurt.
8. Chopped spring onions.
9. Pineapple pieces rolled in finely chopped mint.
10. Finely chopped ginger.

618 FLAMING ORANGE FILLET STEAKS

4 pieces fillet steak
freshly ground black pepper
juice of 1 orange
2 tablespoons brandy
2 oranges, peeled and cut in
    slices

60g [2 oz] butter
extra 2 tablespoons brandy
    for flaming

Rub steaks with freshly ground pepper. Marinate in orange juice and brandy for 4 hours. Gently heat orange slices in a separate saucepan. Melt butter in pan and saute steak until cooked as required. Pour marinade over. Add orange slices. Warm and set alight the extra brandy and pour over the top. Serve immediately with jacket potatoes and hot asparagus.

619 STEAK WITH OYSTER SAUCE

6 pieces fillet steak
1 225g [8 oz] can oysters

300ml [½ pint thick white
    sauce [R 1010]

Make thick white sauce replacing some of milk with liquid from canned oysters. Add oysters and keep warm. Grill steak and pour sauce over.

Variation:
Marinate steak in white wine, sherry or port and use drained marinade in sauce.

620 STEAK WITH ORANGE AND APPLE STUFFING

4 thick rump steaks
4 tablespoons fresh bread-
    crumbs
2 tablespoons chopped
    parsley
rind of 1 orange, finely grated
juice of 1 orange

1 unpeeled Granny Smith
    apple, grated
30g [1 oz] butter, melted
1 egg yolk
salt and pepper
oil

Slit each piece of steak horizontally almost through, and open out.
Mix breadcrumbs, parsley, orange rind, apple, butter, egg yolk and seasoning. Spread stuffing on one half of each piece of steak, fold over, secure with toothpicks, brush with oil and grill. Heat orange juice and pour over cooked steak.

621 STEAK SUPREME

For each serving:

1 piece eye fillet, rump or
   porterhouse steak
1 rasher bacon
1 clove garlic, crushed
3 small mushrooms, halved or
   quartered
oil
parsley sprigs to garnish

Marinade

2 tablespoons claret
3 teaspoons grand marnier or
   curacao
3 teaspoons brandy
1½ tablespoons tomato sauce
salt and pepper

Mix marinade ingredients, add steak, marinate 2 hours, turning several times. Fry bacon until crisp. If using eye fillet, wrap bacon around meat and secure with toothpick. Otherwise chop bacon. Heat bacon fat or oil, saute garlic and mushrooms. Remove. Drain steak, reserving marinade and cook over high heat, remove and keep warm. Add marinade, mushrooms, garlic and bacon. Heat, pour over steak and serve garnished with parsley.

622 STEAK AU POIVRE

Quick and impressive for visitors!

750g [1½ lb] grilling steak
30g [1 oz] peppercorns
30g [1 oz] butter
2 tablespoons brandy

⅔ cup dry white wine
2 tablespoons thick cream
salt

Crush the peppercorns roughly with pestle and mortar or in blender. Roll steak in peppercorns until coated.
Fry steak quickly in butter, until just cooked to taste. Take steak out of pan, keeping hot on serving dish. Pour off fat from pan, leaving pepper in bottom. Pour in brandy, heat and set alight then add wine and cream, stir well, add salt, pour over steak and serve.

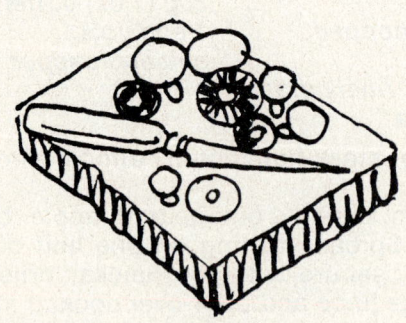

623 STEAK WITH CHOCOLATE SAUCE (ARAGON STEAK)

1 kg [2 lb] rump steak
oil
salt and pepper
2 onions, chopped
2 tablespoons tomato ketchup
    or sauce
1 tablespoon chopped parsley
150ml [¼ pint] dry white wine
30g [1 oz] chocolate, grated

Rub steak with oil, salt and pepper. Fry onions, in oil until soft, add ketchup and parsley and blend in well. Slowly stir in wine and chocolate. Season and keep hot. Grill steak and serve with sauce.

624 BEEF BRAISED IN RED WINE

1.5kg [3 lb] piece topside,
    oysterblade or Scotch fillet
1 teaspoon crushed garlic
1 teaspoon oregano
salt and freshly ground black
    pepper
3-4 tablespoons olive oil
2 tablespoons butter
1 onion, chopped
1 carrot, chopped
1 stick celery, chopped
1-2 rashers bacon, chopped
1¾ cups beef stock
500g [1 lb] tomatoes, skinned
    and chopped
¾ cup dry red wine
1 bay leaf

Mix garlic, bacon, oregano, salt, pepper. Make small incisions all over the meat with a sharp knife and insert small amounts of the mixture into them. Heat oil in a heavy frypan and brown meat on all sides. Put pan aside for later use. Melt butter in a heavy casserole just large enough to hold meat and cook onions, carrots and celery and bacon for 10 mins, stirring frequently until lightly browned. Place meat on top of vegetables, add tomatoes, beef stock and bay leaf. Cover and cook at 350°F (180°C) until meat is tender. Slice meat and arrange on serving platter or leave in one piece for carving at the table. Add wine to frypan and boil rapidly until reduced to ⅓ of its volume, scraping the sides and bottom of the pan to loosen any browned fragments. Add reduced wine to meat juices. Strain sauce, pressing vegetables through a sieve to thicken it. Skim off any excess fat, correct seasoning and pour over meat.

Food, beautiful food!
Food, beautiful food!
Whether it's boiled or stew-ew-ewed
It's still beautiful food!

                                                            Anon.

625 SAUERBRATEN

2-2½kg [4-5 lb] piece of
  topside
1 lemon
2 cups vinegar
2 cups water
1 large onion, sliced

2 tablespoons sugar
2 teaspoons salt
10 peppercorns
1 bay leaf
oil

Slice lemon into quarter inch slices. Place meat in a deep bowl, add lemon. Combine all other ingredients, heat until boiling and pour over meat. Cool, cover and refrigerate for three days, turning meat once each day.

Remove meat and drain, strain and reserve marinade.

Brown meat on all sides in 2-3 tablespoons of oil. Add 2 cups of marinade, bring to boil, cover and simmer 2-3 hours until tender. Serve with gravy.

Gravy
60g [2 oz] butter
60g [2 oz] flour

3 cups of liquid from meat and
  marinade
8 ginger snaps, crumbled

Melt butter, blend in flour, cook 1 minute, gradually add liquid, and a little water if necessary. Stir in ginger snaps. Bring to boil, and cook rapidly until thick.

HUSSARS ROAST (R 2413)

626 POT ROAST WITH PRUNES IN SWEET AND SOUR GRAVY

24 prunes
2kg [4 lb] piece round topside,
  rolled chuck or bolar blade
4 tablespoons flour
2 onions, sliced
3 tablespoons oil
2 bay leaves, sprig rosemary
  [optional]

¼ teaspoon nutmeg
¼ teaspoon cinnamon
salt and pepper
4 cups hot stock
4 carrots, sliced
2 potatoes, sliced
juice of 3 large lemons
2 tablespoons golden syrup

Soak prunes in water overnight. Dust meat with flour. Fry onions in hot oil until golden. Remove, add meat and brown on all sides. Add onions, bay leaves, rosemary, nutmeg, cinnamon, salt and pepper. Pour hot stock over. Cover tightly and simmer 3-4 hours until meat is tender. Remove meat and keep warm. Discard bay leaves and rosemary. Add drained prunes, carrots, potatoes, lemon juice and golden syrup. Cook 15 mins or until vegetables are tender. Serve prunes, carrots and potatoes with meat and pour the sweet and sour gravy over.

Cold Beef

627 SPICY CORNED BEEF

1-1.5kg [2-3 lb] corned silver-
   side
½ teaspoon ground cloves
freshly ground black pepper
2-3 cloves garlic
1 tablespoon chopped fresh
   parsley and thyme

water to cover
½ cup red wine
1 sprig each thyme, oregano
   and rosemary or ¼ teaspoon
   each dried
1 bay leaf
1 onion

Rub meat well with cloves and pepper. Cut garlic into slivers
and roll in chopped herbs. Cut slits in meat and insert garlic
slivers. Place all ingredients in large pan. Bring slowly to boil,
and simmer very gently until tender, about 1½ hours. Allow to
cool in liquid. Remove, cover lightly with foil or plastic wrap,
then refrigerate. Slice thinly to serve.

628 PICKLED BEEF

This dish *must* be made at least 12 hours before serving.

2 onions, finely sliced
3 tablespoons oil
½ cup vinegar
1 teaspoon sugar
2 cloves garlic
1 bay leaf, crushed
1 teaspoon chopped parsley
sprinkle of sage and rosemary

salt and pepper
1 cup white wine or vermouth
1 284g [10 oz] can condensed
   consomme
⅔ cup water
1kg [2 lb] cold cooked beef,
   sliced very thinly

Brown onion in oil, add vinegar and seasonings. Cook over
high heat for 10 mins or until reduced to ¼ cup. Add wine,
soup and water. Pour over slices of meat, cover and refrigerate
for 12 hours. Serve with pickles, olives, champignons and
artichoke hearts.

*If fat catches fire, smother it by covering quickly with a saucepan lid. Do
not pour water on it or try to blow it out—this only fans the flames.

Lamb

629 LAMB CHOPS CALIFORNIAN STYLE

1kg [2 lb] lamb or mutton
  chops
seasoned flour
2 large onions, sliced
250g [8 oz] prunes, stoned
2-3 cooking apples, peeled
  and sliced

brown sugar
1½ cups chicken stock
2 medium potatoes, peeled
  and sliced

Trim fat from chops and toss in flour. Fill greased casserole with alternate layers of chops, onions, prunes and apples, sprinkling prune and apple layers with brown sugar. Add chicken stock and top with layer of sliced potatoes. Cover and bake in moderate oven 1½-2 hours.

Variations:

1. Omit prunes, apples and 1 cup stock, and substitute 4 tomatoes, peeled and sliced and 1 sprig fresh or ¼ teaspoon dried rosemary.
2. Omit prunes and apples, substitute ½ cup chopped celery, 1 cup sweetcorn and ½ cup tomato puree.
3. Add 125g (4 oz) chopped bacon.

630 LAMB AND BEANS

1.25-1.5kg [2½-3 lb] shoulder
  or leg of lamb, boned
30g [1 oz] butter
125g [4 oz] bacon, chopped
1 onion, chopped
1 clove garlic, crushed
2 tablespoons flour
1 cup stock or wine
1 425g [15 oz] can tomatoes,
  undrained or 250g [8 oz]
  fresh tomatoes

1 300g can baby butter beans,
  soya beans or red kidney
  beans, undrained
1 tablespoon chopped fresh
  herbs or 1 teaspoon dried
salt and pepper
2 parsnips, peeled and
  chopped
4 sticks celery, chopped

Trim fat from meat, cut into 1½" cubes. Melt butter, fry meat until golden brown and place in casserole. Fry bacon until just crisp. Fry onion and garlic until golden. Add flour to pan, stir well. Gradually add stock, bring to boil stirring constantly. Add other ingredients, pour over meat and place bacon on top. Cover, bake at 350°F (180°C) for 1 hour or until lamb is tender.

631 LAMB AND BACON

750g [1½ lb] lamb neck chops
125g [4 oz] bacon pieces
1 large onion, chopped
1½ tablespoons flour
1½ cups chicken stock [made
  with cube if desired]
1 teaspoon worcestershire
  sauce
1 tablespoon tomato sauce
salt and pepper
½ green pepper, chopped

Trim fat from chops. Fry bacon lightly, remove from pan. Add chops and onion and fry lightly, adding a little butter if necessary. Remove chops and onion. Add flour and cook until brown. Add stock, sauces, salt and pepper and gradually bring to boil. Return chops, onion and bacon to pan and simmer 1¼ hours or put all in casserole and bake at 350°F (180°C). Add green pepper and cook further 15 mins.

Variation: Add 2 teaspoons curry powder to flour, substitute 2 fresh peeled and sliced tomatoes for tomato sauce and reduce stock to ½ cup. Add 3 tablespoons sweet sherry if desired.

632 LAMB AND PINEAPPLE

6 chump chops
1 tablespoon flour
salt and pepper
3 rashers bacon
1 tablespoon margarine
6 slices pineapple
1 cup pineapple juice or syrup
  from can

Trim fat from chops, toss in seasoned flour. Fry bacon lightly, remove from pan and add margarine. Brown chops on both sides. Place in greased casserole, put a slice of pineapple, then a piece of bacon on each. Cover with pineapple juice. Cover and bake at 350°F (180°C) for 45 mins or until cooked.

633 LAMB AND APRICOTS

8 chump chops
2 tablespoons flour
salt and pepper
1 tablespoon oil
1 onion, chopped
1 green pepper, chopped
1 425g [15 oz] can
  apricot halves, undrained
2 tablespoons soya sauce

Trim fat from chops, coat in seasoned flour. Heat oil, brown chops on both sides, remove from pan. Add onion and pepper and brown lightly. Add undrained apricots and soya sauce, stir until boiling. Add chops, cover and simmer about 45 mins or until meat is tender.

634 LAMB PROVENCALE

6 chump chops
500g [1 lb] tomatoes, peeled
  and sliced
2 onions, peeled and sliced
1 clove garlic, crushed

salt and pepper
1 tablespoon chopped fresh
  herbs or 1 teaspoon dried
  herbs

Trim fat from chops. Mix tomatoes, onion and garlic and put half in base of casserole. Arrange meat on top, then add remaining tomato mixture. Sprinkle with salt, pepper and herbs, cover and cook at 350°F (180°C) for 1 hour or until tender. Add a little water if necessary. Delicious served with cauliflower.

CHOPS IN SPICY SAUCE (R 605)

635 LAMB LAYERED WITH VEGETABLES

750g [1½ lb] lamb neck chops
1 clove garlic, crushed
125g [4 oz] mushrooms,
  sliced
2 onions, chopped
2 tomatoes, sliced
1 zucchini, sliced [optional]

salt and pepper
2 teaspoons paprika
¼ cup dry sherry or red wine
1 teaspoon worcestershire
  sauce
1 tablespoon chopped mint
1 green pepper, sliced

Trim fat from chops and place in one layer in greased casserole. Spread garlic on top, then add mushrooms, onions, tomatoes, zucchini, salt and pepper, paprika, and combined sherry and worcestershire sauce. Cover and bake at 325°F (160°C) for 30 mins. Add mint and green pepper and bake further 15 mins or until meat is tender.

Variations:

1. Add or substitute for another vegetable, ¼ cauliflower, in flowerets, or 1 stick celery.
2. Substitute 1 454g (1 lb) can tomato soup or puree for tomatoes.
3. Omit mushrooms and zucchini, add 1 cup sweetcorn kernels.

*Brewers Yeast
Add one tablespoon to: meat gravies, casseroles, meat loaves, rissoles and other minced meat dishes, bread, curries.

636 LAMB AUBERGINE CASSEROLE

4 chump chops
2 tablespoons oil
2 onions, chopped
1 large aubergine, unpeeled
and cut in chunks
1 cup rice
4 tomatoes, peeled and
chopped

1 tablespoon chopped fresh
herbs or ¼ teaspoon mixed
dried herbs
1 cup beef stock or 1 cup
water with beef cube dis-
solved in it
salt and pepper
bay leaf

Remove fat and bone from lamb and fry quickly on all sides in oil. Add onions and aubergine and fry a few mins. Add rice and stir until transparent. Add tomatoes, seasonings and stock. Simmer gently 1 hour or more, adding more water if it begins to dry.
Variation: Replace some of the stock with wine.

637 BARBECUE CHOPS CHINESE STYLE

6 forequarter chops
1 454g [1 lb] can tomato soup
1½ tablespoons soya sauce
1 tablespoon honey

1 small onion, finely chopped
¼ teaspoon ground ginger
1 teaspoon worcestershire
sauce

Trim fat from chops. Place in shallow casserole. Combine other ingredients in small saucepan and cook over low heat for 5 mins or until well combined. Pour over chops, cover and bake at 350°F (180°C) for 30 mins. Remove cover and allow sauce to thicken. Cook further 15 mins or until chops are tender.

638 SAVOURY CHOPS

1kg [2 lb] stewing chops
½ cup plum jam
¼ cup worcestershire sauce
1 onion, finely chopped

1 cup water
salt and pepper
¼ cup gravy

Trim fat from chops. Mix jam and sauce, spread on both sides of chops. Stand 2 hours then add onion, water, salt and pepper. Simmer 1½ hours, add gravy and cook further ½ hour or until meat is tender.

639 LANCASHIRE HOT POT

6 medium potatoes, peeled
   and sliced
1kg [2 lb] forequarter chops,
   trimmed
125g [4 oz] fresh or canned
   mushrooms
2 sheep or lamb kidneys,
   skinned and sliced
1 small [100g] can smoked
   oysters, drained
salt and pepper
2 medium onions, sliced
1 beef cube dissolved in
1 cup boiling water
chopped parsley

Clean and slice mushrooms if fresh. Place half of potato slices in base of large casserole. Cover with chops, mushrooms, kidney slices and smoked oysters. Season. Add onions and remaining sliced potatoes. Pour in beef stock and bake covered in moderate oven for 1½ to 2 hours. Serve sprinkled with chopped parsley.

640 LAMB PIE

1kg [2 lb] boned lamb or
   mutton, cubed
2 tablespoons oil
1 onion, sliced
2 tablespoons flour
2 cups beef stock
salt and pepper
½ cup diced carrot
½ cup diced turnip
1 cup peas
mixed herbs
2 tablespoons chopped parsley
125g [4 oz] short crust pastry
   [R 1301]
1 beaten egg for glazing

Trim fat from meat and cut into 1" cubes. Heat oil in large pan, brown onion, remove. Add lamb and brown. Blend in flour, add stock and seasonings, cover and simmer until tender. Add onion and other vegetables and herbs and simmer 15 mins. If necessary thicken further by adding equal parts of flour and butter mixed together, and simmer for 5 mins. Turn into greased deep pie-dish and sprinkle with parsley.
Roll out pastry to fit top, moisten edges of pie dish and cover with pastry, press down edges, slit top once or twice, brush with beaten egg and decorate with leaf shapes cut from left-over pastry. Glaze with egg.
Bake at 400°F (200°C) for 15-20 mins.

*For a change, cover nearly cooked grilled chops with cheese, or with chutney with mustard, ginger, or curry added if desired, and grill a few more mins.

641 LAMB, PRUNE AND PEPPER PILAF

1.25kg [1½ lb] lean lamb,
   cubed
3 cups stock
2 tablespoons butter or oil
1 onion, chopped
2 large red peppers, chopped

250g [8 oz] prunes, soaked
   in water and stoned
1 cup raw brown rice
juice of ½ small lemon
salt and pepper
½ teaspoon oregano

Heat butter in large saucepan, saute onion and lamb for about 10 mins until colour has changed. Add stock and simmer 20 mins. Add other ingredients, mix well. Cover and simmer or bake at 350°F (180°C) for 1 hour or until lamb is tender and rice has absorbed all stock. Fluff with fork.

642 BRAISED CHOPS IN MUSHROOM GRAVY

4 barbecue chops, trimmed
2 tablespoons oil
2 medium onions, finely sliced
1 beef cube, dissolved in 1½
   cups water

1 small [190g] can mushrooms
salt and pepper

Trim chops and brown on both sides in hot oil. Remove chops and fry onions until golden, pour off fat, lower heat and return chops to pan. Add stock, cook chops gently until tender (approx 20 mins). Add mushrooms, season and heat through.

643 DEVILLED LAMB SHANKS

4-6 lamb shanks
1 sprig each of fresh rosemary,
   marjoram, thyme and mint
   or ½ teaspoon of each, if
   dried
2 tablespoons oil
1 tablespoon curry powder

2 tablespoons tomato sauce
½ cup white wine
½-1 cup water
2-3 tomatoes, peeled
1 green pepper, sliced into
   rings
salt and pepper

Heat oil in deep pan, brown shanks, add curry powder, tomato sauce, water and wine. Simmer until tender, at least 1 hour. Add tomatoes, pepper rings, salt and pepper and simmer further 10-15 mins.

BRAISED LAMB SHANKS (R 1805)

*If you want to add yeast extract to a casserole, do so just prior to serving so that the vitamin content is not destroyed by lengthy cooking.

644 LAMB KEBABS

500g [1 lb] lean lamb [leg or
  shoulder]
juice of 2 large lemons
½ cup oil
salt and pepper
1 tablespoon chopped fresh
  parsley
1 tablespoon chopped fresh
  oregano or ¼ teaspoon dried

1 large onion
2 tomatoes
1 green pepper
mushrooms
bayleaves

Cut lamb into cubes about 1" square. Marinate for 1-2 hours in lemon juice, oil, salt and pepper, herbs and a little of the onion, chopped. Cut tomatoes, green pepper and remaining onion into thick chunks. On large skewers place pieces of meat, tomato, pepper, onion, mushroom, bayleaf and so on until skewers are full. Grill, basting several times with remaining marinade. Serve with rice.

Variations:

1. Use a different marinade (R 1209-1036).
2. Add quartered lamb kidneys, small whole white onions, or pieces of bacon.
3. Substitute beef or pork for lamb.
4. If time is short, do not marinate meat but baste prepared skewers liberally with marinade.

645 LAMB IN SOYA SAUCE

500g [1 lb] lean lamb, cubed
  [leg or shoulder]
6 tablespoons thick soya
  sauce
1 teaspoon black pepper
¼ cup oil for frying

3 cloves garlic, crushed
1 large onion, sliced into rings
½ cup canned green peas
¼ cup canned sweetcorn
¼ cup diced carrots

Mix soya sauce and pepper well and marinate meat for 30 mins. Heat oil in pan and brown garlic. Fry lamb, adding any excess marinade. When meat is nearly cooked, add carrots and onion rings. When meat is tender and all moisture absorbed, add green peas and sweet corn. Mix well and reheat. Do not add salt as soya sauce is salty.

*Apple slices fried in butter, topped with a teaspoon of mint jelly (R 1915) make a delicious accompaniment to grilled chops.

646 CUTLETS WITH ORANGE STUFFING

6 thick lamb cutlets
1 cup soft white breadcrumbs
1 tablespoon finely chopped
  onion
1 tablespoon chopped parsley
2 teaspoons finely grated
  orange rind

2 tablespoons seasoned flour
1 egg, beaten
dry breadcrumbs
orange slices for garnishing

Mix breadcrumbs, onion, parsley and rind. Cut a large slit in side of each cutlet, fill with stuffing. Seal with toothpick. Coat in seasoned flour, then egg and breadcrumbs. Bake on greased tray covered with foil at 375°F (190°C) for 45 mins. Serve topped with slices of orange.
Variation: Stuff with a mixture of onions and mushrooms, sauteed in a little butter until onion is translucent. Add some soft breadcrumbs if mixture is too moist.

647 CUTLETS HAWAIIAN

4 chump chops
¼ cup seasoned flour
1 egg, beaten
½ cup dessicated coconut
1-2 tablespoons dripping
1 425g [15 oz] can sliced
  pineapple

1 tablespoon flour
1 cup water
1 teaspoon vinegar
salt and pepper

Trim excess fat from chops, coat with seasoned flour. Dip into beaten egg, then into coconut. Heat dripping in baking dish, add chops, baste with dripping. Bake uncovered at 350°F (180°C) for 45 mins or until tender. Remove meat and keep warm. Make gravy in baking dish. Add a little more dripping if necessary to make up to 1 tablespoon. Stir in flour, cook 2-3 mins. Drain pineapple, reserving syrup. Warm 4 slices pineapple in oven. Add syrup, water, vinegar, salt and pepper to flour, blend in well and stir until boiling. Boil several mins. Serve meat topped with pineapple slices and accompanied by gravy.

*To give roast lamb a different flavour, cut slits in meat and insert tiny slivers of garlic or rosemary.

*For quick roast lamb, skewer or tie 2-6 chops together, with bacon and onion rings or stuffing (R 1037) between them.

648 ROAST SEASONED FLAPS

2 boned lamb or mutton flaps, or breasts
Seasoning

1 cup soft breadcrumbs
½ teaspoon mixed herbs
1 tablespoon grated onion
salt and pepper

1 tablespoon chopped
* parsley*
1 teaspoon chopped mint
1 egg, beaten

Trim excess fat from outside of flaps. Mix ingredients for seasoning and spread over one flap, cover with other flap and fold fairly tightly. Tie with string.

Bake on rack in roasting pan approximately one hour in moderate oven, basting occasionally. Good with roast potatoes and mint sauce.

649 ROAST LOIN OF LAMB

1-1.5kg [2-3 lb] loin of lamb,
* boned [ask butcher for the*
* number of chops you*
* require]*

1½ cups stuffing [R 1037]
2 rashers bacon, chopped
* [optional]*

Spread stuffing and bacon over inside of meat, roll up and tie securely. Roast in a moderate oven 350°F (180°C) about 1½ hours. Serve with gravy.

Variations:
1. Roll the stuffed, tied meat in seasoned flour, then beaten egg and finally breadcrumbs. If possible refrigerate for 30 mins before roasting.
2. Omit bacon, substitute 1 tablespoon grated orange rind and 1 tablespoon orange juice. Add 1 tablespoon orange juice and 1 teaspoon red currant jelly to gravy.

Cold Lamb

650 PUMPED LEG OF LAMB

1 pumped leg lamb or mutton
water to cover
1 tablespoon vinegar

2 tablespoons brown sugar
1 bay leaf
6 peppercorns

Place all ingredients in large pan, bring slowly to boil and simmer gently until tender, about 1½-2 hours. Allow meat to cool in liquid. Remove meat, cover lightly with foil or plastic wrap, then refrigerate. Slice thinly to serve.

Pork

651 PORK CHOPS BAKED

4-6 thick pork chops or 750g   salt and pepper
  [1½ lb] pork fillet   2 tablespoons oil
1-2 tablespoons flour

Trim fat from chops, dredge in seasoned flour, brown in hot oil and place in casserole. Then select one of the following, cover and bake at 350°F (180°C) for 1 hour.

1. **With sour cream:**
   Insert one clove in each chop. Mix together ½ cup sour cream, ½ cup water, 2 tablespoons vinegar, 1 tablespoon brown sugar, salt and pepper and pour over chops. Add 1 bay leaf.

2. **With tomato sauce:**
   Mix together ½ cup chopped celery, 1 chopped green pepper, 1 chopped onion, salt, ½ teaspoon paprika and sprinkle over chops. Add 454g (1 lb) can tomato soup and a little water if necessary or 500g (1 lb) chopped tomatoes.
   Variation:
   Put ½" layer of uncooked rice on base of casserole before adding meat and above ingredients plus ½-1 cup vermouth or red wine.

3. **With burgundy and pineapple:**
   Blend 1 cup burgundy, 2 tablespoons mustard, 1 tablespon brown sugar, 1 tablespoon cornflour and 1 und-drained can pineapple pieces (size according to number of chops) in saucepan and stir until mixture boils and thickens. Pour over chops.

4. **With bacon, prunes, and beans:**
   Fry 1 finely chopped onion until golden, add to casserole with 1 chopped apple, 1 small (300g) can three bean mix, salt, pepper and ½ cup stock. Cover and bake for 45 mins, add 8-12 stoned chopped prunes and 4-6 slices bacon. Bake uncovered further 15 mins and sprinkle with 1 tablespoon chopped parsley.

5. **With apple sauce:**
   Add 1 sliced onion, 2 cups (approx) cooked, sieved apples or 2 sliced cooking apples, 1 tablespoon brown sugar, 1 cup water, and either 1 tablespoon chopped parsley with ½ teaspoon mixed herbs or ½ cup raisins with 1 teaspoon cinnamon. Bake 1 hour and if desired sprinkle with breadcrumbs and butter and bake further 15 mins.

652 PORK AND VEGETABLES CHINESE STYLE

500g [1 lb] pork fillet [cubed] or lean pork pieces,
marinate for 1-2 hours, and stirred occasionally.

Marinade:

1 tablespoon dry sherry
1 tablespoon soya sauce
1 tablespoon brown sugar

sprinkle of monosodium
  glutamate
1 tablespoon cornflour

Vegetables:

Prepare and chop any vegetables available, eg, spinach, cabbage, beans, beans shoots, carrot, green or red peppers, onion and place in plastic bag or crisper until ready to use.

Heat 6 tablespoons of oil in large pan, frypan or wok and fry drained pork over high heat, stirring constantly for approximately 5 mins. Remove and keep warm. Reheat pan and add vegetables, saute few mins. Thicken with ½ tablespoon cornflour blended with ½ cup water, stir until thickened, add pork, heat through and serve with boiled or fried rice (R 831).

653 HUNGARIAN PORK STEW

1 kg [2 lb] pork fillet or
  shoulder cut in strips
3-4 tablespoons oil
2 onions, chopped
1 clove garlic, crushed
60g [2 oz] smoked bacon or
  ham, chopped
1 tablespoon paprika

¼ cup [approx.] water
2 peppers, sliced
2 tomatoes, peeled and
  quartered
1 teaspoon salt
300ml [½ pint] sour cream
30g [1 oz] flour

Heat oil, fry onions, garlic and bacon. When onions are golden brown, stir in paprika. Add meat and a little water. Cover, simmer until pork is cooked, adding more water as it evaporates. Add peppers, tomatoes and salt. Simmer 5 mins. Mix sour cream with flour and add to stew, stirring as it reheats. Do not boil.

Then plight our faith anew
Three puddin'-owners true,
Who bodly claim
In Friendship's name
The noble Irish stoo,
Hurrah, Hurrah, Hurroo!

Norman Lindsay, *The Magic Pudding*

654 FESTIVAL PORK CHOPS

6 loin pork chops
1½ cups apple cider
1 tablespoon brown
  sugar
1 teaspoon salt
1 teaspoon curry powder

2 teaspoons beef extract
6 dessert prunes, pitted
12 dried apricots
1 tablespoon cornflour
1 tablespoon water

Trim rind and fat from chops. Brown chops in deep frying pan for 5 mins. Pour off any fat. Combine apple cider, sugar, salt, curry powder and beef extract. Pour over the chops in the fry pan and place the prunes and apricots on the top. Cover and cook very slowly for ½ hour or until chops are tender. When chops are cooked, remove from pan and place in a heated serving dish. Spoon the prunes and apricots over. Combine cornflour and water and add to the liquid in the pan, stirring constantly. Bring to the boil and cook until thick. Pour sauce over the chops and serve with vegetables in season.

655 PORK CHOPS STUFFED AND SEASONED

6 middle loin pork chops, 1"
  thick
60g [2 oz] butter
1 medium onion, finely
  chopped
1 cup sliced celery
½ cup day-old breadcrumbs

¼ cup raisins, chopped
1 teaspoon finely chopped
  fresh sage or ½ teaspoon
  dried
salt and pepper
oil
red currant jelly

Melt butter in saucepan and fry onion and celery until tender. Add to breadcrumbs, raisins, sage, salt and pepper in basin, blend well. Trim rind and fat from the chops. Cut a pocket in the chops and fill with stuffing. Secure opening with toothpicks or skewers. Heat oil in a frying pan and brown chops slowly on both sides. Transfer chops to a baking dish, cover and bake in a moderate oven 350°F (180°C) for 1 hour or until meat is tender. Strain off any fat. Place a teaspoonful of red currant jelly on each chop, return to the oven and bake a further 10 mins.

*Cooking a roast dinner? See page 338 for instructions.

Ham

656 HAM STEAKS WITH MUSHROOM AND TOMATO SAUCE

1 ham steak per person—if too salty, place in a pan of cold water and bring to boil then remove.

Sauce

*250g [4 oz] fresh
    mushrooms
½ cup water
1 cup white wine
30g [1 oz] butter
pepper
2 tomatoes, skinned and
    chopped*

*1 clove garlic, crushed
2 teaspoons brown sugar
2 teaspoons flour
½ cup cream
chopped parsley*

Place in saucepan mushrooms, water, wine, butter and pepper and simmer until mushrooms are tender, approximately 5 mins. Strain, returning liquid to saucepan. Reheat liquid, add tomatoes, garlic and sugar and cook rapidly until it is reduced to half. Remove from heat and add blended flour and cream, return to stove and cook until thickened, add mushrooms and heat through.

Place ham steaks in flat dish, pour sauce over and heat through in moderate oven for 15-20 mins. Serve sprinkled with chopped parsley.

Variation: This sauce is excellent over cooked chicken pieces or sauteed veal slices.

657 HAM STEAKS WITH CAMEMBERT CHEESE

*4-6 ham steaks
1 teaspoon mustard
4-6 slices pineapple*

*1 140g [5 oz] can camembert
    cheese, well chilled*

Spread ham steaks with mustard. Place in shallow baking dish. Top with pineapple and bake in moderate oven for 30 mins. Cut cheese into 4-6 slices, place a slice on top of each pineapple.

*Plain-spoken turnips; honest beets;
The carnal gusto of red meats;
The insipidity of lamb;
The wood-fire pungence of smoked ham;
Young veal that's smooth as natural silk;
The lavish motherliness of milk.*

Louis Untermeyer

658 HAM AND POTATOES (SCHINKEN KARTOFFELN)

6 potatoes, thinly sliced
4 onions, thinly sliced
4 green peppers, thinly sliced
750g [1½ lb] ham, cut in
  chunks

salt [optional]
2 eggs
1½ cups milk
grated parmesan cheese

Butter a deep casserole. Make layers of potatoes, onions, green peppers and ham. Repeat until all these ingredients are used. Add salt if desired. Beat eggs and milk together and pour into casserole. Bake at 350°F (180°C) for 45 mins or until vegetables are tender and the eggs and milk set like custard. Before serving sprinkle with grated cheese.

Variations:
1. Substitute lightly cooked, chopped bacon for ham.
2. Omit eggs and milk and substitute cream or evaporated milk.
3. Add layers of grated tasty cheese to casserole.

659 HAM AND BEANS

3 spring onions, chopped
½ green pepper, chopped
1 cup chopped ham
2 tablespoons butter
1 140g [5 oz] can tomato paste

1 cup red wine
salt and pepper
1 300g can kidney beans,
  drained
8 slices bacon

Saute onions, pepper and ham in butter. Add tomato paste to wine and seasoning. Mix all ingredients except bacon and place in buttered casserole. Put bacon slices on top. Bake at 350°F (180°C) for 30 mins or until bacon is cooked.

660 HAM, ONIONS AND CREAM

4 large onions, boiled until
  tender
1 tablespoon butter
1 cup diced ham

2 eggs, beaten
1 cup cream
salt and freshly ground black
  pepper

Cut onions into quarters and arrange in a shallow casserole with butter. Bake at 350°F (180°C) until golden, about 15-20 mins. Add ham. Beat eggs, cream, salt and pepper together, pour over onions and bake at same heat until brown, about 30 mins.

Veal

661 VEAL, BACON AND PINEAPPLE

125g [4 oz] bacon, chopped
1kg [2 lb] veal, diced
1 tablespoon flour
garlic salt, mustard, nutmeg
1 large onion, chopped
1 clove garlic, crushed
1 cup chopped celery
1 425g [15 oz] can pineapple
  pieces, undrained

1 454g [1 lb] can chicken soup
  or 1 packet chicken noodle
  soup mixed with 2 cups
  water
1 tablespoon worcestershire
  sauce
3 teaspoons vinegar
1/3 cup sherry [optional]
1 tablespoon chopped parsley

Fry bacon until crisp and remove. Coat meat in flour seasoned with garlic salt, mustard and nutmeg. Fry meat in bacon fat until browned. Add onion, celery, undrained pineapple, soup, worcestershire sauce and vinegar. Simmer 1-2 hours. Add sherry and parsley just before serving.

662 VEAL AND MUSHROOMS

750g [1½ lb] veal, diced
2 tablespoons butter
2 tablespoons flour
1 large tomato, sliced
1 bay leaf
1 onion, minced

125g [4 oz] mushrooms, fresh
  or canned
1 tablespoon tomato paste
1½ cups bouillon or stock
salt and pepper

Brown veal in butter. Remove from pan and blend in flour. Stir in tomato, onion, mushrooms, tomato paste and bouillon and add bay leaf. Bring to boil, add browned meat. Season to taste. Simmer for 1 hour, adding more liquid if needed. Excellent with either fried rice (R 831) or buttered noodles.

Variation: Add 125g (4 oz) chopped bacon.

663 VEAL WITH CAPERS

2 tablespoons oil
750g [1½ lb] veal, diced
1 large onion, chopped
1 cup stock

salt and pepper
1 large dill cucumber, diced
2 tablespoons capers

Heat oil and brown veal. Add onion and saute for a few mins. Add stock, salt and pepper and dill cucumber. Simmer until tender, about 1 hour. Add capers and cook 5 mins more. Serve with rice.

*For a different, delicious taste try using wholemeal flour in casseroles, gravies and sauces (even white sauce).

664 VEAL SWEET AND SOUR

1kg [2 lb] veal, diced
1½ tablespoons oil
1 onion, chopped
1 425g [15 oz] can pineapple
  pieces
¼ cup water
1 tablespoon cornflour

2 teaspoons brown sugar
1½ teaspoons salt
1 tablespoon vinegar
1 tablespoon soya sauce
½ cup chopped celery
1 small green pepper, chopped

Heat oil, fry veal quickly until brown, add onion, syrup from can of pineapple and water. Cover and simmer until cooked, about 1½ hours. Mix cornflour, sugar, salt, vinegar and soya sauce and add to meat with celery and green pepper. Simmer 5 mins then add pineapple pieces.

665 VEAL SUPREME

1kg [2 lb] stewing veal
1 large white onion, chopped
3 stalks celery, chopped
2 carrots, chopped
pinch mixed herbs
2 cloves
2 strips lemon rind
stock or water
salt and pepper

milk
125g [4 oz] butter
4 tablespoons flour
juice of 1 lemon
2 egg yolks
6 tablespoons cream
salt and pepper
chopped parsley

Dice meat and place in large saucepan with onion, celery and carrots. Add herbs and cloves stuck in lemon rind (enables you to find them easily). Just cover meat and vegetables with stock or water, add salt and pepper, cover and simmer 1½ hours or until tender. Strain off stock and retain. Place meat in basin. Discard lemon and cloves.
Make stock up to two cups with milk. Make white sauce with butter, flour and stock, stir in lemon juice and yolks mixed with cream, add meat and vegetables, reheat and serve sprinkled with chopped parsley.

CITRUS VEAL (R 2402)

MUSHROOM AND TOMATO SAUCE (R 656)

They dined on mince, and slices of quince,
Which they ate with a runcible spoon;

Edward Lear, *The Owl and the Pussy-Cat*

666 VEAL PAPRIKA

1kg [2 lb] veal cutlets
flour
125g [4 oz] butter
2 medium white onions,
   sliced
1 clove garlic, crushed
1½ cups chicken stock
2 teaspoons prepared
   mustard

2 teaspoons paprika
3 tablespoons chopped
   parsley
60g [2 oz] blanched almonds
1 small [190g] can champignons
½ cup sour cream or plain
   yoghurt

Place half of butter in frypan, saute onion and garlic. Remove and mix with stock, mustard, paprika and parsley.
Flour veal slices, add remaining butter to pan and saute veal until brown on both sides. Add onion and stock mixture to veal, cover and simmer for 45 mins. Add almonds, drained champignons and sour cream. Serve with jacket potatoes and salad.

667 VEAL AND HAM

2 small veal cutlets
   per person
flour, beaten egg, dry breadcrumbs
60g [2 oz] butter
2 tablespoons oil
1 small green pepper, sliced

1 small [113g] can tomato
   paste
¾ cup chicken stock
½ teaspoon thyme
½ teaspoon oregano
1 slice of ham per person

Crumb the veal and brown in hot butter and oil. Remove from pan. Saute mushrooms and pepper until tender, add tomato paste, stock, herbs and seasonings. Blend well and simmer for a few mins.
Place in greased casserole in layers—first veal, then ham, then sauce. Cover and cook for 45 mins in moderate oven.

668 VEAL BAKE

4 veal chops
4 slices cheese
4 slices ham

1 packet cream of chicken soup
2 cups milk

Put chops in deep ovenproof dish. Cover with cheese then ham. Combine soup and milk, pour over chops and bake at 350°F (180°C) for 1-1¼ hours.

Variation: Omit soup and milk, pour tomato sauce (R 1013) over chops and bake as above.

669 VEAL WITH HERBS AND CREAM

veal chops [1-2 per person]
60g [2 oz] butter
salt and pepper
⅓ cup white wine
½ cup sour cream

herbs—parsley, chives, basil,
and tarragon [1 teaspoon
each of fresh or ½ tea-
spoon dried]

Saute chops in butter with salt and pepper until cooked and golden, remove and keep hot. Add wine to pan, stir well, reduce heat and add cream, do not allow to boil. Pour over chops and sprinkle with herbs.

Variations:
1. Omit wine and substitute 2 tablespoons each sherry and lemon juice.
2. Substitute veal slices for chops and roll in flour. Omit wine and cream and substitute ½ cup marsala and ¼ cup water.

VEAL AND CHEESE ROLLS (R 2407)

670 VEAL CORDON BLEU

6 thin slices veal
6 small slices ham
6 small slices Swiss or gruyere
* cheese*
flour

1 egg, beaten
dry breadcrumbs
125g [4 oz] butter
salt and pepper

Pound veal if necessary until very thin. Put a slice of ham on each piece of veal, then a slice of cheese. Fold in half, secure with toothpick. Dip in flour, beaten egg and breadcrumbs. Refrigerate. Heat butter in large frying pan, fry veal until cooked through, about 20 mins. Drain well, season and remove toothpicks.

671 WIENER SCHNITZEL

thin slices of veal
anchovy sauce
lemon juice
salt
paprika
flour

1 egg, beaten
breadcrumbs
butter or oil for frying
lemon and hard boiled egg for
* garnishing*

Rub meat with anchovy sauce, lemon juice, salt and paprika. Allow to stand 30 mins. Dip consecutively in flour, egg and breadcrumbs. Fry until coating is brown and crisp. Serve garnished with wedges of lemon and slices of hard boiled egg.

Sausages

672 SAUSAGE AND POTATO CASSEROLE

1kg [2 lb] sausages
 [Continental sausages or
 frankfurters are delicious]
454g [16 oz] can cream
 chicken soup
2½ cups hot mashed potato
 [instant will do]

¼ cup sour cream
125g [4 oz] grated tasty
 cheese
1 egg
¼ cup breadcrumbs
butter

Grill sausages and place in a buttered casserole. Heat undiluted soup and pour over the top of sausages. Cream potatoes, beating in sour cream, cheese and egg. Pile on top of sausages. Sprinkle with breadcrumbs and dot with butter. Bake in moderately hot oven 45 mins or until golden brown.

673 FRANKFURT AND TOMATO CASSEROLE

500g [1 lb] smoked frankfurts
 [this is the only type to use]
1 medium onion
oil or butter

500g [1 lb] tomatoes, skinned
 and chopped
2 teaspoons cornflour mixed
 with ½ cup water

Slice the onion thinly and saute in a little oil or butter. Add tomatoes and simmer covered for a few mins, then thicken with cornflour. Meanwhile cut the frankfurts into half-inch lengths and place in a casserole. Add the tomato and onion mixture, place in moderate oven until frankfurts have heated through. If you are really in a hurry the frankfurts can be put in the saucepan with the tomato and onion.

674 TOAD IN THE HOLE

500g [1 lb] sausages
125g [4 oz] flour
¼ teaspoon salt

1 egg
1 cup milk and water mixed

Sift flour and salt. Make a well in the centre and add egg and a little of the mixed milk and water. Beat the mixture gradually, drawing in the flour from the sides of the bowl and adding the remaining milk and water to make a smooth batter. (Some milk and water may be left over.) Allow to stand 30 mins if possible. Place sausages in ovenproof dish and bake in hot oven for 15-20 mins. Leave fat in dish and pour the batter over sausages. Cook in hot oven for about 30 mins until well raised and brown.

94

675 SAUSAGES IN BARBECUE OR CURRY SAUCE

Prick sausages and brown on all sides in a little butter or margarine. Place in casserole. Then either:

1. Saute 1 sliced brown onion, blend in 2 tablespoons plain flour, 3 tablespoons vinegar, 2 tablespoons brown sugar, 1 tablespoon worcestershire sauce, 1 tablespoon chutney, ½ teaspoon mustard and 1 cup water. Simmer until thickened. Add ¾ cup diced celery, salt and pepper to taste. Pour over sausages in casserole, cover and cook 30 mins in a moderate oven. (Barbecue Sauce.)
   or
2. Saute 1 diced carrot, onion, apple, banana, tomato and stick of celery until tender. Blend 1 tablespoon curry powder, 1 tablespoon flour, 1 cup of stock or water, 2 teaspoons coconut, 1 teaspoon brown sugar and add to vegetables and fruit. Stir until thickened and cook 1 min, add salt and pepper to taste, ½ cup sultanas and pour over sausages in casserole. Cover and cook in moderate oven 45 mins. (Curry Sauce.)

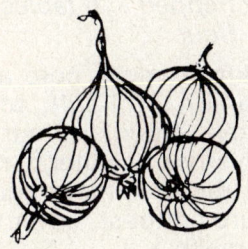

676 OX TAIL WITH OLIVES

1 ox tail, cut in joints
1 tablespoon flour
salt and pepper
1 onion, chopped
1 cup dry wine
bay leaf

1 clove garlic, crushed
1 sprig parsley
water
250g [½ lb] olives, preferably
*   black and stoned*

Remove excess fat from tail, and roll pieces in flour, salt and pepper. Place in casserole, add onion, wine, bay leaf, garlic and parsley, and enough water to barely cover the pieces. Cover casserole and cook at 270°F (140°C) until tender, about three hours. Skim fat by holding sheets of greaseproof paper against the surface. Then add olives and cook another hour or more. Serve with boiled rice or potatoes.

Savoury Meats

677 KIDNEYS IN RED WINE

12 lamb kidneys	salt and pepper
60g [2 oz] butter	sprinkle of garlic powder
1 tablespoon flour	1 cup red wine
handful of parsley	¼ cup water

Cut kidneys in half. Remove skin and core. If desired soak in salt and water for 30 mins. Saute kidneys in butter quickly. If you own a blender, blend the rest of the ingredients—parsley too—and add to the kidneys and butter and stir. If no blender, mix in flour, then add seasonings, chopped parsley, then wine and water. Reduce heat, stir, cover and simmer for 30 mins. Stir occasionally to prevent catching. Serve with toast.
N.B. Always saute or fry kidneys quickly to seal, then simmer gently. They will remain tender this way.

678 KIDNEYS IN SOUR CREAM

8 lamb kidneys	stock or water
60g [2 oz] butter	salt and pepper
1 white onion, finely chopped	6 tablespoons sour cream
1-2 tablespoons plain flour	

Wash the kidneys, skin, remove core and slice thinly. Heat butter in pan. Saute onion until soft, add kidneys and fry 1-2 mins each side. Remove. Sprinkle flour into pan, blend with juices and add enough stock or water to make a smooth sauce, season. Stir in cream, return kidneys and reheat for serving.
Variation: Place mixture on toast, cover with a slice of cheese and grill until cheese melts.

679 KIDNEYS WITH TOMATOES AND MUSHROOMS

500g [1 lb] kidneys, halved, skinned and cored	1 teaspoon sugar
oil	basil or marjoram to taste
2 rashers bacon, chopped	¾ cup chicken stock
1 onion, chopped	1 tablespoon flour
3 tomatoes, chopped	250g [½ lb] mushrooms or small can mushrooms
salt and pepper	parsley

Quickly saute kidneys in oil to seal, then add bacon and cook gently until transparent. Set aside. Brown onion in oil, add tomatoes, seasonings and then blended stock and flour. Cook for 10 mins. Add mushrooms, kidneys and bacon. Cook for a further 10 mins. Serve sprinkled with chopped parsley.

680 BRAISED TONGUE

1 ox tongue, unsalted or 8
   lamb tongues
1 stalk celery, diced
½ carrot, diced
1 small onion, diced
60g [2 oz] butter

2 tablespoons flour
1 teaspoon beef or yeast
   extract
salt and pepper
1 small [190g] can champignons, drained [optional]

Cook tongue in simmering salted water until tender (2 hours for lamb tongue and 3 hours for ox tongue). Drain and reserve 2 cups of the liquid. Remove skin and bone from tongues, cut in half lengthwise and place in casserole. Cover with diced vegetables. Melt butter in saucepan, add flour and cook until browned. Gradually stir in the reserved liquid. Cook, stirring constantly until sauce boils, add the beef or yeast extract. Season with salt and pepper and pour over the vegetables. Cover and cook in moderate oven for approx 45 mins or until vegetables are tender. If liked, add drained champignons just before serving. Serve with boiled potatoes, tossed in butter and chopped parsley. Reserve any remaining liquid for soups or stock.

681 TONGUE IN SPICY SAUCE

1 ox tongue, cooked, skinned
   and sliced [R 680]
2 tablespoons oil
2 large onions, sliced
3 fresh tomatoes, sliced [or
   1 can with juice reserved]
1 tablespoon flour

½ cup water, stock or tomato
   juice from can
1 tablespoon worcestershire
   sauce
1 tablespoon champignons
2 tablespoons sultanas
salt and pepper

Heat oil and saute onions, add tomatoes and cook few mins. Blend flour with liquid and worcestershire sauce and add to pan, stir until thickened and cook 1 min. Add sliced tongue, champignons and sultanas, salt and pepper. Simmer gently for few mins. Sprinkle with parsley and serve with plain or fried rice (R 831).

Variation: Omit champignons and substitute almonds, cut in strips.

Serenly full, the epicure would say,
Fate cannot harm me, I have dined today.

Sydney Smith

682 TONGUE IN SOYA SAUCE

1 ox tongue
5 cups water
6 tablespoons soya sauce

1 teaspoon salt
3-4 slices fresh ginger

Wash tongue, cook in 5 cups water. Simmer until the skin can be removed. Carefully skin tongue. Return to water. Add soya sauce, salt and ginger and continue cooking until the tonque is done. Total cooking time approx 3 hours. If the tongue is served hot, the juice may be used as gravy.

683 COLD TONGUE

Soak in water as many tongues as needed, approx 1 hour. Drain and cook in water for 2-3 hours. To this water add 3-4 peppercorns, 2-3 cloves, 2 teaspoons sugar and 1 tablespoon vinegar. If convenient, cook with other salted meats, e.g. corned beef, pickled pork etc. After cooking put in bowl of cold water, then peel, trim and separate meat. Place meat in small mould, put saucer on top and press down hard with brick or something heavy. When set put in refrigerator. Try small calf tongue for a change. For a different flavour add a quartered unpeeled orange to the water.

684 LAMB'S FRY AND BACON

1 lamb's fry
250g [8 oz] bacon, diced
4 teaspoons cornflour

1 cup water or ½ cup claret
and ½ cup water
salt

Soak the lamb's fry in salted water for 20-30 mins. Fry bacon until well cooked, remove. Skin and slice lamb's fry thinly. Saute until fry is lightly cooked on both sides. Combine cornflour with water and add to the mixture in frying pan. Simmer until gravy is thick. Add bacon and seasoning if necessary. Can be served with vegetables or on toast.

*Finely chopped liver can be added to hamburger recipes where it won't be noticed, and also to minced steak in spaghetti bolognese.

685 LAMB'S FRY WITH VEGETABLES

4 tablespoons oil
1 onion, diced
1 clove garlic, crushed
1 green pepper, diced
1 carrot, grated
2 sticks celery, chopped
2 large tomatoes, skinned
   and chopped
1 cooking apple, peeled and
   chopped
1 lamb's fry, skinned and
   finely sliced
wheat germ or flour
salt and pepper

Soak lamb's fry in salted water for 20-30 mins. Heat half the oil in heavy-based pan and saute onion and garlic until tender. Add green pepper, carrot, celery, tomatoes and apple and cook gently 4-6 mins, turning frequently. Season, remove and keep warm.

Heat remaining 2 tablespoons oil in pan, dip liver in wheat germ and cook 1-2 mins. Pile into centre of platter and surround with vegetables. Serve at once.

Variation: Lamb's fry with herbed mushrooms.
Saute floured lamb's fry or 500g (1 lb) chicken livers until colour changes. Omit vegetables but add a small (220g) can mushrooms in butter sauce or 250g (8 oz) fresh mushrooms, chopped parsley, chives, tarragon, shallot or garlic, and a little lemon juice. Cook gently 3 mins, stirring frequently.

686 LAMB'S FRY CASSEROLE

2 rashers bacon
1 tablespoon butter
750g [1½ lb] lamb's fry,
   skinned and sliced
3 tablespoons flour
1 onion, sliced
1 cup celery, chopped
2 large tomatoes, peeled and
   sliced
¾ cup beef stock
salt and pepper

Soak lamb's fry in salted water for 20-30 mins. Cut bacon into pieces and cook until crisp. Remove from pan. Melt butter, fry sliced, four-dredged liver. Brown with onion. Place celery in casserole, then liver and onion, arrange tomato slices on top. Add bacon, stock and seasonings. Cook 45 mins in moderate oven.

Variation: Put seasoned flour or gravy or a packet of soup mix in bottom of casserole dish, roll liver in this. Add slices of tomato and bacon. Onion and celery can be omitted but add 1 tablespoon tomato paste and 1 teaspoon sugar with stock, and 1 tablespoon sherry if desired.

687 BRAISED CHICKEN LIVERS

1 tablespoon oil
1 onion, chopped
185g [6 oz] bacon pieces
500g [1 lb] chicken livers, sliced
3 tablespoons tomato sauce
2 tablespoons soya sauce
2 cups stock
2 tablespoons parsley
⅓ cup wholemeal flour
½ cup water

Blend flour and water. Heat oil, fry onion. Add bacon pieces, lightly brown. Add chicken livers, cook until they have changed colour. Add sauces, seasoning and stock. Cover and simmer for 15 mins. Add parsley and blended flour. Bring to boil, cook 3 mins.

CHICKEN LIVER PATE (1) (R 119)

CHICKEN LIVER PATE (2) (R 120)

688 TRIPE CATALANE

1kg [2 lb] tripe
4 cups or more water
1 cup white wine or cider
3 onions, chopped
2 carrots, chopped
2 leeks, chopped
5 sprigs parsley, one chopped
1 tablespoon chopped fresh thyme [or 1 teaspoon dried thyme]
2 bay leaves
4 tomatoes
2 tablespoons oil
1 tablespoon chopped fresh herbs, eg. basil, marjoram, [or 1 teaspoon dried mixed herbs]
¼ teaspoon nutmeg
salt and pepper
1 clove garlic, crushed

Put tripe in saucepan with water, a little of the wine, 2 onions, carrots, leeks, 4 sprigs parsley, ½ of the thyme and one bay leaf. Simmer for at least two hours or until tender. Remove and chop. Use vegetables as desired or discard.
Chop remaining onion, skin and chop tomatoes. Saute tripe, onion, and tomatoes in oil. Add half the chopped parsley, and remaining herbs, nutmeg, salt and pepper and half the garlic. Cook gently, pour remaining wine over, and allow to reduce a little. Then cover pan and simmer for about 5 mins. Sprinkle remaining garlic and remaining chopped parsley over tripe.

*Immediately after purchasing, freeze brains in ice cube container. They will remain fresh until required and the skins will then come off easily.

689 BRAINS

Have you ever tried *not* peeling brains? Remove any bits that really offend you, but peeling is unnecessary. If you aren't faced with peeling them you are much more likely to use them.

Rinse them in cold water, and cook a few minutes in boiling water to cover, to which you have added 1 teaspoon salt and 1 tablespoon vinegar. Drain. Then use them in sandwiches (R 1801) or in parsley sauce (R 1010) or as below.

1. Dipped consecutively in flour, egg and breadcrumbs and fried until coating is crisp and brown. Serve with bacon.
2. Chopped up and stirred into beaten eggs (1-2 eggs per set of brains) with salt, pepper, worcestershire and/or tomato sauce. Melt 2 tablespoons butter, add mixture and cook, stirring, until just firm.
3. With Black Butter—a gourmet but simple dish. Slice brains and saute in butter until delicately brown. Remove and keep warm Add a little more butter to pan and heat until it is dark brown. Add a squeeze of lemon juice and pour over brains.

Minced Steak

690 CONTINENTAL MEATBALLS

250g [8 oz] *minced steak*
250g [8 oz] *minced pork*
250g [8 oz] *minced veal*
2 *medium onions, finely*
  chopped
½ *cup fine soft breadcrumbs*
  soaked in 2 tablespoons
  cream or milk

2 *eggs, lightly beaten*
salt and pepper
½ *teaspoon allspice*
2 *tablespoons butter*
2 *tablespoons oil*

Fry onions in butter until golden brown. Mix meats in bowl, add fried onions, breadcrumbs, eggs, salt and pepper, allspice. Refrigerate. Roll into 1" balls, fry in hot oil and butter until brown.

Variation: Add 2 finely chopped anchovy fillets to meat. Heat 3-4 cups stock until boiling, drop meatballs in and simmer gently about 20 mins. Remove with perforated spoon and keep warm. Make roux with 60g (2 oz) butter and 45g (1½ oz) flour, add stock and stir until sauce boils and thickens. Blend 2 egg yolks with 2 tablespoons sour cream, and add to sauce (preferably in double boiler). Add 2 tablespoons lemon juice and 1 tablespoon capers. Pour over meatballs, and sprinkle with chopped parsley.

691 HAMBURGERS DE LUXE

500g [1 lb] minced steak
250g [8 oz] lamb's fry, minced or chopped finely
1 egg
1 onion, minced or grated
1 tablespoon bacon, minced
1 tablespoon chopped parsley
1 teaspoon mustard powder
1 teaspoon salt
1 teaspoon worcestershire sauce
oil

Beat egg in a large bowl, add all other ingredients and mix well. If very moist flour your hands before shaping into hamburgers. Chill for 30 mins. Heat oil and cook hamburgers for a few mins on each side.

692 MEATBALL MEXICANA

500g [1 lb] minced steak
2 tablespoons butter
4 rashers bacon, diced
salt and pepper
1 onion, chopped
½ cup green pepper strips
1 284g [10 oz] can red kidney beans
1 284g [10 oz] can tomato soup
½ cup water
1 teaspoon chili powder
½ teaspoon salt
125g [4 oz] cooked macaroni

Melt butter and cook bacon until crisp. Drain on paper. Combine minced steak, salt and pepper and shape into twenty balls. Saute in bacon fat until browned. Place meat balls in buttered casserole dish. Add onion and pepper to pan and cook 3-4 mins. Stir in undrained kidney beans, soup, water, chili powder, salt and cooked macaroni. Pour over meat balls in casserole, top with bacon and cook ¾ to 1 hour.

MEATBALLS WITH BARBECUE DIP (R 117)

693 PORCUPINES

500g [1 lb] minced steak
¼ cup grated onion
½ cup uncooked white rice
salt and pepper
flour
2 tablespoons oil
1 454g [1 lb] can tomato soup
½ cup water

Mix steak, onion, rice, salt and pepper. Form into small balls, roll in flour, fry in hot oil until light brown on all sides. Mix soup and water, pour over balls, cover and simmer about 45 mins or until rice is tender.

694 SAUSAGE MEAT LOAF

500g [1 lb] sausage meat
500g [1 lb] minced steak
1 284g can soya beans in
   tomato sauce
1 cup day old breadcrumbs,
   preferably wholemeal

1 onion, chopped
1 carrot, grated
½ teaspoon each salt,
   mustard, curry powder
¼ teaspoon each pepper
   and mixed herbs

Mash or slice soya beans with seasonings, combine with breadcrumbs and stand for 5 mins. Combine all ingredients. Pack lightly into greased 9" by 5" loaf tin. Bake in moderate oven for 1¼ hours, or until meat shrinks from pan sides. Serve hot or cold.

695 DELICIOUS MEAT LOAF

500g [1 lb] minced steak
2 rashers bacon, chopped

½ packet French onion soup
250g [8 oz] ricotta cheese

Mix ingredients together until cheese is absorbed into the meat. Bake in meat loaf tin in moderate oven for about 1 hour. Serve hot or cold.

696 MEAT LOAF WITH APPLE

2 cooking apples, peeled,
   cored and grated
500g [1 lb] minced steak
1 tablespoon flour
2 tablespoons tomato sauce
1 heaped teaspoon yeast
   extract

1 cup soft breadcrumbs
1 onion, finely chopped
1 egg, lightly beaten
salt and pepper
4 tablespoons grated cheese

Mix well all ingredients except cheese. Put in greased loaf tin. Sprinkle with cheese and bake at 350°F (180°C) for 1 hour or until cooked.

Variations:
1. Omit breadcrumbs and flour and substitute 1½ cups cooked mashed potato or rolled oats or bran or wheatgerm.
2. Omit onion and tomato sauce and substitute 3 tablespoons tomato chutney.
3. Add ¼ cup coarsely grated carrot and 1 tablespoon chopped parsley.
4. For adults add ½ cup peanuts.

103

697 HIGH PROTEIN MEAT LOAF

1 tablespoon safflower oil
1 clove garlic, crushed
1 green pepper, chopped
1 onion, chopped
500g [1 lb] minced steak
1 egg, beaten,
⅓ cup skim milk powder

⅓ cup wheat germ
3 tablespoons chopped
  parsley
¼ teaspoon each basil,
  thyme and paprika
salt and pepper

Heat oil, add garlic, green pepper and onion, saute lightly. Add remaining ingredients, combine well and pack into an oiled loaf tin, sprinkle with paprika and bake in a moderate oven for 40-50 mins.

698 MINCED STEAK CASSEROLE

2 tablespoons butter or margarine, melted
500g [1 lb] minced steak
1 medium onion, chopped
500g [1 lb] can tomatoes

salt and pepper
4 medium potatoes, sliced
125g [4 oz] tasty cheese,
  sliced

Fry meat in melted butter until browned. Add onion, tomatoes, salt and pepper. Place ⅓ of mixture in greased casserole, cover with ½ potato slices. Add another layer of meat and cover with remaining potatoes. Top with remaining meat and cover with cheese slices. Cook uncovered in a moderate oven for about an hour.

699 LAYER CASSEROLE

1 cup uncooked rice
1 cup finely chopped onion
1 cup whole kernel corn,
  frozen or canned, drained
375g [¾ lb] minced steak

2 cups tomato puree, juice or
  soup
1 cup stock or water
4 rashers bacon
salt and pepper

Arrange all ingredients in layers in casserole in order given, sprinkling each lightly with salt and pepper. Cover and bake in moderate oven for 1¼ hours.

699A MOCK CHOW MEIN

500g [1 lb] minced steak
2 onions, chopped
2 tablespoons butter
3 tablespoons uncooked rice
3 stalks celery, chopped

½-1 cup shredded cabbage
3 cups water
1 packet chicken noodle soup
2 teaspoons curry powder
½ cup frozen beans [optional]

Fry onions in butter. Add other ingredients and simmer gently 30 mins.

104

99B PEPPERS STUFFED WITH MINCED STEAK

4 green peppers
500g [1 lb] minced steak
1 onion, chopped
1 tablespoon oil

½ cup chopped raisins
salt and pepper
2 cups cheese sauce [R 1010]
  or tomato sauce [R 1013]

Put peppers in small saucepan, cover with cold water, boil 5 mins. Remove, halve lengthwise and drain well. Place in shallow baking dish. Cook meat and onion in hot oil until browned. Add raisins, salt and pepper. Mix well and fill peppers. Pour sauce over and bake at 350°F (180°C) about 30 mins.

99C AFRICAN CURRY

750g [1½ lb] minced steak
1 large potato, sliced
1 large cooking apple, sliced
1 large onion, sliced
2 tablespoons oil
2 teaspoons curry powder
½ teaspoon turmeric
½ cup vinegar

½ cup sultanas
¼ cup chopped almonds
salt
1 teaspoon sugar
½-¾ cup apricot jam
4 bananas
1 egg, beaten
½ cup milk

Brown meat, potato, apple and onion in hot oil, add curry powder and turmeric and stir well. Add vinegar, cover, and simmer very gently about 30 mins or until cooked. Add sultanas, almonds, salt and sugar. Stir well and put in shallow casserole dish. Spread jam thinly over top. Cut bananas in halves lengthwise and place on jam. Mix egg and milk and bake at 350°F (180°C) for about 30 mins or until browned.

9D CHILI CON CARNE

500g [1 lb] minced steak
2 tablespoons oil
1 onion, chopped
1 teaspoon salt
1 tablespoon vinegar

4 tablespoons tomato sauce
1 tablespoon chili powder
1 284g [10 oz] can red kidney
  beans

Fry minced steak in oil until lightly browned. Add other ingredients and simmer for 10-15 mins. Add kidney beans and simmer another 10 mins. Good with rice, tossed salad and French bread.

105

699E TAGLIARINI

1kg [2 lb] minced steak
2 tablespoons oil
1 cup chopped onion
1 green pepper, chopped
2 cloves garlic, crushed
  [optional]
1 825g [1 lb 13 oz] can
  tomatoes
1 113g [4 oz] can tomato paste

285g [10 oz] can whole kernel
  corn, drained
2 teaspoons salt
1 teaspoon sugar
1 teaspoon oregano
½ teaspoon pepper
¼ teaspoon allspice

Saute onion, green pepper and garlic in oil. Add meat and brown. Add remaining ingredients and simmer for ½ hour.

Variations:
1. Put into greased casserole, top with 1 cup grated cheese and bake in moderate oven 15 mins or until cheese has melted.
2. Add 250g (8 oz) cooked noodles, spaghetti or macaroni just before serving.

699F MOUSSAKA

500g [1 lb] minced lamb or
  steak
1 onion, finely chopped
1 clove garlic, crushed
2 tablespoons oil
250g [8 oz] zucchini or
  aubergine, sliced

250g [8 oz] tomatoes or
  mushrooms, sliced
½ green pepper, finely
  chopped [optional]
1 tablespoon chopped fresh
  herbs
salt and pepper

Topping:

250g [8 oz] cottage cheese
½ cup plain yoghurt
1 egg, beaten

salt and pepper
2 tablespoons grated cheese

Fry onion in hot oil until transparent, add garlic, zucchini, tomatoes, and green pepper and saute lightly. Remove from pan. Brown meat and cook about 15 mins. Allow meat to cool, skim fat off top. Put alternate layers of meat and vegetables in well greased casserole dish or loaf tin. Mix topping ingredients except grated cheese and spoon on top of meat. Sprinkle cheese on top. Bake at 350°F (180°C) for 40 mins. Allow to stand for 5 mins before cutting into squares.

Topping variations:
1. 2 cups cheese sauce (R1010).
2. 2 beaten eggs, 1¼ cups milk, 2 tablespoons grated cheese, cayenne pepper.

9G FRIED MINI CURRY PIES

Pastry:

3 cups flour
2 teaspoons baking powder
¼ teaspoon salt

125g [4 oz] butter or margarine
2 eggs, beaten
cold water

Sieve flour, baking powder and salt into a bowl, rub in butter, add well beaten eggs. Mix into a stiff dough with a little cold water.

Filling:

500g [1 lb] minced steak
1 onion, chopped
2 tablespoons butter
2 tablespoons curry powder

2 tablespoons chopped parsley
2 cloves garlic, crushed
salt and pepper

Fry onion in butter until golden brown and add curry. Add minced steak, parsley, garlic, salt and pepper. Simmer gently until cooked. Cool by spreading on a large platter. Roll out pastry. Cut into squares and place a spoonful of mixture on to each one. Fold over into a triangle, moisten edges and press to seal. Deep fry in hot oil until well browned.

MEAT PIES (R2113).

9H CORNISH PASTIES

500g [1 lb] short crust pastry
500g [1 lb] lean minced steak
1 large potato
1 carrot
1 turnip
1 parsnip

1 onion
3 sprigs parsley
3 tablespoons peas
salt and pepper
milk for glazing

Finely chop vegetables (except peas) and parsley, or mince coarsely. Add peas and meat and mix well. Roll pastry and cut into circles (an upturned saucer is useful for this). Re-roll any leftover pastry and make more circles until all pastry is used. There should be about 16. Place meat mixture on half of each circle. Dampen edges of pastry and fold over. Using a fork, press around edges and prick tops several times. Brush with milk. Bake on greased oven tray at 425°F (220°C) for 25 mins, then turn down to 375°F (190°C) and bake for another 25 mins or until cooked and brown.

699J MEAT SLICE

250g [8 oz] shortcrust pastry
   [R 1301]
500g [1 lb] sausage meat
1 onion, minced
1 cup celery, minced

1 egg, beaten
125g [4 oz] tomatoes, thinly
   sliced
1 cup crushed potato chips

Roll the pastry thinly and use half to line a 9" lamington tin. Mix together the minced celery, minced onion and egg, spread on to the pastry, cover with a layer of thinly sliced tomato. Press the crushed potato chips into the remaining pastry with a rolling pin and lift over the meat to cover. Bake in a moderate oven 40-50 mins. Serve hot with vegetables or cold with salad.

Variation: Add 125g (4 oz) sliced mushrooms on top of tomato.

699K BEEF CRUST PIE

500g [1 lb] minced steak
1 egg
1 cup soft breadcrumbs
   or rice
3 tablespoons tomato sauce

1 tablespoon chopped parsley
1 small onion, chopped
¼ teaspoon mixed herbs
   [optional]
salt and pepper

Combine all ingredients and press into greased dish. Bake in a moderate oven for about 30 mins.

Filling for Crust

1 cup cooked rice
½ cup shredded cheese
salt and pepper
½ cup chopped celery

½ cup chopped red pepper
2 tomatoes, peeled and
   chopped
extra cheese

Lightly mix all ingredients together and spoon into pie crust. Sprinkle a little cheese on top. Bake a further 20 mins.

699L CABBAGE ROLLS

6 large cabbage leaves
250g [8 oz] minced steak
1 cup cooked rice
1 white onion, chopped

¼ teaspoon mixed herbs
salt and pepper
1 cup tomato soup or juice

Cut out thick centre stalk from base of each leaf and wash leaves. Pour boiling water over them and drain. Mix together meat, rice, onion and seasonings. Place small quantity on each leaf, roll up, tucking in the sides to form a parcel. Fasten with toothpicks. Place in greased casserole, cover with soup or juice and bake 1 hour in moderate oven.

NOTE: If cooking on top of stove, cover base of saucepan with chopped, discarded stalks to prevent sticking and add flavour.

9M ABERDEEN SAUSAGE

500g [1 lb] buttock or topside
  steak or lean minced steak
250g [8 oz] bacon
2 cups fresh breadcrumbs
1 egg, beaten
1 tablespoon worcestershire
  sauce

1 tablespoon tomato sauce
¼ teaspoon mixed herbs
salt and pepper
dried breadcrumbs

Mince steak and bacon together or if steak is already minced, chop bacon finely. Mix well with all ingredients except breadcrumbs. Form into roll about 8" long. Tie firmly in well floured pudding cloth. Lower into saucepan of boiling water, making sure it is well covered. Boil covered for 2 hours. Alternatively steam in pudding basin for 2½ hours. Drain and cool. Remove cloth and roll sausage in dried breadcrumbs.

MINCED STEAK PIZZA (R 414)

Re-Runs

9N LAMB PATTIES

2 cups cooked lamb, minced
½ cup left-over gravy or thick
  white sauce [R 1010]
1½ cups cooked rice
2 tablespoons green pepper,
  finely chopped

1 tablespoon chopped onion
1 tablespoon worcestershire
  sauce
salt and pepper
½ cup dry breadcrumbs
8 rashers bacon

Make white sauce if you have no gravy left over. Mix rice with lamb, green pepper, onion, worcestershire sauce, seasonings and gravy or white sauce. Shape into 8 round patties and roll in breadcrumbs. Wrap bacon around each and fasten with a toothpick. Grill 10-15 mins. Serve with tomato sauce.

Variations:
1. Replace breadcrumbs with stuffing mix.
2. Rissoles: Omit rice and substitute 1½ cups hot mashed potato. Omit breadcrumbs, gravy and bacon and add 1 tablespoon tomato sauce. Form into flat patties, dust lightly with flour and fry in hot oil until golden brown, turning once.

6990 SHEPHERD'S SURPRISE PIE

1 425g [15 oz] can pineapple slices

1½ cups cooked vegetables, either leftover or combination of freshly cooked vegetables: carrots, celery, peas, cauliflower, parsnip, etc.

2 cups cold meat, minced

1 cup gravy or stock

salt and pepper

2 cups hot mashed potatoes [approx 4 medium raw potatoes]

melted butter

Drain pineapple, chop one slice finely and add to vegetables. Place in buttered pie dish. Combine meat, gravy or stock, seasonings and spoon over vegetables. Cover with mashed potatoes, arrange remaining pineapple slices over potatoes and sprinkle with melted butter. Bake in hot oven 400°F (200°C) for 20 mins, or until potatoes and pineapple are lightly browned.

699P DELECTABLE MINCE

1 cup cooked meat, minced, or can of corned beef

2 large potatoes

1 small onion, minced

parsley, chopped

oil

2 eggs

salt and pepper

Cook and mash potatoes. Combine meat, potatoes, onion and parsley. Heat some oil or dripping in a frypan and pour in the mince. Make two hollows and drop an egg into each. Cook over moderate heat until eggs are set and mixture is crusty underneath. If eggs do not set to your liking put a lid on the pan. Serve with a green vegetable and tomato cooked in pan at the same time.

CURRY SAUCE (R 675)

Tinned Australian, and other preserved pieces of meat are valuable additions to the store-box of the traveller or sportsman, but they require very delicate handling, because they are almost always overdone. The really nutritious part of a tin of Australian meat is the gravy that surrounds it.
Wyvern's Indian Cookery Book, 1904

Fur & Feathers

Fur and Feathers

700 POULTRY AND GAME

Chicken

701 ORANGE AND ALMOND CHICKEN

1 roasting chicken, jointed
salt and pepper
1 teaspoon paprika
1/3 cup butter

1 cup orange juice
2/3 cup slivered almonds,
  toasted

Wash and dry chicken. Mix salt, pepper and paprika and rub into chicken until coated. Melt butter in large frying pan. Saute chicken pieces until golden on all sides. Cover pan and reduce heat. Simmer 25-30 mins or until cooked. Remove chicken and keep warm. Pour juice into pan, stir to loosen all browned particles, then reduce heat and simmer a few mins. Pour over chicken and sprinkle with almonds.

702 CHICKEN IN SOYA SAUCE

1 roasting chicken, jointed
1/2 cup soya sauce
1/4 cup sugar
1/2 cup water
2 tablespoons sherry

1 teaspoon ginger
1/2 onion, grated
1/2 teaspoon each of
  cinnamon, cloves and
  nutmeg

Mix all ingredients, except chicken, and bring to boil. Add chicken, simmer slowly until tender—about 45 mins. Remove from sauce and keep warm. Thicken and reduce sauce by boiling over high heat, or add 1 tablespoon cornflour mixed with 1/4 cup water and stir until thick. Serve chicken and sauce separately.

703 CHICKEN WITH CHERRIES

1 roasting chicken, jointed
  or 1.5kg [3 lb] chicken pieces
2 tablespoons oil
3 tablespoons flour
1/2 teaspoon paprika

1 500g [1 lb] can cherries,
  or fresh cooked cherries
  and 1 cup syrup
1 cup dry white wine
salt and pepper

Heat oil and brown chicken well on all sides. Remove from pan. Add flour and paprika to pan, add wine and syrup from cherries, stir until thickened. Return chicken and cook gently until tender, approx 1 hour. Add stoned cherries, salt and pepper 10 mins before serving.

112

704 CHICKEN AND APRICOTS

1.5kg [3 lb] chicken pieces
60g [2 oz] butter
2 medium onions, chopped
1 tablespoon cornflour
1 425g [15 oz] can apricot
  nectar
salt and pepper
125g [4 oz] dried apricots,
  halved
½ green pepper, sliced in thin
  strips
½ cup sour cream

Melt butter in frypan, brown chicken pieces, remove. Add onion to pan and saute until tender. Blend cornflour with nectar a little at a time, add to pan, stir until it boils and thickens. Season, add dried apricots and chicken, cover and simmer 15-20 mins or until chicken is tender. Stir occasionally. Add green pepper, cook 5 mins, stir in cream, reheat gently and serve.

If sauce is too thick, add a little water or chicken stock.

To Freeze: Do not add green pepper and cream—chill thoroughly, seal and freeze.

To Serve: Thaw overnight—heat gently, add green pepper and cream.

Variation: Add 310g can drained red kidney beans.

705 CHICKEN VERONIQUE

1 roasting chicken, jointed
salt
2 teaspoons sweet paprika
125g [4 oz] butter
1 onion, finely chopped
1 clove garlic, crushed
250g [8 oz] fresh mushrooms
60g [2 oz] flour
1 teaspoon sugar
1¼ cups chicken stock
1 tablespoon lemon juice
250g [8 oz] seedless grapes*

Sprinkle chicken pieces with salt and paprika. Melt half the butter, brown chicken and set aside. Add rest of butter, onion and garlic and cook over low heat for 5 mins. Keep aside 8 mushroom caps, slice the remainder and add to the pan—saute for 2 mins, then blend in the flour and sugar. Add chicken stock and lemon juice, bring to boil, stirring well. Add chicken, cover and simmer for 30 mins until tender. Add grapes for the last 5 mins of cooking time. Arrange chicken on a serving dish and pour sauce over. Garnish with sauteed mushroom caps.

*NOTE: If using tinned grapes, omit the sugar.

113

706 CHICKEN SUPREME

1 roasting chicken, jointed
60g [2 oz] butter
125g [4 oz] bacon, chopped
1 onion, chopped
1 tablespoon chopped parsley
pinch thyme
¾ cup dry sherry

1 chicken cube, dissolved in
1 cup boiling water
1 tablespoon extra butter
1 tablespoon plain flour
1 125g [4 oz] can champignons, drained
salt and pepper

Melt butter in pan and lightly fry chopped bacon and onion until tender, place in casserole dish. Saute chicken until golden, add to casserole, add parsley, thyme and cover with sherry and chicken stock. Cook in moderate oven for 1 hour or until chicken is tender. Make a roux from 1 tablespoon butter blended with 1 tablespoon flour. Remove chicken and thicken sauce with roux. Add champignons and chicken and reheat.

Variation: Omit champignons and arrange 250g (8 oz) sliced tomatoes on chicken before baking. Omit sherry and if desired, substitute white wine for chicken stock. Substitute basil for thyme.

707 CHICKEN AND PINEAPPLE

1 roasting chicken, jointed or
1-1.5kg [2-3 lb] chicken
pieces
1 packet French onion soup

1 425g [15 oz] can pineapple
pieces, undrained
½ cup chicken stock or water

Cut chicken into serving pieces and place in casserole. Sprinkle with dry soup. Add pineapple pieces, juice and stock. Bake in moderate oven for 1½ hours.

They had a Cook with them who stood alone
For boiling chicken with a marrow-bone,
Sharp flavouring powder and a spice of savour.
He could distinguish London ale by flavour,
And he could roast and seethe and boil and fry,
Make good thick soup and bake a tasty pie.
Geoffrey Chaucer, *The Canterbury Tales*,
14th century, trans. N. Coghill

708 CURRIED CHICKEN WITH PEACHES OR PEARS

1.5-2kg [3½ lb] roasting
chicken, jointed
2 tablespoons oil or butter
1 medium size onion, finely
chopped
1 tablespoon curry powder
1 tablespoon flour
2 cups chicken stock [R 202]
1 clove garlic, crushed
⅔ cup coconut milk [made by
pouring 1 cup boiling
water on 2 tablespoons
coconut and standing for
1 hour]

1 tablespoon redcurrant or
quince jelly or juice of 1
lemon mixed with
2 teaspoons sugar
1 teaspoon cornflour
3-4 tablespoons cream
2-3 fresh peaches or pears,
peeled and sliced

Brown chicken in oil in flameproof casserole. Remove. Brown onion gently, then add curry powder, flour, chicken stock and garlic and simmer for 20 mins. Return chicken to pot, and allow to cook gently for further 45 mins. Add strained coconut milk, redcurrant jelly, and cornflour mixed to a paste with 1 tablespoon of the nut milk or stock. Add cream and fresh fruit about 10 mins before serving, as the fruit only needs warming. If liked add the coconut remaining from the nut milk. Serve with boiled rice.

709 CRUMBED MARINATED CHICKEN

Make a marinade with 2 tablespoons oil, 2 tablespoons brandy, salt and pepper and leave chicken pieces in it for 1-2 hours.
Roll each piece of chicken in breadcrumbs, place in greased baking dish and bake for 1 hour at 400°F (200°C). For softer consistency of meat, place 600ml (one pint) of chicken stock in bottom of baking dish and place chicken pieces on rack in dish.

There never was such a goose. Bob said he didn't believe there ever was such a goose cooked. Its tenderness and flavour, size and cheapness, were the themes of universal admiration. Eked out by apple-sauce and mashed potatoes, it was a sufficient dinner for the whole family.
Hollo! A great deal of steam! The pudding was out of the copper. A smell like a washing day! That was the cloth. A smell like an eating-house and a pastrycook's next door to each other, with a laundress's next door to that! That was the pudding!

Charles Dickens, *A Christmas Carol*

710 CHICKEN IN SPICY SAUCE

Place required number of chicken pieces in greased baking dish.
Mix together:

3 tablespoons butter, melted	*½ teaspoon oregano*
3 tablespoons worcestershire sauce	*¼ teaspoon paprika*
	1 clove garlic, crushed
1 teaspoon curry powder	*1 chicken cube, crushed*

Pour mixture over chicken, bake uncovered in moderate oven for 1 hour.

711 CHICKEN IN LEMON SAUCE

1 roasting chicken, jointed	*½ cup melted butter*
1 tablespoon flour	*salt and pepper*
1 tablespoon sweet paprika	

In large paper or plastic bag mix together flour, paprika, salt and pepper. Place chicken pieces in bag and shake to coat thoroughly. Place chicken in large roasting pan skin side down, covering chicken well with melted butter. Bake in moderate oven uncovered for 30 mins. Pour the following sauce over.

1 tablespoon soya sauce	*1 clove garlic, crushed*
1 tablespoon oil	*juice and grated rind of 2 lemons*

Cook further 30 mins. Serve with rice. This dish can be cooked ahead of time and reheated.

712 MARINATED CHINESE CHICKEN

12 pieces of chicken	*2 tablespoons brown sugar*
¼ cup soya sauce	*2 tablespoons honey*
¼ cup white vinegar	*2 cloves garlic, crushed*
3 teaspoons chili sauce or ½ teaspoon tabasco	*2-3 slices ginger*
	salt and pepper
¼ cup tomato sauce	*oil*

Mix together all ingredients except chicken to make a marinade. Place chicken pieces in the marinade for 2-3 hours. Remove and drain. Saute in hot oil until they have changed colour. Place in greased baking dish, cover with foil and cook in moderate oven until tender, 30-35 mins.
Note: If preparing early in the day, the chicken pieces can be taken to the browned stage, then kept in the refrigerator until ready to cook. They will take a little longer to cook if placed in oven directly from refrigerator.

713 CHICKEN BREASTS SWISS STYLE

4 whole chicken breasts
seasoned flour
90g [3 oz] butter
1 small clove garlic, crushed
1 small onion or 3 shallots,
    finely chopped
¾ cup white wine or chicken
    stock

1 bay leaf
8 slices ham
8 slices Swiss or gruyere
    cheese
½ cup cream
salt and pepper

Divide each breast into two pieces, dust lightly with seasoned flour. Heat butter, add chicken and saute gently until golden, remove from pan. Add garlic and onion, saute until transparent. Add wine and bring to boil. Add chicken and bay leaf. Simmer, covered for 20 mins or until chicken is tender. Place chicken in flat casserole or heatproof serving dish. Put a slice of ham then a slice of cheese on each piece of chicken. Bake uncovered in moderate oven 10 mins or until cheese has melted. Meanwhile allow liquid in pan to boil uncovered until reduced to ½ cup. Reduce heat, add cream, salt and pepper. Serve sauce over chicken.

714 CHICKEN POT ROASTED IN ORANGE GRAVY

1.5-1.75kg [3-3½ lb] chicken
salt and pepper
2 tablespoons flour
3 tablespoons butter
1 large onion, chopped
2 bay leaves
4 peppercorns
½ teaspoon oregano

2½ cups orange juice
2 tablespoons orange marma-
    lade
4 tablespoons lemon juice
3 tablespoons cream
4 oranges, peeled and seg-
    mented

Rub chicken with salt and pepper and dust lightly with flour. Heat butter and fry onion until lightly brown. Add chicken and cook on all sides until golden. Add bay leaves, peppercorns, oregano, orange juice, marmalade and lemon juice. Cook covered until tender, about 2 hours. Remove chicken and keep warm. Skim off any fat from the juices, add cream, stir well and scrape in all the brown fragments. Heat orange segments in sauce, place them around chicken and serve orange gravy separately.

*When you've had roast chicken for dinner don't discard the carcass before boiling it for stock. (R 202).

715 CHICKEN WITH HONEY

1 roasting chicken
1 cup cooked brown rice
125-185g [4-6 oz] butter,
   melted

½ cup honey
salt and pepper

Melt butter and blend with honey. Stuff the chicken with rice and drizzle in half amount of melted butter and honey. Baste the whole bird with rest of the honey and butter mixture, season. Bake in moderate oven in covered casserole ½-¾ hour, remove lid, baste, then keep turning and basting every 15 mins until golden brown and cooked. (The aroma is incredible and when served, the stuffing is nutty and sweet.) Can be served with jacket baked potatoes topped with sour cream, and a plain tossed salad.

716 CHICKEN WITH PEANUT BUTTER

1 roasting chicken
salt and pepper
cashew nut stuffing [R 1038]
2 tablespoons peanut butter

2 tablespoons soya sauce
¼ cup white wine
½ cup chicken stock
1 tablespoon oil

Season and stuff chicken. Spread lightly with peanut butter. Combine soya sauce, wine, stock and oil. Roast chicken in moderate oven for 1½ hours or cook on spit, basting frequently with sauce mixture.

Pre-Cooked Chicken

717 SMOKED CHICKEN

1 roasting chicken
salt
4 tablespoons brown or raw
   sugar

2 teaspoons sesame oil

Salt the chicken inside and out and refrigerate overnight. Place in a steamer or on a rack in a large saucepan over boiling water and steam for 1 hour. Drain well.

Place several thicknesses of foil in the bottom of a large (preferably old) saucepan and sprinkle sugar on to the foil. Place chicken on a rack over the sugar. Line the saucepan lid with foil and cover tightly so that no smoke can escape. Cook on a medium-high heat for 10 mins. Leave lid on for a further 10 mins. Brush chicken with sesame oil. Serve hot or cold.

718 SWEET AND SOUR CHICKEN

1 chicken, cooked and diced
Marinate for one hour in the following:

1 tablespoon soya sauce
1 tablespoon sugar
½ teaspoon salt

1 tablespoon dry sherry
1 egg yolk
½ cup chicken stock

While chicken is in marinade, prepare the following:

2 tablespoons oil
2 onions, sliced
125g [4 oz] fresh mushrooms,
    sliced
1 red pepper, sliced

½ large cucumber, peeled
    and cut into chunks
1 425g [15 oz] can crushed
    pineapple, drained, juice
    reserved
8 spring onions, chopped

Heat oil in frypan and fry onions, mushrooms and red pepper for 1 min over high heat. Add cucumber, pineapple, and spring onions. Place in casserole or saucepan and add drained chicken. Make sauce from the following.

1 tablespoon cornflour
pineapple juice from can

¼ cup vinegar
1 tablespoon tomato sauce

Blend, add marinade and bring to boil. Season and pour over chicken and vegetables. Reheat gently.

719 CHICKEN SPANISH STYLE

1 chicken, cooked and diced
1 tablespoon oil or butter
1 large onion, chopped
250g [8 oz] tomatoes,
    chopped
2-4 teaspoons allspice

1 425g [15 oz] can tomato soup
salt and pepper
1 teaspoon mustard
2 teaspoons worcestershire
    sauce

Saute onion in oil, add all other ingredients. Simmer gently 15 mins. Serve with Island rice (R 832) or plain boiled rice.

720 CHICKEN HAWAII

1 chicken, cooked and diced
1 tablespoon oil
2 green peppers, sliced
1 clove garlic, crushed
1 425g [15 oz] can cream of
    chicken soup

1 425g [15 oz] can pineapple
    pieces, drained
90g [3 oz] blanched almonds,
    toasted

Cut chicken into bite size pieces. Saute pepper and garlic in a little oil. Add soup and simmer, then add chicken pieces and pineapple pieces. Heat through and add almonds. Serve with buttered rice.

721 CHICKEN CROQUETTES

375g [12 oz] chopped cold
   chicken
125g [4 oz] chopped cold
   cooked mushrooms
small onion, chopped finely
thick binding sauce of 30g
   [1 oz] butter, 30g [1 oz]
   flour, ½ cup milk

2 eggs
breadcrumbs
oil
mushroom sauce [R 656]

Make sauce, add chicken, mushrooms and onion. When cool add 1 egg beaten well. Mix thoroughly. Spread evenly ½" thick on plate and leave until cold. Shape into croquettes about 3" x 1". Dip in egg and breadcrumbs and deep fry in oil until golden brown. Serve with mushroom sauce.

722 CHINESE CHICKEN AND ALMONDS

1.5kg [3 lb] chopped cooked
   chicken
3 tablespoons oil
1 tablespoon butter
60g [2 oz] blanched almonds
125g [4 oz] mushrooms,
   skinned and finely chopped
1 bunch spring onions,
   chopped [green stalks too]

250g [8 oz] bean shoots
1 tablespoon cornflour
1 cup chicken stock
salt and pepper
1 tablespoon soya sauce
3 cups cooked rice for serving

Heat one tablespoon oil with butter and fry almonds gently until golden brown. Remove and add remaining oil to pan. Add chicken, mushrooms, spring onions and bean shoots and heat gently, stirring frequently. Sprinkle in flour, add stock, salt and pepper and soya sauce. Stir until it boils and thickens. Add nuts. Heat rice, add small amount to chicken mixture and use rest as border on large serving dish, with chicken in middle. Serve with green peas and carrots cut in julienne strips.

CHICKEN STOCK (R 202)

CHICKEN CUSTARD (R 1808)

Art is not a special sauce applied to ordinary cooking; it is the cooking itself if it is good.
               W. R. Lethaby, Form in Civilization, Art and Workmanship

723 CHICKEN CASSEROLE IDEAS

Mix 1 cooked, diced chicken with one of the following combinations and reheat gently.

1. 1 454g (1 lb) can asparagus soup, 1 cup drained asparagus pieces, ¼ cup cream. Sprinkle with 125g (4 oz) grated cheese.
2. 1 454g (1 lb) can chicken or celery soup, ¼ cup cream, 125g (4 oz) chopped cooked bacon, and 60g (2 oz) almonds.
3. 1 packet cheese and leek soup, 1½ cups boiling chicken stock or water, 1 cup white sauce (R 1010), 1 cup drained asparagus pieces.
4. 1 packet chicken noodle soup simmered in 1½ cups boiling water or stock for 7 mins, 1 cup white sauce (R 1010), 1 tablespoon chopped parsley, 1 small (298g, 10½ oz) can sweetcorn drained, 125g (4 oz) chopped, cooked bacon (optional).
5. 1 440g (15½ oz) can mushroom or tomato soup, ¼ cup white wine.
6. Melt 1½ tablespoons butter, blend in 1½ tablespoons flour, gradually add 1½ cups chicken stock and ½ cup syrup from canned green gooseberries. Stir until sauce boils and thickens, add chicken, salt and pepper and 1 cup gooseberries.

Cold Chicken

SMOKED CHICKEN (R 717)

724 CHICKEN MOUSSE

1 chicken, cooked
1 297g [10½ oz] can tomato
  soup
½ cup sour cream
1-2 teaspoons lemon juice
salt and pepper
6 teaspoons gelatine

¼ cup cold water
1 soup can warm water
¾ cup chopped dill
  cucumber or gherkin
½ cup stuffed olives, sliced
1 onion, cooked and chopped

Bone chicken and chop meat finely. Blend soup and sour cream adding lemon juice, salt and pepper. Soften gelatine in a little cold water then add one soup can of warm water. Stir over low heat until dissolved. Blend this with the already prepared soup mixture. Chill until slightly thickened, then fold in chicken, cucumber, olives and onion. Pour into mould or individual serving dishes and chill.

Duck

725 ROAST DUCK WITH CHERRY SAUCE

1 duck
salt and pepper
1 cup white wine
2 tablespoons sugar
2 tablespoons vinegar
1 tablespoon butter
2 tablespoons flour
1 cup stock
3 tablespoons grated orange
 rind

½ cup orange juice
3 tablespoons lemon juice
1 tablespoon grated lemon
 rind
1 454g [16 oz] can dark
 cherries, undrained
2 tablespoons brandy

Clean duck and rub with salt and pepper. (If possible season the day before.) Roast on a rack at 450°F (230°C) for 20 mins. Drain off fat, remove rack and pour wine over duck. Reduce temperature to 350°F (180°C) and continue roasting for 1½ hours or until tender. Remove from pan, carve and keep warm.

Sauce:
Place sugar and vinegar in saucepan and cook until dark brown. Melt butter and add flour. Add stock and stir until boiling. Cook over low heat for 10 mins stirring occasionally. Add orange and lemon juices and rinds, 1 cup cherry juice and brandy, stirring well. Add sugar and vinegar mixture, then ¼ cup pan drippings skimmed of all fat. Cook over low heat for 15 mins then add cherries and reheat. Serve with duck.

726 DUCK WITH LYCHEES (PAN-FRIED)

1 1.75kg [3½ lb] duck, roasted
 and cut in thin strips
90g [3 oz] oil
500g [1 lb] green beans, cut
 in thin strips
3 medium green peppers, cut
 in thin strips
1 root ginger, finely grated

1 clove garlic, crushed
2 cups chicken stock
2 tablespoons soya sauce
1 tablespoon arrowroot
2 tablespoons water
1 565g [20 oz] can lychees,
 drained

Heat oil and fry beans, then green peppers. Reheat oil and lightly fry ginger and garlic. Add stock and soya sauce. Bring to boil and thicken with arrowroot mixed with water. Simmer until clear. Add duck, beans, green peppers and lychees. Reheat, check seasoning and serve immediately.

727 DUCK WITH ORANGE SAUCE

1 duck
salt and pepper
1 lemon, halved
1 small onion, sliced
1 small apple, sliced
2-3 celery stalks with leaves on
1 clove garlic

300ml [½ pint] chicken stock
juice and grated rind of 2
 oranges
juice of 1 lemon
2 tablespoons cognac
2 tablespoons sugar
2 tablespoons water

Wipe duck and sprinkle cavity with salt and pepper. Rub with cut lemon, and place the onion, apple and celery inside cavity. Prick skin all over with a fork and rub with the cut clove of garlic, salt and pepper. Place breast side up on a rack in a roasting pan and place in 350°F (180°C) oven for 30 mins. Baste well and continue cooking allowing 20 mins to each 500g (1 lb) until duck is tender. Remove and keep warm.

Skim fat from the pan juices, add chicken stock, scraping in all the crusty bits. Stir in the orange and lemon juices and cognac. Blend sugar with 2 tablespoons water and cook over low heat until caramelised. Add to the sauce and cook gently until reduced by half.

Carve duckling, place on a heated serving platter, pour over sauce and sprinkle with the grated orange rind.

Rabbit

728 CURRIED RABBIT

1 large rabbit
cold salted water
60g [2 oz] oil
1 tablespoon seasoned flour
1 tablespoon curry powder
2 onions, sliced
1 clove garlic, crushed

2 tomatoes, sliced
1 green pepper, sliced
1¼ cups chicken stock [dis-
 solve a bouillon cube in
 water]
1 tablespoon fruit chutney

Soak the rabbit for two hours in cold salted water, dry and cut into neat serving portions. Heat oil in a large pan, roll rabbit pieces in seasoned flour and fry until brown. Add curry powder, onions and garlic, continue cooking 4-5 mins. Add tomatoes, and green pepper, then chicken stock. Cover and cook gently for 30-40 mins. Add fruit chutney and lemon juice. Serve with boiled rice.

729 RABBIT CASSEROLE

1 rabbit, jointed
2 tablespoons vinegar
2 tablespoons flour
¼ teaspoon mixed herbs
salt and pepper
2 tablespoons oil or butter
2 rashers bacon, chopped

½ cup chopped celery
2 teaspoons peanut butter
1 tablespoon chopped parsley
3 tomatoes, skinned and
chopped
½ cup water
3 tablespoons dry sherry

Soak rabbit in vinegar and water for a few hours. Wash in clear water, dry and roll in seasoned flour. Fry lightly in oil until golden brown and arrange pieces in casserole. Add bacon, celery, peanut butter and chopped parsley. Combine tomatoes with water and sherry, pour into casserole. Cook in moderate oven 1½ hours or until tender. If desired thicken gravy with cornflour.

730 RABBIT IN MUSTARD SAUCE

1 large rabbit, jointed
4 tablespoons prepared
French mustard
2-3 tablespoons flour,
seasoned with salt and
pepper
2 tablespoons butter or oil

2-3 rashers bacon, coarsely
chopped
1 onion, finely chopped
1 clove garlic, crushed
½ cup cream
2 tablespoons finely chopped
parsley

Start this dish the day before you want to eat it. Soak rabbit joints for 1-2 hours in cold, salted water. Drain well and cover joints all over with mustard. Leave in refrigerator overnight. Next day, dip joints of rabbit in flour, lightly brown in hot butter or oil and remove and put to one side. Add bacon pieces, onion and garlic and brown, then return rabbit to pan, cover with tightly fitting lid and simmer for 30 mins on top of stove or in moderate oven. Add cream and cook a further 45 mins making sure rabbit does not stick to bottom of pan. Garnish with chopped parsley.

Fresh from the Garden

Fresh From the Garden

I'd like to be able to say a good word for parsley, but I can't. And after all what can you find to say for something that even the dictionary dismisses as a biennial umbelliferous plant?

Ogden Nash

800 VEGETABLES

The following vegetable recipes have been selected as they are a little different from our usual daily fare. However always remember that fresh young vegetables, straight from the garden or market, need nothing more than the simplest cooking. Steam or boil them in very little water and serve tossed with butter and the appropriate herbs, always "under" rather than "over" cooked, still at the "crunchy" stage, thus retaining as many vitamins as possible. Do not throw vegetable water away. Add it to gravies, soups and casseroles.

Bake potatoes in their skins, and serve topped with a dob of cream, yoghurt, butter and parsley, or sprinkled with nutmeg or crumbled cooked bacon.

Cabbage *is* delicious. Shred very finely, pour boiling water over, bring back to the boil, strain and add butter and pepper and for a different taste a sprinkle of caraway seeds, dried or chopped fresh dill.

Always remove the seeds from pumpkin as soon as it is bought, cut into pieces for cooking and store in plastic bag in refrigerator—do not peel, the skin is delicious, either boiled, steamed or roasted. Try pumpkin chips, prepared and cooked as for potato chips, or mixed and served together.

Zucchini, sliced lengthwise, par-boiled, then sprinkled with grated cheese and grilled, is a great treat. Alternatively, after par-boiling, toss them in a pan of melted butter to which has been added 1 tablespoon finely chopped fresh rosemary, juice of ½ lemon, salt and pepper. Give peas a lift by simmering in chicken stock, then mixing with sauteed cubed ham and chopped spring onions or sliced champignons.

Green beans are delicious tossed with butter and toasted almonds.

Vegetable combinations are endless, so be adventurous and create some new dishes and never forget one of the most nutritious greens, parsley, so easy to grow, and an asset to any dish.

126

801 STUFFED AUBERGINE (EGGPLANT)

1-2 large aubergines
2 large onions, chopped
4 tablespoons oil
2 cloves garlic, crushed
1 medium carrot, grated
4 stalks celery, chopped

½ cup chopped parsley
4 mint leaves, chopped
1 cup canned tomatoes
1 teaspoon salt
¼ teaspoon pepper
2 tablespoons uncooked rice

Saute onions in oil until lightly browned. Add garlic, carrot, celery, mint, parsley, tomatoes, salt and pepper. Cook gently for 30 mins. Meanwhile, slice a lid from top of aubergine and carefully spoon contents out into basin, sprinkle lightly with salt. Chop, add to cooked vegetables, continue cooking until tender. Add rice. Stuff aubergine with vegetable mixture. Set "lid" on top and secure with toothpicks. Place in casserole or baking dish. Cover. Put in a slow oven 300°F (150°C) and cook 1½ hours. Cut in slices to serve.

802 BEETROOT IN HOT RELISH

12 small beetroot
½ cup brown sugar
1 tablespoon cornflour
½ cup brown vinegar

½ cup water
2 tablespoons butter
salt and pepper

Cook beetroot and cut into cubes. Mix brown sugar and cornflour in saucepan and add vinegar and water. Bring to boil, stirring,and simmer for 5 mins. Add beetroot and simmer gently for 15 mins more. Before serving, add butter, salt and pepper.

BROCCOLI SAVOURY (R 430)

BARBECUED BEANS (R 432)

803 CABBAGE BAKED WITH SOUR CREAM

¼ cabbage
½ cup sour cream or ½ cup
*   fresh cream mixed with 1*
*   teaspoon vinegar*

1 egg
¼ teaspoon nutmeg
1 tablespoon butter
salt and pepper

Cook cabbage in boiling, salted water until tender but still crisp. Mix together sour cream, egg and nutmeg. Drain cabbage and fold butter through it. Then pour cream mixture over and blend well together. Add salt and pepper Pour into buttered casserole dish and bake in moderate oven until browned on top.

Can be prepared hours before required and placed in oven ½ hour prior to serving.

804 RED CABBAGE

red cabbage, shredded,
amount as desired
1 small onion, chopped
1 rasher streaky bacon,
chopped
1 cooking apple, chopped
butter

1 tablespoon brown sugar
1 tablespoon vinegar
few sultanas
peppercorns, mixed spice,
tarragon

Fry onion, bacon and apple in a little butter. When tender, add the shredded, washed cabbage, brown sugar, vinegar, sultanas, spices and herbs. Cover tightly and cook for at least 2 hours on the lowest possible heat or in non stick saucepan for 30 mins over medium heat. If you have time, cook for longer. Can be prepared hours before needed, as red cabbage can be reheated and tastes all the better for it unlike most vegetables. Serve it in its own delicious liquid—there will not be much of it.

Variation: Use white cabbage instead of red, with caraway seed and nutmeg instead of mixed spice and tarragon.

805 CANDIED CARROTS

3 medium carrots
2 tablespoons butter
¼ cup brown sugar

¼ cup honey
¼ cup sweet vermouth

Peel carrots and slice into strips or rounds. Cook until tender. Drain and place in greased casserole. Melt together butter, brown sugar, honey and sweet vermouth. Pour over carrots, re-heat and serve.

Can be prepared in advance, ready to re-heat.

CARROT RICE CASSEROLE (R 433)

806 CARROTS DELICIOUS

6 medium carrots, thinly sliced
1 apple, thinly sliced
2 tablespoons butter
salt

1 teaspoon grated lemon rind
2 tablespoons water
½ cup grated cheese
1 tablespoon chopped parsley

Arrange carrots and apple in alternate layers in saucepan. Dot with butter, sprinkle with salt, lemon rind and water. Cover, cook over gentle heat until tender about 20 mins. Sprinkle with cheese, cover, steam further 5 mins. Serve sprinkled with parsley.

807 CARROTS TURKISH STYLE

1 bunch baby carrots
1 beaten egg
½ cup breadcrumbs
butter

1 cup chilled yoghurt
1 clove garlic, crushed
chopped mint

Cook carrots then dip in beaten egg and coat with breadcrumbs. Saute until golden brown in butter. Serve with chilled yoghurt flavoured with garlic. Sprinkle with chopped mint.

808 CELERY SPEARS ALMONDINE

4 stalks celery
60g [2 oz] butter

salt and pepper
almond flakes

With a sharp knife, slice celery stalks diagonally producing thin spears. Saute in the butter until tender, but still crisp. Sprinkle with salt, pepper and almonds.

809 SWEETCORN CASSEROLE

250g [8 oz] bacon, chopped
butter for frying
1 cup fresh breadcrumbs
½ cup chopped green pepper

1 small onion, chopped
1 454g [1 lb] can creamed
  sweetcorn

Saute bacon until brown. Pour any drippings over fresh breadcrumbs in basin. Add green pepper and onion to bacon in pan and cook slowly 5 mins. Add sweetcorn and mix together. Layer in greased casserole with crumb mixture ending with crumbs on top. Bake in moderate oven for 25 mins or until brown.

SWEETCORN FRITTERS (R 412)

810 MUSHROOMS AND CABBAGE CHINESE STYLE

250g [8 oz] mushrooms
2 tablespoons oil
2 cups cabbage, sliced
3 sticks celery, sliced

1 white onion, sliced
250g [8 oz] bean shoots
salt and pepper
1 tablespoon soya sauce

Wash mushrooms, remove stems and slice thickly. Heat oil in large pan, add cabbage, celery and onion, and saute until tender. Season. Add mushrooms and bean shoots and cook over high heat until mushrooms are tender. Sprinkle with soya sauce and serve.

CHINESE VEGETABLES (R 912)

811 MUSHROOMS AND ZUCCHINI ITALIAN STYLE

2 tablespoons oil
3 medium zucchini, finely
  sliced
250g [8 oz] mushrooms

¼ cup white wine
¼ cup sour cream
salt and pepper
chopped parsley

Heat oil in large pan. Add zucchini and saute gently until tender. Add mushrooms, then pour white wine over. Stir until mushrooms are tender. Add sour cream and mix well. Season and serve sprinkled with parsley.
Variation: Omit wine and cream, add 1 crushed clove garlic. Saute all in oil or butter until browned and tender.

KASHA (Buckwheat with mushrooms and onions) (R 2414)

VEGETABLE CUPS (R 1049)

812 PEAS AND BACON

2 rashers bacon, chopped
250g [8 oz] peas [fresh or
  frozen]
6 spring onions, chopped
1-2 tablespoons water

salt and pepper
1 teaspoon sugar [if using
  fresh peas]
marjoram

Cook bacon until crisp, add other ingredients. Cover tightly and cook for 15 mins. Drain and serve immediately.

813 PEAS AND LETTUCE

lettuce [no longer suitable for
  salad]
2 tablespoons oil
30g [1 oz] butter

1 onion, sliced
250g [8 oz] peas
water

Slice lettuce finely. Heat oil and butter in pan and saute onion. Add lettuce and peas and very little water. Steam until tender.

PEPPERS STUFFED WITH MINCED STEAK (R 699B)

*Use patty pans to bake potatoes, apples and tomatoes. They remain in position and can all be removed at once.

130

814 PEPPERS STUFFED WITH SOUR CREAM AND MACARONI

6 green peppers
2 cups cooked macaroni
1 egg
1 cup sour cream
2 teaspoons prepared mustard

1 tablespoon grated onion
salt and pepper
125g [4 oz] grated cheddar
cheese

Cut off tops of peppers. Remove seeds and parboil peppers 3 mins in salted water. Drain. Stand in baking dish. Stuff with half of the macaroni. Mix egg, cream, mustard, onion, salt and pepper. Put half in peppers, then add half the cheese. Spoon remainder of macaroni into peppers, add remaining sauce mixture, top with remaining cheese. Bake in moderate oven for 30 mins.

815 GNOCCHI

1kg [2 lb] potatoes
250g [8 oz] flour

30g [1 oz] butter or margarine
2 eggs
salt and pepper

Cook potatoes, drain well and mash thoroughly. Add flour, butter and eggs and season well. Roll into a long sausage shape ½″ in diameter. Cut "sausage" into ¾″ lengths and drop these into a large saucepan of boiling salted water. Cook for 3 mins (they will float to the top when done). Drain well and cover with melted butter and grated parmesan cheese.
Serve as they are or with Bolognese sauce (R 507) or Pesta (R 509).

816 HOT POTATO SALAD

This dish is delicious with barbecued steak and can be prepared beforehand or while the steak is cooking.

1kg [2 lb] potatoes
½ teaspoon salt
3 rashers bacon

½ cup French dressing
[R 1004]
parsley, chopped

Peel and dice potatoes, place in cold salted water and bring to boil, simmer 4-5 mins. While potatoes are cooking, fry bacon, then chop. When potato cubes are just tender, drain. Add chopped bacon to potatoes and pour French dressing over. Sprinkle with parsley. Fold through until potatoes and bacon are coated with dressing. Serve hot. Any left-overs can be reheated gently in the oven.
Variation: Use yoghurt or mayonnaise instead of French dressing.

817 SCALLOPED POTATOES

750g [1½ lb] potatoes [4
 medium size]
salt and pepper

2 tablespoons butter
1¼ cups [approx] warm milk

Peel potatoes and slice thinly. Sprinkle with salt and pepper. Put into well greased casserole dish, add milk to barely cover, dot with butter and bake covered in a moderate oven for about 1 hour. Remove lid and bake further 30 mins or until potatoes are cooked and top is golden.

Variations:
1. Add 1 finely chopped onion or 1 clove garlic, crushed.
2. Sprinkle top with 2 tablespoons cheese.
3. Add ¼ teaspoon nutmeg or 1 teaspoon paprika.
4. Replace ¼ cup milk with ¼ cup sherry.
5. Replace milk with chicken stock. Make layers of potatoes, finely chopped garlic and gruyere cheese.
6. Omit milk and substitute 1 454g (1 lb) can asparagus soup and ¼ cup cream.
7. Add 1 packet creamy French onion or chicken soup and extra ¼ cup milk.
8. Serve sprinkled with parsley.

818 HUNGARIAN STYLE POTATOES

1 large onion, finely sliced
60g [2 oz] butter
2 teaspoons paprika
3 tomatoes, peeled, seeded
 and sliced

1 cup stock
6 large potatoes, peeled and
 sliced
salt and pepper
chopped parsley

Fry onion in butter in large pan. Add paprika and cook until onion is translucent. Add tomatoes and stock and bring to boil. Dry and season potatoes and place in baking dish. Pour sauce over potatoes. Place in moderate oven and bake until tender, 45-60 mins. Sprinkle with chopped parsley and serve.

---

*To shorten the cooking time of baked potatoes insert a skewer or a clean 4" nail into the centre of the potato.

---

*Store left-over mashed potato in a straight-sided glass. Remove by running a knife around it and cut into shaped potato cakes.

819 POTATOES WITH CHEESE FILLING

4 medium to large size
  potatoes for baking
1 egg, beaten

1 cup grated cheese
salt

Bake potatoes in hot oven until soft in the centre (about 1 hour). Cut potatoes in half and scoop out centres, leaving skins intact. Mash all the potato insides together in basin, add egg, beat well, add cheese and salt. Spoon mixture back into potato shells. Bake 5-10 mins in hot oven until golden brown.

OVEN BAKED POTATOES WITH SOUR CREAM SAUCE
(R 2418·1)

820 POTATO PANCAKES (LATKES)

1kg [2 lb] potatoes
2 tablespoons S.R. flour
salt and pepper

1 egg, beaten
grated onion [optional]

Peel and grate potatoes into bowl of cold water, then strain. Place strained potatoes in a bowl, add flour, salt, pepper and egg. Mix thoroughly. Drop tablespoons of the mixture into hot oil and fry on both sides until brown. A little grated onion may be added to mixture before cooking.

821 CANDIED SWEET POTATOES

3 large sweet potatoes
¾ cup brown sugar or ½ cup
  honey
1 cup water

¼ teaspoon nutmeg
¼ teaspoon allspice
salt and pepper

Peel sweet potatoes and cut into ¼ inch slices. Combine other ingredients in saucepan and simmer 5 mins. Place potato slices in ovenproof dish and pour syrup over. Cover and cook for 30 mins, basting several times.

822 ORANGE SWEET POTATOES

sweet potatoes
butter
grated orange rind

juice of 1 orange
freshly ground black pepper

Cook sweet potatoes in jackets, then peel. Mash with plenty of butter, orange rind, orange juice and pepper.

133

823 PUMPKIN CASSEROLE

4 cups cooked, mashed
  pumpkin
¼ cup brown sugar
salt and pepper
¼ teaspoon nutmeg

½ teaspoon ginger
¼ teaspoon cinnamon
1 teaspoon grated lemon rind
1 teaspoon grated orange rind
¼ cup melted butter

Combine all ingredients. Turn into buttered casserole. Bake at 350°F (180°C) for 1 hour or until top is lightly brown.

824 CARRIED AWAY SPINACH

1 packet frozen spinach or
  375g [¾ lb] fresh spinach
½ teaspoon caraway seeds

2 teaspoons butter
1 teaspoon lemon juice

Cook spinach according to directions on package, drain thoroughly. Add caraway seeds, butter and lemon juice and toss.
Variation: Substitute Brussels sprouts for spinach and cook them in a little chicken stock before tossing as above.

825 TOMATOES PROVENCALE

4 medium tomatoes
salt and pepper
30g [1 oz] butter]

4 tablespoons breadcrumbs
1 clove garlic, crushed

Halve tomatoes, sprinkle with salt and pepper. Melt butter and mix with breadcrumbs, garlic, salt and pepper. Place equal quantities on each tomato half and grill until well browned.

TOMATOES IN CHEESE SAUCE (R 431)

EGG IN A NEST (R 1807)

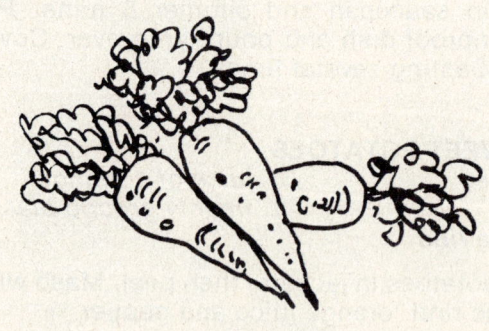

826 RATATOUILLE

1 large green pepper	1 tablespoon tomato paste
oil	½ teaspoon dried sweet basil
1 large aubergine	1 clove crushed garlic
2 medium tomatoes	vegisalt [or preferred
500g [1 lb] zucchini	seasoning]

Slice vegetables coarsely. Heat oil in frypan or large skillet, then one at a time fry the vegetables. Allow 3-4 mins per vegetable, then set it aside. Add oil as necessary. When each has been fried in this manner, combine all the vegetables, add tomato paste, basil and garlic, season, then allow to simmer on low heat with lid off for at least 20 mins, but up to one hour to allow flavours to combine. (Lid can be replaced if mixture appears to be drying out too much.)

BACON RATATOUILLE (R 434)

827 GRILLED ZUCCHINI

Cook whole zucchini in boiling salted water until barely tender. Trim ends, halve lengthwise and sprinkle with one of the following, then grill until topping is browned.

1. Breadcrumbs seasoned with salt and pepper, chopped parsley and finely chopped garlic, and mixed with 2 table-spoons butter.
2. Prepared stuffing mix.
3. Garlic salt, freshly ground black pepper and grated cheese (parmesan is tasty).
4. Bechamel Sauce (R 1018) with cheese added.

But there's nothing the matter with butter,
And nothing the matter with jam,
And the warmest of greetings I utter
To the ham and the yam and the clam.
Bring salad or sausage or scrapple,
A berry or even a beet
Bring an oyster, an egg, or an apple,
As long as it's something to eat.

Ogden Nash

828 ZUCCHINI AND TOMATOES

750g [1½ lb] tomatoes,
  chopped
1 onion, finely chopped
2 tablespoons butter

salt and pepper
500g [1 lb] zucchini, thinly
  sliced
1 tablespoon chopped parsley

Saute onion in butter until transparent. Add tomatoes, salt and pepper and simmer until cooked to a thick sauce. Add zucchini and simmer about 15 mins. Sprinkle with parsley.

Variations:

1. Cook zucchini in fresh tomato sauce (R 1013).
2. Turn mixture into greased casserole dish, sprinkle with ¾ cup grated cheese and bake at 350°F (180°C) for 20 mins or until golden brown.
3. Saute zucchini with onion. Slice tomatoes and make layers of tomatoes, salt and pepper, grated cheese, zucchini and onion finishing with cheese. Bake at 350°F (180°C) for 30-45 mins.
4. Parboil whole zucchini 10 mins. Trim ends, cut in half lengthwise and mix pulp with onion and tomato mixture and 1 cup soft breadcrumbs. Fill zucchini and bake in moderate oven 15-20 mins.

829 ZUCCHINI SLIPPERS

6 medium zucchini
1½ cups grated tasty cheese
½ cup ricotta cheese
  [optional]

2 tablespoons chopped
  parsley
salt and pepper

Cut ends off zucchini. Simmer in salted water, 10-12 mins. Remove, cut in half lengthwise. Scoop out pulp and invert each slipper to drain. Mix pulp, cheese, parsley, salt and pepper and fill each shell with mixture. Bake uncovered in moderate oven for 5 mins or until cheese topping is browned. Serves 6.

*Green tomatoes are delicious served as a vegetable. Slice, dredge with flour, sprinkle with a little raw sugar and saute in butter.

830 PILLAU

500g [1 lb] long grain rice
4 tablespoons oil
12 almonds, blanched and
  sliced
1 large onion, sliced
extra oil
½ teaspoon saffron powder

1 cinnamon stick
4-6 cloves
2½ cups chicken stock [made
  from 4 stock cubes]
garnish: almonds, onion,
  slices of hard boiled egg

Heat oil. Fry almonds, remove and set aside. Fry onion until golden brown, set aside. Add a little more oil, saffron and rice. Fry for 2 mins. Make sure the rice is thoroughly mixed with the oil and the saffron. Add cinnamon stick and cloves. Add stock, lower heat, stir well with a fork. Cover and simmer for 15 mins or until stock is absorbed or rice tender. Stir well with a fork. Remove from heat and add sultanas. For best results cook about 1 hour before serving.

To serve: Remove cinnamon stick and cloves, heat thoroughly and garnish.

Variation: Omit nuts and sultanas. After frying the rice, add peas, finely sliced beans and cubed or grated carrots.

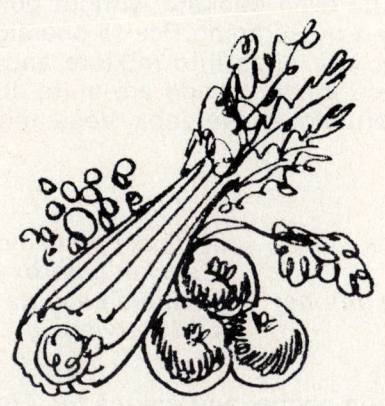

*Lemon peel added to cauliflower helps to retain whiteness.

*Place an unpeeled wedge of lemon in the water when cooking cabbage or cauliflower to lessen the odour.

*Cook a few of the pea pods with the peas to preserve the colour.

831 FRIED RICE

This dish can be as simple or as elaborate as you wish to make it. It is a tasty way of using up small amounts of vegetables, chicken, pork or seafood. The rice is nicer if cooked the day before but this is not absolutely essential. Vegetables and other additions should be cut to a uniform size.

500g [1 lb] cold, cooked rice
1 tablespoon oil
155g [5 oz] bacon or ham, chopped

2 tablespoons chopped spring onions
2 eggs
1 tablespoon soya sauce

Include any of the following:
185g [6 oz] pork or chicken
125g [4 oz] prawn, crab meat or crayfish
125g [4 oz] mushrooms
60g [2 oz] bamboo shoots
60g [2 oz] bean shoots
60g [2 oz] cooked fresh or uncooked frozen peas

125g [4 oz] whole kernel sweetcorn
2 sticks celery
1 green or red pepper
60g [2 oz] salted peanuts [optional]
60g [2 oz] sultanas

Beat eggs and set aside. Chop or slice vegetables. Heat oil in large pan or wok. Add bacon, fry quickly then add rice. Add all other ingredients except eggs and soya sauce. Stir continually to ensure even cooking without burning. Make a hole in centre of pan by scraping rice to one side. Pour eggs into hole and cook. Stir eggs into mixture and keep stirring until eggs have been mixed in and are quite dry. Lastly add soya sauce. Be careful not to overcook. Vegetables should still be slightly crisp.

832 ISLAND RICE

1 small green pepper chopped
6 shallots or spring onions, chopped
3 cups cooked rice

1 tablespoon soya sauce
1 packet [approx 125g, 4 oz] salted peanuts
oil for frying

Heat oil and fry green pepper and onions for 2 mins. Add rice, soya sauce and peanuts and toss well.

CURRIED RICE (R 314)

*To skin tomatoes place them in boiling water for a few minutes, then plunge into cold. The skins will slip off easily. Peaches and grapes etc., can be peeled in the same way.

The Salad Bowl

The Salad Bowl

900 SALADS

Salads are not just a summer time addition to the menu—they can enhance almost any meal throughout the year.

Take a little extra time and effort in the blending of different vegetables and fruits and experiment with dressings and sauces. You will find many "sneaky" ways of enticing your fussy eater to enjoy raw fruit and vegetables.

Salads do not always have to be accompanied by cold meat. Place them on the table with grilled chicken or steak, baked fish, crumbed veal or omelettes. For garnishes (R 1045-1061).

901 SALAD IDEAS

Easy, interesting salad combinations.

1. Tomato, parboiled cauliflower and parboiled French beans, all cut into sections. Sliced raw mushrooms can be added. Moisten with French dressing.
2. Raw mushrooms, sliced paper-thin and marinated in French dressing.
3. Tomato, cucumber and onions, all sliced.
4. Grated pineapple and finely grated carrot (no dressing required).
5. Cooked French beans (whole if small, sliced if longer), tossed in French dressing, sprinkled with garlic powder and covered with toasted slivered almonds.
6. Grated raw zucchini, sprinkled with salt, and left for 30 mins before draining, and grated cheese.
7. Crushed pineapple, diced cheddar cheese, raisins and chopped celery, all tossed in mayonnaise.
8. Diced fresh canteloupe and chopped tomatoes with French dressing.
9. Parboiled broccoli or raw cauliflower flowerettes, or both, with French dressing.
10. Chopped tomatoes, stoned black olives and chopped green pepper with French dressing.
11. Apple and celery, both chopped, with walnuts and mayonnaise or with tomato wedges.
12. Tinned, drained artichoke hearts, cut in halves with tomato wedges.
13. Diced watermelon and sliced white onion rings.
14. Sliced, peeled oranges and tomatoes.

902 BEAN SALAD

1 cup green beans	⅔ cup white wine vinegar
1 cup yellow wax beans	½ teaspoon freshly ground
1 cup red kidney beans	black pepper
1 medium onion, grated	1 teaspoon salt
½ cup sugar	¼ teaspoon mixed herbs
½ cup salad oil	1 green pepper, cut in rings

Cook beans if fresh, or drain if canned. When cool, mix all ingredients and marinate for 24 hours. Drain off excess dressing and arrange in lettuce-lined bowl. Garnish with green pepper rings.

Variations:
1. Any other fresh, canned or frozen beans can be added or substituted.
2. Quick and easy:

1 large [450g] can 3 bean mix, drained	½ cup French dressing chives
1 425g [15 oz] can crushed pineapple	salt and pepper

Mix beans and pineapple then add French dressing, chives, salt and pepper to taste.

903 JELLIED BEETROOT

Jellied is the only civilised way to serve beetroot. It avoids flavouring everything else on the plate and is very quick and easy to prepare.

1 425g [15 oz] can beetroot, drained with liquid reserved	2 teaspoons gelatine water

To the reserved juice add sufficient water to make one cup. Stir gelatine into a little warm water until it is dissolved. Melt over hot water and add it to the beetroot juice. Chop the beetroot and put in an appropriate receptacle (glass is pleasant), pour liquid over and leave it to set, preferably in refrigerator.

---

*When you have an abundance of home-grown herbs, freeze what you can't use at once. Chop finely, place in ice-cube containers and cover with water. When frozen remove blocks and store in a plastic bag.

904 CARROT BALLS

1 250g packet [8 oz] cream
  cheese

1 cup raisins, chopped
1 carrot, finely grated

Soften cream cheese, beat in raisins, then shape into balls about the size of large marbles. Roll in grated carrot and place in refrigerator until firm. Serve in salads, or as after school or lunch snacks.

905 CARROT RAISIN SURPRISE

4 carrots
4 apples
lemon juice
2 stalks celery
1 cup raisins

4 tablespoons mayonnaise
  [R 1003] [optional]
lettuce for serving
½ cup chopped nuts
1 tablespoon chopped mint

Shred carrots and apples and sprinkle with lemon juice to prevent browning. Chop celery finely. Add raisins, mix all together. Toss with mayonnaise if desired. Serve on lettuce and sprinkle with nuts and mint.

CARROT RICE CASSEROLE (R 433)

906 CUCUMBER AND GREEN PEPPER SALAD

1 green cucumber
1 small green pepper
1 clove garlic, crushed

French dressing as desired,
  made with lemon juice
  [R 1004]

Wash cucumber, do not peel. Score cucumber lengthwise with prongs of fork and slice thinly. Slice green pepper thinly in rings, remove seeds and white fleshy material. Arrange cucumber and green pepper in alternate layers in serving dish, sprinkling with garlic to taste. Pour French dressing over and chill well before serving.

Variation: Add sesame seeds or poppy seeds.

Everybody was terribly kind and cooperative at dinner and it took all four of us ceaselessly moiling and toiling from kitchen to studio and back again to organise and consume a simple meal of soup, steak and onions, peas and potatoes and salad. And even then the process was simplified by my just leaving the loaf of bread, just simply forgetting it and leaving it at the bottom of the shopping-bag.

Elaine Dundy, The Dud Avocado. 1958

907 CUCUMBERS IN SOUR CREAM

1 large cucumber, peeled and   *2 tablespoons finely chopped*
   sliced finely   *chives*
salt and pepper   *1 teaspoon fresh or*
1 cup sour cream   *¼ teaspoon dried dill*

Arrange cucumber in dish, sprinkle with salt and leave in refrigerator for one hour. Mix together sour cream, chives, salt and pepper, and chill. Just before serving, drain off liquid from cucumber and pour the cream over. Sprinkle with dill.

GRAPES IN ASPIC (R 2405)

908 COLESLAW

Coleslaw can be as varied and interesting as your pantry permits. If your cabbage is a little tired, soak it in salted cold water. Shred approximately half a cabbage and add any combination of the following:

1 or 2 carrots

2 tablespoons grated white onion, or chopped spring onions or chives

chopped green pepper

1 unpeeled apple, chopped

125g [4 oz] dried apricots or 6 fresh ones, chopped

125g [4 oz] sultanas

125g [4 oz] dates

125g [4 oz] nuts [almonds, cashews, walnuts or peanuts]

1 425g [15 oz] can crushed pineapple or fresh pineapple

sliced or grated cooked beet-root

2-3 gherkins, chopped

1 tablespoon capers

2-4 celery stalks, chopped

125g [4 oz] fresh sultana grapes

½ cucumber, chopped

1-2 dill cucumbers

1 fresh pear, banana or other fruit in season, chopped

125g [4 oz] cheese, diced or grated

dressing [R 1000]

Toss ingredients together in salad bowl and moisten with a dressing of your choice.
Coleslaw improves if made 2 hours before serving.

*To obtain onion juice put a small piece of onion through a garlic crusher.

*Chill onions in refrigerator to prevent crying when slicing them.

*Soak onion rings in iced, salted water for an hour before adding to salads. They will be mild yet crisp.

909 POTATO SALAD

500g [1 lb] potatoes
1 cup mayonnaise [R 1001] or
   yoghurt
salt and pepper

1 tablespoon finely chopped
   spring onions or chives
1 tablespoon chopped parsley
¼ teaspoon nutmeg

Scrub potatoes and boil until just tender. Peel, cut into cubes and while still warm, mix in mayonnaise, taking care not to break potatoes. When cool add other ingredients and chill well.

Variations:
1. Use mint instead of parsley.
2. Add 1 teaspoon curry powder.
3. Use French dressing instead of mayonnaise.
4. Speedy Potato Salad: Cut potatoes into cubes, cook for exactly 5 mins, drain carefully, mix with mayonnaise etc.

TOMATO SALAD (R 2418)

910 SAUERKRAUT SALAD

Salad
500g [1 lb] drained sauerkraut
   [available in cans or at a
   good continental
   delicatessen]
½ cup finely sliced celery
1 green pepper, grated
1 cup grated carrot

Dressing
½ cup oil
½ cup vinegar
¼ teaspoon pepper
1¼ cups sugar

Mix salad ingredients. Mix dressing ingredients and pour over salad.

911 TOMATOES IN MINT JELLY

3 teaspoons gelatine
½ cup cold water
1 cup hot water
¼ cup sugar

½ cup chopped mint
½ cup vinegar
12 small tomatoes
salt

Soften gelatine in ½ cup cold water. Add to cup of hot water and stir until dissolved. Add sugar, mint and vinegar. Leave until cold. Peel tomatoes, sprinkle lightly with salt. Arrange in serving dish then pour in mint jelly when it is thickening. Allow to set. Serve with cold meat or poultry.

912 CHINESE VEGETABLES

2 tablespoons oil
½ inch green ginger root, peeled and sliced [obtainable from greengrocers]
1 small white onion, chopped
1 small carrot, cut in julienne strips
1 stalk celery, thinly sliced
1 small green pepper, chopped
125g [4 oz] frozen beans
125g [4 oz] mushrooms, peeled and sliced
1 cup bean shoots
1 tablespoon soya sauce
2 spring onions, finely chopped

Saute ginger slices for 2 minutes in oil, remove and add onion, saute until tender, but still crisp. Add the other vegetables except mushrooms, bean shoots and spring onions. Cook quickly 2-3 mins. Add mushrooms and bean shoots. Cook 1 min. Add soya sauce and sprinkle with spring onions. Cool and use as salad or serve hot over noodles or rice.

Variations:

1. Add cooked diced chicken, ham, flaked tuna, shrimps or lightly fried strips of steak and serve hot as main dish.
2. Add or substitute shredded cabbage with carrot etc.
3. Add or substitute water chestnuts and bamboo shoots with mushrooms etc.

913 MARINATED VEGETABLE SALAD

3 carrots
2 onions
250g [8 oz] green beans
1 red and 1 green pepper
6 small zucchini
250g [8 oz] button mushrooms
2 cups cauliflower sprigs
salt and cayenne
1½ cups French dressing [R 1004]

Slice carrots and onions thinly, cut beans diagonally in ½" lengths, cut peppers in strips, slice zucchini diagonally ¼" thick, and trim stems of mushrooms. Put onions in cold water, bring to boil and drain. Drop cauliflower, carrots and beans into boiling water and boil 5 mins. Drain and rinse quickly under cold water. Drop pepper and zucchini into boiling water for 1 min then drain. Arrange layers of mushrooms and still-warm vegetables in large glass jar or bowl, seasoning each layer. Pour dressing over, cover and chill at least 24 hours.

914 FRENCH SALAD

French salad need not be merely lettuce leaves tossed with French Dressing (R 1004). There are many different salad greens available. Try one or a combination of these:

endive	mignonette lettuce
fennel	watercress
chicory	cucumber
cos lettuce	chives
silver beet leaves	zucchini
spinach leaves	leftover cooked peas or beans
tender leafy part of celery	parsley or other herbs
mustard and cress	sweetcorn kernels

Add a diced avocado as a touch of luxury or drained, canned artichoke hearts.
Consult your greengrocer for suggestions; ask him the name and use of the unfamiliar green leaves he has.

915 TOSSED SALAD ALMONDINE

whole blanched almonds	orange sections
mixed salad greens [R 914]	French dressing [R 1004]
green pepper slices	

Toast almonds in shallow pan in moderate oven. When cool, toss with other ingredients.

916 SPINACH SALAD

1 bunch spinach	½ cup French dressing—with
2 hard boiled eggs, chopped	added crushed garlic if
2 rashers bacon, cooked and	desired
chopped	2 tablespoons chopped spring
1 tablespoon almonds,	onions
toasted and chopped	

Wash spinach, remove stalks and dry well. Break into bite-size pieces. Place in bowl with eggs, toss with dressing. Sprinkle with bacon, almonds and spring onions.

Variation: Add 1 155g (5 oz) can water chestnuts, drained.

---

*Mix French dressing in the base of the salad bowl. Place salad greens on top and toss just before serving.

917 NEIMAN MARCUS SALAD

This is an attractive, unusual salad to serve, especially if you have a vegetarian guest. The dressing is rich and blends well with the mildness of cottage cheese.

Salad

Almost any fruit, chopped or scooped into balls (e.g. banana, water-melon, apple, apricot). Arrange fruit on individual lettuce leaves, pour dressing over fruit and serve with ½ cup of cottage cheese for each person.

Zodiac Dressing

¾ cup sugar	1 teaspoon onion juice
1 teaspoon dry mustard	⅓ cup wine vinegar
1 teaspoon salt	

Beat all together and then add:

1 cup salad oil	cochineal or green colouring
1½ teaspoons poppy seeds	

Stir very well to mix in the colouring.

918 PEACH SALAD

6 fresh firm peaches	60g [2 oz] cheese, grated
1 or 2 tablespoons	lettuce
mayonnaise [R 1001]	lemon juice
60g [2 oz] nuts, chopped	chopped parsley
½ cup chopped celery	

To the mayonnaise add nuts, cheese and celery. Chill. Just before serving, peel and halve peaches, sprinkle with lemon juice and fill with the mayonnaise mixture. Lay them in crisp lettuce leaves. Sprinkle with finely chopped parsley.

919 PEACH OR PEAR APPETIZER

1 822g [1 lb 13 oz] can peach or pear halves	60-90g [2-3 oz] walnuts, chopped
125g [4 oz] cream cheese, softened and mixed with a little cream	60g [2 oz] glace ginger, chopped
1 tablespoon chopped chives	lettuce for serving

Drain fruit. Mix cream cheese, chives, walnuts and ginger and place in fruit halves. Chill. Serve on lettuce leaves.

920 PIQUANT FRUIT CREAM SALAD

1 apple, chopped
2 bananas, sliced
1 orange, chopped

small carton sour cream
4 lettuce cups
nuts

Mix apple, bananas, orange and sour cream. Just before serving, pile in crisp lettuce cups. Garnish with nuts.

921 AVOCADO CHEESE SALAD

1 large avocado
2 cups chopped ripe tomatoes
1 small onion, chopped
1/3 cup cottage cheese

2 tablespoons lemon juice
3 tablespoons olive oil
salt and pepper

Peel avocado, remove stone and dice flesh. Toss well with remaining ingredients until thoroughly combined.

922 FRUIT CHEESE SALAD FOR ONE

lettuce leaves
1 carrot, grated
1 pear, sliced
lemon juice

1 tablespoon raisins
60g [2 oz] cottage cheese
2 stalks celery

Place grated carrot on lettuce. Cover with pear slices (sprinkled with lemon juice to prevent browning), raisins and cottage cheese. Add stalks of celery on side.

Celery, raw,
Develops the jaw,
But celery stewed,
Is more quietly chewed.

Ogden Nash

923 RICE SALAD

A well known standby, wonderful if catering for large numbers, and capable of infinite variation.

Cold boiled rice is the foundation. Cook the kind you like (short grain, long grain, brown, wild) the way you like to cook it. Add any combination of the following, prepared by dicing or chopping to appropriate size:

asparagus	olives
bean shoots	pineapple chunks
beans	radishes
cashews, walnuts or peanuts	raw carrot, grated
celery	peas
cheese	parsley
chicken	salami pieces
gherkins or dill cucumbers	spring onions
green pepper	sultanas, raisins or dates
ham or cooked bacon	sweetcorn
hard boiled eggs	tomatoes, peeled
mushrooms	or anything else

Moisten with French dressing or mayonnaise (R 1001, 1004).
Variation:
Try this combination.
mandarin segments, cooked peas, chopped spring onions, chopped walnuts and French dressing.

BACON RATATOUILLE (R 434)

RATATOUILLE (R 826)

924 CURRIED RICE SALAD

1 cup rice
½ cup French dressing
   [R 1004] and
1 tablespoon curry
   powder blended together

1 white onion, diced
½ cup sultanas
½ cup diced celery
½ large green pepper, diced

Boil rice in water until cooked, strain and place in salad bowl. While still warm, mix in French dressing and curry powder. When cool, mix in onion, sultanas, celery and green pepper.

*When boiling rice, add a few drops of lemon juice or vinegar to the water to prevent sticking and a tablespoon of oil or butter to prevent boiling over.

925 MACARONI SALAD

Salad
500g [1 lb] packet small
   macaroni or shell noodles
4 hard boiled eggs, chopped
185g [6 oz] ham, diced
3 tomatoes, skinned and
   quartered

Dressing
¾ cup oil
¼ cup white vinegar
½ cup mayonnaise
2 cloves garlic, crushed
salt and pepper
½ cup finely chopped
   parsley

Cook macaroni or noodles until tender, drain and pour dressing over noodles while hot, mix well. Add eggs, ham and tomatoes. Leave to stand several hours. Serve at room temperature. If too dry, add a little more dressing.

MUSHROOMS A LA GRECQUE (R 2422)

See end of fish, meat and poultry sections for cold dishes to serve with salads.

For me, food not only interrupts everything while people eat it and sit about waiting for more of it to be served, but also casts a spell of vacancy before and after. No other sensual activity must take place at a set time to be enjoyed by anybody at all, or comes up so inexorably and so often. Some of the stuff I can stand. Fruit slides down, bread soon goes to nothing, and all pungent swallowables have a value of their own that transcends mere food. As for the rest of it, chewing away at the vile texture of meat, pulling bones out of tasteless mouthfuls of fish or encompassing the sheer nullity of vegetables is not my idea of a treat. At least sex does not demand a simultaneous outflow of talk, and drink needs no mastication.
Kingsley Amis, *The Green Man.* 1971

The Added Touch

The Added Touch

Hunger is the best sauce in the world.

Miguel Cervantes, Don Quixote

1000 DRESSINGS, MARINADES, SAUCES, STUFFINGS AND GARNISHES

The addition of the right sauce can turn an ordinary meal into something special. Be adventurous with sauces, but never let the sauce overpower the flavour of the food it is meant to complement.

Dressings

1001 MAYONNAISE

1 egg yolk at room
  temperature
½ teaspoon salt
1/8 teaspoon white pepper

1 teaspoon mild vinegar or
  lemon juice
1 cup salad oil

Place yolk, salt, pepper and lemon juice in bowl and beat with wooden spoon. Add oil *drop by drop* beating continually. The egg yolk will absorb the oil and become creamy. If the mayonnaise is to be kept, the addition of 1 tablespoon of boiling water after it is mixed will help prevent separation. Water can also be added if a thinner consistency is required. Keep in refrigerator.

Variation: Thousand Island Dressing: Add finely chopped chives, gherkins and capers.

1002 COOKED MAYONNAISE

2½ tablespoons sugar
1 tablespoon butter
2½ tablespoons vinegar

1 teaspoon mustard
2 eggs, beaten

Beat butter and sugar until well mixed. Add all other ingredients and cook slowly over low heat (preferably in double saucepan), stirring until it thickens like custard. Keep in refrigerator and thin with milk or cream as required.

*Keep an eye dropper for food colourings or essence—it is quicker and more accurate.

152

1003 QUICK MAYONNAISE

1 can [400g] sweetened
   condensed milk
1½ teaspoons mustard

1 teaspoon salt
1 cup vinegar or lemon juice
1 egg [optional]

Beat all together until well mixed. Keep in refrigerator. It will thicken and may be thinned with a little cream before use.

1004 FRENCH DRESSING

1 cup vinegar or lemon juice
1½ cups salad oil
1 teaspoon salt
1 teaspoon sugar

1 teaspoon mustard
2 cloves garlic, peeled
¼ teaspoon black pepper

Mix all together in blender or put in bottle and shake well. Store in refrigerator.

1005 ITALIAN DRESSING

oil
vinegar] equal quantities
1 large clove garlic, peeled

1/8 teaspoon sugar
salt and pepper
basil [optional]

Make incisions with a sharp knife in the garlic. Place all ingredients in a screw top jar and shake well. If fresh basil is available, chop and sprinkle on salad before adding dressing.

MACARONI SALAD DRESSING (R 925)

ZODIAC DRESSING (R 912)

SAUERKRAUT SALAD DRESSING (R 910)

1006 YOGHURT DRESSING

1 cup plain yoghurt
2 teaspoons lemon juice
½-1 teaspoon paprika

salt
freshly ground black pepper

Mix well together.

1007 BLUE CHEESE DRESSING

125g [4 oz] blue cheese
½-1 tablespoon French
   dressing [R 1004]

1 teaspoon mustard
1 cup mayonnaise [R 1001,
   1002, 1003]

Blend cheese to a soft creamy paste with French dressing. Blend in mustard and mayonnaise and mix well.

Savoury Sauces

1008 SOUR CREAM SAUCE
1 cup sour cream
2 tablespoons tarragon
  vinegar
2 teaspoons finely chopped
  chives

½ teaspoon sugar
salt
sprinkle cayenne pepper

Mix well just prior to using.

SOUR CREAM SAUCE (R 2418.1)
TOMATO AND SOUR CREAM SAUCE (R 510)

1009 TARTARE SAUCE
Delicious served with fried fish.

½ cup mayonnaise [R 1001,
  1002, 1003]
1 teaspoon capers
1 teaspoon chopped gherkins
2 teaspoons chopped parsley

5 stuffed olives, sliced
1 tablespoon thick or semi-
  whipped cream
1 teaspoon lemon juice

Mix all together.

1010 WHITE SAUCE
30g [1 oz] butter
30g [1 oz] flour
1-1½ cups milk

½ teaspoon salt
sprinkle cayenne pepper

Melt butter, add flour and cook for 1 min without browning. Add milk gradually, stirring constantly until it thickens and the desired consistency is reached. Cook for 3-5 mins. Add salt and pepper. Reheat if necessary.

Variations: to each 1-1½ cups add:
1. Cheese: ½ cup grated tasty cheese.
2. Caper: 1 tablespoon capers and a little of the caper vinegar
3. Parsley: 1 tablespoon finely chopped parsley
4. Mustard: 2-3 teaspoons English mustard
5. Fish: substitute fish stock for milk
6. Mushroom: **60-125g [2-4 oz] thinly sliced mushrooms** gently cooked in 15-30g [½-1 oz] butter for 15-20 mins.

BOLOGNESE SAUCE (R 507)

PESTA (R 509)

BARBECUE DIP (R 117)

BARBECUE SAUCE (R 675)

011 MINT SAUCE

½ cup finely chopped
mint leaves
1 tablespoon sugar

4 tablespoons boiling water
½ cup vinegar

Cover mint with sugar, add water, stirring to dissolve. Cool and add vinegar.

Variation: For easy mint jelly, soften 1 teaspoon gelatine in ½ tablespoon water and add to above. A few drops of green colouring improves the colour.

012 SWEET AND SOUR SAUCE

½ cup pineapple juice
1 tablespoon brown sugar
1 tablespoon oil
2 tablespoons vinegar

2 teaspoons soya sauce
½ teaspoon pepper
1 tablespoon cornflour

Mix all together and cook over low heat until thick.

013 TOMATO SAUCE

60g [2 oz] butter
60g [2 oz] flour
500g [1 lb] tomatoes
1 large onion, chopped
1 clove garlic, crushed
1 small carrot, chopped
1 bay leaf

¼ teaspoon thyme and
nutmeg
1 tablespoon chopped fresh
basil or 1 teaspoon dried
1 tablespoon vinegar
1 cup of stock

Place all ingredients except butter and flour into a saucepan and bring to the boil.

Simmer uncovered until reduced and thickened. Press through a sieve or puree in a blender and if necessary add more stock to make 600ml (1 pint). Make a roux with butter and flour and slowly add the tomato sauce, stirring well. Cook for a few mins.

SPICY SAUCE (R 681)

014 SEAFOQD SAUCE

3 tablespoons tomato sauce
2 teaspoons worcestershire
sauce
1 tablespoon lemon juice

1 tablespoon dry sherry
1 tablespoon cream
salt and pepper

Mix all ingredients together well. Chill until ready. Serve with oysters, prawns or pour over any combination of seafood.

OYSTER SAUCE (R 619)

1015 HORSERADISH SAUCE

A marvellous accompaniment to beef, can be prepared in advance and kept for later use. Fresh horseradish is not easy to buy but many people have it growing in their gardens.

horseradish

white vinegar, enough to cover horseradish

brine, 1 teaspoon salt to 2 cups water

Grate horseradish finely and immerse immediately in brine to prevent discolouring. Drain well and pack into small clean jars. Bring vinegar to boil and pour over horseradish. Cover. This gives you concentrated horseradish.

To make sauce, mix:

2 tablespoons well drained, concentrated horseradish with 1 cup thick cream and 1 teaspoon sugar

or

2 tablespoons well drained, concentrated horseradish with ½ cup mayonnaise.

1016 BERNAISE SAUCE

(Make 1¼ cups)

For steak, fish, chicken, egg dishes, green vegetables or globe artichokes.

3 tablespoons wine vinegar
3 tablespoons dry white wine
1 tablespoon chopped shallots or spring onions
1 tablespoon chopped fresh tarragon [or 1 teaspoon dried tarragon]
3 egg yolks

30g [1 oz] cold butter
155g [5 oz] melted butter
¼ teaspoon salt
¼ teaspoon pepper
2 extra tablespoons fresh chopped tarragon or parsley

Boil vinegar, wine, shallots, and 1 tablespoon tarragon over moderate heat until reduced to about 2 tablespoons. Cool. Beat egg yolks until thick, strain in the vinegar mixture and beat well. Add 15g cold butter and stir egg yolk mixture in the top of a double boiler until thickened. Remove from heat, beat in remaining 15g cold butter (this stops yolks from further cooking), then add melted butter *drop by drop,* beating all the time. Add salt and pepper to taste, then beat in extra tarragon or parsley.

CURRY SAUCE (R 675)
SATAY SAUCE (R 613)
CHOCOLATE WINE SAUCE (R 623)

1017 HOLLANDAISE SAUCE
(Makes 1-1½ cups)

185-250g [6-8 oz] butter
3 egg yolks
1 tablespoon cold water
1 tablespoon lemon juice
¼ teaspoon salt
30g [1 oz] cold butter
extra salt, pepper or lemon
 juice

Melt butter over low heat and set aside. Place egg yolks in saucepan and beat well. Add water, lemon juice and salt and beat again. Add 15g cold butter (do not beat in) and place saucepan over low heat (or use double saucepan) and stir yolks until they thicken to a smooth cream—about 2 mins. Remove from heat and beat in remaining 15g cold butter to cool yolks and stop them cooking further. Pour in melted butter *drop by drop* beating all the time. Season to taste with extra salt, pepper or lemon juice.

Variations:
1. For poached eggs or steamed fish add a mixture of chopped parsley, chives and tarragon.
2. For egg dishes, add a puree of artichokes, asparagus tips or cooked shellfish.
3. For asparagus or broccoli, use only 155g (5 oz) butter, omit water and substitute 1 tablespoon orange juice. Then beat in 2-4 tablespoons orange juice and grated rind of 1 orange to sauce.

1018 BECHAMEL SAUCE
1½-2 cups milk
1 small onion or shallot,
 chopped
1 small carrot, chopped
½ blade mace
1 tablespoon butter
1 tablespoon flour
salt and pepper
2 tablespoons cream

Simmer milk with onion, carrot and mace for 10 mins. Melt butter, add flour and cook 2 mins. Strain milk and add to flour mixture, stirring constantly until it thickens. Add salt and pepper, then cream. Reheat but do not boil.

GREEN ALMOND SAUCE (R 511)

MUSHROOM ANCHOVY SAUCE (R 512)

MUSHROOM AND TOMATO SAUCE (R 656)

Sweet Sauces

1019 CHOCOLATE SAUCE [1]

6 tablespoons golden syrup
6 tablespoons cocoa
1 tablespoon butter

1 teaspoon vanilla
1½ cups water
3 cups sugar

Mix in *large* saucepan. Boil 3 mins. Serve hot or cold.

1020 CHOCOLATE SAUCE (2)

2½ tablespoons cocoa
1 cup sugar
1 tablespoon butter

¼ teaspoon cream of tartar
½ cup water

Cook all together until slightly thickend. Serve hot over ice-cream.

1021 CHOCOLATE SAUCE (3)

(Quickly mixed)
4 tablespoons icing sugar
1 tablespoon cocoa
cream, evaporated milk, or
   top of milk

1 teaspoon vanilla

Sift sugar and cocoa together. Add sufficient cream or alternative until sauce reaches desired consistency. Add vanilla.

1022 FUDGE SAUCE CAFE

2 teaspoons instant coffee
½ cup water
½ cup sugar
4 squares chocolate, grated

1 tablespoon cream
¼ teaspoon salt
1 tablespoon butter
½ teaspoon vanilla

Dissolve coffee in hot water. Place sugar, chocolate, cream and salt in saucepan over low heat, add coffee and stir until slightly thickened. Remove from heat and blend in butter and vanilla. Serve warm or cool.

1023 CARAMEL SAUCE

½ cup sugar
½ cup cream

1 tablespoon golden syrup
1 tablespoon butter

Cook all together over water for 40 mins.

158

1024 ALMOND SAUCE

1 cup milk
30g [1 oz] castor sugar
15g [½ oz] cornflour
little cold milk

1 teaspoon almond essence
2 tablespoons brandy or
* kirsch*
1 teaspoon butter

Bring milk and sugar to boil. Add cornflour mixed with a little cold milk and cook for 3-4 mins. Add almond essence and liqueur and stir in butter.

1025 ORANGE RAISIN SAUCE

1½ cups orange juice
3 teaspoons cornflour
½ cup sugar

¼ cup raisins
1½ tablespoons butter

Blend cornflour to a paste with a little orange juice. Add sugar and raisins to remaining orange juice and heat to boiling point. Stir in cornflour mixture and cook 2 mins. Remove from heat and stir in butter. Serve with steamed pudding or chocolate ice-cream.

ORANGE SAUCE (R 1153)

1026 HARD SAUCE FOR CHRISTMAS PUDDING

125g [4 oz] butter
1 cup icing sugar

¼ cup brandy
sprinkle nutmeg

Cream butter and add sugar gradually. Beat well and add brandy drop by drop. Pile in dish, sprinkle top with nutmeg and refrigerate.

1027 RUM CREAM SAUCE

(for Christmas Pudding or to serve with berry fruit)
¾ cup rum or brandy
¼ cup sugar

2 egg yolks
300ml [½ pint] cream

Combine rum and sugar and allow to stand 1 hour. Beat egg yolks until thick and creamy and add gradually to rum mixture, beating well. Cover and stand 1 hour. Just before serving whip cream and fold into sauce.

1028 HOT TODDY SAUCE

1 tablespoon chopped
  raisins
1 tablespoon chopped glace
  cherries
2 tablespoons rum, brandy
  or sherry

3 tablespoons golden syrup
150ml [¼ pint] water
2 teaspoons cornflour
juice of 1 lemon
1 tablespoon almonds,
  blanched and chopped

Soak fruit in rum 1 hour. Heat golden syrup in small heavy saucepan until lightly caramelized. Remove from heat and add water gradually. Blend flour in lemon juice. Add to syrup and stir over low heat until boiling. Boil several mins. Cool and then add fruit and nuts. Store in jar in refrigerator until required. Serve hot over ice-cream.
Variation: Add 1 tablespoon finely chopped ginger.

Marinades

A marinade is a mixture of oil, wine vinegar or lemon juice and sometimes wine together with herbs and spices, used for soaking meat, fish or vegetables in order to season or tenderize them. Combine all ingredients in a shallow dish and marinate meat overnight or for several hours. Spoon the marinade over meat while cooking and any left over may be heated, strained and served as a sauce.

1029 MARINADE

Suitable for lamb chops.
2-4 teaspoons soya sauce
1 tablespoon chili sauce
¼ teaspoon pepper

1½ tablespoons oil
¼ teaspoon garlic salt
2 teaspoons lemon juice

1030 RED WINE MARINADE

Particularly suitable for beef.
¾ cup red wine
¼ cup oil
1 onion, sliced
1 clove garlic, crushed

6 peppercorns
1 bay leaf
parsley stalks, chopped

1031 DEVILLED MARINADE

2 tablespoons tomato sauce
2 tablespoons plum jam
1 tablespoon vinegar
1 tablespoon sugar
salt and pepper

1 tablespoon worcestershire
  sauce
1 tablespoon soya sauce
½ cup red wine

160

032 MARINADE
Excellent for seafood, chicken, kebabs or steak.

½ cup soya sauce
1 inch green ginger, minced

½ cup sherry
1 clove garlic, crushed

033 MARINADE
This is a good marinade for kebabs.

1 cup tarragon vinegar
2 fresh chili peppers, finely
   chopped [or ½ teaspoon
   dried crushed chili peppers]
¼ teaspoon saffron

½ cup water
3 cloves garlic, crushed
1 teaspoon salt
12 peppercorns
3 tablespoons olive oil

034 MARINADE
Excellent for lamb kebabs.

1 small bottle stout
1 medium onion, finely
   chopped

salt and pepper

035 PINEAPPLE MARINADE

1 cup pineapple juice
1 tablespoon chopped
   preserved ginger

1 clove garlic, crushed
1 tablespoon soya sauce
¼ cup dry sherry

036 MARINADE
Particularly nice for lamb or mutton.

1 apple, chopped
2 onions, chopped
1 lemon
4 tablespoons vinegar
2 tablespoons chutney
1 tablespoon curry powder

1 tablespoon sugar
1 tablespoon tamarind
1 cup boiling water
1 cup dried apricots [soaked
   or stewed]
2 bay leaves or lemon leaves

Fry apple and onion until golden brown. Add remaining ingredients and bring to the boil. Leave to cool completely and pour over meat. Marinate in refrigerator for 2 days. Boil marinade, strain and serve with meat.

OTHER MARINADES (R 621, 652, 709, 712, 718)

LAMB KEBABS (R 644)

Stuffings

1037 HERB

1 cup soft breadcrumbs
1-2 tablespoons chopped
   fresh herbs
   or ½ teaspoon mixed
   dried herbs

½ onion, chopped
1 tablespoon melted butter
salt and pepper
1 egg, beaten

Saute onion in butter, mix with other ingredients.

1038 CASHEW NUT

125g [4 oz] cashews, finely
   chopped
1 small onion, chopped
30g [1 oz] butter
grated rind 1 lemon
1 cup soft breadcrumbs

2 tablespoons chopped mixed
   herbs including parsley
1 egg, beaten
¼ teaspoon cinnamon
salt and pepper

Saute onion in butter, add nuts, cook 3-4 mins, cool slightly, add other ingredients.

1039 CELERY, APRICOT AND WALNUT

60g [2 oz] dried apricots,
   chopped and soaked overnight
1 onion, finely chopped
45g [1½ oz] butter

3-4 sticks celery, thinly sliced
125g [4 oz] walnuts, chopped
1¼ cups soft breadcrumbs
1 tablespoon chopped parsley
salt and pepper

Drain apricots. Cook onion in butter until soft. Add celery and walnuts. Cook 4 mins. Allow to cool, add other ingredients.

1040 SAGE AND ONION

(For pork or poultry)
4 medium onions
1 teaspoon powdered sage
salt and pepper

1 cup soft breadcrumbs
1 tablespoon butter, melted

Parboil onions and chop finely. Mix all ingredients well together.

1041 CHESTNUT

3-4 cups chestnuts [or 360g
   [12 oz] can chestnut puree]
60g [2 oz] butter

salt and pepper
1 cup soft breadcrumbs
¼ cup cream

Boil the chestnuts for 20 mins, then shell them and rub through a coarse sieve while still warm. Add other ingredients and mix well.

1042 FRUIT

1 cup chopped dried apricots   2-3 cups unpeeled diced apple
1 cup chopped prunes   ¼ teaspoon cinnamon

Soak apricots overnight in water to cover. Drain and combine with other ingredients, mixing well.

1043 APPLE

1 large apple, peeled, cored   ½ cup soft breadcrumbs
  and diced   1 egg, beaten
125g [4 oz] raisins   salt and pepper
1 tablespoon chutney

Mix all together.

Variations:
1. Add chopped apple and raisins to a packet of commercial stuffing.
2. Add to the above 3 rashers of bacon, chopped and cooked, and if desired 60g (2 oz) chopped walnuts can be substituted for raisins.
3. Substitute sultanas for raisins, omit chutney and add 1 small onion, grated, ¼ teaspoon cinnamon or nutmeg and 1 tablespoon sherry.

ORANGE (R 646)

ORANGE AND APPLE (R 620)

CELERY AND RAISIN (R 655)

MINT (R 648)

1044 FLAVOURED BUTTERS

For grilled meats and fish, in bread sticks, sandwiches or on dry biscuits.

To 2 tablespoons of butter add one of the following combinations:
1. 1 tablespoon finely chopped parsley, juice of ½ lemon, salt and pepper.
2. 2 teaspoons of prepared French mustard.
3. 2 mashed anchovy fillets, pepper, few drops of pink food colouring.
4. 1 crushed clove of garlic, 2 teaspoons finely chopped parsley.
5. 2 teaspoons grated tasty cheese, 2 teaspoons finely chopped parsley.
6. 2 teaspoons sesame seeds, 1 teaspoon lemon juice.
7. 1 tablespoon finely chopped mint.

Garnishes

Garnishes give a professional finish to special meals. However the attractiveness of a colourful garnish in family meals should not be overlooked. They need not be complicated or time consuming—something as simple as paprika or chopped parsley sprinkled on creamed potatoes or a white sauce can make a plain meal look festive.

A garnish can provide a contrast in textures e.g. crisp croutons in a creamy soup.

1045 LEMON FLOWERS

To make a flower-like edge to your lemon slices, cut narrow strips of peel length-wise from the lemon, thus showing strips of yellow and white. Slice the lemon thinly cross-wise and the serrated edge will give the appearance of a flower. Slice may be sprinkled with chopped parsley.

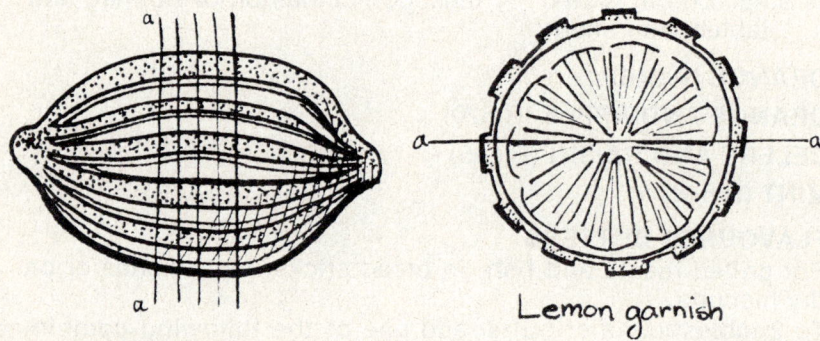

Lemon garnish

1046 LEMON BOATS

Cut lemons in half lengthwise and carefully remove the pulp, taking care not to break the skin. Serrate the edges with a sharp knife and use the boats as containers for chutneys, pickles, etc.

1047 LEMON FANS

Cut lemon slices into halves and arrange them in a fan-shaped overlapping fashion.

164

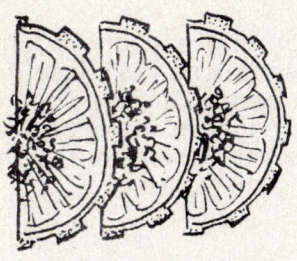

Lemon fans

Lemon bows

1048 LEMON BOWS

Cut a wedge out of the opposite sides of lemon slices, taking care not to break the slice in the middle. Put a tiny strip of red pepper or tomato across the centre to form the loop of the bow.

1049 VEGETABLE CUPS

Cut large carrots into 2" lengths and cook until tender, but not broken. Hollow out carefully with a spoon or pointed knife and fill with cooked green peas.

1050 CELERY CURLS

Cut 3" lengths of cleaned celery. Beginning on the curved side, cut in very thin slices about 1" deep to form a fringe, then cut the other side in the same manner. Put in cold water with a dash of lemon juice to crisp and curl the fringes.

His mouth watered for mutton stewed with butter and cabbages, for rice speckled with strong-scented cardamoms, for the saffron-tinted rice, garlic and onions, and the forbidden greasy sweetmeats of the bazaars.
Rudyard Kipling, Kim

1051 RADISH ROSES

Cut off the stem and leave the root long enough to form a "pistil". Cut the red skin into narrow sections 1/8" deep, from the root almost to the stem, to form petals. Slip the point of a sharp knife under each petal section to loosen and prise it from the centre of radish. Place in cold water for an hour or more and the petals will curl back.

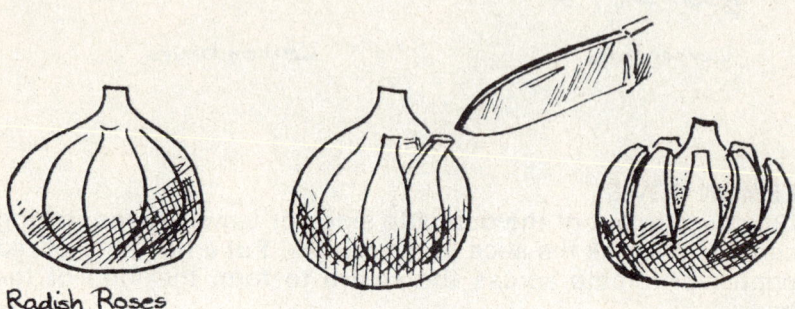

Radish Roses

1052 BEETROOT FLOWERS

Choose very small cooked beets. With an apple corer, cut down around the centre of the beet, taking care not to cut right through. Divide the outer part into petals by cutting from the top downwards in narrow sections, but do not separate at the root end. Open petals out carefully with the point of a knife

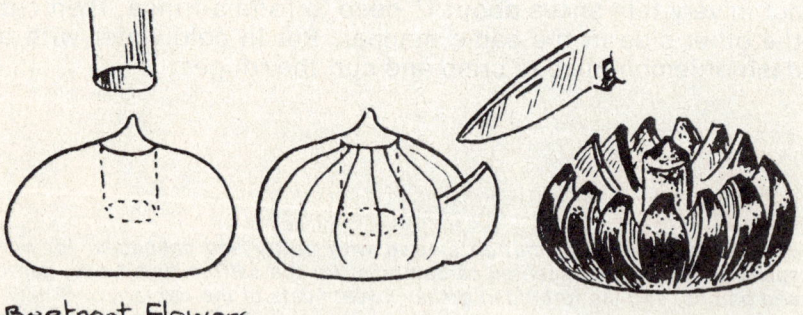

Beetroot Flowers

166

1053 TOMATO FLOWERS

Cut down sides of small tomatoes to form petals, and with the point of knife loosen the petals from the centre pulp. Open petals out carefully, taking care not to break them off. Press the yolk of a hard boiled egg through a sieve and sprinkle over centre as pollen.

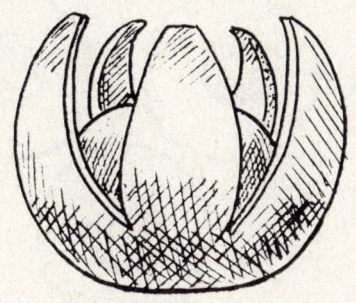

Tomato flowers

1054 TOMATO BASKETS

Cut 2 wedge-shaped pieces from the upper half of a firm tomato (see diagram), leaving a ¾" strip over the top as a handle. Carefully remove the pulp with a small spoon and serrate the edge of the basket with a small saw-edged knife.
Note: A saw-edged knife is always best for cutting tomatoes, whether into plain slices or fancy shapes.

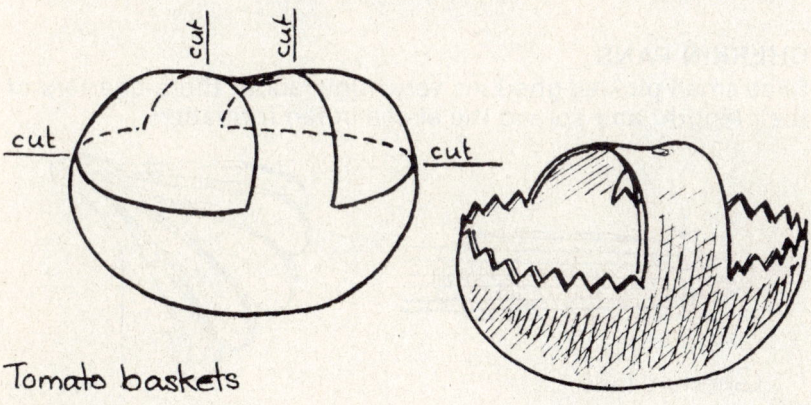

Tomato baskets

1055 CUCUMBER DAISIES

Peel a cucumber and run the prongs of a fork lengthwise down it, pressing into the cucumber. This gives a serrated edge. Cut into slices and form a yellow centre with a small round of cooked carrot. Fasten with a tooth pick. These make a most effective garnish round a salad.

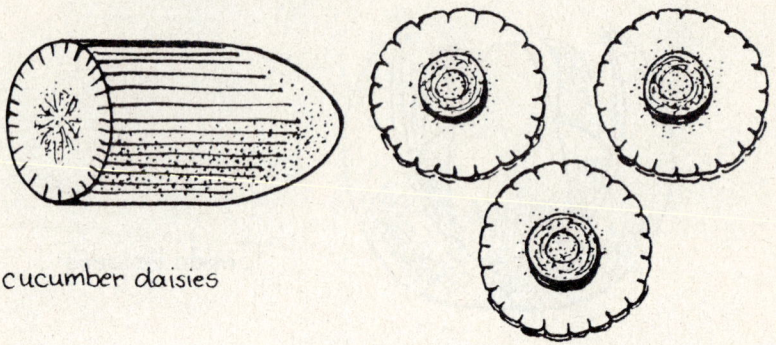

cucumber daisies

1056 CUCUMBER BOATS

(for individual salad)
Select thick cucumbers, peel and cut them lengthwise. Hollow out with a teaspoon, being careful not to break the boats. Chop the pieces of cucumber and then mix with diced beets, chopped onion and diced carrots. Add a little mayonnaise and seasoning and fill the boats with the mixture. Serve on a crisp, green lettuce leaf.

1057 GHERKIN FANS

Slice small pickled gherkins very thinly about three-quarters of their length, and spread the slices in fan formation.

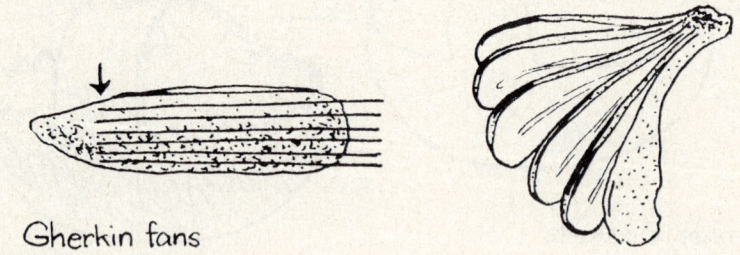

Gherkin fans

168

058 FRILLS FOR CHOPS OR CHICKEN DRUMSTICKS

Double a strip of plain writing paper to form a length about
5" x 2". Cut the folded edge to about half its depth, making a
fine fringe. Turn the paper inside out, twist the double plain
edge round a pencil and fasten it with a bit of stamp edging.
Slip on to the bone of a chop or end of drumstick when
cooked.

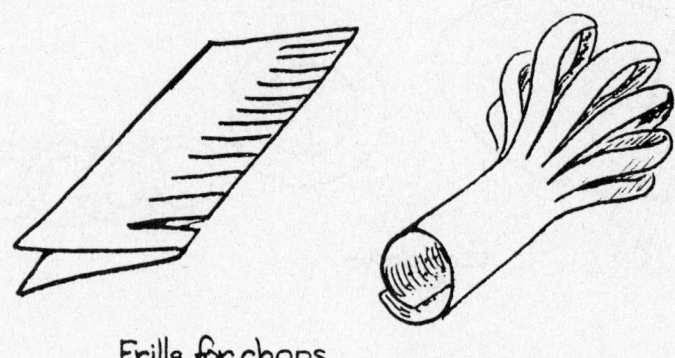

Frills for chops

059 EGG FLOWERS

Egg flowers are made by cutting hard boiled eggs lengthwise
into halves. Remove the yolks and press them through a sieve.
Cut the whites into petals lengthwise and arrange them in
cartwheel fashion in the centre of a salad. Pile the sieved yolk
in the middle.

Egg flowers

1060 EGG CHAIN
Slice hard boiled eggs and carefully remove the yolks. Arrange the rings of white round the salad (or down the centre), slightly overlapping like the links of a chain.

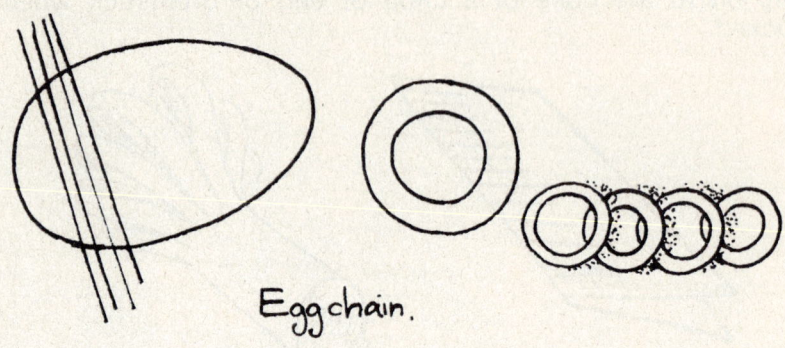

Egg chain.

1061 CARROT CURLS
Use a medium-sized carrot and square it off at the sides and both ends. Using a vegetable peeler, peel off thin slices lengthwise. Roll each slice carefully and secure it with a toothpick. Drop into iced water and leave for an hour. The toothpick can then be removed.

Carrot curls

Fabulous Finishes

Fabulous Finishes

Eat away, chew away, munch and bolt and guzzle,
Never leave the table till you're full up to the muzzle.

Norman Lindsay, The Magic Pudding

1100 DESSERTS

The quickest, easiest and best dessert is fresh fruit. However, most people have a sweet tooth so try some of these to delight your family and friends.

1101 FRUIT FLAN

Short pastry
315g [10 oz] flour
155g [5 oz] unsalted butter

5 tablespoons castor sugar
1 egg yolk
5 tablespoons water

Mix well, refrigerate for at least 30 minutes if possible. Roll out and line sides and base of a 15" flan tin. Prick base with pointed knife.

Filling
2 pears, peeled and thinly
   sliced
2 peaches, peeled and thinly
   sliced
20 cherries, stoned
1 orange or 2 mandarins,
   peeled and segmented

12 prunes, stoned
2 eggs
300ml [½ pint] cream
3 tablespoons sugar
icing sugar [optional]

Prepare fruit and arrange neatly in flan. Beat eggs, add sugar, then cream. Beat well, and pour over tart. Bake at 375°F (190°C) for 40 mins, then turn to 400°F (200°C) and bake for further 10 mins. Cool, sprinkle with icing sugar if desired.

1102 FILLINGS FOR PRE-COOKED PASTRY OR CRUMB SHELLS

Make several shells, (R 1300) pre-cook and store in vacuum container. They will keep for several weeks. Alternatively, if you have a freezer, wrap them in foil and store uncooked. Thaw and cook before adding filling. For crumb shells, see R 1142. Many of these fillings are good made simply in a pie dish if you haven't a pastry or crumb shell.

172

1. Apple Cream

Fill shell to three quarters full with cooked, pulped, sweetened apple. Beat 150ml (¼ pint) cream until just thick. Cover apples with half the cream. Colour remaining cream pale pink and pipe or spoon in swirls on top.

2. Banana

Stir ½ cup sugar into 1 cup mashed bananas. Add 1 tablespoon butter and juice of 1 lemon and mix together in a double saucepan. Add 1 beaten egg and stir over gentle heat until thick. Cool before filling case.

3. Banana Passionfruit Custard

Mix 1 tablespoon custard powder with ¼ cup milk. Heat 1 cup milk and 2 tablespoons sugar. Add custard powder mixture and stir until it boils and thickens. Remove from heat, add 2 bananas which have been sliced and soaked in juice of 1 lemon, and pulp of 2 passionfruit. When cool, fill shell.

4. Blackberry (R 1125)

5. Brandied Fruit

Put 250g (8 oz) mixed dried fruit into saucepan with one tablespoon brandy or juice of one orange, one tablespoon water and two teaspoons sugar. Add one teaspoon cornflour mixed with one tablespoon of water and stir until thickened. Fill case. Sprinkle with coconut if desired.

6. Caramel

Boil 1 400g (14 oz) can sweetened condensed milk for at least 2 hours. When cool pour into case. Decorate with sliced bananas sprinkled with lemon juice and whipped cream.

7. Cherry

Beat together 250g (8 oz) cream cheese and ¼ cup sugar. Add ¼ cup milk, 1 teaspoon grated lemon rind, 2 teaspoons cointreau (optional) and 1 can cherry pie filling. Reserve some cherries for decoration. Fill shell and decorate.

8. Chocolate (R 1190)

9. Glazed Fruit

Fill cooled wholemeal short crust pastry flan (R 1304) with drained fresh or canned fruit. Place 1 cup fruit juice, 1 heaped teaspoon arrowroot and 1 tablespoon apricot or other jam in saucepan and bring to boil. Allow to cool a little and spoon or brush over fruit. Alternatively, make small fruit tarts, pressing 4" rounds of pastry into patty tins, and proceed as above.

10. Jam Custard
Spread base with 3 tablespoons red jam and then cover with just under 600ml (1 pint) thick custard. Sprinkle with desiccated coconut, place under griller to brown. Serve hot or cold.

11. Lemon (R 1127), (R 1131)

12. Peanut Butter
Put a layer of stewed, drained fruit in case and top with setting peanut butter mixture (R 1157).

13. Pineapple (R 1140)

14. Ricotta Cheese
Beat 250g (8 oz) ricotta cheese until smooth, add yolk of one egg, 3-4 tablespoons castor sugar, 1 teaspoon vanilla, 1 teaspoon brandy or cointreau, 1 teaspoon mixed peel and 150ml (¼ pint) whipped cream. Beat white of one egg until stiff and fold into mixture. Pour straight into pie shell or put some drained, canned or fresh fruit in bottom of shell and spoon topping over.

1103 SPONGE TOPPING FOR FRUIT
1 cup wholemeal SR flour   *1 egg, well beaten*
½ cup sugar   *90g [3 oz] butter, melted*
½ cup milk

Mix altogether, adding butter last; beat well and pour over hot, drained, stewed or canned fruit in a deep pie dish or oblong casserole. Bake for 30 mins at 375°F (190°C).
Variation: Cream together sugar and only 1 tablespoon butter, add egg, flour and milk. Beat well and pour over hot fruit.

MOTHER'S YUMMY CRUMMY PASTRY (R 1305)

1104 PUFF PASTRY IDEAS (R 1310)
Roll out pastry, leaving quite thick.
1. Cut into oblongs about 2" x 4", put into hot oven for about 10 mins. Cool, split in half and fill with jam or cold custard, and cream. Put other half on top, and add dob of cream.
2. Cut into squares about 2" x 2". Bake in hot oven, cool and place in an airtight container. When time is short, take the required number of pieces, warm in the oven and serve with hot stewed fruit and cream.

1105 CRUMBLE TOPPINGS FOR FRUIT

Use 3-4 cups any stewed or raw fruit. Drain juice, sweeten if necessary, and place fruit in bottom of pie dish. Mix topping ingredients together and spread over fruit. Bake in a moderate oven for 30 mins or until topping is golden.

1. 2 tablespoons wholemeal SR flour
   2 tablespoons raw sugar
   2 tablespoons wheat germ
   2 tablespoons lecithin
   2 tablespoons desiccated coconut or crushed walnuts

   ¼ teaspoon cinnamon, mixed spice, nutmeg, ginger or cloves
   60g [2 oz] butter

2. 1½ cups grated soft cheese
   3 tablespoons brown sugar

   ¼ cup finely chopped walnuts

3. 125g [4 oz] butter or margarine, melted
   ¾ cup flour [wholemeal is excellent]
   ¼ cup brown sugar

   2 teaspoons cinnamon
   ¾ cup crushed cornflakes, rolled oats, or other cereal, or coconut

This topping will keep in the refrigerator for at least 4 weeks.

Variation:
Omit flour and reduce butter to 60g (3 oz).

4. 60g [2 oz] butter, melted
   4 slices bread, cut into small cubes

   ½ cup sugar
   ¼ teaspoon mixed spice

Toss bread cubes in butter. Add brown sugar, and lastly spice.

5. 1 cup stale cake crumbs
   ½ cup coconut

   ¼ cup sugar
   1 teaspoon cinnamon

6. See also R 1144 and R 1617.

HOT FRUIT (R 1701)

*If butter is too cold to mix in with flour, try grating it.

175

1106 FRUIT FOOL

300ml [½ pint] fruit [any
   fresh berry or stewed,
   drained fruit]
30g [1 oz] castor sugar
1 tablespoon gelatine, dissolved in 5 tablespoons
   water

2-3 egg whites, beaten until
   stiff
150ml [¼ pint] cream,
   whipped

Puree fruit in blender, combine ingredients in order above and refrigerate.

Variation: Simply mix equal quantities sweetened pureed fruit and thick cream.

1107 FRUIT AND NUT FILL-UP

½ cup nuts
1 apple, unpeeled, chopped

1 tablespoon orange or blackcurrant juice or water

Place all ingredients in blender and blend to desired consistency.

Variation: Add 1 tablespoon sesame seeds, 1 teaspoon honey, extra fruit.

1108 FRUIT SALAD IDEAS

1. Add a little canned fruit juice or undiluted cordial.
2. Add a small amount of liqueur e.g. grand marnier and preferably leave in refrigerator for 30 mins before serving.
3. Some unusual additions: watermelon or rockmelon balls, grapefruit segments, stoned grapes, Chinese gooseberries (Kiwi fruit), chopped nuts, coconut, chopped marshmallows, raisins, diced dried apricots soaked in brandy, canned mandarin segments, guavas, gooseberries, lychees.
4. Dissolve a little honey in some boiling water for extra juice.
5. Winter fruit salad: Use dried fruits such as raisins, apricots, prunes and peaches. Add a little honey to fruit and almost cover with boiling water. Leave for two hours, then just before serving bring to boil for two mins and serve hot.
6. Serve in a halved unskinned pineapple.

GLAMOROUS FRUIT SALAD (R 2420)

1109 FRUIT BOWL WITH COCONUT

This may be used either as a dessert or a salad.

1 large [822g, 1 lb 13 oz] can
  pineapple pieces, drained
1 can [230g, 8 oz] mandarin
  pieces, drained
1 cup tiny marshmallows, or
  chopped marshmallows

1 cup seedless grapes
125g [4 oz] flaked coconut
2 cups sour cream
¼ teaspoon salt

Combine all ingredients and chill overnight.

1110 FRUIT SALAD DELIGHT

1 small [425g, 15 oz] can fruit
  salad
1 packet pineapple jelly
  crystals
1 cup boiling water

1 egg [optional]
2 teaspoons sugar
  [optional]
1 cup milk or yoghurt

Drain fruit and place in small casserole dish or bowl with large base area. Dissolve jelly crystals in boiling water. Beat egg and sugar, add milk and mix well. When jelly mixture is cool, combine with egg mixture. Pour over fruit and place in refrigerator to set.

Variations:
1. Use different fruit and jelly flavours e.g. passionfruit and lemon jelly, punnet of strawberries and strawberry jelly.
2. For Spanish Cream effect, beat egg whites separately and fold into mixture.
3. When mixture is almost set, decorate top with coloured coconut, chopped nuts, etc.

JELLY WHIP (R 2114)

*QUICK JELLY VARIATIONS
1. Instead of jelly crystals, make jelly with 1 teaspoon gelatine for each cup of fruit juice and add sugar if desired.
2. Substitute 1 cup milk for 1 cup of water.

1111 APPLES AND BISCUIT PASTRY IDEAS (R 1306)

1. Sweet Apple Tart
Line a tart plate with pastry. Spread with jam (preferably apricot or berry) and cover with thin slices of apple. Top with another thin layer of jam or sprinkle with brown sugar. Bake in a hot oven for 10 mins, turn down to moderate and bake further 20-25 mins. Serve with cream or custard.

2. Mince Tart
Grate cooking apple into a basin and add all or any of the following ingredients: sultanas, currants, mixed peel, raisins, glace cherries, cinnamon and/or mixed spice. Mix well and place in a tart plate which has been lined with biscuit pastry. Place strips or shapes of pastry on top of mixture to decorate. Bake in hot oven as above. Serve with cream or custard.

3. Apple Pasties
Peel apples and cut into eighths. Remove core from each piece. Roll out biscuit pastry and cut into circles with a scone cutter. Wrap each piece of apple in a circle of pastry and crimp edges as though it were a miniature pastie. Brush tops with milk and sprinkle with sugar. Bake as above and serve with cream.

4. Applings
Form pasties as above, but drop them into a large saucepan of boiling sweetened water and cook until they float (a few mins). Remove, pour melted butter over them and serve with cinnamon and sugar.

5. Apple Slice
Line a greased scone tray with pastry. Add a combination of sliced apples, sultanas, chopped nuts, glace cherries and a little cinnamon. Top with sugar and crumbled almond meal or ground almonds. Bake in a moderate oven about 40 mins and cut into slices while still warm.

6. Dutch Tart (R 1412)

7. Macaroon Slice (R 1522)

1112 STUFFED APPLES

6 large apples
3 tablespoons chopped
 almonds
½ cup finely crushed
 macaroons

1 tablespoon finely chopped
 ginger
6 tablespoons honey, warmed

Remove core of apple with sharp knife or apple corer, taking care not to cut right through. Slit skin around middle of apple. Mix ingredients, except honey, and stuff apples. Place in well buttered dish. Pour one tablespoon of warm honey into and over each apple. Bake uncovered in a moderate oven 30-40 mins.

Variations:
Fill apples with one of the following combinations:
1. ½ cup crushed cereal, 1 tablespoon coconut, 1 tablespoon plum jam, 1 tablespoon sugar, ½ teaspoon cinnamon. Pour over apples juice of one orange and 1 tablespoon water.
2. Finely chopped walnuts, bananas mashed with a little lemon juice, sugar to taste. Pour maple syrup over apples.
3. Chopped dates, brown sugar, softened butter and a little cinnamon. Combine 1 cup boiling water, ½ cup sugar and juice of 1 lemon and pour over and around apples.
4. Chopped peppermint creams. Add a little water to baking dish.

1113 CARAMEL APPLES

4-5 cooking apples
½ cup sugar
1 tablespoon golden syrup

1 tablespoon butter
1 tablespoon flour
1 cup boiling water

Peel, core and quarter apples, place in flat buttered ovenproof dish. Combine sugar, syrup, butter and flour and very slowly add boiling water. Pour over apples and bake uncovered in a moderately hot oven for about 1 hour.
Variation: Substitute pears for apples.

1114 APPLE APRICOT CRUMBLE

500g [1 lb] cooking apples
½ cup apricot jam

½ cup water
crumble topping [R 1105.1]

Peel and core apples, cut into quarters. Mix jam and water, pour over apples. Add topping and bake in a moderate oven for 30-45 mins.
Variation: Omit jam and substitute marmalade plus grated rind of one orange.

1115 APPLE DATE PUDDING

2 eggs
¾ cup raw sugar
3 heaped tablespoons wholemeal SR flour
1 teaspoon cinnamon

¼ teaspoon nutmeg
2 cups diced tart apples
¾ cup chopped dates
30g [1 oz] butter

Beat eggs and sugar together. Sift in flour and spices. Stir in apples and dates. Put in greased ovenproof dish and dot with butter. Bake in moderate oven for 30 mins. Serve with cream or ice-cream.

Variation: Use only 2 tablespoons flour and add 1 tablespoon coconut.

1116 GERMAN APPLE CAKE

Cake
125g [4 oz] butter
90g [3 oz] sugar
1 cup plain or SR flour, sifted
1 egg

Filling
3 cooking apples
2 tablespoons sultanas
1 tablespoon raw sugar
½ teaspoon cinnamon
¼ teaspoon nutmeg
juice of 1 lemon

Cake: Melt butter in a large saucepan, add sugar and stir until it is beginning to dissolve. Add flour and stir well, beat in egg. Grease a 7" cake tin and using fingers spread a little more than half the cake mixture over the bottom.
Filling: Peel, core and slice apples, place half of these in layers over cake mixture. Mix together sultanas, sugar and spices and sprinkle over apple slices. Cover with rest of apple, sprinkle with lemon juice. Spread remaining cake mixture on top, in spoonfuls. Cook in moderate oven for 45 mins.

*Use an egg slicer to cut evenly sized slices of banana for decorating cakes etc.

*To sour milk add 1 tablespoon lemon juice or white vinegar to 1 cup of milk and let stand for five minutes. Results are even better if milk is warmed slightly first.

*Use a vegetable peeler to slice apples very thinly for tarts or strudel.

117 APPLE STRUDEL

Strudel Dough
250g [8 oz] flour
salt
1 egg yolk, beaten

1 tablespoon melted
  unsalted butter
⅔ cup [approx] warm water

Sift flour and salt into warmed basin. Make a well in centre and stir by hand the egg yolk, butter and enough warm water to make a soft dough. Knead thoroughly on a warmed, well floured board. When smooth, place in a warm bowl and cover with a cloth. Set aside.

Filling:
60g [2 oz] dry breadcrumbs
125g [4 oz] unsalted butter,
  melted
750g [1½ lb] cooking apples
60g [2 oz] currants

60g [2 oz] raisins
125g [4 oz] castor sugar
½ teaspoon cinnamon
extra sugar and cinnamon or
  apricot jam for serving

Melt butter (keep aside 2 tablespoons for glazing pastry).
Fry breadcrumbs in butter until brown. Peel, core and slice apples very thinly into a large basin, add rest of ingredients and breadcrumbs and mix thoroughly, being careful not to break up apple slices.

Cover the table with a clean tea towel, dust with flour, place dough in centre and roll out as thinly as possible with floured rolling pin. Slip your hands under dough and gently pull it out thinner from the middle, working toward the edges. Ideally it should be thin enough to see the pattern of the tea towel clearly, but this takes practice.

Spread filling evenly over dough leaving 1" of dough all around the edge. Fold this 1" over filling, then roll up as for a Swiss roll. Brush with melted butter, and lift carefully on to a buttered oven tray. Bake in hot oven for 20 mins, then lower temperature to moderate and bake a further 30 mins. Brush with melted butter 2 or 3 times during baking.

Serve either hot or cold sprinkled with extra cinnamon and sugar or brushed with a little melted apricot jam.

*Try cooking rhubarb in orange juice rather than water.

1118 APPLE CRUMB TART

1⅓ cups sweet biscuit
   crumbs
30g [1 oz] or more butter,
   melted
¼ teaspoon each cinnamon
   and nutmeg
2 eggs, separated

1⅓ cups sieved stewed apple
1 400g [14 oz] can sweetened
   condensed milk
2 tablespoons lemon juice
grated rind of 1 lemon
¼ teaspoon salt

Mix crumbs, butter, cinnamon and nutmeg. Spread half mixture over bottom of a 7" springform tin or deep cake tin lined with foil. Beat yolks well, add condensed milk, lemon juice, rind and stewed apple. Beat egg whites and salt stiffly, fold into mixture, spoon into tin and top with remaining crumbs. Bake in moderate oven about 50 mins. Serve warm or cold.

1119 APPLE CHOCOLATE CRACKLE

Base

60g [2 oz] copha
1½ cups rice bubbles

1½ tablespoons cocoa
2 tablespoons icing sugar

Melt copha and combine with other ingredients. Mix well and press into base of lamington tin. Refrigerate until firm.

Filling

125g [4 oz] cream cheese
juice and grated rind of
   1 lemon
2 tablespoons castor sugar
1 cup sweetened, drained
   stewed apple

3 teaspoons gelatine dis-
   solved in ¼ cup water
grated chocolate

Beat cheese until smooth, gradually add other ingredients except chocolate and beat well. Cover chocolate crackle base with apple mixture, sprinkle with chocolate and return to refrigerator to set.

APRICOT ALMOND SOUFFLE (R 2409)

120 BANANAS IN HONEY

6 bananas
2 tablespoons lemon juice

2 tablespoons butter
½ cup honey

Peel bananas, halve lengthwise and dip in lemon juice. Melt butter and honey and fry bananas gently until cooked and glazed, or bake in 325°F (160°C) oven for 15 mins.

Variation: Omit lemon juice and honey. Substitute ½ cup orange juice, ¼ cup brown sugar, 1 cup coconut. Mix together juice, sugar and bananas. Dot with butter and sprinkle with coconut. Bake as above.

121 FLAMED BANANAS

1-2 bananas per person
30g [1 oz] butter per person
2 teaspoons brown sugar per person

2 teaspoons desiccated coconut per person
¼ cup brandy or rum

Melt butter in frying pan. Slice bananas lengthwise or leave whole if very small. Sprinkle with brown sugar and coconut. Cook until bananas are soft. Warm brandy, ignite and pour over bananas.

122 BANANA CARAMEL

1¾ cups brown sugar
¼ cup butter
¼ cup cream or top of milk
1 teaspoon vanilla

4-6 bananas, peeled and sliced
whipped unsweetened cream

Mix brown sugar, butter, cream or top of milk together, and stir over low heat until thick. Remove from heat and add vanilla. Arrange bananas in serving dishes, pour sauce over and allow to cool. When ready to serve, top with cream.

123 BANANA BAKE

4 bananas, sliced diagonally in 1" pieces
juice of 1 large lemon
2 eggs, beaten

2 tablespoons sugar
1 cup coconut
2 tablespoons apricot jam

Slice bananas, put into an ovenproof dish and sprinkle generously with lemon juice. Beat together eggs and sugar until thick and creamy. Add coconut and jam, stir well. Pour over bananas and bake uncovered in moderate oven until golden brown, about 30 mins.

1124 BANANA DISHES
(Quick and easy)
1. Bananas sliced lengthwise, covered with whipped cream, chopped dates and nuts.
2. Sliced bananas, wheatgerm and cream.
3. Sliced bananas, jam and cream.
4. Mashed bananas, orange juice and cream.
5. Sliced bananas, cream and nutmeg.

Even quicker banana dishes—as above but leave bananas whole.

1125 BLACKBERRY MOUSSE

1 cup blackberries, drained
1 tablespoon gelatine
1 cup blackberry juice and water

½ cup sugar
2 eggs, separated
1 cup cream, lightly whipped
8" pie shell [optional]

Dissolve gelatine in juice. Beat egg yolks and sugar until thick and creamy. Add dissolved gelatine and blackberries. Whip egg whites until soft peaks form and fold into setting blackberry mixture. Fold in cream. Pour into individual glass bowls or 8" pie shell and chill.

BRANDIED CHERRIES (R 1933)

1126 CHERRIES JUBILEE

500g [1 lb] can cherries
½ cup syrup from cherries
1 tablespoon butter
¼ cup brown or white sugar
1 tablespoon cornflour

¼ teaspoon cinnamon
1 tablespoon kirsch
2 teaspoons lemon juice
¼ cup brandy
vanilla ice-cream

Drain and stone cherries, reserving syrup. Melt butter, add sugar. Blend cornflour with a little syrup. Add cherries to pan, then cornflour mixture, cinnamon, lemon juice, remaining syrup and kirsch. Stir until sauce boils and thickens. Warm brandy, ignite and pour over cherries. Serve immediately over ice-cream.

Variation: Substitute peaches for cherries and brandy for kirsch.

---

*To dissolve gelatine soak it first in 1-2 tablespoons cold water in a small bowl or cup. When gelatine has swelled the bowl can then be stood in boiling water or hot liquid can be added to dissolve the gelatine. Three teaspoons of gelatine will set 600ml (1 pint) of liquid.

1127 LEMON MERINGUE PUDDING

2½ cups water
1 cup sugar
grated rind of 1 lemon
juice of 2 lemons
4 tablespoons cornflour

2 eggs, separated
1 tablespoon butter
extra 3 tablespoons sugar for
meringue

Place 2 cups water in saucepan with 1 cup sugar, lemon rind and juice. Blend cornflour smoothly with remaining water. Slowly bring lemon mixture almost to boiling point, then stir in cornflour. Continue stirring until it boils and thickens, simmer 3 mins. Allow to cool slightly, then stir in egg yolks and butter. Pour into pie dish and allow to become cold. Beat egg whites until stiff, adding remaining sugar gradually. Spoon over mixture in pie dish. Bake in slow oven 300°F (150°C) for about 30 mins until meringue browns slightly. Serve cold.

Variation: Bake mixture in pre-cooked pastry shell (R 1300).

1128 LEMON OR ORANGE DELICIOUS PUDDING

1 tablespoon butter
½ cup sugar
2 eggs, separated
2 tablespoons flour

2 lemons or oranges [juice of
both and grated rind of one]
1¼ cups milk

Cream butter and sugar. Add egg yolks, flour, grated rind and juice. Mix well after each addition. Add milk slowly. (In an emergency combine all these ingredients in blender.) Whisk egg whites until stiff and fold into mixture. Bake in a buttered dish, standing in a pan of water, at 350°F (180°C) for approximately 40 mins, or until the top springs back when lightly pressed with a finger.

Variation: Add pulp of 2 or 3 passionfruit.

1129 LEMON SOUFFLE (Cold)

1 tablespoon gelatine
1 cup water
3 eggs, separated
185g [6 oz] sugar

2 teaspoons grated lemon
rind
2 tablespoons lemon juice
1 cup cream

Dissolve gelatine in water. Beat egg yolks, add sugar, lemon rind and juice, and beat again. Add dissolved gelatine and stir quickly. Whip cream lightly and fold in. Beat egg whites stiffly and fold in lightly. Pour into serving bowl and chill.

1130 LEMON SYLLABUB

juice and thinly cut rind of 1
   lemon
60g [2 oz] castor sugar
2 tablespoons brandy

1 liqueur glass sherry
300ml [½ pint] whipped
   cream.

Chop rind coarsely and put in a bowl with lemon juice. Add sugar, brandy and sherry and leave overnight. Strain. An hour or so before serving, add cream and beat until mixture forms soft peaks. Spoon into individual glasses.

1131 LEMON GINGERNUT PIE
Crumb Crust

250g [8 oz] gingernut
   biscuits, crushed
125g [4 oz] butter, melted

1 tablespoon brown sugar
1 teaspoon ground ginger

Combine all ingredients and press on to base and sides of greased 8" spring form tin. Refrigerate.

Filling

150ml [¼ pint] cream
400g [14 oz] can sweetened
   condensed milk
juice of 2 lemons and rind of 1

1 can [1¾ cups] evaporated
   milk, chilled
1 teaspoon vanilla
2 teaspoons gelatine dissolved
   in 2 tablespoons water

Whip cream, fold in condensed milk, Add lemon juice and rind. Beat evaporated milk, add vanilla and dissolved gelatine. Put in prepared crumb crust and chill well in refrigerator. Alternatively, this can be frozen until 1 hour before serving.

CITRUS CREAM (R 2419)

1132 ORANGE TART
Crumb Crust

2½ cups cornflakes, crushed
125g [4 oz] butter, melted

¼ cup castor sugar

Combine ingredients and press into pie plate lined with foil.

Filling

2 teaspoons gelatine
¾ cup orange juice
4 eggs, separated

½ cup castor sugar
½ cup chopped walnuts
whipped cream, chopped nuts
   to garnish

Dissolve gelatine in a little orange juice. Beat egg yolks, add sugar, remaining juice and gelatine. Cook until mixture starts to thicken but do not boil. Cool and add walnuts. Beat egg whites until stiff, fold into mixture and pour into crust. Garnish with whipped cream and chopped nuts.

133 PEACH BRULEE

500g [1 lb] fresh or canned, drained peaches
sugar [optional]

300ml [½ pint] cream, whipped
3 tablespoons brown sugar

Skin, stone and slice fresh peaches. Place fruit in ovenproof dish and sprinkle with a little sugar if desired. Cover fruit well with whipped cream. Refrigerate overnight. Immediately before serving sprinkle with brown sugar and place under hot griller until sugar starts to caramelise, about 1 min.

Variations:
1. Add a little almond essence or liqueur to cream.
2. Add 1 cup desiccated coconut to cream.
3. Add chopped blanched almonds to peaches.
4. Substitute apricots, pears or grapes for peaches.

134 PEARS BAKED IN HONEY

4 pears
½ cup honey
½ cup water

1 tablespoon or more lemon juice
¼ teaspoon mixed spice
½ teaspoon cinnamon

Make a syrup of honey, water, lemon juice and spices. Peel pears and arrange them whole in a fire-proof dish. Pour syrup over them and bake in a moderate oven until tender about 45 mins, basting occasionally.

135 STUFFED PEARS

Peel and core large pears. Stuff with dates or raisins, chopped nuts and tart marmalade. Place in baking dish, cover bottom of pan with a little water and bake slowly for 1 hour or until tender.

136 CURRIED PEARS

125g [4 oz] butter
½ cup brown sugar
2 teaspoons curry powder

½ teaspoon salt
12 canned pear halves, drained

Mix butter, sugar, curry and salt. Place pears in shallow ovenproof dish and spoon mixture carefully into centre of pears. Grill until filling is bubbly.

1137 GINGERBREAD PEARS

1 cup flour
1 cup S.R. flour
¼ teaspoon salt
3 teaspoons ground ginger
1 teaspoon allspice
½ cup golden syrup
½ teaspoon bicarbonate of
   soda

60g [2 oz] butter
125g [4 oz] brown sugar
1 large egg, beaten
½ cup warm milk
extra 60g [2 oz] brown sugar
extra 60g [2 oz] butter, melted
6-8 canned pear halves,
   drained

Sift flour, salt and spices. Place syrup, soda, butter and sugar in saucepan and stir over low heat until sugar is dissolved. Cool and stir in dry ingredients, then egg and milk. Combine extra sugar and butter and spread over base of well greased 8" square tin. Place pears on this, and then spread mixture on top. Bake in a moderate oven 30-45 mins. Cut into squares and serve hot or cold with cream or custard.

"GIANT STRAWBERRIES" (R 2424)

1138 PEARS IN RED WINE

6 firm pears
300ml [½ pint] water
250g [8 oz] brown or white
   sugar
2 sticks cinnamon

3 whole cloves
1 twist lemon peel
300ml [½ pint] red wine
1 tablespoon brandy
   [optional]

Peel pears leaving stalks on. Combine water, sugar, cinnamon, cloves and lemon peel in a saucepan. Bring to boil and simmer 5-8 mins, then add wine and brandy. Place in a deep ovenproof dish, cover and bake in 275°F (140°C) oven for 2-3 hours until pears are transparent and tender. Baste several times during cooking. Serve hot or cold.

Note: Brown sugar gives a rich deep crimson colour, white sugar gives a pinky-red translucent look.

1139 RUMMY PEARS

For the unexpected guest or when everything else has gone wrong, this is a quick and delicious dish. A halved tinned or stewed pear is covered with ice-cream and *hot* chocolate sauce liberally laced with rum and raisins. Well, all right, just raisins.

1140 PINEAPPLE MERINGUE

1 small [425g, 15 oz] can
   crushed pineapple
1 large or 2 small eggs,
   separated

2 teaspoons custard powder
2 tablespoons castor sugar

Put pineapple, egg yolks and custard powder into saucepan. Mix well and stir over moderate heat until thickened. Transfer to ovenproof dish but do not allow to become cold. Beat egg whites with a pinch of salt until thick and gradually add sugar. Pile meringue on to thickened pineapple taking care to cover it completely. Place in a hot oven until tinted or a cooler oven for a longer time if a crisper meringue is desired.

1141 PINEAPPLE IN JELLY

1 small [425g, 15 oz] can
   pineapple rings
boiling water

1 packet orange jelly crystals
125g [4 oz] cottage cheese
6 glace cherries

Drain syrup from pineapple and add boiling water to make up to 1½ cups liquid. Bring to boil and add jelly crystals. Stir until dissolved. Divide into two parts and cool. Add cottage cheese to one part and stir to blend. Turn into oblong tin and chill until firm. Arrange drained pineapple slices on cheese layer and place a cherry in the centre of each. Carefully pour remaining jelly over pineapple and chill again. Cut in squares to serve.

1142 PINEAPPLE CREAM CHEESE PIE

Crust:

185g [6 oz] plain sweet
   biscuits

90g [3 oz] butter, melted

Crush biscuits finely. Mix with butter. Press into base of 9" springform pan. Refrigerate for at least 20-30 mins.

Filling:

1 small [425g, 15 oz] can
   crushed pineapple
1 tablespoon cornflour

250g [8 oz] cream cheese
⅓ cup sugar
2 eggs
1 teaspoon vanilla

Drain pineapple and reserve liquid. Mix cornflour to paste with a little of the liquid. Add remaining liquid, bring to boil, stirring until thickened. Add pineapple, spoon mixture on to prepared crumb base. Beat cream cheese until smooth. Add sugar, eggs and vanilla. Beat well. Pour over pineapple. Bake at 300°F (150°C) for 40 mins or until set. Turn off heat and leave in oven until cold then refrigerate. Serve with cream or ice-cream.

PINEAPPLE UPSIDE-DOWN CAKE (R 1414)

1143 PRUNE SNOW

250g [8 oz] prunes
water to cover
2 tablespoons sugar
1 tablespoon lemon juice
1 teaspoon grated lemon
　　rind

¼ teaspoon cinnamon
2 egg whites
6 teaspoons sugar
cream

Place prunes in saucepan, cover with water and simmer gently until soft—about 15-20 mins. Add sugar, drain and sieve or puree in blender. Add lemon juice, rind and cinnamon. Beat egg whites with sugar until stiff. Fold into prune mixture and spoon into glasses. Decorate with cream.

Variations:
1. Substitute apples for prunes and add a little green food colouring.
2. Place fruit mixture and beaten egg whites in alternate layers in glasses.

1144 RHUBARB BAKED WITH RAISINS

1 bunch rhubarb
juice of 1 orange
½ cup sugar
3 tablespoons raisins
½ teaspoon cinnamon or
　　ground ginger

Topping:
30g [1 oz] butter
½ cup S.R. flour
3 tablespoons sugar
3 tablespoons coconut

Wash rhubarb well, cut into 1" pieces. Mix with other ingredients and place in shallow ovenproof dish. Combine topping ingredients and sprinkle on top of rhubarb. Bake in a moderate oven for 40 mins.

1145 STRAWBERRY IDEAS

Wash and drain 500g (1 lb) strawberries (2 punnets). Hull, sweeten and combine with one of the following:—
1. 300ml (½ pint) cream, whipped and flavoured with 2 table-spoons cointreau, kirsch or other liqueur.
2. 125g (4 oz) cream cheese, beaten until soft, with ¾ cup cream added.
3. Juice of 1 orange and 300ml (½ pint) cream, whipped.
4. 1 tablespoon raspberry jam mixed with 2 tablespoons water, 1 tablespoon brandy, ¼ cup chopped blanched almonds and 1 cup whipped cream.
5. Equal quantities fresh, diced pineapple and 2 tablespoons rum, port or brandy.

146 JELLIED PLUM PUDDING

125g [4 oz] sultanas
30g [1 oz] currants
60g [2 oz] raisins
1 cup hot water
125g [4 oz] drained cherries
30g [1 oz] crystallised ginger
60g [2 oz] shredded peel
60g [2 oz] prunes or figs,
  chopped
2 bananas, sliced

150ml [¼ pint] sherry
4 tablespoons sugar
2 tablespoons lemon juice
  and a piece of lemon rind
1 tablespoon gelatine dissolved in 3 tablespoons hot
  water
30g [1 oz] almonds, blanched
  and cut in strips

Cook sultanas, currants and raisins in hot water for 15 minutes and strain, saving the water. Mix all the fruit well together and cover with 2 tablespoons of the sherry. Leave covered. Bring ½ cup of the water you have saved to the boil with sugar, lemon juice and rind. Strain, add dissolved gelatine, and water to make 1 ¼ cups. Add balance of sherry and pour over fruit. Add nuts. Allow to set in a pudding basin, and unmould before serving with cream. Serves 8-10.

1147 "LEAD US NOT" BREAD PUDDING

300-450ml [½-¾ pint] milk
¼ teaspoon salt
500g [1 lb] fresh breadcrumbs
4 eggs, lightly beaten
2 tablespoons brandy
375g [12 oz] mixed diced fruit
60g [2 oz] candied peel

60g [2 oz] raw sugar
125g [4 oz] shredded suet
2 level teaspoons mixed spice
grated rind 1 lemon
grated nutmeg
castor sugar

Place milk and salt in saucepan and bring to boil. Pour over breadcrumbs. Stir, cover and leave for 30 mins. Stir in eggs and brandy and add fruit, peel, sugar, suet, spice and lemon rind. Mix well and transfer to well greased 9" x 7" x 1" tin with smooth surface. Grate nutmeg over top. Bake at 350°F (180°C) for 1½ hours. Cool slightly and turn out. Dredge with castor sugar. Cut in squares.

*Wash strawberries before taking stems off to prevent loss of juice.

1148 JAM ROLY POLY

½ cup butter
2 cups S.R. flour
cold water
jam

½ cup sugar
1 tablespoon butter
1 cup boiling water

Rub butter into flour until it looks like breadcrumbs. Add enough cold water to make a fairly firm dough. Roll out and spread with jam then roll up like a Swiss roll and put in pie dish. Make a syrup of sugar, butter and boiling water. Pour over roll and bake in fairly hot oven for 30 mins.

1149 GOLDEN DUMPLINGS

Sauce:
1 cup water
½ cup sugar
1 tablespoon golden syrup
1 tablespoon butter

Dumplings:
1 cup S.R. flour
1 tablespoon butter
1 egg, lightly beaten
little milk

Place sauce ingredients in pan and heat. Rub butter into flour, stir in egg and enough milk to make a fairly stiff dough. Roll into little balls and drop into the boiling syrup for about 5-10 mins.

1150 TIPSY CAKE

375g [12 oz] stale sponge
   cake
185g [6 oz] seedless raspberry
   jam
6 tablespoons sherry or
   madeira

6 tablespoons brandy or rum
300ml [½ pint] cream
halved toasted almonds,
   angelica, cherries for
   decoration

Break cake into pieces, place in bowl. Warm jam and pour over cake. Mix well until cake is coated with jam. Add sherry and brandy and blend well. Turn mixture into pudding basin and press down firmly with back of wooden spoon, smoothing over top. Put a small plate or saucer to fit exactly inside top of basin and place a weight on it. Refrigerate overnight. Run a knife around edge and unmould. Whip cream until thick. Use half to cover. Put remaining cream in piping bag to decorate. Arrange nuts, angelica, and cherries on top.

HAZELNUT GATEAU (R 2404)
STRUESEL KUCHEN (R 1617)
HALVA CAKE (R 1424)

1151 TRIFLE

1 8" sponge cake
3-4 tablespoons raspberry or strawberry jam or 1 [284g, 10 oz] packet frozen raspberries or 250g punnet fresh raspberries

¼ cup sherry or fruit juice
600ml [1 pint] warm custard [sweetened with 3 tablespoons sugar]
150-300ml [¼-½ pt] thick cream

For decoration: *blanched and halved almonds, glace cherries, diamonds or strips of angelica.*

Split sponge cake in two, sandwich together with jam and put in bottom of a glass bowl. Place raspberries on top and sprinkle sherry over cake. Prepare custard, and while still hot, pour over cake. Then leave until cold. Lightly whip cream and spread some of it in a layer over custard. Beat rest until stiff and pipe in a lattice work pattern over top. Decorate with almonds, cherries and angelica.

PASSIONFRUIT OR STRAWBERRY SHORTCAKE (R 1413)

RAISIN SQUARES (R 1519)

SAVARIN OR RUM BABA (R 1618)

1152 BAKED CUSTARD

600ml [1 pint] milk
2 eggs
2 tablespoons sugar

½ cup powdered milk
¼ teaspoon salt
½ teaspoon vanilla

Puree all ingredients in blender until smooth. Place in casserole and stand in dish of water. Bake in moderate oven approx. 1½ hours, or stir over low flame until it thickens.

Variations:
1. Sprinkle top with coconut, cinnamon or nutmeg.
2. Use dark brown sugar instead of white.
3. Add 2 tablespoons honey.
4. Add 1 tablespoon cocoa or coffee.
5. Add 3 tablespoons sultanas or ½ cup chopped dried apricots.
6. Line the casserole with caramel, made by boiling 1 cup sugar and ½ cup water until a light caramel colour. Do not stir.

*To prevent a skin forming on custard or white sauce place a sheet of wet greaseproof paper on the surface as it cools.

1153 CUSTARDS WITH ORANGE SAUCE

Custard:
4 eggs
3 tablespoons sugar
½ teaspoon vanilla
600ml [1 pint] milk
125g [4 oz] cream cheese, chopped
grated nutmeg

Orange Sauce
2 teaspoons cornflour
1 tablespoon lemon juice
1¼ cups orange juice
1 tablespoon white curacao or brandy
1 tablespoon sugar
2 teaspoons grated orange rind
toasted flaked coconut

Beat together eggs, sugar and vanilla. Place milk and cream cheese in a saucepan and heat to lukewarm, stirring constantly until cheese melts. Pour over eggs and mix well. Pour mixture into 8 well greased small moulds and sprinkle a little grated nutmeg on top. Place moulds in a water bath and bake at 350°F (180°C) for 35 mins or until set. Allow custards to cool, then chill in refrigerator. Blend cornflour with lemon juice. Place orange juice, curacao, sugar and orange rind in saucepan. Bring to boil and stir in blended cornflour. Cook, stirring constantly until sauce boils and thickens. Cool. To serve: unmould custards on to individual serving dishes and spoon orange sauce over. Sprinkle with toasted coconut.

1154 RICE PUDDING DELICIOUS

¾ cup rice
boiling water
3-4 cups milk
¼ cup sultanas

grated rind of 1 lemon
½-¾ cup sugar
2 teaspoons butter

Turn oven to slow. Place rice in greased dish, barely cover with boiling water, stand in oven approximately 10 mins until water is absorbed. Add 3 cups milk and stand another 10 mins in oven. Add sultanas, lemon rind, sugar and butter and stir. Put dish in a baking dish of water, bake until rice is thoroughly cooked, stirring occasionally at first. Add more milk if necessary. After about 1 hour, leave so top can brown. Total cooking time about 2½ hours.

Variation: Omit sultanas and butter. Put ½ cup rice and ½ cup water in saucepan and bring to boil. Gradually add 4 cups milk and simmer 30 mins. Add sugar and lemon rind and simmer further 10 mins. Pour into bowls and chill well. Just before serving, sprinkle with cinnamon.

1155 YOGHURT DESSERTS

Combine 250g (8 oz) plain yoghurt, (R 1935, R 1936) with one of the following combinations:
1. 2 grated apples, grated rind and juice of 1 orange, 1 tablespoon castor sugar or honey, 30g (1 oz) chopped walnuts, almonds or hazelnuts, ½ cup chopped dates (optional).
2. 1½ cups stewed fruit, e.g. apricots, peaches, stoned prunes, apple puree or rhubarb.
3. 3 mashed bananas, 2 teaspoons lemon juice, 1 tablespoon sugar, 2 tablespoons wheatgerm (optional).
4. Small can frozen orange concentrate.
5. Pulp of 4 passionfruit and 1 tablespoon sugar.
6. Raspberry jam.
7. 3 tablespoons sultanas or currants.
8. Sugar and cinnamon.

1156 HONEYED CHEESE

1 small carton plain creamed   4 teaspoons honey
   cottage cheese   nutmeg

Mix cheese and honey, spoon into individual glasses, and top with nutmeg.

FRENCH "PANCAKE" (R 1206)

1157 PEANUT BUTTER WHIP

2 teaspoons gelatine   ½ cup peanut butter
1½ tablespoons water   ¼ cup sugar
1 can [1¾ cups] evaporated   ½ teaspoon vanilla
   milk at room temperature

Soften gelatine in water. Stir over low heat until dissolved. Cool. Mix evaporated milk and peanut butter. Low speed on mixer is ideal. Slowly add cooled gelatine then sugar and vanilla. Beat until well blended and sugar is dissolved. Chill until set. Delicious with stewed fruit.

*When measuring syrup or honey, dip the spoon into boiling water first. If using a cup, rinse with boiling water or grease the inside or dust with flour.

1158 LIME PARFAIT

1 packet lime jelly
1 cup boiling water
250g [8 oz] cream cheese
¼ cup sugar
¼ cup orange juice
2 teaspoons lemon juice
2 teaspoons grated lemon
  rind
few drops green colouring
300ml [½ pint] cream,
  whipped
cherries to garnish

Dissolve jelly in water. Beat cheese until smooth, add sugar, juices, rind, jelly and colouring. Chill until almost set. Fold in whipped cream, and pour into individual glasses. Decorate with cherries.

1159 RUM SOUFFLE (Cold)

4 eggs, separated
½ cup castor sugar
3 teaspoons gelatine
¾ cup water
300ml [½ pint] cream,
  lightly whipped
1½ tablespoons rum
grated chocolate and extra
  cream for decorating

Beat egg yolks and sugar in electric beater or over hot water until light and creamy. Dissolve gelatine in water and add to egg yolks. Stir in cream and rum. Beat egg whites until soft peaks form and fold lightly into mixture. Decorate with grated chocolate and whipped cream.

1160 ALMOND SOUFFLE (Hot)

125g [4 oz] ground almonds
1 cup milk
60g [2 oz] butter
60g [2 oz] castor sugar
30g [1 oz] flour
30g [1 oz] cornflour
5 eggs, separated
1 teaspoon vanilla
1 teaspoon almond essence

Make a foil collar for the souffle mould. Grease mould with butter and dredge with sugar. Place ground almonds in a saucepan with milk and bring to boil. Cream butter and sugar until light and creamy and mix in flour and cornflour. Pour hot milk mixture over and stir vigorously. Return to saucepan and cook for a few mins. Remove from heat and allow to cool slightly. Add egg yolks one at a time beating well after each addition. Add vanilla and almond essence. Whisk egg whites stiffly and blend one third into mixture then fold remainder in gently. Do not overmix. Fill souffle dish and bake at 400°F (200°C) for 20-25 mins. Just before removing from the oven dust liberally with icing sugar. Serve with almond sauce. (R 1024).

1161 PAVLOVA

4 egg whites
8 tablespoons castor sugar
¼ teaspoon salt
½ teaspoon vanilla

1 teaspoon vinegar
whipped cream and fruit or
flavouring

Preheat oven to 350°F (180°C). Beat egg whites and salt until stiff. Add sugar very gradually, beating constantly. Fold in vanilla and vinegar. Cover scone tray with lightly greased foil and spoon mixture on to it, making either a circle, square or rectangle, and building up outer edges a little. Turn oven down to 250°F (130°C), put pavlova on lowest shelf and cook for 1½-2 hours. Allow to cool in oven. Before serving cover with either:
1. Whipped cream flavoured with creme de menthe and with some grated peppermint crisps folded through or
2. Whipped cream flavoured with rum and sugar and topped with grated chocolate or
3. Whipped cream and fresh fruit, e.g. passionfruit and sliced bananas, raspberries, strawberries, etc.
N.B. If varying the size allow 2 tablespoons sugar to every egg white. Increase vinegar accordingly ¼ teaspoon per egg. Use yolks for scrambled eggs, lemon butter, custard or zabaglione.

Variation: Using electric beater, beat together for 10 mins 2 egg whites, 1½ cups castor sugar, ½ teaspoon vanilla, 1 teaspoon vinegar, 1 teaspoon cornflour, and 4 tablespoons boiling water. Place on greased foil or scone tray, as above, and bake at 300°F (150°C) for 1¼-1½ hours.

1162 WALNUT MERINGUE

3 egg whites
1 cup sugar
125g [4 oz] plain dry biscuits,
   crushed

125g [4 oz] walnut pieces
whipped cream

Beat egg whites and sugar until stiff. Mix biscuits and walnut pieces, add egg mixture. Brown in slow oven for 30-45 mins until golden. Decorate with whipped cream.

1163 ZABAGLIONE

6 egg yolks
½ cup sugar

1 cup marsala or sweet
sherry

Beat egg yolks and sugar until thick and lemon coloured. Stir in marsala, pour mixture into top of double boiler (or basin set over simmering water). Beat constantly with rotary beater or electric beater until mixture is very light and begins to thicken. When mixture begins to rise, remove from heat. Serve hot by itself or poured over ice-cream, sprinkled lightly with cinnamon if desired. For each serving, allow 1 egg yolk, 1 teaspoon sugar, 1 tablespoon marsala. Do not use rum or any other strong spirit or eggs will curdle.

Variation:
If thicker consistency is desired, continue to beat over hot water. It can then be served warm or chilled.

1164 PASHKA (Russian Easter Dessert)

1 cup sultanas
hot water
½ cup candied fruit
   [cherries, ginger, angelica,
   pineapple, apricots, peel,
   etc]
500g [1 lb] cream cheese

300ml [½ pint] sour cream
1 cup castor sugar
½ teaspoon vanilla
½ teaspoon almond essence
walnuts or blanched almonds
   and whole crystallised
   cherries to garnish

Soak sultanas in hot water for 30 minutes. Chop the candied fruit very finely. Sieve or beat cream cheese well, add sour cream and beat until very smooth. Continue beating and slowly add sugar, vanilla and almond essence. Drain sultanas and fold into cheese mixture with candied fruit. Mix thoroughly. The mixture should be very firm. Pile up in a pyramid shape using a fork to roughen it. Garnish with walnuts or almonds and crystallised cherries.

*If you miss the "mushy" stage when making ice cream and find it already frozen, do not panic, remove from freezer, allow it to soften sufficiently to mix, then beat vigorously and refreeze.

1165 CHEESECAKE

250g [8 oz] plain sweet
  biscuits
90g [3 oz] butter, melted
375g [12 oz] cream cheese
½ cup castor sugar

2 eggs
2-3 drops vanilla
150ml [¼ pint] cream,
  whipped
4 passionfruit

Crush biscuits in blender and add to melted butter. Press into base and about 1" up sides of greased tin. Chill 20-30 mins at least. Mix cheese, sugar, eggs and vanilla in blender. Pour into case. Bake at 300°F (150°C) for 45 mins or longer. Cool in oven. Decorate top with cream and passionfruit.

Variation: Continental Cheesecake.
Add ¼ cup sultanas, ¼ cup raisins and 2 teaspoons finely chopped mixed peel (optional).

1166 CHEESECAKE (No bake)

Crumb Crust

185g [6 oz] sweet biscuit
  crumbs
75g [2½ oz] butter, melted

½ teaspoon cinnamon
½ teaspoon nutmeg
1 tablespoon sugar

Combine ingredients and press into buttered 8" springform cake tin. Put in refrigerator to harden.

Filling

250g [8 oz] cream cheese
2 grapefruit
1 400g [14 oz] can sweetened
  condensed milk

1 teaspoon gelatine
¼ cup lemon juice
1-2 egg whites, stiffly beaten

Peel grapefruit and chop into small segments reserving any juice. Grate a little rind. Dissolve gelatine in lemon juice. Beat cheese until smooth and add 1 teaspoon grated rind. Add condensed milk, dissolved gelatine, grapefruit segments and juice. Finally fold in stiffly beaten egg whites and pour into prepared crust.

Variations:
1. **Lemon:** Omit grapefruit, increase lemon juice to ½ cup and add 2 teaspoons grated lemon rind.
2. **Chocolate:** Use chocolate ripple biscuits for crust. Omit grapefruit, increase lemon juice to ½ cup and add 125g (4 oz) melted chocolate (optional) and 1 teaspoon vanilla. Decorate with chopped almonds or hazelnuts.

199

1167 AMERICAN SPIKED PIE
Crust:

220g [7 oz] chocolate biscuits   75g [2½ oz] butter, melted
   or gingersnaps, crushed

Mix well and press into 9" springform tin. If desired bake in moderate oven for 10 mins and cool. Alternatively, chill for at least 30 mins.

Filling:

3 teaspoons gelatine   ¼ cup liqueur, e.g. cognac,
¼ cup water   creme de cacao, creme de
⅔ cup sugar   menthe, cointreau, any fruit
salt   brandy
3 eggs, separated   1 cup cream, whipped

Soak gelatine in water, heat slightly until dissolved, add ⅓ cup of sugar, salt and egg yolks. Mix well and cook slowly over low heat, stirring constantly until mixture thickens. Do not boil. Remove from heat, stir in liqueur. Chill until mixture starts to set. Beat egg whites stiffly, add remaining sugar and beat well. Fold into thickened liqueur mixture. Fold in whipped cream. Pour into crust and chill. Freeze if desired.

Ice-Cream

1168 HONEY AND YOGHURT ICE-CREAM

1 cup plain yoghurt   ¼ teaspoon salt
2 teaspoons lemon juice   ¼ cup honey
½ cup orange juice   2 egg whites

Blend together first 5 ingredients thoroughly. Freeze until mixture starts to set. Remove from trays, beat until smooth. Beat egg whites stiffly then fold in. Refreeze.

Variation: Add 12 stoned prunes, finely chopped or pureed in blender.

1169 HEALTH ICE-CREAM

3 eggs   1 teaspoon gelatine,
300ml [½ pint] chilled   dissolved in
   evaporated milk   ¼ cup water
   or cream   1 teaspoon vanilla
½ cup honey or brown sugar

Beat eggs, add milk and beat until thick and creamy. Add honey, gelatine and vanilla and beat until blended. Freeze.

1170 EASY ICE-CREAM

2 cans [3½ cups] evaporated
   milk
1 400g [4 oz] can sweetened
   condensed milk

1 teaspoon vanilla

Mix 3 cans of milk together, add vanilla, freeze. When partially frozen beat until quantity is doubled. Makes 2¼ litres (4 pints).

Variation: Omit condensed milk and add 8 tablespoons powdered milk and 125g (4 oz) sugar.

1171 MILK ICE-CREAM

600ml [1 pint] milk, warmed
   to blood heat
3 tablespoons powdered milk
½ can [200g] sweetened
   condensed milk
2 tablespoons sugar
   [optional]

2 teaspoons gelatine
   dissolved in
¼ cup water
¼ teaspoon salt
1 teaspoon vanilla

Combine milks, sugar and dissolved gelatine and mix well. Freeze to stiff mush. Beat until smooth and creamy adding salt and vanilla. Refreeze.

Variations:
1. Dissolve a flavoured junket tablet in a little water and add to mixture in the first mixing stage.
2. Add 150ml (¼ pint) cream.
3. Omit vanilla and substitute a different flavouring, e.g. grated orange or lemon rind or 125g (4 oz) melted chocolate.
4. To make a larger quantity, add 2 beaten eggs and increase condensed milk to 1 can.

1172 POWDERED MILK ICE-CREAM

2 teaspoons gelatine
1 tablespoon butter
¾ cup [approx] water
1½ cups powdered milk

¾ cup sugar
1¾ cups boiling water
2 teaspoons vanilla

Dissolve gelatine and butter in ¼ cup water. Mix milk and sugar to a smooth paste with about ½ cup cold water. Add boiling water, gelatine mixture and vanilla. Mix well, partially freeze, then beat in chilled bowl until very thick. Re-freeze.

1173 CUSTARD ICE-CREAM

2 tablespoons flour
½ cup sugar
1¼ cups milk
2 eggs, separated

¼ teaspoon salt
1 cup cream, whipped
1 teaspoon vanilla

Mix flour and sugar thoroughly. Stir in milk and make smooth paste. Cook over hot water until mixture thickens. Cook further 10 mins. Beat egg yolks lightly, pour into mixture and cook 2 mins longer, then cool.
Fold in stiffly beaten egg whites to which the salt has been added. Fold in cream and vanilla, pour into tray and freeze partially, beat again then refreeze.

Variation:

Omit flour and make custard with milk, sugar and beaten eggs (unseparated). Remove from heat, add vanilla, allow to cool. Fold in whipped cream or 1 can (1¾ cups) chilled, whipped evaporated milk, and freeze. Beat again and refreeze.

1174 TROPICAL FREEZE

2 eggs, separated
juice of 2 oranges
3 bananas, mashed

1 cup crushed pineapple
5-6 tablespoons sugar [if
    using fresh pineapple]

Beat egg yolks, mix in juice, fruit, and sugar if used, freeze to mush. Beat egg whites until stiff and add to mixture. Refreeze.

1175 PINEAPPLE ICE-CREAM

1 medium pineapple or
  1 425g [15 oz] can crushed
  pineapple
juice of 1½ lemons

185g [6 oz] sugar
300ml [½ pint] water
300ml [½ pint] cream,
  whipped

If using fresh pineapple the shell can be kept for serving. Cut pineapple in half lengthwise including top. Remove hard core and discard. Remove all flesh and chop finely. Mix chopped pineapple, pineapple and lemon juice. Dissolve sugar with water over low heat and cool. Add this to pineapple and freeze until almost set. Whisk until light and fold in whipped cream. Freeze until firm.

Blender method: Put pineapple flesh, juice and lemon juice into blender, blend for 2 minutes then add cooled sugar syrup.

1176 CHEESE FRUIT FRAPPE

250g [8 oz] cream cheese
¼-½ cup honey
½ cup cream, whipped

1 cup chopped dates
1 425g [15 oz] can crushed
   pineapple, drained

Beat cheese until smooth, add honey and combine well, then add cream and mix together. Add dates and pineapple, mix well. Place in freezer tray until mixture firms. Serve cut into small slices (with added cream if desired).

1177 FRUIT SALAD CREAM

This is quick, easy and delicious and nice enough for a special occasion.

1 large 822g [1 lb 13 oz] can
   fruit salad, drained
2 apples, peeled and chopped
2 bananas, thinly sliced
2 tablespoons lemon juice
¼ cup stoned, fresh or
   canned, or glace cherries,
   halved

½ cup sugar
300ml [½ pint] cream,
   whipped
1 cup coconut, toasted if
   desired

Mix fruit salad, apples, bananas, lemon juice, cherries and sugar. Fold in whipped cream. Sprinkle half coconut on base of a large refrigerator tray lined with foil. Spoon mixture in carefully. Top with remaining coconut and freeze. Remove from refrigerator 1 hour before serving. Serve cut into small slices.

1178 BANANA CHOCOLATE ICE-CREAM

1¼ cups milk
1½ tablespoons cocoa,
   dissolved in 2 tablespoons
   hot water
3 tablespoons raw sugar
2 eggs, separated

¼ teaspoon vanilla
¾ cup evaporated milk,
   chilled
3 large ripe bananas, mashed
chopped walnuts or almonds
   to decorate

Stir milk and cocoa until blended. Add sugar, then beaten egg yolks, and stir over low heat until mixture thickens. Cool. Beat egg whites stiffly, fold into mixture with vanilla. Whip evaporated milk and fold in, then add mashed bananas. Freeze. Beat again when mixture has become mushy. Serve topped with nuts.

BANANA PASSIONFRUIT ICE-CREAM (R 1180)

203

1179 BANANA FREEZE

3 cups cornflakes, crushed
90g [3 oz] butter, melted
2 tablespoons sugar
1 teaspoon cinnamon
3 eggs, separated
¼ cup milk

½ cup sugar
3 large bananas
1 tablespoon lemon juice
300ml [½ pint] cream,
  lightly whipped

Line a deep refrigerator tray or large cake tin with foil and leave enough at sides to fold over top. Mix cornflake crumbs, butter, sugar and cinnamon and spread half on base of tray. Combine egg yolks, milk and sugar and cook, stirring, over a low heat until thickened. Cool. Mash bananas with lemon juice and stir into cooled custard. Beat egg whites stiffly and fold in. Whip cream lightly and add to mixture. Pour over crumbs and sprinkle remaining crumbs on top. Freeze, cover with foil. Remove from freezer 1 hour before serving. Cut in slices.

1180 AVOCADO ICE-CREAM

1 medium avocado
2 tablespoons lemon juice
½ cup brown sugar
1 cup milk

1 cup orange juice
1 teaspoon grated lemon rind
1 cup cream or evaporated
  milk, whipped

Peel and mash avocado with lemon juice. Combine all ingredients. Partially freeze. Beat again until smooth and fluffy, and refreeze.

Variation:
Substitute 1 banana for avocado and add pulp of 2 passionfruit.

1181 WHISKY AND PUMPERNICKEL ICE-CREAM

1 cup pumpernickel or other
  dark bread
2 tablespoons whisky or
  brandy
½ cup sugar
4 egg yolks

300ml [½ pint] top of milk
150ml [¼ pint] cream,
  whipped
3 egg whites
¼ teaspoon salt

Crumble bread and soak in whisky. Beat sugar and egg yolks until pale yellow. Over a low heat in double saucepan or thick pan, make a custard of yolks, sugar and milk, cool. Cover with damp greaseproof paper to prevent skin forming. Beat egg whites with salt until stiff. Add bread mixture, cream, then egg whites to custard. Freeze. Makes ¾ litre (1¼ pints). Serves 8.

182 ICE-CREAM VARIATIONS

To 2½-3 cups slightly softened vanilla ice-cream add one of the following combinations—

1. *Apricot:* 1 cup sweetened dried apricot puree and 2 table-spoons brandy.
2. *Banana:* 2 large bananas, sliced and cooked in 60g (2 oz) butter until soft, then mashed with 2 teaspoons lemon juice and 1 tablespoon sugar.
3. *Cassata:* Mixture of dried fruits, mixed peel, grated chocolate, chopped nuts.
4. *Cherry-almond:* 1 cup drained, stoned cherries and 4 tablespoons chopped almonds.
5. *Chocolate-peppermint:* 3 tablespoons grated chocolate and 2 tablespoons creme de menthe or a few drops green colouring and 1-2 teaspoons peppermint essence.
6. *Coconut:* 3 tablespoons toasted desiccated coconut.
7. *Date:* ½ cup chopped dates and ½ cup chopped walnuts.
8. *Ginger:* ½ cup chopped glace ginger and 4 tablespoons ginger syrup.
9. *Raisin:* ¼ cup chopped raisins and 2 tablespoons whisky or rum.
10. *Strawberry:* 1 250g punnet strawberries, washed, hulled, sweetened and crushed, and 1 tablespoon cointreau (optional).

HOT TODDY SAUCE (R 1028)

183 FROZEN CHRISTMAS PUDDING

This is easy and delicious and the ingredients can be varied according to taste and availability.

2 litres vanilla ice-cream
125g [4 oz] dark chocolate, grated
60g [2 oz] glace cherries, halved
60g [2 oz] mixed peel, finely chopped
125g [4 oz] sultanas
125g [4 oz] raisins, chopped
125g [4 oz] dates, chopped
60g [2 oz] currants
1 tablespoon brandy or rum
125g [4 oz] almonds, toasted if desired, chopped
2 teaspoons mixed spice

Allow ice-cream to soften slightly. Melt chocolate in double saucepan over low heat. Combine fruit and add brandy. Fold fruit, nuts and spice into chocolate and mix well. Blend into ice-cream. Freeze either in ice-cream containers or in a pudding basin lined with foil.

1184 SPECIALITY ICE-CREAM

600ml [1 pint] whipping cream   1 400g [14 oz] can sweetened
condensed milk

Beat cream until stiff. Fold in milk. Add any of the flavourings below—quantity to taste. Freeze.

Flavourings:
   grated chocolate and/or 2 teaspoons cocoa
   passionfruit
   sherry, rum or brandy
   fruit puree
   mixed dried fruit
   nutmeg, cinnamon, mixed spice
   chopped nuts

CHOCOLATE ICE-CREAM (R 2403)

BOMBE ALASKA (R 2132)

ICE-CREAM BIRTHDAY CAKE (R 2130, 2131)

Sherbets

These can be served as a dessert, a light summer entree, or in between courses to refresh and cleanse the palate.

1185 GRAPEFRUIT SHERBET

1 cup sugar   *1 cup grapefruit juice*
1¼ cups water   *2 egg whites*
juice 1 lemon

Put sugar and water in saucepan and simmer 3 minutes. Cool, add juices, freeze until partly frozen. Beat egg whites until stiff and fold through grapefruit mixture. Refreeze. Can be served in grapefruit shells.

1186 EMERALD SHERBET

¾ cup sugar   *2 egg whites, stiffly beaten*
2 cups water   *2 tablespoons creme de*
thinly pared rind 2 lemons   *menthe*
3 tablespoons lemon juice   *mint to garnish*

Place sugar, water and rind in saucepan and simmer 10 mins. Cool, add lemon juice. Beat egg whites until stiff. Pour strained lemon mixture on to egg whites. Mix well. Pour into refrigerator trays, freeze until mushy. Put back in basin, beat 2 mins, add creme de menthe and freeze just until mushy. Garnish with mint leaves.

187 LEMON OR ORANGE GRANITA

600ml [1 pint] water
250g [8 oz] sugar
300ml [½ pint] lemon juice
  [4-6 lemons] OR

300ml [½ pint] orange juice
[3-5 oranges] plus juice
  of 1 lemon

Place water and sugar in large saucepan and using moderate heat bring to boil, stirring only until sugar dissolves. Cook for exactly 5 mins from the time the mixture begins to boil. Immediately remove from heat and allow to cool to room temperature. Stir in juice. Pour into ice cream tray. Freeze 3-4 hours, stirring every 30 mins and scraping into mixture the ice particles around the edges of the tray. This gives a fine, snowy texture.

For a more authentic Italian effect, use ice cube tray and freeze until solid. Remove cubes and crush in an ice crusher.

188 CHOCOLATE FUDGE SAUCE PUDDING

½ cup SR flour
¼ teaspoon salt
90g [3 oz] sugar
1 tablespoon cocoa
¼ cup milk

1 tablespoon melted butter
Sauce:
½ cup brown sugar
1 rounded tablespoon cocoa
210ml [7 fl oz] very hot water

Sift flour, salt, sugar and cocoa into a bowl. Stir in milk and butter. Into the bottom of a 2 pint casserole, put sauce ingredients and stir. On to sauce put the cake mixture. It does not have to be placed evenly as the cake will rise to the top and the sauce will remain beneath.

Bake for ¾ hour in a moderate oven. Serve with cream or ice cream. For a larger quantity, double the amount of pudding mixture but 1½ times sauce mixture is sufficient.

189 CHOCOLATE FLUFF

125g [4 oz] block
  unsweetened dark
  chocolate
2 teaspoons gelatine
½ cup water

1 can [1¾ cups] evaporated
  milk, chilled
½ cup sugar
cream and chocolate to
  decorate

Melt chocolate in top of double boiler or equivalent. Dissolve gelatine in water. Beat milk until thick and frothy. Add sugar, beat well. Add gelatine and chocolate. Chill in refrigerator and decorate with cream and grated chocolate.

Variation:
Omit chocolate and substitute 2 heaped teaspoons drinking chocolate and 1 heaped teaspoon Milo.

1190 CHOCOLATE CHIFFON

3 teaspoons gelatine
3 tablespoons water
2 eggs, separated
½ cup sugar
5 tablespoons cocoa or
drinking chocolate

1¼ cups milk
1 teaspoon instant coffee
1 teaspoon vanilla
1¼ cups cream, whipped
almonds and cream to garnish

Soften gelatine in water. Beat egg yolks and sugar until light and creamy. Stir in cocoa and milk. Pour into saucepan and while stirring bring to boil. Add coffee, vanilla and gelatine and remove from heat. Cool until starting to set. Beat egg whites stiffly and fold in. Whip cream and stir in, saving a little for garnishing. Rinse mould in cold water and pour mixture into it. Chill until completely set. Turn out on to cold serving dish. Garnish with almonds and cream.

CHOCOLATE PEPPERMINT PIE (R 2408)

Steamed Puddings

1191 HALF HOUR PUDDING

2 eggs
2 tablespoons sugar
2 tablespoons milk

1 cup SR flour, sifted
¼ teaspoon salt
1 tablespoon melted butter

Beat eggs, add sugar and beat well. Add milk and then flour and salt. Lastly add butter. Place in a greased uncovered basin and steam for 30 mins.

Variations:
1. Place 2 tablespoons dark jam in basin before adding batter.
2. Add grated rind of 1 lemon.
3. Add 1 tablespoon marmalade.
4. Add 2 tablespoons cocoa, an extra tablespoon milk and flavour with vanilla.

*Make chocolate curls by "peeling" with a vegetable peeler a block of chocolate at room temperature.

208

1192 CHOCOLATE FRUIT PUDDING

1 cup flour
½ teaspoon bicarbonate of
    soda
1 teaspoon cream of tartar
1 tablespoon cocoa
½ cup mixture chopped
    dates, sultanas and
    walnuts

½ cup milk [approx]
Sauce:
2 teaspoons golden syrup
¼ cup sugar
60g [2 oz] butter
1 cup boiling water
1 tablespoon coconut
    [optional]

Mix all ingredients together, add enough milk to make soft dough and turn into greased pudding basin. Combine sauce ingredients. Pour over dough, steam for 30 mins with lid on saucepan but no cover over basin. Does not spoil if boiled longer.

1193 DATE PUDDING

1 cup flour
½ cup sugar
1 teaspoon bicarbonate
    of soda
1 teaspoon mixed spice

1 cup dates, raisins or
    mixed fruit
1 tablespoon butter dissolved
    in
1 cup hot milk

Mix dry ingredients, add fruit, then gradually stir in milk and butter mixture. Turn into greased pudding basin, cover with lid or greaseproof paper and steam for 2-2½ hours.

1194 CITRUS APPLE PUDDING

½ cup marmalade
1 tablespoon brandy
1 lemon, juice and grated
    rind
60g [2 oz] butter
½ cup sugar

1 egg
¼ cup water
1½ cups SR flour
3 tablespoons powdered milk
2 cups diced apples

Heat marmalade, brandy and lemon juice to boiling and cook over low heat for 3 mins. Cool slightly and pour into well greased basin. Cream butter, sugar and lemon rind. Add egg, beat well then gradually add water. Sift together flour and powdered milk and fold through creamed mixture Add apples and mix well. Spoon into basin on top of marmalade mixture. Cover basin with lid or greaseproof paper and place in saucepan of rapidly boiling water. Reduce heat and steam for 1½ hours.

1195 SAGO PLUM PUDDING

4 tablespoons sago soaked
   overnight in 1 cup milk
½ cup sugar
1 cup soft wholemeal
   breadcrumbs
2 tablespoons melted butter
1 cup raisins
½ cup sultanas

1 teaspoon bicarbonate of
   soda dissolved in
1 tablespoon boiling water
1 tablespoon finely chopped
   preserved ginger [optional]
2 teaspoons finely chopped
   mixed peel [optional]

Mix all ingredients except soda well. If not moist enough, add a little more milk. Lastly add bicarbonate of soda. Pour into greased pudding basin, cover with lid or greaseproof paper and steam for 3 hours.

1196 CHRISTMAS PUDDING

250g [8 oz] cooking apples,
   peeled
500g [1 lb] raisins
250g [8 oz] currants
250g [8 oz] sultanas
125g [4 oz] almonds,
   chopped
6 eggs, well beaten
500g [1 lb] raw sugar
250g [8 oz] flour
375g [12 oz] soft
   breadcrumbs

1 teaspoon cinnamon
½ teaspoon ginger
½ teaspoon nutmeg
1 teaspoon salt
2 tablespoons treacle
2 tablespoons rum or sherry
juice and grated rind of 1
   orange and 1 lemon
500g [1 lb] suet, finely
   chopped

Mince apples, raisins and sultanas. Add other ingredients and mix well together. Stand for 24 hours.
Place in well buttered basin, leaving 1" at top, cover with two circles of buttered greaseproof paper, then a large piece of foil and tie this around rim of basin.
Place in large saucepan of boiling water, with water reaching half way up sides of basin.
Boil for 6-8 hours. As water boils down, replace with boiling water, so that the heat remains constant. Serve with Rum Cream Sauce (R 1027) or Hard Sauce (R 1026),

He may live without love—what is passion but pining?
But where is the man that can live without dining?

Owen Meredith

Better Batter

Better Batters

1200 BATTERS AND PANCAKES

To ensure that your batter does not part company with the food it is coating, always make sure that the meat, fish or fruit is quite dry. Toss in flour before dipping in batter. Shallow or deep fry in hot oil. If the batter is being used for fruit it can be sweetened by the addition of 1-2 teaspoons of sugar.

1201 BATTER (1)

125g [4 oz] flour
¼ teaspoon salt
1 tablespoon oil

150ml [5 fl oz] warm water
1 teaspoon baking powder

Sift flour and salt. Mix with oil and a little water until smooth, beat well, then add gradually rest of water until batter coats the back of the spoon. Just before using, stir in baking powder.

1202 BATTER (2)

125g [4 oz] flour
¼ teaspoon salt

150ml [5 fl oz] milk
1 egg yolk

Sift flour and salt, make a well in the centre, pour in egg yolk and stir gently. Add milk gradually, then beat well to make it smooth and light. Allow to stand about 30 mins before using.

1203 BATTER (3)

A tasty batter for use with fish
125g [4 oz] SR flour
1 tablespoon olive oil
½ teaspoon basil
½ teaspoon rosemary
150ml [5 fl oz] milk or milk and
   water mixed

1 tablespoon brandy
¼ teaspoon salt
1 egg white, stiffly beaten

Mix all ingredients except egg white. Beat well and allow to stand 30 mins. Just before using, fold in stiffly beaten egg white.

212

204 BEER BATTER

250g [8 oz] flour
¼ teaspoon salt
1 tablespoon oil or melted
 butter

¼ cup beer
warm water
1 egg white, stiffly beaten

Sift flour and salt, add oil, gradually stir in beer and enough water to make thin consistency. Allow to stand. Just before using, fold in stiffly beaten egg white.

1205 PANCAKES

125g [4 oz] flour [not whole-
 meal]
¼ teaspoon salt
1 egg + 1 yolk extra

300ml [½ pint] liquid—250ml
 milk, 50ml water
1 tablespoon melted butter
1 teaspoon oil for frying

Sift flour and salt, make a well in the middle, and break in the egg and yolk and stir. Add liquid gradually (or mix all in blender) and continue stirring until all the flour is absorbed. Beat well until smooth. Allow to stand for one hour, then add melted butter. Heat oil in small frying pan, drain and pour in a small quantity of batter. Tilt so that it covers the whole pan very thinly. Cook quickly until edges come away from sides of pan, toss or turn with a spatula and cook other side. Fill and serve. Pancakes may be made in advance, filled if desired, rolled and brushed with melted butter. Reheat on a greased oven tray in 400° oven for 4-5 mins. Alternatively they can be allowed to cool, formed into a stack with a piece of grease-proof paper between each one, and frozen until required.

Filling ideas:
1. Lemon juice, castor sugar.
2. Ricotta cheese, sugar, cinnamon, sultanas.
3. Berry jam. Serve with cream.
4. 250g (8 oz) fruit mince softened in 1 tablespoon brandy.
5. 125g (4 oz) cream cheese, 2 teaspoons lemon juice, 4 tablespoons chopped walnuts.
6. Chocolate sauce.
7. Honey or golden syrup.
See R 435 and R 1811 for savoury fillings.

1206 FRENCH "PANCAKE"

60g [2 oz] butter   60g [2 oz] S.R. flour
2 eggs   300ml [½ pint] milk
60g [2 oz] sugar

Cream butter. Beat eggs until frothy, then add sugar gradually and beat well. Slowly add mixture to creamed butter, stir in flour, mix well and lastly add milk. Beat for a few mins. Pour into a buttered ovenproof dish and bake at 425°F (220°C) for 20 mins or until set. Serve with lemon and sugar, or jam and cream.

1207 CORNMEAL PANCAKES

2 eggs   1⅓ cups cornmeal [polenta]
1½ cups milk   1 teaspoon bicarbonate of soda
3 teaspoons lemon juice   ⅔ cup sifted flour
1½ tablespoons melted butter
   or margarine

Heat frying pan to 350°F (180°C) and grease.
Beat eggs, milk, lemon juice and melted butter. Then add dry ingredients and blend to a smooth batter. Pour batter to make 5" diameter pancakes. Use sweet or savoury filling.

ORANGE AND DATE PIKELETS (R 1441)

MARMALADE PIKELETS (R 1704)

*When draining fried food on paper-towels place some greaseproof paper underneath to prevent bench top becoming greasy. (Why not use old brown-paper bags intead of expensive paper towels? Good for ecology and economy.)

*Grated lemon rind added to batter counteracts greasiness and gives a fresh flavour.

With a Rolling Pin

With a Rolling Pin

Promises and pie-crust are made to be broken.

Jonathan Swift

1300 PASTRY

The recipes in this section have been selected to complement other recipes in the book, rather than to provide a comprehensive range of pastries. If possible make pastry in advance and chill for at least 30 mins to allow for shrinkage. Pastry freezes well so any that is not used can be frozen and if desired, mixed in with a later batch at room temperature. Remember cold, clean hands are essential when making most pastries, so it follows that the surface and utensils should not be warm unless otherwise specified. Pastry is harder to handle on a hot day.

1301 SHORT CRUST PASTRY (1)

250g [8 oz] S.R. flour
¼ teaspoon salt
125g [4 oz] butter or
*   margarine [straight from*
*   the refrigerator]*

½ cup lemon juice
*   and cold water, mixed*
*   together*

For meat pies 1-2 tablespoons meat fat gives added flavour. For fruit tarts, add 1 tablespoon sugar to sifted flour. Sift flour and salt. Rub butter into flour with fingertips until mixture resembles breadcrumbs. Mix into a stiff dough with lemon and water mixture, using a knife. Add more cold water if dough is still very dry. Turn on to floured board and knead a little. Roll to size required and place in refrigerator for 30 mins.

1302 SHORT CRUST PASTRY (2)

(Quick and tasty)
125g [4 oz] butter or
*   margarine, melted*

5 tablespoons cold milk
250g [8 oz] S.R. flour, sifted

Add milk to melted butter, stir in the flour. Roll out between 2 sheets greaseproof paper.

1303 SWEET SHORT CRUST PASTRY

125g [4 oz] S.R. flour
125g [4 oz] flour
¼ teaspoon salt
125g [4 oz] butter

2 tablespoons castor sugar
1 egg yolk
3 tablespoons water

Sift flour and salt, rub in butter. Add sugar. Mix to a dough with yolk and water. Work into ball.

SHORT CRUST PASTRY WITH UNSALTED BUTTER (R 1101)

1304 WHOLEMEAL SWEET SHORT CRUST PASTRY

(Quick and crunchy)

185g [6 oz] wholemeal flour
1 tablespoon sugar or
* warmed honey*

125g [4 oz] butter
2-3 tablespoons cold water

Sift flour, add sugar. Cut butter into flour and rub in lightly with fingers. Using flat knife, mix in water. Roll out, line 8"-10" flan ring or pie tin. Prick bottom. If possible put in freezer for 30 mins. Bake blind (see P 359) at 375°F (190°C) for 10 mins.

Variation:
Substitute 2 tablespoons cornflour or soya bean flour for 2 tablespoons wholemeal flour.

1305 MOTHER'S YUMMY CRUMMY PASTRY

(Very good for apple pie)
60g [2 oz] butter
60g [2 oz] sugar [raw sugar
* adds to flavour]*
¼ cup milk

2 cups wholemeal S.R. flour,
* sifted*
1 egg

Melt butter, sugar, milk slowly in saucepan, leave to cool slightly, then add flour and egg. Mix all this together in saucepan. Place on well floured board, roll and shape to pastry plate. This makes a warm, soft dough. Bake approximately 30 mins at 325°F (160°C).

1306 FOUNDATION BISCUIT PASTRY

125g [4 oz] butter
125g [4 oz] castor sugar OR
   4 tablespoons icing sugar
1 egg

125g [4 oz] flour
125g [4 oz] S.R. flour
a few drops of vanilla

Cream butter and sugar, add egg and blend in thoroughly, add sifted flours and vanilla. Mix to a smooth dough. If using for biscuits knead on board to a creamy consistency. If using for a biscuit or slice base, press into two 7" greased sandwich or lamington tins.

STRUDEL DOUGH (R 1117)

1307 BISCUIT PASTRY

(Quick and easy)
250g [8 oz] butter, melted
3 eggs, beaten
1½ cups flour

1½ cups S.R. flour
¾-1 cup sugar
vanilla

Melt butter in a large saucepan. Add beaten eggs, flour, sugar and vanilla. When well mixed remove pastry and place in greaseproof paper in the refrigerator. This mixture keeps for a long time and is a great time saver. It can be the basis for many desserts, slices and pies.

1308 ALMOND PASTRY (1)

90g [3 oz] plain flour
90g [3 oz] butter

60g [2 oz] ground almonds
30g [1 oz] icing sugar

Blend well together without kneading too much. Roll carefully between 2 sheets of greaseproof paper or press into pie plate. Bake blind (see page 359).

1309 ALMOND PASTRY (2)

1¼ cups plain flour
125g [4 oz] soft butter
3 tablespoons castor sugar

60g [2 oz] ground almonds
2 egg yolks
½ teaspoon vanilla

Knead well together. Work into a ball and chill before rolling between 2 sheets of paper.

218

1310 PUFF PASTRY

(Quickly made)

250g [8 oz] flour	*2 tablespoons water*
¼ teaspoon salt	*squeeze lemon*
185g [6 oz] butter	

Sift flour into basin with pinch of salt, cut butter into flour, then chop with a knife. Mix into dough with water and lemon, roll out very thinly, fold over 3 times, and roll out 3 times.

PUFF PASTRY IDEAS (R 1104)

1311 QUICHE PASTRY

125g [4 oz] butter, melted	*125g [4 oz] flour*
125g [4 oz] cottage cheese	

Melt butter and rub into cheese and flour until smooth. Press into 9" round quiche dish or tin. Chill for 30 mins before filling.

QUICHE (R 415)

1312 CHOUX PASTRY

60g [2 oz] butter	*salt*
½ cup water	*2 eggs*
½ cup flour, sifted	

Bring butter and water to boil, remove from heat and add sifted flour and salt. Return to heat, all the time beating mixture with wooden spoon until it forms one ball and leaves side of saucepan (up to 3 mins). Cool slightly and beat in each egg thoroughly. The mixture is then ready for use, and is easily handled in a forcing bag. For uses see R 1404, R 1405, R 122.

RICH CREAM DOUGH (R 1620)

SOUR CREAM PASTRIES (R 2411)

Who Cares about Calories?

Who Cares About Calories?

1400 CAKES, LOAVES, SCONES AND ICINGS

Cakes

Who does not love cakes? Even if we have to watch our weight, and our vitamins, there is no need to go without cakes altogether, just be sensible. Try replacing white flour in whole or in part with wholemeal flour in darker coloured cakes (e.g. fruit, chocolate). It gives these cakes a nuttier texture and varies the taste but it also makes them drier so add an extra tablespoonful of liquid. Some cakes using milk can have skimmed powdered milk added to the dry ingredients. Many of the cakes in this section are also good as desserts, served hot or cold with cream, custard or ice-cream.

Basic cakes can be made by either of two methods. In one, the butter or margarine is creamed, in the other, it is softened or melted. The latter is a quicker method although the result may be a little drier, thus it lends itself to flavoured cakes.

1401 BASIC PLAIN CAKE

125g [4 oz] butter
125g [4 oz] sugar
2 eggs, well beaten
250g [8 oz] S.R. flour
¼ teaspoon salt
½ cup milk
½ teaspoon vanilla

Grease an orange cake tin. Heat oven to 350°F (180°C). Sift flour and salt. Beat butter and sugar until light and creamy. Add beaten eggs gradually. Add flour and salt alternately with milk and vanilla. Put in tin and bake for 40-45 mins.

1402 PATTY CAKES

As R 1401 but in paper patty cases. Makes approximately 24. Instead of icing these cakes, try adding one tablespoon of any of the following toppings before cooking:

1. Grate a mixture of plain dark chocolate and walnut pieces over cakes until there is a ¼" layer of mixed chocolate and walnuts.
2. Colour a small quantity of desiccated coconut with food colouring and sprinkle over cakes.
3. Mix finely chopped lemon and orange peel, or red and green cherries and moisten with a little sieved apricot jam, and spread over cakes.

Bake for 12-15 mins.

222

1403 CHERRY CAKES

As R 1402 but add 60g (2 oz) chopped cherries and 1 cup crushed cornflakes to basic patty mixture. May require a little extra milk. Place on well greased oven tray in tablespoonfuls or bake whole mixture in orange cake tin.
Bake for 12-15 mins.

1404 ECLAIRS

1 quantity choux pastry [R 1312]   *chocolate icing*
whipped cream

Heat oven to 400°F (200°C).
Pipe out "sausages" about 3"-5" long on to greased and floured baking sheet. Bake for 30 mins until brown, risen and hollow. Remove and place on wire rack. Slit side with sharp knife and if there is any soft mixture left inside, scoop out, otherwise eclair will go soft.
Fill with whipped cream and pour thin chocolate icing over.

Variation:
1405 CREAM PUFFS

Pipe out rounds the size of a tablespoon on to greased and floured baking sheet. When cool, fill with whipped sweetened cream and dust with sieved icing sugar.

1406 CREAM CAKES

2 eggs   *1 cup S.R. flour, sifted*
¾ cup cream, fresh or sour   *1 teaspoon vanilla*
¾ cup sugar   *jam*

Heat oven to 400°F (200°C). Break eggs into a cup and fill to the top with cream. Add sugar and beat. Stir in flour and vanilla. Place in patty pans and cook for 12-15 mins. When cool, fill with jam. Ice or dip in partially set jelly.

Variation:
1407 LAMINGTON CAKE

Cook in loaf tin in moderate oven 350°F (180°C) for 35-40 mins. When cool, cut in two, join with raspberry jam. Ice with chocolate icing (R 1443) and sprinkle with coconut.

FRUIT TARTS (R 1102-9)

JAM TARTS (R 2125)

1408 ROCK CAKES

250g [8 oz] S.R. flour
¼ teaspoon salt
½ teaspoon cinnamon
¼ teaspoon nutmeg
125g [4 oz] butter
90g [3 oz] sugar

½ cup sultanas
½ cup dates
60g [2 oz] walnuts, in small pieces
1 egg, beaten
3 tablespoons milk

Grease an oven tray. Sift flour, salt and spices, rub in butter, add sugar, fruit and nuts. Mix into firm dough with egg and milk. Heat oven to 375°F (190°C). Allow mixture to stand for 10 mins. Place teaspoonfuls on tray. Bake 12-15 mins.

1409 SIMPLICITY CHOCOLATE CAKE

2 tablespoons margarine or butter
2 tablespoons cocoa
1 cup S.R. flour
1 cup sugar

½ cup milk
2 eggs
½ teaspoon vanilla
½ teaspoon instant coffee

Grease an 8" ring tin. Heat oven to 350°F (180°C). Melt butter. Put all other ingredients in basin and add butter. Beat for 3 mins. Put in tin. Bake for 30 mins. Can also be cooked by placing tin on asbestos mat in frypan at 420°F (220°C).
This is even simpler if the saucepan used to melt the butter is also used to melt a little extra butter to grease sides of ring tin, and is then retained further to melt butter to make an icing for cake once it is cooled.

Variations:
Omit cocoa and coffee and add 2 additional tablespoons S.R. flour plus—
1. Coffee—1½ tablespoons coffee essence or 3½ teaspoons instant coffee mixed with 3 tablespoons hot water then cooled.
2. Orange—grated rind of one orange and 2 tablespoons orange juice.
3. Lemon—grated rind of one lemon plus few drops lemon essence or lemon juice.
4. Ginger—3 teaspoons powdered ginger, and 1 teaspoon golden syrup added to butter when melting it.
5. Cinnamon—1 heaped teaspoon cinnamon.
6. Banana—one ripe mashed banana. If desired use less sugar.
7. Fruit—2 tablespoons sultanas or mixed fruit.
8. Wholemeal—use wholemeal S.R. flour.

1410 CHOCOLATE APPLE CAKE

4-6 apples
2 teaspoons bicarbonate of
   soda
125g [4 oz] margarine
1 cup brown sugar
2 teaspoons cinnamon
½ teaspoon nutmeg
1½ teaspoons cocoa
2 cups S.R. flour
¼ teaspoon salt

Grease a 7" square tin. Stew apples in as little water as possible. While still warm, add bicarbonate of soda, and put through a sieve. Allow to cool. Heat oven to 350°F (180°C). Cream margarine and sugar together until sugar is well dissolved. Add apple mixture. Fold in cinnamon, nutmeg, cocoa, salt and flour. Bake for 45 mins. This cake remains moist, especially if kept in refrigerator.

GERMAN APPLE CAKE (R 1116)

1411 APPLE TEA CAKE

60g [2 oz] margarine
60g [2 oz] brown sugar
1 egg
4 tablespoons milk
lemon essence
125g [4 oz] wholemeal S.R.
   flour, sifted
salt
1 apple, peeled and sliced
Topping:
¾ teaspoon cinnamon
1 tablespoon castor sugar

Grease a 7" tin. Heat oven to 350°F (180°C). Cream butter and brown sugar. Add egg and beat well. Mix in milk, essence, flour and salt. Place in tin. Arrange apple slices on top. Sprinkle with cinnamon and sugar. Bake for 25-30 mins.

1412 DUTCH TART

Heat oven to 375°F (190°C). Line a 7" sponge tin with biscuit pastry (R 1308), and spread with raspberry jam or a layer of drained fruit. Then add the following cake mixture:

3 tablespoons butter
½ cup sugar
1 egg, beaten
¼ cup milk
3 tablespoons S.R. flour
1 teaspoon cinnamon
2 teaspoons mixed spice
2 tablespoons walnuts,
   chopped

Cream butter and sugar. Add egg and milk. Mix in the other ingredients. Spread into the lined tin and bake for 15 mins, then reduce temperature to 350°F (180°C) and bake further 30 mins. When cold, ice with lemon icing.

1413 PASSIONFRUIT SHORTCAKE

Shortcake
250g [8 oz] S.R. flour
125g [4 oz] butter or margarine
125g [4 oz] sugar
1 egg
a little extra sugar

Filling
1 cup icing sugar
1½ tablespoons softened
butter
passionfruit [or orange or
lemon juice]

Grease well an 8" sandwich tin. Heat oven to 350°F (180°C).
Sift flour into a basin. Rub in butter and add the sugar. Beat
the egg and add to the mixture, making a rather dry, crumbly
dough. Pack into the tin. Rough the surface with a fork and
sprinkle with a little castor sugar. Bake about 30 mins and
cool. Cut the shortcake through the centre, making 2 thin
layers. Cream the butter for the filling and gradually work in
the icing sugar and enough passionfruit (or substitute) to give
the consistency of whipped cream. Spread on one layer of the
shortbread and cover with the other half.

Variation: A good dessert is made by substituting whipped
cream and strawberries for the filling. Sieve icing sugar lightly
over top.

1414 PINEAPPLE UPSIDE-DOWN CAKE

1 quantity Basic Plain Cake
mixture [R 1401]
60g [2 oz] light brown sugar
60g [2 oz] butter

1 425g [15½ oz] can sliced
pineapple [or peach or pear
halves], drained
30g [1 oz] glace cherries

Heat oven to 350°F (180°C). Soften butter and mix with brown
sugar. Spread evenly over base of 8" cake tin. Drain fruit and
arrange in pattern on top of butter and sugar mixture, decorate
with the cherries. Spread the plain cake mixture evenly over the
fruit. Bake for 35-40 mins. Remove from oven and allow to
stand 3-4 mins before inverting on to a serving dish. Most
suitable as a hot dessert, as well as a cake.

HEDGEHOG CAKE (R 1533)

*To soften icing sugar which has gone hard, place in a hot oven for a few
minutes.

1415 WALNUT LAYER CAKE

Grease a deep 7" tin (springform if possible). Heat oven to 350°F (180°C). Make as R 1401 but separate eggs. Beat whites stiffly, beat yolks and add to creamed butter and sugar. Fold in flour, salt, milk, and vanilla then fold in stiffly beaten egg whites. Spread half the mixture in tin.

Filling
75g [½ cup] brown sugar   2 tablespoons melted butter
¾ cup chopped walnuts   2 tablespoons plain flour
2 teaspoons cinnamon

Mix all ingredients thoroughly and spread half of this filling on mixture in tin. Spread over remainder of cake mixture, then remainder of filling. Bake 45-50 mins.

1416 SPONGE CAKE (1)

4 eggs, separated   1 teaspoon cream of tartar
155g [5 oz] castor sugar   salt
15g [½ oz] plain flour   1 teaspoon vanilla
90g [3 oz] cornflour   1 tablespoon boiling water
½ teaspoon bicarbonate of
  soda

Grease a 12" x 9" baking dish. Heat oven 375°F (190°C). Beat egg whites until stiff. Gradually add sugar, beat well. Add egg yolks. Sieve all dry ingredients together twice and fold into mixture. Add vanilla. Fold in boiling water. Bake 20 mins or until centre springs back when lightly pressed with thumb.

Variations:
1. Ginger: Sieve 1 teaspoon ginger with flour, omit vanilla but gradually fold in 1 teaspoon warmed golden syrup to mixed dry ingredients.
2. Cocoa: As above but substitute cocoa for ginger.
3. Spice: As above but substitute spice for ginger.
4. Powder Puffs: Place teaspoonfuls of mixture on a hot greased tray and bake in hot oven for 5 mins. Store in airtight jar until required. Six hours before serving, cream, join in pairs and dust with icing sugar.

*To give a sponge cake a professional effect, spread base and sides of cake tin with a paste of 1 tablespoon melted copha and 1 tablespoon plain flour.

1417 SPONGE CAKE (2)

4 eggs
185g [6 oz] castor sugar
185g [6 oz] S.R. flour

3 tablespoons lukewarm
water

Grease and flour two 8" sandwich tins. Heat oven to 375°F (190°C). Beat eggs until very thick and light, add sugar gradually. When all sugar has been added, continue beating for 10-15 mins. Add 1 tablespoon water and fold in. Sift flour over top of mixture and carefully fold in, then add remaining water. Fold in gently but thoroughly. Divide mixture evenly into two tins. Bake for 25-30 mins. Turn out, cool and fill with jam and/or whipped cream.

1418 BOILED FRUIT CAKE

(A favourite with NMAA members).

375g [12 oz] mixed dried fruit
1 cup water [substitute part
   or whole with sherry,
   brandy, or rum if you like]
125g [4 oz] butter
125g [4 oz] sugar
1 teaspoon mixed spice
1 teaspoon bicarbonate of soda

2 eggs, beaten
125g [4 oz] wholemeal S.R.
   flour
125g [4 oz] wholemeal plain
   flour
2 tablespoons wheat germ,
   [optional]

Grease and line a 7" square tin. Place fruit, water, butter, sugar and spice in large saucepan. Bring to boil and simmer gently 1 min. Allow to cool. Heat oven to 350°F (180°C). Stir in remaining ingredients and mix well. Pour mixture into tin and bake for 1¼-1½ hours, reducing heat to 325°F (160°C) after 15 mins.

Variations:
1. Add some chopped walnuts.
2. Add 425g (15 oz) can crushed pineapple. Drain, keep fluid and make up to 1 cup with water to replace water as above. Mix crushed pineapple into fruit mixture after it has cooled.

DESPERATION CAKE (R 1431)

*Use any left-over whipped cream to pipe stars and swirls on a sheet of foil, and freeze. When frozen hard, lift them carefully. Drop into a screw-topped jar and store in the freezer, for quick decoration of cakes, desserts, etc. Place them in position while still frozen—they thaw in a few minutes.

1419 PUMPKIN FRUIT CAKE

This is a moist, wholesome cake and cheap to make when pumpkins are in season.

1 cup mashed pumpkin
500g [1 lb] mixed dried fruit
125g [4 oz] raw sugar
1 tablespoon golden syrup
1 cup water
1 teaspoon bicarbonate of
  soda

2 eggs
125g [4 oz] wholemeal plain
  flour
125g [4 oz] wholemeal S.R.
  flour

Grease a round 8" tin. Boil and mash pumpkin. Cool. At the same time put fruit, sugar, syrup and water in a saucepan and bring to the boil. Remove from heat and add bicarbonate of soda. Cool. Heat oven to 325°F (160°C). Beat eggs. Add cold pumpkin and fruit mixture and beat until smooth. Stir in flour and bake for 1½ hours.

1420 CARROT CAKE

3 eggs
1 cup white sugar
¾ cup cooking oil
1⅓ cups flour
½ teaspoon salt
1⅓ teaspoons bicarbonate of
  soda

1⅓ teaspoons baking powder
1⅓ teaspoons cinnamon
2 cups grated raw carrot
½ cup nuts
1 teaspoon vanilla

Grease a square 8" tin. Heat oven to 300°F (150°C). Beat eggs and sugar until frothy. Add oil, stir in sifted dry ingredients and lastly fold in carrot, nuts and vanilla. Bake for 1 hour. When cool, ice as below.

Icing:
Combine—

4 oz cream cheese,
250g [½ lb] icing sugar

3 tablespoons butter
1 teaspoon vanilla

*When separating eggs and some of the yolk escapes into the white it can be easily removed using a piece of eggshell.

1421 GLACE FRUIT CAKE

250g [8 oz] dessert dates
250g [8 oz] glace pineapple
125g [4 oz] glace apricots
250g [8 oz] shelled hazelnuts
60g [2 oz] glace cherries—red
60g [2 oz] glace cherries—
   green
125g [4 oz] raisins

2 eggs
½ cup brown sugar
1 teaspoon vanilla
1 tablespoon brandy
90g [3 oz] softened butter
½ cup wholemeal S.R. flour
salt
2 tablespoons brandy [extra]

Grease and line a 9" x 5" loaf tin. Heat oven to 275°F (140°C). Stone and chop dates. Chop pineapple and apricots into fairly large pieces, halve nuts crosswise; leave cherries and raisins whole. Beat eggs until light and fluffy, add sugar, vanilla, brandy and butter. Continue beating until well blended. Sift flour and salt, add to creamed mixture with fruit and nuts. Mix well. Spoon into tin. Bake for approximately 1½ hours. Remove from oven and while hot pour extra brandy over cake. Cool in tin standing on a wire rack. When completely cool, take out of tin and wrap in foil or put in airtight container.

1422 DATE CAKE

250g [8 oz] dates, chopped
½ cup boiling water
½ teaspoon bicarbonate of
   soda
125g [4 oz] butter
90g [3 oz] sugar
2 eggs

2 heaped tablespoons S.R.
   flour
2 level tablespoons plain
   flour
1 tablespoon cocoa
3-4 tablespoons desiccated
   coconut

Soak dates one hour or more in boiling water and bicarbonate of soda. Heat oven to 375°F (190°C). Line a 7" square tin with paper. Cream butter and sugar, add eggs and beat well. Sieve flours and cocoa together and fold into the mixture. Fold in dates and coconut. Bake for 45 mins. When cool, ice with pink coconut icing.

*Home-made baking powder
1 level tablespoon bicarbonate of soda
2¼ level tablespoons cream of tartar
Sift together several times to ensure even distribution and store in a screw-top jar. Do not store longer than 1 week. The correct proportions for most cakes and pastries are 15g (4 teaspoons) to 500g (1 lb) flour.

*Make extra working space on baking day by opening a top drawer under a bench and resting a tray or pastry board on it.

423 FRUIT CAKE

250g [8 oz] butter
250g [8 oz] sugar
4 eggs, beaten
vanilla or rum essence
250g [8 oz] plain flour
60g [2 oz] S.R. flour
1 teaspoon mixed spice
1 teaspoon cinnamon
½ teaspoon ground ginger
375g [12 oz] sultanas
250g [8 oz] seeded raisins,
  chopped

250g [8 oz] currants
125g [4 oz] mixed peel
60g [2 oz] blanched almonds
30g [1 oz] crystallized cherries
¼ teaspoon bicarbonate of
  soda
1 tablespoon water
1 teaspoon golden syrup or
  1 tablespoon brandy

Line bottom and sides of 8" tin with a double layer of brown paper cut to size and extending 1½" above top of sides. Heat oven to 400°F (200°C). Cream butter and sugar. Beat eggs and add gradually. Add essence. Sift together flour and spices. Split almonds in half (saving 6 whole ones for garnish). Mix fruit and almonds into flour. Dissolve bicarbonate of soda in water and add golden syrup or brandy. Pour on to fruit and flour mixture, add butter, sugar and eggs, stir until thoroughly blended. Place in lined tin and decorate with 6 whole almonds. Bake, lowering heat after 10 mins to 325°F (160°C). Check after 2 hours and lower temperature to 300°F (150°C) if browning easily. Cook 4 hours in all.

424 HALVA CAKE

185g [6 oz] butter
185g [6 oz] castor sugar
4 eggs
juice and rind of 1 orange
315g [10 oz] semolina
2 teaspoons baking powder
125g [4 oz] ground almonds

Syrup
250g [8 oz] sugar
¼ pint water
small stick cinnamon
3 tablespoons orange juice
1 tablespoon lemon juice

Grease 7" square cake tin. Heat oven to 350°F (180°C). Cream butter and castor sugar until very light and fluffy. Beat in the eggs one at a time and stir in rind and juice of 1 orange. Add semolina, baking powder and ground almonds and mix well. Pour into tin and bake for 40 mins until top is golden. Meanwhile boil sugar, water, cinnamon, orange and lemon juices. Simmer until slightly thickened. Remove cake from the oven and pour hot syrup over it. Allow to cool. Serve cut into squares—may be served with cream as a dessert if desired.

1425 CHRISTMAS CAKE

125g [4 oz] glace cherries
125g [4 oz] glace pineapple
125g [4 oz] prunes, stoned
125g [4 oz] dried apricots
125g [4 oz] currants
250g [8 oz] sultanas
250g [8 oz] raisins
6 tablespoons rum
1 cup honey
250g [8 oz] butter
2 teaspoons grated lemon rind
5 eggs

1 tablespoon plum jam
315g [10 oz] plain flour
½ teaspoon cinnamon
¼ teaspoon nutmeg
¼ teaspoon mixed spice
1 cooking apple, grated
125g [4 oz] mixed peel
125g [4 oz] almonds
¼ teaspoon bicarbonate of
  soda
1 tablespoon boiling water
2 tablespoons brandy

Chop cherries, pineapple, prunes and apricots, add currants, sultanas and raisins, mix well together, pour rum over, leave overnight.

Next day, line 8" square tin with 3 thicknesses of paper, greasing paper next to mixture. Heat oven to 350°F (180°C). Cream honey, butter and lemon rind, add eggs one at a time. Mix in plum jam. Sift flour and spices and fold into the mixture. Add apple, peel, soaked fruits and almonds. Mix in soda dissolved in 1 tablespoon boiling water. Turn into tin. Hollow out centre of cake slightly and bake for 1 hour, then lower oven to 300°F (150°C) for further 1-2 hours. Sprinkle with brandy when cooked.

Loaves

Loaves freeze well but must be securely wrapped first. Slice and butter to serve, although they are nice even without butter when freshly made.

1426 BANANA DATE LOAF

90g [3 oz] butter
½ cup raw sugar
grated rind of 1 orange
2 eggs
1 cup chopped dates

3 large bananas, mashed [the
  riper the better]
2½ cups wholemeal S.R.
  flour
⅓ cup orange juice

Grease two 9" x 5" tins and line with greased paper. Heat oven to 350°F (180°C). Cream butter and sugar, add orange rind, then eggs. Beat well. Add dates and bananas. Sift flour and add it alternately with orange juice. Place mixture into tins and bake for 50-60 mins. Slice and butter.

427 BANANA LOAF

125g [4 oz] butter or margarine
¾ cup raw sugar
1 egg
1 cup wholemeal plain flour
½ cup wholemeal S.R. flour
¾ teaspoon salt
1¼ cups mashed bananas,
  2 large or 3 small
¼ cup yoghurt or buttermilk

Grease a 9" x 5" loaf tin. Heat oven to 375°F (190°C). Cream butter and sugar until very light and creamy. Add egg, beat well. Combine bananas and yoghurt, stirring just enough to mix. Add flours and salt alternately with banana mixture to creamed butter, stirring just enough to combine well. Turn into tin. Bake for 50 mins. Cool for 10 mins in tin, then turn out on to wire rack.

428 LEMON BREAD

90g [3 oz] butter or margarine
1 cup castor sugar
2 eggs
1½ cups plain flour
1 teaspoon baking powder
¼ teaspoon salt
½ cup milk
1 tablespoon grated lemon
  rind
1 tablespoon lemon juice
½ cup sultanas
½ cup chopped dried
  apricots

Grease an 8" x 4" loaf tin. Heat oven to 375°F (190°C). Melt butter, mix in sugar. Add eggs, one at a time, beat well. Add sifted flour and dry ingredients alternately with milk. Fold in lemon rind, juice, sultanas and apricots. Pour into tin. Bake for 50-60 mins. While still hot, gradually spoon lemon syrup over the bread.

Lemon syrup
Stir 2 tablespoons lemon juice and ½ cup castor sugar over low heat until sugar dissolves.
This loaf freezes particularly well. To freeze, wrap in foil, then put in plastic bag. To serve, remove plastic bag, place foil wrapped loaf in warm oven for about one hour. Slice and butter.

*No time to ice that plain cake you're baking? Grate apple on top and sprinkle with cinnamon and sugar before baking.

1429 FRUIT LOAF (BROWN BETTY)

¾ cup raw sugar
1 teaspoon mixed spice
1 cup mixed dried fruit
1 cup milk and water mixed
2 cups S.R. flour or 1¾ cups
   S.R. flour and ¼ cup
   wheat germ

salt
2 tablespoons butter
coconut

Grease and line a 9" x 5" loaf tin. Heat oven to 400°F (200°C). Mix sugar, spice, fruit, and milk and water in small bowl. Sift flour and salt into large bowl and rub in butter. Add contents of small bowl to flour mixture and mix to a fairly wet consistency. Turn into baking tin and sprinkle liberally with coconut. Bake for 30-45 mins. Remove from oven and leave to cool in cake tin for 1 hour. This loaf can be cooked in a small sized billy without the lid. Slice and butter.

Variations:

1. Substitute for mixed fruit and spice, 1 cup chopped dates, 1 heaped teaspoon ginger.
2. Instead of sprinkling top with coconut before cooking, rub top with knob of butter and sprinkle with a mixture of sugar and cinnamon while still hot after taking loaf out of oven.

1430 BRAN LOAF

1 cup bran
1 cup milk
½ cup brown or raw sugar

1 cup wholemeal S.R. flour
1 tablespoon golden syrup
1 cup sultanas

Grease 9" x 5" loaf tin. Combine bran with golden syrup, sugar, milk and sultanas, and allow to stand 2 hours or longer, until bran is softened. Heat oven to 375°F (190°C). Sift flour and stir in. Bake for approximately 50-60 mins. Alternatively, spoon mixture into 2 well greased soup tins. cover with **greaseproof paper, stand in large saucepan or boiler with** boiling water ⅓ of the way up tins. Keep water gently boiling for 1½ hours.

Variations:

1. Replace sultanas with chopped, dried apricots.
2. Replace sultanas with chopped dates and nuts.
3. Add 1 well-mashed banana as well as sultanas.
4. Use 3 whole wheat breakfast biscuits instead of bran.
5. Cook mixture in patty pans for 15-17 mins.

234

431 DESPERATION CAKE

75g [2½ oz] butter
1 cup sultanas
1¾ cups S.R. flour, not sifted
1 cup brown sugar

1 teaspoon vanilla
¼ teaspoon salt
1 teaspoon baking powder
½ cup milk

Turn oven on to 350°F (180°C), put butter in fruit cake tin and place in oven. Measure out sultanas, mix with flour and shake in a paper bag to coat them well. Take out the tin, rinse with the melted butter and drain it into a bowl. Add sugar, vanilla and salt and mix well. Stir in all other ingredients, return to buttered tin, cook about 45 mins. Serve with butter.

432 BARM BRACK

500g [16 oz] mixed dried fruit
   e.g. dates and raisins OR
   500g [16 oz] currants
1 cup brown sugar

1 cup cold black tea
2 cups S.R. flour
1 egg

Soak fruit with sugar in the tea overnight. Heat oven to 300°F (150°C). Grease 9" x 5" loaf tin. Add flour and well beaten egg to fruit mixture. Place in tin. Bake for 2 hours in middle shelf of oven. Serve in buttered slices.

433 APPLE BARM BRACK

3-4 apples
250g [8 oz] S.R. flour
125g [4 oz] butter or margarine

125g [4 oz] sugar
250g [8 oz] dried fruit

Grease 9" x 5" loaf tin. Stew apple in a little water and cool. Heat oven to 350°F (180°C). Sift flour, rub in shortening. Add remaining ingredients and mix well. Pour into greased loaf tin. Bake for approximately 1¼ hours.

434 PEANUT BUTTER BREAD

2 cups flour
3 teaspoons baking powder
1 teaspoon salt
½ cup sugar

1 cup milk
2 eggs
1 cup peanut butter

Grease a 9" x 5" loaf tin. Heat oven to 350°F (180°C). Sift first three ingredients. Add sugar. Beat milk, eggs and peanut butter well. Add to dry ingredients and beat until blended. Pour into tin and bake for one hour.

1435 NUT LOAF

185g [6 oz] S.R. flour
¼ teaspoon salt
½ teaspoon mixed spice
1 teaspoon butter

60g [2 oz] mixed nuts and
raisins, chopped
60g [2 oz] sugar
½ cup milk

Grease 8" x 4" nut loaf tin. Heat oven to 350°F (180°C). Sift flour, salt and spice. Rub in butter, add nuts and sugar. Mix into a soft dough with milk. Half fill tin with mixture and put in oven. Bake for 25-30 mins. If you do not have a nut loaf tin, two soup cans with the lids removed can be used instead. Fill to within 2" of top to allow for rising of loaf. Stand on oven tray. Slice and butter to serve.

1436 COCONUT LOAF

This would not win a prize for nutrition but is very easy when you need a "plate" for meetings, etc.

1 cup coconut
1 cup S.R. flour

¾ cup sugar
¾ cup milk

Heat oven to 375°F (190°C). Mix all ingredients together and cook in well greased loaf tin for 40-45 mins.

1437 HONEY LOAF

250ml [8 fl oz] milk
125g [4 oz] raw sugar
125g [4 oz] runny honey

280g [9 oz] wholemeal S.R.
flour

Heat oven to 350°F (180°C). Grease a 9" x 5" loaf tin. Heat half quantity of milk and stir in sugar and honey. Add rest of milk. Fold in the flour. Bake 1 hour. Delicious with butter when fresh, and honey later on if it ever gets to that stage.

1438 SOYA SELF-RAISING FLOUR

When making white scones and drop scones, soya bean flour gives extra nourishment and flavour. Keep a supply of this made up specially.

220g [7 oz] plain flour
30g [1 oz] soya bean flour

3-4 teaspoons baking powder

Sift together 3 times.

Scones

439 SCONES

250g [8 oz] S.R. flour
½ teaspoon salt
2 tablespoons powdered skim milk [optional]

1 tablespoon butter
1 cup milk
milk or egg yolk for glazing

Heat oven to 425°F (220°C). Grease scone tray or oven slide. Sift flour, salt and skim milk. Cut butter into flour and using fingers rub in lightly. Mix to a soft dough with milk. Turn on to a floured surface and knead slightly. The less the dough is handled, the lighter the scones will be. Flatten out with heel of hand to approx ½" in thickness. Stamp out with scone cutter or glass dipped in flour. Place scones touching each other on tray, glaze tops with milk or egg yolk. Bake 8-10 mins.

Variations:

1. Yoghurt: Use yoghurt instead of milk or ½ yoghurt and ½ milk.
2. Cheese: Add 2 tablespoons grated cheese.
3. Date: Add ½ cup chopped dates and 1 tablespoon sugar.
4. Egg: Crack an egg into measuring cup, fill to 1 cup with milk, beat together before mixing into flour.
5. Wholemeal honey: Use wholemeal S.R. flour, omit butter and add 2 tablespoons honey dissolved in the milk.
6. Savoury: Add 2-3 tablespoons finely chopped cooked bacon, 2 tablespoons finely chopped cooked onion, 1 teaspoon curry powder, and 2 teaspoons finely chopped parsley.

440 DROP SCONES

½ cup wholemeal flour
4 tablespoons powdered milk
1½ teaspoons baking powder
½ cup milk

½ teaspoon salt
1 tablespoon golden syrup, sugar or honey
1 egg

Heat frypan or griddle to 350°F (180°C) and grease lightly. Mix all ingredients together. Drop tablespoonfuls on to greased frypan, cook until mixture bubbles, then turn to other side until brown.

·If you haven't any SR flour, substitute baking powder and plain flour (4 teaspoons to 500g, 1 lb).

1441 ORANGE AND DATE PIKELETS

1 cup S.R. flour
4 tablespoons castor sugar
salt
bicarbonate of soda
1 egg [2 eggs make a tastier pikelet]

½ cup milk
rind of 1 orange, grated
¼ cup orange juice
⅓ cup finely chopped dates

Heat frypan or griddle to 350°F (180°C) and grease lightly. Sift flour, sugar, salt and bicarbonate of soda into basin. Make well in centre of dry ingredients, add egg and milk, beat well to make a smooth batter. Add orange juice and rind, and dates. Beat thoroughly. Drop tablespoonfuls of mixture on to pan. Cook until bubbles rise to surface, but do not break. Turn and cook other side until golden brown. Serve buttered. Makes approximately 24.

MARMALADE PIKELETS (R 1704)

Icings

1442 ROYAL ICING

250g [8 oz] pure icing sugar
1 egg white

1 teaspoon lemon juice

Put egg white in bowl, beat slightly with wooden spoon. Add sugar very gradually, beating with spoon. When thick and smooth add lemon juice and beat again.

1443 LEMON GLACE ICING

1 cup icing sugar
2 teaspoons melted butter

1 tablespoon lemon juice
¼ teaspoon lemon essence

Variations:
1. Almond: Omit lemon juice and essence and substitute 1 teaspoon vanilla, ¼ teaspoon almond essence and a little water.
2. Coffee: Omit lemon juice and essence and substitute 1 teaspoon instant coffee dissolved in 1 tablespoon water.
3. Chocolate: Omit lemon juice, essence and butter and substitute 2 tablespoons grated chocolate or 1 tablespoon cocoa and 1½ tablespoons hot water.

LEMON ICING (R 1520, R 1531)
CREAM CHEESE ICING (R 1420)
MARSHMALLOW ICING (R 2128)

238

The Biscuit Barrel

The Biscuit Barrel

1500 BISCUITS AND SLICES

Homemade biscuits and slices have a distinction all of their own. Firstly the ingredients are known to mother, and secondly, baked in quantity they provide a supply that economically surpasses any bought ones. While most mothers encourage their children to eat fruit, a biscuit often satisfies that desire for something sweet. You may find it easier and quicker to make some of these biscuit recipes as slices and cut them into squares after cooking.

Biscuits

1501 FOUNDATION BISCUIT MIXTURE

125g [4 oz] butter
125g [4 oz] sugar [castor or
  icing]
1 egg
flavouring
125g [4 oz] S.R. flour
125g [4 oz] plain flour

Cream the butter and sugar, add egg and flavouring, mix thoroughly. Add sifted flours and mix to a smooth dough. Knead to a creamy consistency on a floured surface. Roll and cut as you wish. Bake on greased tray in moderate oven 350°F (180°C) for 15-20 mins.

Variations:

1. **Almond:** Use almond essence as flavouring. Place in small teaspoonfuls on greased oven tray. Place ½ almond on top of each.

2. **Chocolate:** Omit 1 tablespoon flour, add 1 tablespoon cocoa and a few drops rum essence and/or grated chocolate or chocolate chips.

3. **Cinnamon:** Omit 1 tablespoon flour, add 2 teaspoons cinnamon.

4. **Coconut:** Omit 3 tablespoons flour, add 3 tablespoons coconut.

5. **Cherry and Coconut:** Omit 1 tablespoon flour, add 1 tablespoon coconut, 90g (3 oz) chopped cherries, grated rind 1 lemon, 1 tablespoon lemon juice. Roll in small balls in extra coconut.

6. **Bran:** Substitute bran for plain flour. Roll to 1/8" thickness, cut into fingers. Serve with butter and honey.

7. **Oatmeal:** Omit 125g (4 oz) plain flour, substitute 90g (3 oz) oatmeal, chopped finely in blender, few drops vanilla. Use wholemeal S.R. flour. Roll out thinly, cut into shapes.

1502 MACAROONS

3-4 egg whites [at room
   temperature]
250g [8 oz] castor sugar
125g [4 oz] ground almonds

squeeze lemon juice or grated
   rind one orange
icing sugar

Whip egg whites stiffly, add sugar slowly, until all absorbed, add ground almonds, and lemon juice or orange rind. Drop a teaspoonful at a time on to greaseproof paper or rice paper sprinkled with sugar, or pipe with forcing bag with a plain or star nozzle. Dust with sifted icing sugar to make tops crack. Bake in a slow oven 325°F (160°C) for 30-40 mins. Cool on a cake rack.

Variation: Omit ground almonds, add 125g (4 oz) coconut.

MERINGUES (R 2126)

1503 SPICE CRINKLES

185g [6 oz] S.R. wholemeal
   or white flour
¼ teaspoon salt
¼ teaspoon bicarbonate of
   soda
1 teaspoon cinnamon

½ teaspoon mixed spice
¼ teaspoon grated nutmeg
60g [2 oz] butter or margarine
60g [2 oz] raw sugar
1 tablespoon honey
1 egg

Sift together wholemeal flour, salt, soda, cinnamon, spice, and grated nutmeg. Cream shortening and sugar with honey. Beat in egg gradually. Mix in dry ingredients. Cool until firm. Roll into small balls. Dip tops in sugar. Place with sugar sides up on greased tray, allowing space for spreading. Cover cookies with a wet cloth and press lightly. Remove cloth and bake at 350°F (180°C) for 10-15 mins.

1504 BURNT BUTTER BISCUITS

125g [4 oz] butter or margarine
125g [4 oz] castor sugar
1 egg

1 teaspoon vanilla
155g [5 oz] S.R. flour
approx 24 blanched almonds

Melt the butter and allow it to become light brown in colour but do not burn. Cool slightly, add sugar and beat well. Add the egg and vanilla. Beat again. Add flour and mix well. Roll mixture into small balls about the size of a walnut and place on baking tray allowing room for biscuits to spread. Put almond in centre of each biscuit. Bake slowly for 10-12 mins.

If no castor sugar is available, put ordinary sugar in paper bag and roll with rolling pin or puree in blender.

1505 PEANUT BISCUITS

½ can [200g] or more sweetened condensed milk

1 cup peanut butter
2 cups cornflakes

Mix condensed milk and peanut butter, add cornflakes and mix
well until firm. Place teaspoonfuls on greased oven tray and
bake at 350°F (180°C) for 10-12 mins.

Variations:
1. Add ½ cup raw peanuts for added texture.
2. Add ½ cup coconut.
3. Omit peanut butter, add 1 cup dried fruit.

1506 HONEY CRACKLES

1 tablespoon honey
2 tablespoons sugar

3 tablespoons butter
4-5 cups cornflakes

Place butter, honey and sugar in saucepan. Bring to the boil
and cook for 1 min. Remove from heat and stir in cornflakes.
Place in paper patty pans and bake in moderate oven for 8-10
mins until slightly brown. When cold they will be very crisp.

1507 GINGERBREAD MEN (OR GINGERNUTS)

125g [4 oz] butter or margarine
2 tablespoons golden syrup
185g [6 oz] sugar
1 egg, beaten

315g [10 oz] S.R. flour 2¼-2½
¼ teaspoon salt
2 teaspoons ground ginger

¾

Grease oven tray. Melt butter and golden syrup in a saucepan,
then add the sugar and the egg. Lastly, add the sifted flour,
salt and ginger. Mix well. For gingernuts, drop in teaspoonfuls
on to tray. For gingerbread men, mould into shape or use
cutter, and make faces with currants and peel. Bake at 325°F
(160°C) until a delicate golden brown, approx 10-12 mins.

1508 ORANGE CORNFLAKE CRUNCHIES

⅓ cup butter or margarine
¾ cup brown sugar
1 teaspoon grated orange rind
1 egg, beaten
1 tablespoon orange juice

1¼ cups plain flour
1 teaspoon baking powder
¼ teaspoon salt
2 cups cornflakes
1 cup mixed dried fruit

Cream together butter and sugar and orange rind. Add beaten
egg and orange juice. Sift flour with the baking powder and
salt and add to the creamed mixture. Stir in cornflakes and
mixed fruit. Place spoonfuls on a greased tray and bake in
moderate oven for 12-15 mins.
Variation: Use cherries instead of mixed fruit.

242

1509 SHORTBREAD

375g [12 oz] plain flour
60g [2 oz] cornflour or rice
    flour

250g [8 oz] butter
125g [4 oz] castor sugar
¼ teaspoon salt

Rub butter into flour. Add all other ingredients, form into long roll and cut into small rounds about ¼" thick. Bake about 30 mins at 350°F (180°C), reducing to 300°F (150°C) after 5 mins. Alternatively, pat into rounds 6" in diameter and mark pieces while cooling, or cut into Christmas shapes and decorate by icing when cold.

1510 CHOCOLATE PEANUT BUTTER CRUNCHIES

1½ cups flour
½ teaspoon baking powder
½ teaspoon bicarbonate of
    soda
¼ teaspoon salt
½ cup peanut butter

½ cup butter
½ cup brown sugar
½ cup sugar
1 egg
½ cup milk
box [90g] chocolate bits

Sift flour, baking powder, bicarbonate of soda and salt. Cream butter and peanut butter. Gradually blend in sugars, add egg and mix thoroughly. Stir in flour mixture alternately with milk. Fold in chocolate bits. Place teaspoonfuls on greased trays. Bake in moderate oven 350°F (180°C) for about 12 mins.

1511 LUNCHBOX COOKIES

90g [3 oz] butter or margarine
½ cup brown sugar
½ cup castor sugar
1 egg
1 teaspoon vanilla
1¼ cups wholemeal plain
    flour
½ teaspoon bicarbonate of
    soda

¼ cup S.R. flour
½ teaspoon salt
½ teaspoon cinnamon
½ teaspoon ground ginger
1¼ cups rolled oats
¼ cup marmalade
1 cup chopped raisins, or
    sultanas

Cream butter and sugar, beat in egg and vanilla. Sift dry ingredients, add to creamed mixture, then fold in oats, marmalade and raisins. Place teaspoonfuls on greased tray, bake at 375°F (190°C) for 15 mins until brown. Makes about 4C.

BUMBLE BEES (R 2143)

ROCK CAKES (R 1408)

1512 ANZACS

1 cup rolled oats
½ cup S.R. flour
½ cup plain flour
¾ cup coconut
¾ cup sugar [raw, brown or white]

½ teaspoon bicarbonate of soda
2 tablespoons boiling water
125g [4 oz] butter, melted
2 tablespoons golden syrup

Mix all dry ingredients. Dissolve soda in boiling water and add to melted butter and golden syrup. Add to dry ingredients and mix well. Place in teaspoonfuls on greased slide or press into greased tray and cut into squares while still hot. Bake in moderately slow oven 325°F (160°C) for 15 mins.

Variations:
1. Nutties: Add 30g (1 oz) crushed nuts.
2. Rolled oat cookies: Add 30g (1 oz) sultanas or raisins.
3. Muesli biscuits: Omit 1 cup rolled oats, add 1 cup muesli (R 1703).

Slices

1513 OLD ENGLISH MATRIMONIALS

1½ cups S.R. flour
185g [6 oz] butter
½ cup rolled oats
1 cup coconut

1 cup brown sugar
¾ cup raspberry jam [or other dark jam]

Sift flour, rub in butter, add rolled oats, coconut and brown sugar. Divide into two, pressing one half into greased lamington tin (11" x 7"). Warm the jam in a saucepan, spread evenly over mixture in tin. Sprinkle remainder of mixture over jam to cover it. Bake in moderately hot oven 375°F (190°C) for 30 mins. Allow to cool slightly in tin, then cut and loosen edges. Remove from tin when cold. Makes 12-18.

1514 ALMOND FINGERS

biscuit pastry [R 1501]
apricot jam
60-90g [2-3 oz] almonds, chopped

Icing:
1 egg white
125g [4 oz] icing sugar

Line a Swiss roll tin with biscuit pastry. Spread with apricot jam. Make icing by stiffly beating egg white and stir in icing sugar. Spread thickly over jam. Sprinkle with chopped almonds and bake in a moderate oven for approximately 25 mins or until golden brown.

1515 APRICOT DATE BARS

125g [4 oz] dried apricots
hot water
1 cup raw sugar
2 cups S.R. flour
¾ cup coconut

½ cup chopped dates
¼ teaspoon salt
185g [6 oz] butter or
   margarine, melted

Soak chopped apricots in hot water for 30 mins, drain. Put in bowl with sugar, sifted flour, coconut, dates, salt, add melted butter, mix well. Spread mixture into greased 11" x 7" lamington tin. Bake in moderate oven approximately 25 mins or until cooked. remove from oven, allow to cool, and cut into squares

Variations:
1. Omit dried apricots, and double quantity of dates.
2. Omit ¼ cup of flour and substitute ¼ cup wheatgerm.

516 APPLE SLICE

4-6 apples
2 tablespoons butter or
   margarine
½ cup sugar
1 egg
2 cups S.R. flour

½ teaspoon bicarbonate of
   soda
1 teaspoon mixed spice
little milk
extra sugar and cinnamon

Stew apples with as little water as possible. Allow to cool. Cream butter, sugar, add egg. Fold in flour, soda and spice. Add a little milk to make firm dough. Flatten out into two circles to fit cake tins. Put in greased tin with stewed apple between. Sprinkle with sugar and cinnamon. Bake for 25 mins in moderate oven.

1517 HONEYCOMB SLICE

Base: Biscuit pastry [R 1501] or Yeast Dough [R 1620]
Press pastry about ¼" thick into baking tin (yes, your large baking dish). Pour topping over pastry and bake in moderate oven 350°F (180°C) for 25-30 mins. Topping should be sticky. Cut into squares when cold.

Topping:
125g [4 oz] butter
125g [4 oz] sugar
45g [1½ oz] almonds, finely
   chopped

2 tablespoons milk
vanilla or almond essence

Melt butter, add other ingredients, boil until sugar dissolves.

1518 PRUNE BARS

2 eggs
¼ teaspoon salt
½ cup brown sugar
185g [6 oz] dessert prunes
1 cup S.R. flour
1 teaspoon mixed spice

½ cup rolled oats
30g [1 oz] margarine, melted
30g [1 oz] walnuts, finely
    chopped
icing sugar

Beat eggs on high speed until frothy, add salt and brown sugar and beat until creamy. Remove stones and chop prunes. Sift flour and spice and fold into egg mixture with oats, melted margarine, prunes and walnuts. Spread mixture over the base of a greased 11" x 7" tin. Bake in a moderate oven for 20 mins. Cut into bars, cool, and dust with icing sugar before serving.

1519 RAISIN SQUARES

125g [4 oz] butter
1 cup sugar
2 eggs, well beaten
½ cup flour
½ teaspoon salt

3 tablespoons cocoa
⅔ cup raisins or mixed fruit
½ cup chopped nuts
1 teaspoon vanilla

Cream butter and sugar. Add eggs, beat thoroughly. Sift flour, cocoa and salt together and add to mixture. Add nuts, fruit and vanilla. Mix thoroughly. Pour in to well-greased 11" x 7" tin and bake in moderately hot oven for about 45 mins. Cool slightly and cut into squares for school lunches, or serve with ice-cream or cream for dessert.

1520 BANANA SLICE

1 banana [small to medium]
1 cup S.R. flour
½ teaspoon cinnamon
¼ teaspoon ground cloves
60g [2 oz] butter or margarine

½ cup sugar
1 egg
¼ cup milk
¼ cup chopped walnuts

Peel and mash banana. Sift flour with spices. Cream butter and sugar, add banana. Beat for two mins. Add egg, beat well. Add alternately milk and sifted flour. Stir in chopped nuts. Put into greased 11" x 7" lamington tin. Bake at 350°F (180°C) for 25-30 mins until cooked and slightly browned. While warm, top with lemon icing. Cut into slices.

Lemon icing:

15g [½ oz] butter or
    margarine
1 teaspoon hot water

¾-1½ cups icing sugar
few drops lemon essence or
    1 tablespoon lemon juice

Melt butter, mix all ingredients together.

1521 PEANUT CRUNCH

185g [6 oz] *butter, melted*   *1 cup coconut*
60g [2 oz] *salted peanuts*   ½ *cup brown sugar*
1 cup S.R. flour

Melt butter, add other ingredients. Press into 11" x 7" tin. Bake in moderate oven for 15-20 mins. Ice with chocolate icing (optional).

1522 APRICOT MACAROON SLICE

Biscuit pastry [R 1501]   *jam*

Put thin layer of pastry in two 7" sandwich tins. Cover with apricot, raspberry or plum jam.
Spread the topping below evenly over the jam and bake at 350°F (180°C) for 25-30 mins.

Topping: Mix all together:
1 cup coconut   *1 egg*
½ *cup sugar*

Variations: Instead of jam use:
1. Thin slices of apple placed closely together.
2. ½-¾ cup dates, 1 tablespoon butter, 1 cup milk. Boil gently until consistency of jam and allow to cool.
3. Cold, drained, preserved or stewed fruit, e.g. cherries, crushed pineapple, apricots.

Topping Variations: (R 1105)

1523 FRUIT SLAB

1 cup wholemeal S.R. flour   90g [3 oz] *melted butter*
1 cup raw sugar   1½ *cups dried fruit*
1 teaspoon mixed spice   *1 cup coconut*
2 eggs, beaten

Sift flour, add sugar and spice, mix in beaten eggs. Add butter, fruit and coconut. Mix well. Spread on to greased 11" x 7" tin. Bake in moderate oven 15-20 mins. Cool and cut into squares.

Variations:
1. Omit 2 tablespoons flour, 1 cup coconut and add 2 tablespoons wheat germ, 1 cup crushed cornflakes, 2 tablespoons honey. Cool, ice with chocolate or lemon icing.
2. Sultana Slab. Use only 1 egg but increase butter to 125g (4 oz). In a large measuring jug, measure flour, add sugar, coconut, sultanas, and spice. Add to melted butter, then add eggs and mix well.

After Dinner Delights

1524 CHOCOLATE PEPPERMINT SLICE

Biscuit layer
1½ cups S.R. flour
1 cup coconut
½ cup brown sugar
185g [6 oz] butter
Peppermint layer
375g [12 oz] icing sugar,
    sifted
60g [2 oz] copha, melted
    and cooled

3 tablespoons milk
1 teaspoon peppermint
    essence
Chocolate topping
90g [3 oz] copha, melted
½ cup chocolate drinking
    powder
1 teaspoon instant coffee

Mix together dry ingredients for biscuit layer. Melt butter, pour over dry ingredients. Press into base of a greased 11" x 7" tin and bake in a moderate oven for 20 mins. While still hot, mix together ingredients for peppermint layer and spread over biscuit layer. Put aside until cold.

Pour melted and slightly cooled copha over chocolate and coffee. Stir, spread over peppermint layer and just before it sets cut into slices.

1525 CHOCOLATE MARSHMALLOW SLICE

Biscuit layer:
[R 1524] Place mixture in 9" square tin lined with aluminium foil.

Marshmallow layer:
250g [8 oz] sugar
1 cup water
1 tablespoon gelatine

½ teaspoon cream of tartar
peppermint essence or few
    drops of cochineal

Place all ingredients except essence in saucepan and boil 3 mins. Allow to cool. Beat until thick, add essence and pour over biscuit layer. Place in refrigerator to set.

Chocolate topping:
(R 1524). Allow to cool, but not harden, before pouring over cold marshmallow.

Just before the chocolate sets, cut into fingers or squares.

Variation:
Make biscuit base with 4 crushed whole wheat breakfast biscuits, 1 cup coconut, ½ cup raw sugar, 60g (2 oz) chopped walnuts, 185g (6 oz) butter, melted.

Place layer of chopped, drained preserved cherries between biscuit base and marshmallow.

1526 CHOCOLATE CHEWS
(Quick, easy and delicious)

1 cup cornflakes OR
3 whole wheat breakfast
   biscuits
1 cup S.R. flour with ¼
   teaspoon salt
1 cup desiccated coconut
   or 1 cup dried mixed fruit

1 teaspoon vanilla
½-¾ cup sugar
1 tablespoon cocoa
155g [5 oz] butter or
   margarine

Melt butter or margarine, then stir all ingredients into it. Press on to a 7" x 11" tray. Cook 15 mins in moderate oven. Ice while hot with chocolate icing. Cut into 2" squares and leave until cold.

1527 HAZELNUT TRIANGLES

Biscuit pastry [R 1501]
apricot jam

60g [2 oz] chocolate, melted

Press pastry into greased tray 12" x 10". Spread with apricot jam and spread topping over jam. Bake in moderate oven 350°F (180°C) for 30 mins. When cold, cut into 2" squares, then triangles. Melt chocolate over boiling water, dip corners of each triangle daintily into chocolate. Allow to dry on greaseproof paper.

Topping:
125g [4 oz] butter
125g [4 oz] castor sugar
2 tablespoons water

125g [4 oz] minced hazelnuts
125g [4 oz] whole hazelnuts
vanilla

Melt butter, add sugar, water, vanilla. Bring to boil. When slightly cool, add hazelnuts.

1528 ALMOND BREAD

4 egg whites
125g [4 oz] castor sugar
125g [4 oz] plain flour

125g [4 oz] whole
   unblanched almonds

Beat egg whites stiffly, add sugar, beat well. Fold in flour and almonds. Cook in greased loaf tin in moderate oven 350°F (180°C) for 30 mins. When cold, wrap in thick cloth or aluminium foil and store for one week. Slice *very* thinly with sharp knife, toast in moderate oven until light brown and crisp. Store in airtight tin. Will keep indefinitely. Ideal for morning tea or with coffee after dinner.

1529 AFTER DINNER DIP

Combine 250g (8 oz) ricotta cheese, 125g (4 oz) grated chocolate, 1 tablespoon tia maria liqueur and 150ml (¼ pint) cream together, pile into a bowl and serve with vanilla wafers.

"No Bake" Slices and Biscuits

"No bake"—a boon to busy mothers—once mixed, into refrigerator—no worry that baby will be feeding, the telephone ringing, rain falling on the washing or a meeting in progress, when biscuits are ready to come out of the oven.

1530 DATE FINGERS

60g [2 oz] butter or margarine
250g [8 oz] dates, chopped
¼ cup sugar
1 tablespoon fruit juice
½ teaspoon vanilla essence
4 cups rice bubbles
desiccated coconut

Gently cook butter, dates and sugar in saucepan until dates are soft. Mix in fruit juice and vanilla. Pour on to rice bubbles. Mix well. Line 11" x 7" tin with greaseproof paper and sprinkle with coconut. Spread on date mixture, press firmly. Sprinkle top with coconut and allow to set in refrigerator before cutting.

1531 LEMON FINGERS

250g [8 oz] sweet biscuits
90g [3 oz] coconut
125g [4 oz] butter or margarine, melted
½ can [200g] sweetened condensed milk

Icing:
1½ cups icing sugar
juice of 1 lemon [grated rind also if liked]

Crush biscuits, add coconut. Melt butter, add condensed milk. Pour on to mixture, mix thoroughly. Press in 9" square tin or 11" x 7" tin and pour lemon icing on top. Allow to set in refrigerator before cutting.

1532 WHITE CHRISTMAS

1 cup powdered milk
1 cup rice bubbles
1 cup icing sugar
1 cup mixed dried fruit
250g [8 oz] copha, melted
2 teaspoons vanilla

Mix dry ingredients thoroughly, add melted copha (not too hot) and vanilla. Pour into sandwich tray, and allow to set in refrigerator. Cut into squares when firm.

1533 HEDGEHOG CAKE

125g [4 oz] butter
125g [4 oz] sugar
1 egg
2 tablespoons cocoa
vanilla

¼ cup chopped walnuts
¼ cup sultanas [optional]
250g [8 oz] sweet biscuits, crushed

Melt butter and sugar together in saucepan, remove from heat, then add beaten egg, making sure mixture is not too hot or it will curdle, add cocoa. Return to heat, bringing slowly almost to boiling point. Add vanilla and nuts, then biscuits. Press into loaf or orange cake tin. When cold, unmould and cover with chocolate icing. Alternatively, pour into 11" x 7" tin, ice and cut into squares.

1534 CHOCOLATE WAFER FINGERS

1 packet round wafers [available from Continental delicatessens]
Filling:
250g [8 oz] dark plain chocolate
2 egg yolks
1 cup icing sugar

2 tablespoons cream
250g [8 oz] unsalted butter, diced
rum or curacao

Stir filling ingredients except butter over hot water. When hot gradually add butter. Stir until melted. Flavour with rum or curacao. Put filling between layers of wafers, refrigerate and when set, cut into fingers or triangles.

1535 GINGER MALT SLICE

125g [4 oz] malt biscuits, crushed
15 marshmallows, chopped
125g [4 oz] glace cherries, chopped
125g [4 oz] dates, chopped
60g [2 oz] preserved ginger, chopped

60g [2 oz] raisins, chopped
60g [2 oz] walnuts, chopped
½ can [200g] sweetened condensed milk
1 teaspoon sherry
1 cup [approx] coconut

Mix well all ingredients except coconut, form into one or two logs and roll in coconut. Refrigerate. Cut into slices as required.

APRICOT BALLS (R 2141)
FRUITY TRUFFLES (R 2142)

1536 PEANUT HONEY SLICE

125g [4 oz] butter or
   margarine
½ cup brown sugar

2 tablespoons peanut butter
3 tablespoons honey
5 cups rice bubbles

Melt butter, sugar, peanut butter, and honey in large saucepan. Boil 3 mins. Cool slightly. Mix in rice bubbles and press
into greased 11" x 7" tin. Cut into slices.

Variation: Replace 1 cup rice bubbles with 1 cup of coconut
and sprinkle coconut on top, or ice with chocolate icing and
nuts. Ideal for parties for children. (Keeps better in refrigerator during summer.)

1537 HONEY SLICE

¾ cup chopped dried apricots
½ cup water
½ cup almonds, finely
   chopped
1 teaspoon lemon juice
1 teaspoon orange juice

1 cup skim milk powder
1 tablespoon wheat germ
½ cup sultanas
½ cup desiccated coconut
extra coconut
1 cup honey

Combine apricots and water. Simmer until soft. Remove from
heat and combine with remaining ingredients. Divide mixture
into 3, wet hands and form into rolls. Roll in extra coconut.
Refrigerate overnight. Cut into slices.

1538 RUM BALLS

250g [8 oz] Marie biscuits
1 cup coconut
2 tablespoons cocoa
1 400g [14 oz] can sweetened
   condensed milk

rum or rum essence or sherry
extra coconut or chocolate
   splinters

Crush biscuits finely. Add coconut and cocoa and mix well.
Add rum. Stir in condensed milk. Form into balls and roll in
coconut or chocolate splinters. Makes 40 to 50.

*If you have no castor sugar, place ordinary sugar in a blender until correct
consistency is obtained. If blended for long enough it will become icing
sugar.

1539 RUM TRUFFLES

750g [1½ lb] plain cake
    [butter or vanilla is suit-
    able—not too fresh]
250g [8 oz] castor sugar
250g [8 oz] almond meal

2 or 3 tablespoons hot apricot
    jam
sherry or rum to bind stiffly
    [optional]

Sieve cake finely, then mix all ingredients thoroughly. Roll into small balls. Using skewer or steel knitting needle, dip balls in fairly thin chocolate icing (add rum if liked) then roll in chocolate non-pareils. Set in refrigerator on a tray lined with greaseproof paper.

Savoury Biscuits

1540 WATER BISCUITS

To each cup plain flour, use 1 tablespoon butter and ½ teaspoon salt. Rub butter into flour, mix with warm water into pliable but not sticky dough. Roll out very thinly, prick with fork and cut into squares. Make the baking sheet very hot in the oven; it is this which causes the biscuits to blister. Have oven very hot 450°F (230°C), and bake for 3 mins.
Variation: Add 60g (2 oz) finely grated cheese to pastry.

1541 CHEESE BIX

2 cups plain flour
2 cups S.R. flour
2 teaspoons salt
½ teaspoon cayenne pepper
2 teaspoons dry mustard
250g [8 oz] butter

250g [8 oz] tasty cheese,
    grated
4 egg yolks
4 teaspoons lemon juice
little water
poppy or sesame seeds

Sift flours, salt, cayenne, mustard into basin, rub in butter, add grated cheese. Mix to dough with yolks (reserve a little for glazing), juice and water. Roll out thinly, cut into fingers or straws. Brush with extra yolk. Sprinkle with poppy or sesame seeds. Bake in moderate oven, 350°F (180°C) for 15-20 mins. Makes about 120. These make a good Christmas present.

1542 WHEATMEAL CRISPS

1 cup wheatmeal flour
¾ cup flour
½ teaspoon salt

1 teaspoon baking powder
60g [2 oz] butter
2 tablespoons milk

Sift flours, salt and baking powder. Rub butter into flours. Wet with milk. Roll out thinly and cut into fingers. Cook in moderate oven 350°F (180°C) until crisp.

1543 ONION BISCUITS

2 medium onions
250g [8 oz] wholemeal flour
½ teaspoon salt
2 teaspoons baking powder

½ cup sesame seeds
2 eggs, beaten
½ cup water [more if necessary]

Grate onions or puree in blender. Sift flour, salt and baking powder and add to onions. Add sesame seeds, beaten eggs and enough water to make a firm dough. Lightly flour a pastry board and roll dough out thinly. Cut out with round cutter and cook on a lightly greased oven tray in a moderate oven 350°F (180°C) for about 25 mins. Serve with butter.

1544 RYE BISCUITS

155g [5 oz] rye flour
½ teaspoon salt
1 teaspoon baking powder

90g [3 oz] butter
1 egg
2-3 tablespoons water

Sift together rye flour, salt and baking powder. More salt may be desired as the salt taste must come through. Rub in butter until mixture resembles breadcrumbs. Blend in egg and enough water to make a firm dough. Roll out thinly and bake on a greased tray in a moderate oven 375°F (190°C), for 10-15 mins. Cool on a cake rack.

1545 SCOTS OATCAKES

Very good for breakfast with butter and marmalade—use generally in place of bread. Good to take camping as they are sustaining.

250g [8 oz] oatmeal
   [Note: not rolled oats]
125g [4 oz] plain flour
½ teaspoon salt

1 teaspoon sugar
1 teaspoon baking powder
90g [3 oz] butter or lard
cold water

Mix dry ingredients, rub in the butter and add enough cold water to make a stiff dough. Sprinkle a little oatmeal on the board, turn out the dough, knead lightly and roll out to a quarter inch in thickness. Cut into shapes, place on a greased tray and bake in a moderate oven 350°F (180°C) for 20-30 mins. (Makes about 12.)

Variation: Try using half wholemeal flour and half white flour—it gives a slightly crunchier texture.

There's a Bun in the Oven!

There's a Bun in the Oven

The happy occupation of making bread.
R. L. Stevenson, quoted in Lady Jekyll, Kitchen Essays

1600 BREADS AND YEASTS

Baking with yeast is easy if you remember the following: Yeast is a living plant which is killed at high temperatures and is dormant at low temperatures. Therefore, it works best at tepid temperatures (about 85°F or 29°C) and better and quicker results are obtained if flour, water, workplace, bowl and bread tin are warm. Yeast feeds on sweetness—hence the inclusion of sugar or its equivalent in all yeast recipes.

If flour and yeast are bought in bulk, homemade bread is far more economical than the factory-made product—also of course more nourishing and delicious.

Quantities and methods in yeast cookery are always fairly flexible and need not be followed precisely. With a little practice, you will find there is no need to measure quantities. The variations are endless—you are limited only by your imagination. Use different shaped containers—a nut-loaf tin, a casserole or even a flower pot (line it with foil or removing the loaf will be difficult).

All the recipes here use compressed yeast (available from health food shops and delicatessens) but if you find it difficult to obtain, the dried yeast works very well too. 7g (¼ oz) dried yeast is equivalent to 30g (1 oz) compressed yeast.

Compressed yeast can be bought in bulk, divided into 30g (1 oz) portions, wrapped in foil and frozen—it will keep for up to a year in the deep freeze.

To store compressed yeast:
1. Crumble yeast into a dry and clean ice-cream container.
2. Cut 3-4 holes of approx. ¼" diameter into container lid.
3. Place the container with the lid on into a dry corner of the refrigerator.

Stored like this, yeast will keep its activity up to 6 weeks or longer. Browning of the yeast is the natural result of the drying process during storage and does not in any way interfere with the quality and activity of the yeast.

Do not use plastic bowls for mixing as plastic inhibits the action of yeast. Too much salt will have the same effect so use only the specified amount. Do not put salt directly on to yeast but rather mix it in with the flour etc.

Always cream compressed yeast 15-30g (½-1 oz) with one teaspoonful of sugar, and when it is liquid, add half a cup of lukewarm water. It should froth up in 10 mins. However, it is unnecessary to wait for this and the yeast mixture can be added to the flour immediately. If dried yeast of a fine-granular type is used, it can be added to the dry ingredients and all mixed with the warm liquid ingredients. However, coarse dried yeast should be sprinkled on to ½ cup warm water to which 1 teaspoon of sugar has been added. It should then be kept in a warm place until it dissolves and the liquid becomes frothy.

Once all ingredients have been mixed, leave mixture in a warm place to prove—i.e. to rise or double in bulk. Keep the dough covered while proving. Place in warmed greased tins and allow to prove again.

If you like a soft crust, brush your loaves with butter before baking. Use milk for a crisper crust; water makes the crust very crisp, and beaten egg gives a dark, shiny crust. Bread is sufficiently cooked when tapping on the bottom of the loaf produces a hollow sound. When cooked, always turn out immediately and cool on a wire rack.

When making bread rolls for the children, make their initials with poppy seeds or draw a face. If you have never made bread before, do it late in the afternoon so that when the family comes home, the house will be filled with the smell of freshly baked bread. They will think you are wonderful! (A word of warning here—hide a loaf away for breakfast before they get home.) And once you have made French sticks for that special dinner party, you will never want to buy them from the shop again!

If making bread in large quantities to freeze, wrap each cooled loaf in foil and seal tightly. It can then be taken from the freezer when required, and popped straight into the oven for 30 minutes to give you hot, fresh bread again.

1601 WHOLEMEAL BREAD

30g [1 oz] yeast
2 teaspoons brown sugar or
   honey
½ cup lukewarm water
750g [1½ lb] stoneground
   wholemeal flour plus extra
   flour for kneading

2 teaspoons salt
2 tablespoons wheat germ
1 tablespoon treacle or
   molasses
2 cups warm water
sesame or poppy seeds or
   cracked wheat

Dissolve yeast with sugar; cream together until it becomes liquid then add ½ cup lukewarm water, stir well and set aside in a warm place. Mix flour, wheat germ and salt in a large bowl and warm slightly in the oven.

Mix treacle with 2 cups warm water. Make a well in the flour, pour in the frothing yeast mixture, then add the treacle and water, mixing well. (The dough should be very moist and soft.) Cover basin with a cloth and leave in warm place until doubled in size. Add enough flour to make a firm dough, turn on to a floured surface and knead well until elastic and non-sticky. Dough is ready when it springs back after being dented with a finger.

Shape into loaves or rolls, baste with butter or milk and sprinkle with seeds or cracked wheat.

Half-fill warm greased tins with dough, and allow to rise to top.

Bake at 450°F (230°C) for 30-35 mins on the middle shelf of the oven.

Turn out at once and cool on a rack.

Variations:

1. Add 1-2 tablespoons of any or all of the following: wheat germ, powdered milk, whole grains of wheat, cracked wheat or bran.

2. For a lighter loaf, use half plain flour.

3. For a fruit loaf, flatten the dough and sprinkle generously with about 1 cup mixed fruit, cinnamon, nutmeg or mixed spice and brown sugar. Knead this in well and shape as before.

Glaze for fruit loaf:
Boil 2 tablespoons brown sugar with 2 tablespoons milk and ½ teaspoon cinnamon. Brush baked loaf with this as soon as it comes out of the oven.

1602 HEALTH LOAF

750g [1½ lb] plain flour
750g [1½ lb] wholemeal flour
125g [4 oz] soya flour
125g [4 oz] rye flour
125g [4 oz] millet flour
125g [4 oz] rolled oats
125g [4 oz] wheat germ
125g [4 oz] powdered milk
45g [1½ oz] salt
60g [2 oz] yeast
60g [2 oz] brown sugar
6½ cups warm water

Combine yeast, sugar and 60g (2 oz) plain flour. Mix in 2½ cups warm water, stir well and leave for about ½ hour when it will be frothing.

Combine remaining dry ingredients and mix in yeast mixture and remaining water. Turn on to a floured surface and knead well until dough is no longer sticky. Leave in a warm place until doubled in bulk. Punch down and place in warmed greased bread tins. Cover and allow to rise 30-40 mins. Bake at 400°F (200°C) for 40-45 mins.

1603 STEAMED YEASTLESS HEALTH BREAD

(This is a heavy dark bread)

125g [4 oz] stale bread, crusts removed and soaked overnight in 1½ cups water
½ cup molasses
1 teaspoon salt
155g [5 oz] corn meal [polenta]
155g [5 oz] rye flour
155g [5 oz] stoneground wholemeal flour
2 teaspoons bicarbonate of soda
½ cup cold water

Rub the soaked bread through a sieve using the back of a wooden spoon. Add molasses. Mix well and set aside.

Combine salt, flours and bicarbonate of soda. Mix in water and bread and molasses mixture, combining well.

Divide the mixture between two oiled 1½ pint pudding bowls, and cover with oiled aluminium foil tied tightly with string under rim of basin.

Place on a rack in a large saucepan. Add sufficient boiling water to come half way up sides of basins. Cover and steam over low heat for 3-3½ hours.

Remove bread from bowls, and place in 300°F (150°C) oven for 15 mins to remove excess moisture. Serve warm or cold—excellent with cheese and beer!

1604 FRENCH LOAF (Sticks or Rolls)

30g [1 oz] yeast
1 teaspoon sugar
1 cup lukewarm water
1 cup flour

2½ cups warm water
1 tablespoon salt
1-1¼ kg [2-2½ lb] flour
flour or sesame seeds

Cream yeast and sugar and dissolve in lukewarm water. Add flour. Mix well, cover and leave for 6 hours or overnight.

Add warm water, salt and sufficient flour to make a firm, elastic dough. Knead well on a floured surface. Cover again and leave in a warm place to double in bulk.

Punch down and knead 4-5 mins. Divide into 5 or 6 long loaves or "sticks". Place on warmed greased flat baking trays, brush with water and sprinkle heavily with flour or sesame seeds. Make 5 horizontal slashes on the top of each loaf and leave in a warm place 10-15 mins. Bake at 450°F (230°C) for 20 mins, placing a pan of boiling water in the bottom of the oven during baking to create steam and give the typical crustiness to these loaves.

1605 GOLDEN LOAF

(Try this for those difficult children who will eat only white bread)

2 cups milk
500g [1 lb] wholemeal flour
2 teaspoons salt
3 cups plain flour
3 teaspoons gluten [obtain-
    able at health food shops]

30g [1 oz] yeast
1 tablespoon raw sugar
¼ cup warm water
1 tablespoon oil
2 tablespoons wheat germ

Heat milk and cool to lukewarm. Sift the wholemeal flour 2-3 times to remove the grist. Measure 3 cups and add salt, plain flour and gluten. Cream the yeast with the sugar, add warm water, milk and oil. Add wheat germ and flours, reserving 1 cup for kneading. Knead for 10-15 mins. Cover and leave to rise in a warm place. Punch down, place in warmed greased tins and prove again. Bake at 375°F (190°C) for 45 mins

Variation: Golden Fruit Loaf (R 1601.3)

---

*Home-made breads will remain fresh and moist if wrapped securely in foil, plastic wrap or airtight plastic bag. Seal well and place in bread container or cool, dry place.

1606 MILK LOAF

60g [2 oz] powdered milk
600ml [1 pint] warm water
30g [1 oz] yeast

2 teaspoons sugar
1kg [2 lb] plain flour
2 teaspoons salt

Dissolve powdered milk in water. Cream yeast with sugar and mix with warm milk and water mixture. Stir in flour mixed with salt and knead until smooth and elastic. Cover and leave in a warm place to double in bulk. Punch down, and half fill greased bread tins with the dough. Brush with egg glaze (or egg and milk mixed for a lighter coloured crust). Prove until dough reaches top of tins and bake at 400°F (200°C) for 35 mins. Cool on a rack.

Variation: Substitute wholemeal flour for plain flour and omit milk.

1607 HOT CROSS BUNS

30g [1 oz] yeast
90g [3 oz] sugar
300ml [½ pint] warm milk
500g [1 lb] plain flour
1 teaspoon salt
½ teaspoon cinnamon

½ teaspoon mixed spice
60g [2 oz] butter, melted
1 egg, beaten
60g [2 oz] sultanas
60g [2 oz] currants
30g [1 oz] mixed peel

Cream yeast with 1 teaspoon of the sugar, add ½ cup warm milk. Mix well and set aside. Sift flour with salt and spices and add yeast mixture with remaining milk, sugar, melted butter and beaten egg. Mix in the fruit and knead until no longer sticky. Cover and prove in a warm place. Shape into 12 buns and place close together in a greased baking pan 1"-2" deep. Cover and allow to rise until very light. For crosses, pipe on a mixture of 2 rounded tablespoons self-raising flour and 2 tablespoons cold water. Bake at 400°F (200°C) for 15-20 mins. Brush with glaze while still hot.

Glaze:
1 teaspoon gelatine
150ml [¼ pint] water

4 tablespoons sugar
½ teaspoon cinnamon
¼ teaspoon mixed spice

Dissolve gelatine in water. Place in a saucepan with other ingredients and boil 10 mins. Cool on a rack.

---

*If you have difficulty finding a warm place for your yeast dough to prove (rise), try placing it in the car in the sun. Remember to cover it.

1608 SOUR RYE BREAD

Sourbread starter
2 cups plain flour

2 cups warm potato water
[i.e. unsalted water in
which potatoes have been
boiled]

Mix well and place in a non-metal container. Cover with a cloth and leave to ferment in a warm place 2-3 days. (Half of this quantity is used—it can then be replenished with more flour and potato water and will be ready for use again in six hours. It can also be frozen after this stage, but must be thawed for 24 hours before using again.)

3 cups rye flour
3 cups plain flour
2 teaspoons sugar
2 teaspoons salt
1½ cups warm water

1 cup sourdough starter
½ teaspoon bicarbonate of
soda
2 teaspoons caraway seeds
[optional]

Measure rye flour, 1 cup plain flour, sugar and salt into bowl. Mix in the water and starter, and stir until well blended. Cover with a cloth and leave in a warm place for 24 hours by which time it should have doubled in bulk. Stir in one cup of the remaining flour mixed with the bicarbonate of soda. Turn the dough out and knead in the remaining cup of flour with the caraway seeds if used. The dough should be very firm (use more flour if necessary). Divide into two and shape into rounds.
Place on greased trays, cover and leave for 3-4 hours in a warm place until doubled in bulk. Prick all over with a skewer or make slashes with a sharp knife. Brush with water and bake at 400°F (200°C) for 40 mins. Cool on a rack.

1609 RIESKA

2 cups rye or barley flour
2 teaspoons baking powder
¾ teaspoon salt
2 teaspoons sugar

2 tablespoons melted butter
1 cup evaporated milk, cream
or buttermilk

Sift dry ingredients. Mix in melted butter and milk to form a dough. Knead slightly to make a ball. Place on greased tray and pat out to ½" thick, 14" diameter circle. Prick all over with a fork and bake at 450°F (230°C) for 15 mins until lightly browned. Serve warm, cut into wedges which are split and buttered.

1610 LIMPA BREAD (Swedish)

1 cup boiling water
½ cup cracked wheat
1 teaspoon dried dill
1 teaspoon cummin
1½ teaspoons grated orange
   rind
2 teaspoons salt
6 tablespoons molasses

1½ tablespoons oil
30g [1 oz] yeast
¼ cup lukewarm water
1 cup milk
2 cups rye flour
4½ cups plain flour
4 teaspoons gluten
melted butter

Pour boiling water over cracked wheat in a bowl, add dill, cummin, orange rind, salt, molasses and oil. Stir once and leave to cool. Dissolve yeast in lukewarm water and add to mixture. Stir in milk, rye flour, gluten and sufficient plain flour to make a stiff dough. Turn out and knead in remaining flour. Knead well 10-15 mins.

Place dough in a large bowl, cover and leave to prove until doubled in bulk. Punch down, divide into two and shape into 9" round loaves. Place on greased trays. Prove again and bake at 350°F (180°C) for 35 mins. Brush with melted butter and cool on a rack.

1611 MUESLI BREAD

1 cup rolled oats
125g [4 oz] dried apricots,
   chopped
¼ cup raw sugar
2 teaspoons salt
1 tablespoon oil
2 cups boiling water
30g [1 oz] yeast
¼ cup warm water

1 egg, beaten
½ cup sultanas
½ cup currants
125g [4 oz] almonds, chopped
½ cup wheat germ
1½ tablespoons powdered
   milk
2½ cups wholemeal flour
1-2 cups plain flour

Put oats, apricots, sugar, salt and oil in a large bowl. Add boiling water, stir well and allow to cool. Dissolve yeast in ¼ cup warm water and add to oats mixture with beaten egg, fruit, almonds, wheat germ and powdered milk. Stir well. Add the wholemeal flour and one cup plain flour (add more if necessary). Cover and allow to double in bulk. Place in greased tins and prove again. Bake at 400°F (200°C) for 10 mins. Reduce heat to 350°F (180°C) and bake a further 40 mins. Brush with melted butter and cool on a rack.

*Thaw frozen bought bread in original wrapper, unwrap just before serving. Foil-wrapped bread may be thawed and warmed in moderate oven for about 20-30 mins. Unwrap for last 5 mins to crisp the crust.

1612 ONION ROLLS

½ cup finely chopped onion
30g [1 oz] butter
30g [1 oz] yeast
2 teaspoons sugar
1 cup lukewarm milk

1 egg, beaten
3 cups flour
1 teaspoon salt
milk or beaten egg

Saute onion lightly in butter. Cream yeast and sugar and add to lukewarm milk. Add egg and stir in flour mixed with salt. Reserve 2 or 3 tablespoons onion for topping and add remainder to the dough. Mix well and knead until no longer sticky, adding more flour if necessary. Cover and prove in a warm place until doubled. Punch down and shape into round rolls. Flatten and press reserved onion into the tops. Brush with milk or beaten egg and allow to prove again. Bake at 375°F (190°C) for 20-25 mins. Cool on a rack.

1613 PIZZA DOUGH

15g [½ oz] yeast
1 teaspoon sugar
150ml [5 oz] warm water

½ teaspoon salt
250g [8 oz] plain flour

Dissolve yeast with sugar and warm water. Mix salt and flour and add half to yeast mixture. Beat very well for at least 2 mins (can be done with mixer). Add remaining flour and mix until very smooth. Cover and prove for 30 mins. Spread dough on oiled pizza tray (makes 1 large or 2 small pizzas). Spread with desired topping (R 413) and bake at 375°F (190°C) for 20 mins.

BLINI (R 2410)

*Pizza may be frozen cooked or uncooked covered in foil for later reheating or cooking.

1614 CRUMPETS

30g [1 oz] yeast
2 teaspoons sugar
300ml [½ pint] milk
300ml [½ pint] water
4 cups flour

2 teaspoons salt
¼ teaspoon bicarbonate of
  soda
1 tablespoon warm water

Dissolve yeast with the sugar. Heat milk and water to luke-warm and add yeast. Stir into flour gradually, mixing well. Cover and leave in a warm place for about an hour until doubled in size. Dissolve salt and bicarbonate of soda in warm water and stir into mixture. Cover and allow to stand for another hour. Heat a heavy based frying pan (or use electric frypan, 360°F (185°C) or griddle). Grease egg rings and pan with oil. Pour in sufficient batter to almost fill rings and cook until top has set (about 5 mins). Remove rings and turn crumpets to cook the other side. Cool on wire rack. Toast and serve with butter and honey or jam.

1615 DOUGHNUTS

30g [1 oz] yeast
1 tablespoon sugar
½ cup milk
2 tablespoons soft butter
1 egg, beaten

250g [8 oz] plain flour
½ teaspoon salt
oil for deep frying
castor sugar
cinnamon [optional]

Cream yeast with sugar until liquid. Scald milk and add butter to hot milk. Stir until melted, then cool to lukewarm and add to yeast with the egg. Mix flour and salt and add yeast mixture. Mix well and knead only until non-sticky. Allow to rise in a warm place until doubled in bulk. Punch down and roll out ¼" thick. Cut with a plain round cutter (use a smaller cutter to remove the centres for "ring" doughnuts). Allow to prove until very light. Deep fry in hot oil turning once (about 2 mins each side). Drain on crumpled kitchen paper and dust with plain castor sugar or a mixture of castor sugar and cinnamon. Alternatively, ring doughnuts can be iced with glace icing (R 1443).

I never had a piece of toast,
Particularly long and wide,
But fell upon the sandy floor,
And always on the buttered side.

James Payn

1616 CHELSEA BUNS OR COFFEE SCROLLS

250g [8 oz] flour
¼ teaspoon salt
30g [1 oz] butter or
    margarine
15g [½ oz] yeast
150ml [5 oz] warm milk

30g [1 oz] currants or sultanas
30g [1 oz] candied peel
½ teaspoon allspice
30g [1 oz] sugar
30g [1 oz] castor sugar
milk or beaten egg

Mix flour and salt, rub in butter, cream yeast and add flour and milk. Beat well and allow to rise until doubled in bulk.
Knead dough lightly and roll in a square of about 10". Sprinkle with fruit and sugar and roll up like a Swiss roll. Cut roll into 7 pieces and place cut sides up in an 8" sandwich cake tin. Allow to prove until level with top of tin. Brush with milk or egg and bake at 425°F (215°C) for 20 mins. Brush with glaze. Sprinkle with castor sugar. Can be iced with lemon or coffee glace icing (R 1443) when cool.

Glaze

1 tablespoon milk   1 teaspoon sugar

Boil together until sugar is dissolved.

1617 STREUSEL KUCHEN

Dough
30g [1 oz] yeast
1½ cups [approx] warm milk
90g [3 oz] butter, melted
90g [3 oz] sugar
500g [1 lb] flour
½ teaspoon salt
2 eggs
1 teaspoon very finely grated
    lemon peel

Streusel
220g [7 oz] flour
125g [4 oz] butter
90g [3 oz] sugar
jam or stewed or canned fruit
    [e.g. peach or apricot halves]

Heat ½ cup milk, 1 teaspoon sugar and melted butter to luke-warm. Dissolve yeast in this. Sift flour and salt and add remaining ingredients and yeast mixture with enough milk to form a soft dough. Knead on a floured surface until elastic and non-sticky. Cover and leave in a warm place to double in size. Rub flour, sugar and butter together to a crumb-like consistency to make the streusel. Roll dough into a rectangle to fit a buttered baking tray. Cover thinly with jam or drained fruit. Allow to prove again. Cover with the streusel. Bake in a 400°F (200°C) oven for 30 mins.

1618 SAVARIN

15g [½ oz] yeast
4 tablespoons warm water
4 tablespoons warm milk
250g [8 oz] flour
60g [2 oz] sugar

¼ teaspoon salt
2 eggs, beaten
½ teaspoon vanilla
60g [2 oz] softened butter

Mix yeast with warm water and milk and set aside. Sift flour, sugar and salt into a warm mixing bowl. Beat eggs with vanilla and add to dry ingredients with the yeast mixture. Beat well by hand; when the mixture is well blended, spread the softened butter over the surface of the dough, cover and leave in a warm place until doubled in bulk. Punch down and beat well again until dough leaves the side of the bowl.

Place in a deep cake tin (preferably a ring mould or savarin mould). Cover again and leave to rise almost to the top of the tin (about 45 mins). Bake at 400°F (200°C) for 10 mins, lower heat to 350°F (180°C) and bake a further 25-30 mins until cake is rich golden brown. Leave to cool for 5 mins, then turn out on to a rack with a plate underneath and prick all over with a skewer. Saturate with hot syrup while the cake is still warm, re-using what drips into the plate, spooning it over continuously until all the syrup is absorbed.

Syrup
300ml [½ pint] water

250g [8 oz] sugar
6 tablespoons dark rum

Boil sugar and water together until slightly thickened. Add rum.

Variation:

Rum Baba

As for Savarin, but add 60g (2 oz) currants and 30g (1 oz) candied peel to the dough.

1619 CROISSANTS

150ml [5 oz] milk
30g [1 oz] butter
1 teaspoon salt
1½ tablespoons sugar
30g [1 oz] yeast
½ cup warm water

375g [12 oz] flour
125g [4 oz] butter [room temp.]
1 egg yolk beaten with a little
milk for glazing

Scald milk. Place butter and sugar in a bowl. Pour hot milk over. Stir until butter has melted and cool to lukewarm. Add yeast which has been dissolved in water. Add sifted flour and salt and knead until soft, smooth and elastic. Cover with a damp cloth and place in a warm place until doubled in size. Punch down and wrap in plastic wrap. Refrigerate until well chilled.

Roll out the chilled dough to a strip three times as long as it is wide. Spread the softened butter evenly over the strip and fold in each end to form a square. Roll out into another strip of the same size, the other way, and again fold in ends to make a square. Leave in the refrigerator until thoroughly chilled again. Roll and fold twice more at intervals of at least an hour or overnight*. Roll dough into 2 equal circles and cut each circle into 8 pie-shaped wedges.

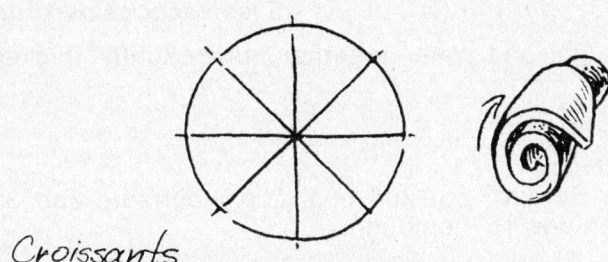

Croissants

Starting at the wide end, roll each portion up. Curve into a crescent shape and place on greased oven tray. Brush with the beaten egg yolk and milk and bake for 15-20 mins at 400°F (200°C). Cool on a rack.

Variation: Danish Pastry
Proceed as above up to *. Roll dough out and cut into varying shapes (e.g. R 1624) and fill with dried fruit, almond paste, jam, nuts etc. Fold and seal edges and brush with a mixture of egg, milk and melted butter. Bake in a moderate oven for 30 mins. Ice with glace icing (R 1443).

1620 RICH CREAM DOUGH

30g [1 oz] yeast
¼ cup warm water
1 cup cream
3 egg yolks
¼ cup evaporated milk

3⅓ cups flour
¼ cup sugar
1 teaspoon salt
½ cup butter
extra softened butter

Dissolve yeast in warm water. Mix with cream, egg yolks and milk and set aside. In a large bowl, sift flour, sugar and salt. Cut in butter. Stir in yeast mixture and mix well. Spread a light film of butter over surface of dough. Cover tightly with plastic wrap and refrigerate overnight. The dough is now ready for use, and can be kept refrigerated for 4-5 days. When using knead on a very lightly floured board.

1621 ALMOND TWIST AND CLAWS

½ quantity rich cream dough
  [R 1620]
250g [8 oz] almond paste

slivered almonds
1 egg white

Twist:
Roll dough to a 24" x 12" rectangle. Cut into three 4" wide strips. Crumble almond paste along the centre of each strip, moisten long edges, fold them to the centre and press to seal. Use two strips for the twist and form them into two overlapping "U" shapes.

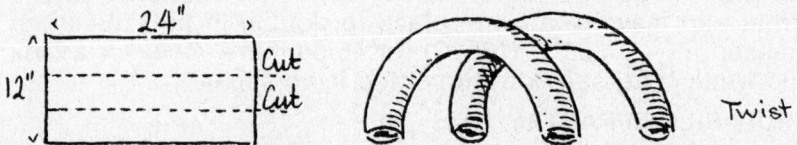

Starting from the left, weave the strands into a braid and tuck edges under. Brush with egg white and sprinkle with almonds.
Claws:
Cut remaining filled strip into 6 sections and make ½" cuts half way across at ½" intervals. Curve the uncut edge so that the cut edge fans out.

Claws

Brush with egg white and sprinkle with slivered almonds. Place twist and claws on greased trays and leave to rise in a warm place until doubled in bulk. Bake at 350°F (180°C) until golden brown (20 mins for Twist and 15 mins for Claws). Cool on a rack.

1622 PANETTONE (Italian)

1 quantity rich cream dough
[R 1620]
½ cup sultanas

½ cup candied peel
2 tablespoons melted butter
icing sugar

Knead fruit into dough. Divide in half and shape into two round smooth balls. Place into 8" greased round cake pans and cut a ¼" deep cross right across the top of each. Brush with melted butter. Allow to rise and bake for 45 mins at 350°F (180°C). Brush again with butter when cooked and sprinkle with sifted icing sugar whilst still hot. Cool on a rack.
Serve cut in wedges and buttered.
(If desired, halve the quantity of fruit and use the half quantity of dough left over from the almond twist and claws.)

1623 STOLLEN (German)

1 quantity rich cream dough,
[R 1620]
½ cup currants
¾ cup chopped, blanched
almonds

½ cup sultanas
¼ cup candied peel
icing sugar, sifted

Knead fruit and almonds into dough (using as little flour as possible—only enough to stop dough sticking). Roll into 10" x 8" oval and make a lengthwise crease just off centre with the blunt edge of a knife. Fold the smaller section over the larger and leave in a warm place to double in bulk. Bake on greased tray at 350°F (180°C) for 45-50 mins. Cool on a rack and when cold, sprinkle with sifted icing sugar.

1624 FRUIT FILLED PASTRY

½ quantity rich cream dough
[R 1620]
250g [8 oz] stoned prunes or
dried apricots
½ cup sugar

1 cup water
egg white
almonds
extra sugar

Simmer prunes or apricots with sugar and water until soft. Drain, puree and leave to cool. Roll dough to 24" x 12" rectangle and cut into 4" squares. Place a tablespoon of filling on the centre of each square. Moisten edges and fold as desired, e.g.

Brush with egg white and sprinkle with almonds. Allow to rise. Bake for 15 mins at 350°F (180°C). Brush with glace icing (R 1443) while hot. Cool on a rack.

1625 CONTINENTAL TEA RING

1 quantity rich cream dough
  [R 1620]
1 cup walnuts
½ cup sugar

1 tablespoon cinnamon
¼ cup melted butter
1 egg white, slightly beaten
2 tablespoons extra sugar

Blend walnuts, ½ cup sugar and cinnamon in a blender until finely ground. Roll dough into a 24" x 20" rectangle. Brush with butter and spread with walnut filling. Roll dough into a Swiss roll, dampen edge to seal. Place seam side down and form into a circle, joining the ends and pressing to seal. Squeeze gently to distribute filling equally all round, and with a sharp knife, make crosswise cuts in the top of the ring 3" apart and just deep enough to reach the filling. Brush with egg white and sprinkle with 2 tablespoons sugar. Place on greased tray in a warm place until doubled in bulk, and bake at 350°F (180°C) for 25 mins.
Ice with glace icing (R 1443) and decorate with red and green cherries and walnut halves.

1626 ALMOND BUNS

1 quantity rich cream dough
  [R 1620]
Almond filling:
2 cups sliced almonds
¼ cup butter

2 tablespoons milk
1 400g [14 oz] can condensed
  milk
⅓ cup raisins
lemon glace icing [R 1443]

Combine all ingredients for filling except raisins in a saucepan and bring to the boil. Cook gently for 5 mins stirring well, until mixture has a glazed look. Stir in raisins and cool. Roll dough to a 15" x 12" rectangle and spread with filling. Roll up lengthwise as for Swiss roll, dampen edge to seal. Cut into 18 even slices and place cut sides up in a greased 13" x 9" x 2" baking pan. Allow to rise in a warm place until doubled. Bake for 25 mins at 350°F (180°C) and drizzle with lemon glace icing (R 1443) while warm.

Why has our poetry eschewed
The rapture and response of food?
What hymns are sung, what praises said
For home-made miracles of bread?

1627 FANCY ROLLS

1 quantity rich cream dough [R 1620]
1 egg white, slightly beaten

melted butter
sesame and poppy seeds

Divide dough into 4 portions. Shape each portion as described below. When shaped allow to rise in a warm place and then bake for 15-20 mins at 350°F (180°C).
(Note: Keep remaining dough chilled whilst preparing each portion.)

Brioche
Roll first portion of dough into 6 balls and pinch a marble size piece of dough off each ball. Place each ball into a greased gem-iron and make a sharp cut across the centre of each. Shape the small pieces into cone shapes (smooth top and tapering bottoms). Insert the the tapered ends into the cuts and press all around to seal. Brush with egg white. Proceed as above. Serve with butter and jam or honey.

Cloverleaf rolls
Divide second portion of dough into 18 small balls (the easiest way is to roll into an 18" long strip and cut into 18" x 1" portions). Place three balls together in greased gem-irons or muffin tins. Proceed as above.

Parkerhouse rolls
Roll third portion of dough into 8" long sausage. Cut 8 portions and roll each into a 2" circle. Crease just off centre with the blunt edge of a knife. Brush with butter and fold smaller section over larger. Press together and proceed as above.

Sesame and Poppy Seed rolls
Cut fourth portion of dough into 12 equal portions and roll each into a ball. Dip tops into egg white then dip 6 into sesame seeds and 6 into poppy seeds. Arrange in greased 8" round pan, and proceed as above.

If music be the breakfast food of love, kindly do not disturb until lunchtime.
James Agee, *Age of Film*

What's for Breakfast?

What's For Breakfast?

Bring porridge, bring sausage, bring fish for a start,
Bring kidneys and mushrooms and partridges legs,
But let the foundation be bacon and eggs.

A. P. Herbert

1700 BREAKFAST SUGGESTIONS

Breakfast can be just as interesting or as monotonous as you wish to make it! In many households breakfast tends to be a rather rushed affair—a cup of tea or glass of milk and a slice of toast swallowed half way out the door to the office or school. Children are often too rushed or excited or sometimes apprehensive to eat a good breakfast before going to school. It is not uncommon for teachers to find young children eating their packed lunches before school starts!

There is no need to sit the family down to a three course meal—let them decide whether they want a cooked breakfast or something lighter, but you can encourage them by varying the menu a little. It may mean getting up 10 minutes earlier to ensure a more relaxed approach—it is worth it—father and the children have a busy day ahead and they will need something sustaining.

Here are a few ideas to brighten the breakfast table:

Cereal—add interest and variety with fresh or stewed fruit, cream or yoghurt (plain or flavoured). Vary the type of cereal and alternate with muesli or porridge. Wheat germ is a tasty addition.

Apple, banana, orange, chopped, with cream, yoghurt, cottage cheese or ricotta cheese. Try coffee flavoured yoghurt over sliced banana.

Fresh fruit and cheese platter.

Grapefruit, halved and grilled for a few minutes.

Grilled prune and bacon rolls.

Grilled banana and bacon rolls.

Sauteed apple rings and bacon.

Bacon pancakes drizzled with warm golden syrup or honey (R 1205).

Fritters—sweetcorn (R 412), banana, pineapple, or apple (R 1201-1204).

Grilled or fried ham steaks with pineapple or egg.

Devilled kidneys.

Delectable mince (R 699P).

274

Thick slices of beef german (or similar) fried lightly in butter.
Black pudding, sliced and grilled or lightly fried.
Smoked fish or kippers, grilled or pan fried and served with lemon.
Baked beans, brightened up with the addition of bacon and tomatoes.
Baked eggs.
Grilled or fried tomatoes and bacon.
Anything on toast! e.g. cheese, bacon, sweetcorn.
Scots oatcakes (R 1545).
Read through Savouries to Sustain (R 400) for more ideas which can be used for breakfast. Recipe ideas using liver, brains, kidneys and sausages can be found in The Butcher's Hook, (R 600).
Small portions of leftovers such as boiled potatoes, fried rice, lasagne or spaghetti meat sauce can be successfully reheated and make a tasty breakfast either on their own or with eggs.
On mornings when the family sleeps in, throw together an egg nog (R 2018) and hand them a piece of fruit as they rush out the door!

1701 HOT FRUIT

2 prunes, stoned
125g [4 oz] dried apricots
125g [4 oz] raisins
2 bananas, cut into thick
  slices

3 tablespoons honey
1 lemon, juice and grated rind
4 tablespoons orange juice
yoghurt [optional]

Soak prunes and apricots overnight in a little water. Drain and place in casserole with raisins, bananas, honey and lemon juice and rind. Dot with butter and bake at 350°F (125°C) for 30 mins. Add orange juice just before serving. May be served with yoghurt or just plain.

1702 NUTRITIOUS BREAKFAST

4 tablespoons rolled oats
4 tablespoons lemon juice
125g [4 oz] nuts, chopped or
  crushed

2 eating apples
60g [2 oz] brown sugar
2 tablespoons yoghurt

Apples may be peeled and chopped or grated. Mix with other ingredients and serve. Oats may be soaked overnight to give a different consistency.

1703 MUESLI

This muesli recipe can be made in bulk and stored for use as desired. All the ingredients are available from health food stores. Do experiment a little, other ingredients can be added and perhaps you may wish to leave some out.

1kg [2 lb] rolled oats
250g [8 oz] wheat germ
250g [8 oz] lecithin meal or granules
250g [8 oz] bran
125g [4 oz] wheat grist
2 tablespoons desiccated coconut

2 tablespoons sesame seeds
250g [8 oz] sultanas or raisins
2 tablespoons sunflower kernels
125g [4 oz] crushed nuts

Mix well together and store in airtight container. Serve with milk and sugar and top with yoghurt or cream.
Try adding 60g (2 oz) dried fruit or stewed or fresh fruit to each serve.

1704 MARMALADE PIKELETS

1 egg
2 tablespoons chunky marmalade
½ cup milk
½ cup flour

½ cup wholemeal flour
¼ teaspoon salt
1 tablespoon butter, melted
4 teaspoons baking powder

Beat egg and marmalade together. Add half the milk then flour and salt sifted together. Mix well, add remaining milk and beat thoroughly with a whisk. Stir in melted butter and gently fold in baking powder. Do not stir any further. Grease frying pan and drop batter in spoonfuls into pan. When bubbles appear on surface, turn quickly and brown. Pikelets are cooked when edges look dry. Place between folds of clean napkin to keep warm while rest are cooking. Serve with butter and honey or more marmalade.

1705 EGG FLUFFS

For each serve:
1 egg, separated
1 slice wholemeal toast

yeast extract
salt and pepper

Separate egg and whip white until fluffy. Spread toast with marmite or vegemite and pile egg white on top. Make a hollow in white and drop in yolk. Place toast on foil covered baking tray and bake at 250°F (125°C) until firm.

*Add a tablespoonful of cornflour to scrambled eggs to prevent them going watery.

706 EGG IN THE HOLE

For each serve: *1 slice bread*
1 egg   *30g [1 oz] butter*

Make a neat hole with a scone cutter in the middle of the bread and retain the piece removed. Melt the butter in a frying pan and put in both pieces of bread. When they are slightly brown drop egg into hole and cook for a few mins. Turn upside down to brown other side. Serve with the piece removed as a "hat" on top of the egg.

EGG IN A NEST (R 1807)

707 PETER'S SCRAMBLED EGG VARIATIONS

"Many things can be used with scrambled egg. I generally operate on the principle of one egg for small persons and two eggs for large persons. You can achieve remarkable degrees of variation by:
mixing them in the blender.
mixing them with the rotating egg whisk.
mixing them with an ordinary light whisk.
hardly mixing them at all.
by cooking them in bacon fat or especially in butter or even simply by themselves in a saucepan.
Depending what leftovers, if any, there may be left around in the kitchen, you can make a ham scramble with a wee bit of ham, pureed in blender with the egg, salt and pepper; or bits of chicken again blended or not as you wish; or by using cheese. Chives are very nice too if you've got them growing in the garden. Ours unfortunately died and we haven't had any lately. Often a delightful mixture can be obtained by adding cream, about a couple of tablespoons for a family of four.
If meringues have been made in the house, thus leaving a residue of egg yolks, or if something has made use of yolks so that whites have been left over, well you chuck them into the scrambled egg, but additional yolks are very much better than additional whites. Make sure that you include at least one whole egg. Tomato sauce is nice too, especially when scrambled egg is cooked in the fat after frying bacon."

SPECIAL SCRAMBLED EGGS (R 409)

POACHED EGGS WITH CHEESE SAUCE (R 408)

OMELETTE (R 407)

1708 BUBBLE AND SQUEAK

A delicious way of using up odd bits of cooked leftover vegetables, in fact it is often worth cooking a few extra at dinner time to be ready for breakfast.

bacon

butter

cooked cold vegetables, sliced

Dice bacon and saute quickly in pan. Add butter and when melted add vegetables. Cook quickly, turning frequently until brown. May be served with fried eggs or grilled tomatoes. Try it for a Boxing Day treat using scraps of poultry and a little redcurrant jelly.

Breakfast at Plumstead Episcopi
The tea consumed was the very best, the coffee the very blackest, the cream the very thickest; there was dry toast and buttered toast, muffins and crumpets; hot bread and cold bread, white bread and brown bread, home-made bread and baker's bread, wheaten bread and oaten bread; and if there be other breads than these, they were there; there were eggs in napkins, and crispy bits of bacon under silver covers; and there were little fishes in a little box, and devilled kidneys frizzling on a hot-water dish; which, by-the-by, were placed closely contiguous to the plate of the worthy archdeacon himself. Over and above this, on a snow-white napkin, spread upon the sideboard, was a huge ham and a huge sirloin; the latter having laden the dinner table on the previous evening. Such was the ordinary fare at Plumstead Episcopi.

Anthony Trollope, The Warden, 1855

The Lunch Box

Lunch Box Inspirations

1800 What do you put in the lunch boxes you prepare for your children or husband? Would you consider their lunch box contains a nutritious meal, or do you take the attitude that it doesn't really matter much, because you make sure your child has a good breakfast, a substantial snack after school and a good evening meal?

Did you know that your child's performance in school is very much related to the quality of food eaten during breaks? Carbohydrate rich food satisfies quickly, but combined with some fat and protein rich food, more energy will be available for concentration for a longer time.

Food brought from home generally makes a better contribution to the nutritive value of the diet than that bought at the school canteen or shop.

Every meal we serve should contain something from each of the five food groups and the lunch box is no exception.
Group 1—milk and milk products.
Group 2—meat, fish, eggs, nuts, dried peas and beans.
Group 3—fruit and vegetables.
Group 4—bread, flour and cereals.
Group 5—butter or fortified margarine—fats.

This is an example of a lunch which was a favourite with one NMAA member's young children. She kept two polythene boxes from ice cream cakes for use as "cool boxes" for the lunches and in each she put two lettuce leaves, 1 whole tomato, 1 chunk of cucumber, 1 chunk of cooked (but not 'vinegared') beetroot, 1 chunk or foil wrapped triangle of cheese, 1 small packet of raisins or some other dried fruit or nuts, a piece or two of cold meat, e.g. grilled chop, one or two biscuits (R 1500) and one or two pieces of wholemeal bread, lightly buttered and sometimes spread with yeast extract.

Each type of food was wrapped separately. Also included was an apple, and a fruit drink in a plastic drink bottle. The drink was frozen overnight and used in the box as an ice block. The bottle was placed in a plastic bag or film before packing for as the drink melts it causes condensation on the outside of the container.

A small can of fruit juice, frozen overnight, is an alternative for the child who is always losing his drink bottle. Older children might like to take to school a vacuum flask with hot soup or an icy cold drink. This mother found that it was a good idea to include once or twice a week a 'surprise', which was always wrapped in foil and sealed with coloured cellotape to make it look a surprise. It often just contained some nuts or dried fruit, or maybe a chocolate biscuit or home-made fudge. But it helped to keep the lunch interesting, and that was very important. She believed and hoped that her children always ate their lunches with gusto. She said that she had many young folk coming home from school with her youngsters asking her to let their mothers know how she packed lunches!

Another NMAA member who lives in the hot inland of Australia, bought her children insulated plastic jars 8cm in diameter, 6cm deep. She freezes the lids overnight, and packs salad or stewed fruit and homemade egg custard in the jars and finds nothing ever comes home as the sandwiches did.

If making sandwiches, save time by making two weeks' supply in advance and freeze in plastic film. Or prepare them the night before, wrap in plastic film and refrigerate. This results in a fresher-tasting sandwich than one cut in the morning from day-old bread. If you have cold meat from the weekend roast, make a loaf of sandwiches and freeze that day, before the meat has a chance to dry on the bone.

Have you thought of using dry biscuits or rolls instead of bread? Other suggestions for inclusion in the lunchbox are:
Slices of ham or sausage wrapped around cubes of cheese, prunes or tomato, and fastened with a tooth-pick; peanut butter, vegemite or cheese sandwiched in carrot or celery sticks; carrot balls (R 904); cheese sticks or wedges; savoury snacks (R 401); hard boiled eggs; cold chicken drumsticks, chops or sausages; wedges of cold egg and bacon pie (R 417) or pizza (R 413); cold Wiener schnitzel (R 671); Cornish pasties (R 6991); hamburgers (R 691); fish balls (R 812); meat loaf (R 694); cold tongue (R 683); drop scones (R 1440); Scots' oatcakes (R 1545).

---

*To shell hard boiled eggs, crack the shell all over, then roll between palms of hands to loosen. Start shelling from the air-pocket end of the egg—you'll be able to peel off the shell in one piece.

1801 SANDWICH FILLINGS

Marmite or Vegemite—with shredded lettuce; grated carrot; cheddar cheese; scrambled egg and parsley; cooked mashed brains; chopped nuts; peanut butter; chopped hard boiled eggs and mayonnaise; baked beans; sliced cold meat; chopped parsley; sliced cucumber; chopped celery; raisins and walnuts; grilled bacon; cooked mashed pumpkin; sliced tomato.

Honey—with raisins soaked in orange juice; grated apple, sultanas and lemon juice; ricotta cheese.

Peanut Butter—with honey; chopped raisins; sliced or grated cheese; bacon; tomato; celery; sliced or mashed banana; sliced or grated apple; sliced pineapple; jam; golden syrup; grated carrot; cream cheese and finely chopped celery; devon sausage and grated carrot.

Ham—with cheese, sliced pineapple and chopped mint.

Cheese—try creamed with chopped dried fruits; nuts; chopped hard boiled eggs and raisins with mayonnaise, nutmeg, cinnamon and salt; bacon; tomato; drained crushed pineapple; onion salt; apple slices sprinkled with lemon juice; grated cucumber; milo and sultanas; chutney and cottage cheese; gherkin; shredded raw cabbage; chopped parsley; chopped chives; flaked tuna with ricotta cheese.

Banana—with brown sugar and orange juice; coconut and chutney; chopped raisins.

Tuna or Salmon—flaked; with shredded lettuce; grated onion; finely chopped tomato; celery with mayonnaise.

Roast beef—with cheese and tomato sauce; horseradish sauce.

Chicken—with crumbled cooked bacon; cottage cheese.

Apple or Almond—with chopped celery and a little cream.

Egg—scrambled or fried with chopped bacon; cold omelettes with sauteed onion and chopped parsley; sliced with ricotta cheese; curry powder.

Brains—with grated walnuts.

Dates—with chopped orange, nuts and raisins; cottage cheese; chopped walnuts, pinch of cinnamon; chopped with raisins, figs, sultanas, dried apricots, crystallized fruit and ginger.

AVOCADO SPREAD (R 104)

1802 MEAT PASTE

¾ cup milk
1 cup cooked meat leftovers
1 cooked potato
2 pickled onions
1 sprig parsley

1 teaspoon worcester-
  shire sauce
½ teaspoon dry mustard
salt and pepper

Place half the meat and all other ingredients in blender, blend for 20 seconds. Add rest of meat and blend further 20 seconds. Chill before using.

1803 LIVER PATE

If your family finds liver hard to stomach, try this pate. It has been included in this chapter as it makes very nourishing sandwiches or a spread for biscuits. Served on toast it also makes a delicious lunch for both children and adults and is a suitable entree for dinner parties.

250-375g [½-¾ lb] calf or
  pig liver, soaked in water
  and few drops vinegar for
  ½ hour
90g [3 oz] bacon scraps

medium onion
medium apple
salt and pepper
garlic if desired and sprinkle
  mace

Mince the lot finely, twice if you want it very fine and smooth. Make thick white sauce:

60g [2 oz] butter
30g [1 oz] flour
150ml [¼ pint] milk

1 egg
anchovy essence

Melt butter, add flour until butter is absorbed. Remove from heat, gradually add milk, stirring all the time to avoid lumps, return to heat after each addition of milk. As it cools, add 1 egg, beaten in, and a few drops of anchovy essence if desired. Mix everything together well. Put in greased oven-proof dish, with butter paper on top. Cook an hour or so in slow oven. Press with weight on top when cooling.

1804 SANDWICH VARIATIONS

Remove crusts from very fresh bread. Spread with fillings and either roll up or make layers with different coloured bread and cut into fingers.

Fillings:
Meat paste and scrambled egg.
Cream cheese with finely chopped ham.
Finely grated celery and carrot with mayonnaise.
Peanut butter and mashed banana.
Drained spear of asparagus.

Weekday Lunches at Home for Children

Toddlers do not need separate foods made for them, for if the family eats well, they can be given the same foods as the family, but cut up finely and in smaller portions. However some mothers have found that coaxing is sometimes necessary to induce their child to eat nutritionally well. Mother often needs to appraise meal times and ask the question: Are the children tired of food or have they lost interest because of the way it is cooked and served? Invariably, it is the latter.

Consider that all meat tastes and looks much the same to the young child so serve it in small portions and add interest with these suggestions:

Serve raw carrot cut in strands with vegetable peeler and made into flowers; cook beans in long lengths and thread them through a ring of tomato; serve finely shredded cabbage cooked lightly in a little butter in a half orange skin saved from the morning's juice, or with a slice of orange twisted to stand upright or a curl of celery (R 1050). See R 1045-1061 for other ideas.

Try cabbage served with a few whole peanuts sprinkled over the top for the older children, and for the younger ones, a spoonful of smooth peanut butter blended into it. Try piping "baskets" of mashed potato and serve the meat in these. Even a very fussy eater might enjoy trying a combination of orange juice, grated carrot, desiccated coconut and raisins. Another idea is to spread peanut butter or yeast extract on to lettuce instead of bread. This can be folded into a sandwich if desired. Serve the meal in different crockery—children love ramekins with a lid or handle.

1805 BRAISED LAMB SHANKS

2 lamb shanks
2 carrots
1 onion [optional]
flour

salt and pepper
60g [2 oz] margarine or oil
1½ cups tomato juice

Cut shanks into 1" pieces (the butcher will do this for you), chop the carrots and the onion finely. Roll the shanks in flour seasoned with salt and pepper, melt the margarine and heat. Brown the shanks in margarine and add tomato juice, cover and cook slowly for one hour. Serve with mashed potato.

DEVILLED LAMB SHANKS (R 643)

284

1806 VEGETABLE WHIP

3 cups potatoes, diced
1 cup carrots, diced
1 apple, sliced and peeled
½ onion, sliced

salt and pepper
butter
milk

Cook all vegetables and apple together with a little water. Drain, season and mash with a little butter and milk. Whip until fluffy. Or, return to saucepan over low heat, and stir in a tablespoon of grated cheese until it melts. This is ideal for children who 'don't like vegetables', and is very quick and easy.

1807 EGG IN A NEST

Cook an assortment of vegetables; mash, arrange in a plate with centre hollowed out. Poach an egg, when cooked pop into the vegetable "nest" and garnish with grated cheese.

Variation:
Use 1½ cups very finely chopped spinach or silver beet. Cook and drain well, mix with 150ml (¼ pint) white or cheese sauce.

1808 CHICKEN CUSTARD

½ cup fine breadcrumbs
¼ cup finely chopped cooked
   chicken
salt

½ teaspoon parsley
   [optional]
1-2 eggs
1 cup milk

Beat eggs and milk; pour over remaining ingredients. Steam or bake in a greased ramekin, soup plate or basin until just set.

1809 CHEESE SOUFFLE PUDDING

1-2 slices of bread, crusts
   removed
softened butter
1 egg, separated

60ml [2 fl oz] milk or cream
45g [1½ oz] grated cheese
¼ teaspoon dry mustard
salt and pepper

Cut slice of bread into triangles, butter both sides and line a ramekin dish so that points stick out above rim. Beat egg yolk lightly with milk. Add grated cheese, mustard and salt and pepper to taste. Beat egg white until stiff and fold gently into cheese mixture. Spoon into bread-lined ramekin dish and bake in moderate oven 375°F (190°C) for 20-25 mins until risen and golden brown.

CHEESE AND BACON CUSTARDS (R 422)

1810 CORNED BEEF FRITTERS ("Burdekin Duck")

This is an old Australian country recipe and the name used above is a North Queensland bush one, which should appeal to children.

leftover cold corned meat,   pancake batter [R 1205]
  finely chopped   oil or fat

Prepare pancake batter and add meat. Heat oil or fat in frying pan, and put in large spoonfuls of the mixture. When bubbles show on the top of each fritter, you'll know it's ready to turn over.

Serve with tomato sauce, grilled tomatoes or fried left over vegetables. Very small children seem to prefer the meat to be flaked into their fritters which makes it easier for them to manage. The size of the meat pieces can be varied to keep every age group happy.

1811 FISH BALLS

375g [12 oz] cooked smoked   salt and pepper
  cod, or cooked fresh fish,   2 eggs
  flaked   flour
1 tablespoon grated onion   butter or oil
4 tablespoons milk
375g [12 oz] cooked, mashed
  potatoes

Combine flaked fish, onion, milk, mashed potato, salt and pepper, and bind well with eggs. If too dry, add a little more milk. Shape into small balls, roll in flour and brown in hot butter or oil.

HONEYED CHEESE (R 1156)

SAVOURY SNACKS (R 401)

OTHER PATES (R 118, 119, 120, 121, 2416)

*Take fresh plums or apricots on a picnic in an egg carton lined with plastic wrap. They won't squash and can all be lifted out together.

The Pantry Shelf.

For the Pantry Shelf

We have rose candy, we have spikenard,
Mastic and terebinth and oil and spice,
And such sweet jams meticulously jarred
As God's Own Prophet eats in Paradise.

James Elroy Flecker, Hassan.

1900 JAMS, MARMALADES, CHUTNEYS, PICKLES AND PRESERVES

Making your own preserves can be a most satisfying occupation and it need not be time consuming or difficult. It certainly is economical, whether using your home-grown fruit and vegetables or buying produce in season. Further economies can be made by buying a bag of sugar and perhaps bulk vinegar at the beginning of the season rather than purchasing in small amounts. It is wise to work out what are your family's needs, as it is better to make small amounts of several varieties. You may have a vision of jam making and preserving as a great dramatic performance—the whole family chopping up fruit all day—waiting interminably for "setting point" to be reached—exhaustion and bad temper! However if you make small quantities you will find the whole operation peaceful, undramatic and easy. A well stocked pantry shelf is a most useful standby and a great source of admiration!

Jams

A general guide for making most types of jam.
To every 500g [1 lb] of prepared fruit use:
   500g [1 lb] sugar
   juice of 1 lemon
   ¼ cup water [if using very ripe or juicy fruit such as plums and berries no water is necessary].

Preparation of fruit depends on the variety used. Wash all fruit well unless it requires peeling such as canteloupe or pineapple. Remove stones and pips and cut fruit into small even pieces. Place prepared fruit, lemon juice, water and any pips or stones from fruit (tied in a muslin bag) in a pan and cook gently until soft. Warm sugar in a low oven and add gradually, keeping the jam at boiling point. Stir in well, and boil rapidly until "setting point" is reached. The time will de-

288

pend on the amount and type of fruit used. A useful test is to place a little cooked jam on a saucer and cool it—if the skin wrinkles, the jam is set. A jam thermometer is a useful aid. "Setting point" is 220°F (105°C) while the jam is boiling. What you have to do is boil until enough liquid has evaporated to give you a mixture of fruit, liquid and sugar which will set when cold.

You may need to skim off froth before pouring jam into clean, warm jars. Seal while hot or when completely cold. Do not seal while lukewarm. If sealing with paraffin wax it is preferable to wait until jam is cold. Label jars and store in cool place.

If the fruit used has a low pectin level use more lemon or a commercially prepared pectin powder to assist setting.

If fermenting occurs after storing it may be caused either by not enough sugar or insufficient cooking after the addition of the sugar.

Shrinkage of jam will occur if jars are not properly covered or are stored in a warm place.

Do not be frightened to experiment a little—try a combination of two or three fruits. Often this greatly improves the flavour and can have the advantage of combining fruits low in pectin with fruits with a high pectin content, such as blackberry and apple.

1901 CARROT JAM

3 medium carrots   *10 cups water*
4 large lemons   *2kg [4 lb] sugar*

Grate carrots. Slice lemons very finely. Cover with water and leave overnight. Then boil the mixture for 1 hour, add the sugar and boil again for 1 hour or until it has reached setting point. Bottle and seal.

1902 ROCKMELON or CANTELOUPE JAM

2kg [4 lb] rockmelon or   *1.5kg [3 lb] sugar*
  canteloupe   *juice of 4 medium lemons*

Peel, seed and dice melon. Cover with half quantity of sugar and stand for 3 hours. Place on stove, bring slowly to boiling point and add rest of sugar. Boil rapidly until setting point is reached—approx 1 hour. Bottle in clean, warm jars and seal.

*Apples added to the other fruit when making jam will increase both the quantity and pectin content.

1903 PINEAPPLE CONSERVE

2kg [4 lb] pineapple
2kg [4 lb] sugar
3 medium lemons

Peel and core pineapple, cut into chunks. Place in a bowl and cover with sugar. Cover and stand for 24 hours. Place pineapple mixture in pan together with lemon juice and lemon peel and pips tied in muslin. Bring to the boil stirring frequently. Cook until setting point is reached. Take out peel and pips. Bottle and seal.

1904 PEAR GINGER

3kg [6 lb] firm pears
1.75kg [3½ lb] sugar
500g [1 lb] preserved ginger,
  sliced
3-4 cups [1½ pints] water

Peel, core and dice pears. Cover with sugar and leave overnight. Next day, add ginger and water and boil until set. Bottle and seal.

1905 RHUBARB and ORANGE JAM

1.5kg [3 lb] rhubarb
5 oranges
1.5kg [3 lb] sugar

Cut rhubarb into 1 inch chunks and place in pan with orange juice and simmer until tender. Add orange skins and pips tied in muslin bag, then sugar, stirring until dissolved. Boil quickly until setting point has been reached. Bottle and seal.

1906 FIG JAM

1kg [2 lb] figs, chopped
  roughly
¾ cup orange juice
¼ cup lemon juice
2 tablespoons sweet sherry
1kg [2 lb] sugar

Place chopped figs with juices and sherry in saucepan. Bring to boil and cook until tender. Add warmed sugar, stirring to dissolve. Boil rapidly until setting point is reached—about 25 mins. Bottle and seal.

Variations:
1. Add 90g (3 oz) preserved ginger, finely chopped.
2. Add very finely sliced peel of 2 large lemons in addition to lemon juice.

1907 RASPBERRY JAM

1kg [2 lb] raspberries   *juice of 1 lemon*
1kg [2 lb] sugar

Place fruit in saucepan and heat gently until the juice has started running. Add warmed sugar gradually, stirring until dissolved. Add lemon juice and boil until setting point is reached. Bottle and seal.

1908 QUINCE JELLY

3-5kg [6-10 lb] quinces   *2 lemons, rind and juice*
water
500g [1 lb] sugar to every 600ml
   [1 pint] of juice

Wash quinces, quarter and place in pan. Barely cover with cold water. Slowly bring to boil and simmer until pulpy. Turn into cheesecloth and allow to drip into basin overnight. Do not squeeze bag or jelly will be cloudy. Measure juice and place in clean pan with sugar. Using a vegetable peeler remove rind from lemons and add to pan with lemon juice. Bring slowly to boil, stirring occasionally to dissolve sugar. Boil rapidly until setting point is reached. Pour into clean warm jars and seal. If desired place a piece of lemon rind in each jar before sealing.
Variation: Substitute crab apples for quinces but for every 600ml (1 pint) juice add 375g (¾ lb) sugar.

MARMALADE

To many of us breakfast is not complete without a little marmalade.
A general guide: Scrub skins of fruit well.
Cut fruit in half and squeeze out juice.
Remove excess pith and pips and tie in muslin.
Cut peel into matchstick strips or longer if you like chunky marmalade.
Place all in pan and cover with water and leave overnight.
Bring to boil and simmer until tender.
Warm sugar by placing in low oven.
Add warmed sugar and boil rapidly until setting point is reached. Remove muslin bag.
Allow marmalade to cool slightly for better distribution of peel.
Pour into clean warmed jars.
Cover and seal (R 1900).

1909 GRAPEFRUIT OR ORANGE MARMALADE

1kg [2 lb] grapefruit or
   seville oranges
2 lemons

10 cups [4 pints] water
3kg [6 lb] sugar

Prepare fruit by squeezing juice and cutting peel into strips. Reserve pips in muslin bag. Place fruit, juice and muslin bag in pan, cover with water and leave overnight. Simmer until soft and add sugar. Boil quickly approx 45 mins until setting point is reached. Remove muslin bag. Cool slightly before bottling. Seal.

1910 LEMON GINGER MARMALADE

1.5kg [3 lb] lemons
3.75 litres [6 pints] water
3kg [6 lb] sugar

125g [4 oz] preserved ginger,
   [may be omitted for plain
   marmalade]

Squeeze juice and remove pips and excess pith—tie in muslin bag. Cut peel into thin strips. Place all in pan and boil until tender. Warm sugar in oven and add, stirring well until dissolved. Add chopped ginger and boil rapidly until setting point is reached. Remove muslin bag. Leave to stand for a few mins, then bottle and seal.

1911 CUMQUAT MARMALADE

cumquats
water, allow 5 cups to each
   500g [1 lb] fruit

sugar, allow 750g [1½ lb] to
   each 500g [1 lb] fruit

Slice fruit, remove pips and place in muslin bag, cover with water and leave for 8 hours. Boil in pan with muslin bag until tender, stand for further 8 hours. Return to stove, add sugar stirring to dissolve and boil until setting point is reached. Remove muslin bag. Allow to stand for few mins, then bottle and seal.

*When making jam, add 1 teaspoon brandy, whisky or rum to cover top of jam before sealing. This prevents any mould and improves the flavour.

*Brush the pan with a little oil to prevent jam frothing up.

*A wooden spoon standing in the jam pan prevents boiling over.

1912 FOUNDER'S MARMALADE

A very economical marmalade made from orange or grapefruit skins which you would normally discard after you have used the fruit. Just keep them in the refrigerator until you have enough. It is not very elegant, but it is easy.

2 cups chopped or minced
orange or grapefruit peel
2½ cups water

juice of 2 large lemons
1kg [2 lb] sugar

Soak peel in water overnight. In morning add lemon juice, and simmer with lid on the saucepan until fruit is soft. Add warmed sugar and boil rapidly until setting point is reached. Bottle and seal.

1913 GRAPEFRUIT AND PINEAPPLE MARMALADE

2 medium grapefruit
2 medium lemons
1 medium to large pineapple

6 cups water
4-6 cups sugar

Remove yellow rind from grapefruit and lemons and shred finely. Squeeze the juice and strain through a fine strainer. Tie white pith and seeds in a piece of muslin. Place peel and juice in a bowl with water and stand overnight. Next day shred pineapple—there should be about 3 cups of shredded pineapple and juice. Place all fruit and muslin bag in pan and simmer until cooked (½-1 hour). Measure the fruit and liquid and to each 1 cup add 1 cup of sugar. Return to heat, stir until dissolved. Boil rapidly until setting point is reached. Remove muslin bag. Cool a little before bottling. Seal.

1914 FIVE FRUITS MARMALADE

500g [1 lb] oranges
500g [1 lb] lemons
500g [1 lb] cumquats
500g [1 lb] mandarins

500g [1 lb] grapefruit
2.5kg [5 lb] sugar
10 cups [4 pints] water

Slice cumquats, reserving pips. Squeeze other fruits and reserve juices. Cut the skins into thin strips. Place any excess pith and all pips into muslin. Place peel, juice and muslin bag in pan and cover with water. Leave overnight. Next day bring to boil and simmer until tender. Add warmed sugar and boil rapidly until setting point is reached. Remove muslin bag. Cool slightly, bottle and seal.

Sauces, Chutneys and Pickles

1915 MINT JELLY WITH APPLE

1.5kg [3 lb] green apples
small bunch fresh mint
2¾ cups water
2¾ cups vinegar

sugar, about 1kg [2 lb]
3 extra tablespoons chopped
   fresh mint
few drops green colouring

Wash apples, quarter and place in preserving pan with water and bunch of mint. Simmer until apples are pulpy, add vinegar and boil 5 mins. Strain overnight through cheesecloth. Measure juice and allow 500g (1 lb) sugar for each 2½ cups juice. Bring sugar and juice to boil stirring until dissolved. Boil rapidly until setting point is reached, add chopped mint and colouring and boil further 3 mins. Bottle and seal.

1916 TOMATO SAUCE

This quantity may be reduced proportionately.

10kg [20 lb] ripe tomatoes,
   chopped
1.5kg [3 lb] apples
30g [1 oz] garlic
125g [4 oz] salt
3 cups vinegar
1kg [2 lb] sugar

½ teaspoon cayenne pepper or
   tabasco sauce [more if
   desired]
30g [1 oz] cloves
30g [1 oz] peppercorns
60g [2 oz] allspice

Wash bottles well and place in low oven for 30 mins.
Peel, core and dice apples. Finely chop garlic. Place together with tomatoes in pan and boil until very soft and pulpy. Strain through a coarse sieve to remove skins. Return to pan with salt, vinegar, sugar, cayenne and spices tied in muslin bag. Boil rapidly for 2 hours. Remove muslin bag. Bottle and seal.

Put bottles or jars in sterilizer, add warm water to come ¾ way up sides of bottles, bring to 170°F (80°C) and hold at this temperature for 30 mins.

1917 PLUM SAUCE

3kg [6 lb] plums
7½ cups vinegar
1kg [2 lb] brown sugar
750g [1½ lb] brown onions

60g [2 oz] salt
15g [½ oz] cloves
15g [½ oz] peppercorns
¼ teaspoon cayenne pepper

Place all ingredients in pan and boil gently until plums are soft and pulpy—about 1½ hours. Strain through sieve, bottle and seal.

Variation: Add 30g (1 oz) bruised ginger or 1 teaspoon of ground ginger.

294

1918 TOMATO CHUTNEY

"My grandparents owned several hotels and Grandmother spent a large part of her spare time (apart from her 14 children) making preserves for the guests. This has been a favourite with family and friends for years."

10kg [20 lb] ripe tomatoes, peeled and cut roughly

1.5kg [3 lb] onions, finely chopped

1.5kg [3 lb] apples, peeled and finely chopped

60g [2 oz] garlic, finely chopped

250g [½ lb] sultanas

2kg [4 lb] sugar

250g [½ lb] salt

4 cups vinegar—use less if tomatoes are very ripe

250g [½ lb] preserved ginger, finely cut

15-30g [½-1 oz] cayenne pepper

60g [2 oz] cloves

60g [2 oz] allspice

[last two ingredients tied in muslin bag]

Place all ingredients in pan with bag of spice. Boil well for 2 hours. Remove bag. Bottle and seal when cold.

1919 MADRAS CHUTNEY

500g [1 lb] apples, peeled, cored, and diced

500g [1 lb] dark plums, peeled, stoned and chopped

500g [1 lb] yellow peaches, peeled, stoned and chopped

500g [1 lb] tomatoes, peeled, and chopped

500g [1 lb] dates, chopped

500g [1 lb] preserved ginger, finely chopped

500g [1 lb] raisins, chopped

1.5kg [3 lb] sugar

45g [1½ oz] salt

7½ cups vinegar

60g [2 oz] garlic

15g [½ oz] hot chillies

15g [½ oz] whole allspice

[last three ingredients tied in muslin bag]

juice and grated rind of 1 lemon

Place all ingredients in pan. Boil gently for 2 hours. Remove muslin bag. Bottle and seal. Particularly nice served with curries.

*If you have no muslin bag an old handkerchief can be used instead.

295

1920 DRIED APRICOT CHUTNEY

500g [1 lb] dried apricots
750g [1½ lb] onions
250g [8 oz] sultanas or raisins
2 cloves garlic, crushed
500g [1 lb] sugar

juice and grated rind of
  2 oranges
3½ cups malt vinegar
½ teaspoon ground allspice
1 teaspoon mustard

Soak apricots overnight in water. Drain and cut into small pieces. Finely chop onions and raisins. Mix all ingredients together in pan. Simmer about 1 hour until thick and soft, stirring occasionally to prevent sticking. Pour into hot, clean jars and seal.

1921 MIXED PICKLES

Suggested vegetables are as follows, but allow your imagination to work for different combinations, or just try two or three.

500g [1 lb] carrots
500g [1 lb] parsnips
500g [1 lb] small onions
500g [1 lb] sugar
1 tablespoon mustard seed

2 teaspoons celery seed
7 cups vinegar
2 red peppers, sliced
2 green peppers, sliced
½ stick celery, chopped

Peel and slice carrots, parsnips and onions. Place in pan with sugar, seeds and half the vinegar. Boil for 15 mins then add remaining vinegar, peppers and celery. Bring back to boil and cook for further 3 mins. Bottle and seal when cold.

1922 MUSTARD PICKLES

1kg [2 lb] French beans
3kg [6 lb] green tomatoes
1kg [2 lb] onions
500kg [1 lb] cauliflower
   flowerets
¾ cup salt
8 cups vinegar
750g [1½ lb] sugar

2 teaspoons cloves
2 teaspoons whole allspice
[tied in muslin bag]
4 tablespoons flour
2 tablespoons mustard
1 tablespoon turmeric
½ teaspoon cayenne

String beans and cut in 1" pieces, chop tomatoes, and slice onions. Place together with cauliflower in bowl sprinkling each layer with salt. Leave overnight. Next day drain off liquid and discard. Bring vinegar and sugar to boil, stirring to dissolve. Add vegetables and spice bag and boil until just cooked, about ½ hour. Mix flour, turmeric, mustard and cayenne to a smooth paste with a little vinegar. Add to pan, stirring constantly until it thickens. Boil for further 5 mins. Remove muslin bag. Bottle and seal.

296

1923 RED CABBAGE PICKLE

1 red cabbage, shredded
½ cup salt [or more if
   cabbage is large]
10 cups vinegar
1 extra teaspoon salt

60g [2 oz] peppercorns
60g [2 oz] mustard seed
2 blades mace
60g [2 oz] green ginger,
   bruised

Spread shredded cabbage on flat dish and cover liberally with salt, leave overnight. Next day drain off liquid and place cabbage in clean jars. Boil all other ingredients together for 5 mins. Strain and pour over cabbage while still hot. Seal.

1924 ZUCCHINI PICKLE

1kg [2 lb] zucchini, thinly
   sliced
2 small onions, thinly sliced
¼ cup salt
2 cups white vinegar

1 teaspoon caraway seed
1 teaspoon turmeric or
   cummin
2 teaspoons mustard seed

Place sliced zucchini and onion in bowl, add salt and cover with water. Stand for 2 hours. Drain well. Bring all other ingredients to boil. Pour over zucchini and stand for further 2 hours. Replace on stove and bring all to boil, simmer for 15 mins. Bottle and seal.

1925 CUCUMBER PICKLE

3-4 unpeeled green
   cucumbers, thinly sliced
3 medium white onions,
   thinly sliced
¾ cup salt

1 cup water
3 cups vinegar
2½ cups sugar
2 tablespoons celery seed
2 tablespoons mustard seed

Arrange cucumber and onion in layers in bowl sprinkling each layer with salt. Cover and stand for 3 hours. Drain off liquid. Combine remaining ingredients in large saucepan and bring to boil, stirring until sugar is dissolved. Boil for 3 mins. Add cucumber and onion and bring nearly to boiling point—but do not boil. Place in jars and seal.

1926 PICKLED ONIONS

Select firm, small onions of the pickling variety. Quantities will depend on the number of onions you wish to pickle.

onions, peeled
salt
5 cups vinegar
2½ cups sugar
1 tablespoon peppercorns
1 tablespoon whole allspice

1 tablespoon cloves
[last three ingredients tied in muslin bag]

Brine: 1 cup salt to 5 cups water

Soak onions overnight in brine. Drain, dry and warm them by placing them on baking trays in a low oven. Combine sugar, vinegar and spice bag in pan and bring to boil, stirring to dissolve sugar. Boil for 3 mins. Cool. Remove spice bag. Place warm onions in jars and pour over vinegar. Seal and leave for 6-8 weeks before use.

Other Fruit Preserves

1927 FRUIT MINCEMEAT

500g [1 lb] raisins
500g [1 lb] sultanas
500g [1 lb] currants
125g [4 oz] mixed peel
250g [8 oz] beef suet, grated
   or finely chopped
500g [1 lb] cooking apples

500g [1 lb] brown sugar
grated rind 1 lemon
grated rind 1 orange
1 teaspoon cinnamon
½ teaspoon nutmeg
½ teaspoon allspice
1 cup brandy or rum

Chop raisins and sultanas finely and mix with currants, beef suet and mixed peel (chop the latter if necessary). Peel, core and chop apples finely and add to mixture with orange and lemon rinds and spices. Dissolve sugar in brandy and pour over mixture. Cover and let stand overnight. Stir well and place in clean dry jars, cover loosely and store in a cool dry place for at least a month before using.

1928 LEMON BUTTER

4 eggs, beaten
4 large lemons

500g [1 lb] sugar
125g [4 oz] butter

Grate rind of lemons and squeeze juice. Place butter and sugar in double saucepan. When melted add juice and grated rind of lemons. Then add eggs. Stir until smooth and thickened—about 20 mins. Bottle and seal. It is best stored in the refrigerator.

Variation: Add 10 passionfruit to eggs and sugar.

1929 APRICOT BUTTER

2kg [4 lb] apricots
juice of ½ lemon
water to cover

sugar, allow 1 cup to each
2 cups of pulp

Chop apricots, cover with water, add lemon juice. Simmer until pulpy. Sieve and measure the pulp. Add sugar and bring to boil, simmering until thickened. Bottle and seal while still hot.

1930 PRESERVED CUMQUATS

When picking cumquats leave a tiny portion of the stalk intact.

1kg [2 lb] cumquats
water to cover

2½ cups sugar
brandy [optional]

Prick cumquats all over well with a needle. Cover with water and bring to the boil. Simmer for 20 mins then strain fruit, reserving the liquid. Add sugar to liquid and boil briskly for 5 mins. Return fruit to syrup and cook gently for approx 30 mins. Let stand overnight to plump fruit then bottle and seal. Keep for 2 weeks before using. If using brandy, replace half the boiled syrup with brandy and stir gently to blend.

1931 CANDIED PEEL

peel of oranges and/or
    lemons

water
sugar

Scrub skins well and cut into strips about ¼ inch thick. Cover with water and bring to the boil. Strain and discard water. Repeat this twice. Measure or weigh peel and add equal quantity of sugar. Add just enough water to dissolve sugar. Bring slowly to the boil and boil until syrup has evaporated. Toss peel in white sugar and spread out on absorbent paper to dry. The drying process will take several hours. Store in airtight containers.

1932 BRANDIED APRICOTS OR PEACHES

apricots or peaches, firm
    but ripe
sugar, 125g [4 oz] for each
    500g [1 lb] of fruit

brandy

Wash fruit and prick all over thoroughly with needle. Pack into clean dry jars. Sprinkle sugar over the fruit and cover with brandy. Stir fruit gently from time to time over the next 24 hours, then seal and store for 3 months before using.

1933 BRANDIED CHERRIES OR BERRY FRUITS

6 cups cherries and/or
    strawberries, logan-
    berries, raspberries

4 cups sugar
2 cups brandy

Cherries are better if stoned. In large screw top jar, place brandy with ¾ cup sugar and 1 cup of fruit. Stir gently to dissolve sugar. For each cup of fruit add ¾ cup of sugar. This can be done over a period of several days as fruit comes to hand. Continue to stir occasionally for a couple of days to ensure sugar is dissolved. Leave to stand for 1-2 months before using. Very good served over ice-cream or apple pie.

1934 COTTAGE CHEESE

5 cups milk
2 tablespoons salt

2 unflavoured junket tablets,
    dissolved in a little water

Heat milk until lukewarm. Stir in salt and junket tablets. Allow to cool and set—about 20 mins. Cut with knife to allow whey to separate. Strain through cheesecloth, old stocking or very fine strainer—this can take up to 12 hours depending on how dry one wants to serve the cheese. Refrigerate to keep. Is pleasant served with lettuce, or on dry biscuits or rye bread.

Variation: Add fresh chopped chives, parsley or carraway seeds.

Yoghurt

Turning milk into yoghurt is dependent on the lactic acid culture and will only occur satisfactorily if the milk is kept at a warmish temperature for quite a long period. Once this process is mastered, it is easy to keep the "plant" going by reserving a cup of the plain yoghurt to use as a starter next time. It is preferable to use the starter yoghurt within 5 days. When able to master the art of yoghurt making, experiment with flavours e.g. honey, malt, coffee, fruit.
For ideas for serving (R 1155).

935 YOGHURT (1)

Quantities may be reduced proportionally.

4 cups cold water   *3½ cups boiling water*
2 cups skim milk powder   *1 cup unflavoured yoghurt*

Place cold water and skim milk in large bowl and whisk until dissolved. Add boiling water then yoghurt and whisk again. Place in thermos flasks, replace lids firmly and leave for 18-24 hours until set. Refrigerate.
Alternatively, place in earthenware casserole with lid, cover with thick towel and stand in warm place.

936 YOGHURT (2)

1 can [1½ cups] evaporated   *6 cups warm water*
  milk   *3 tablespoons unflavoured*
1½ cups skim milk powder   *yoghurt*

Beat well together. Put into jars with lids. Stand jars in warm water up to their necks. Keep water at 105-115° for 4 hours until set. Refrigerate.

1937 YOGHURT (3)

2 cups tepid water
1½ cups powdered milk
2 tablespoons unflavoured
  yoghurt

600ml [1 pint] tepid water
½ can [approx ¾ cup] evaporated milk

Using hand beater, mix 2 cups water, powdered milk and yoghurt in a warmed bowl. Then add remaining water and evaporated milk. Strain (if necessary) into warmed 2½ pint casserole or parfait glasses. Stand on several layers of newspaper in frypan set at 100°F. Check after 5 hours. If necessary leave for further hour until set. Chill.

"There's cold chicken inside it", replied the Rat briefly, "coldtonguecolo. coldbeefpickledgherkinssaladfrenchrollscressandwichespottedmeatginge. beerlemonadesodawater—"

Kenneth Grahame, The Wind in the Willows

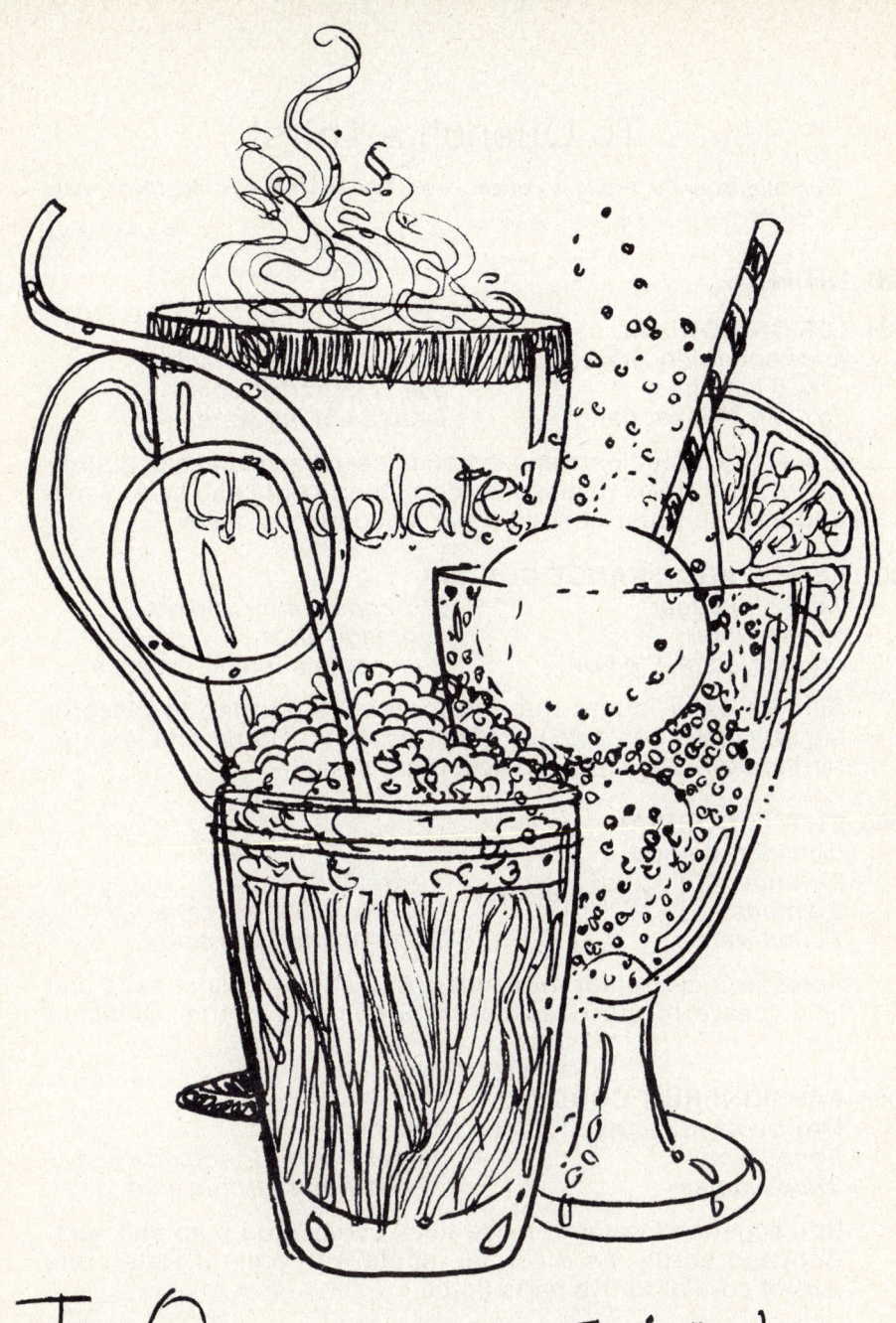

To Quench a Thirst

To Quench a Thirst

Look here, steward, if this is coffee, I want tea; but if this is tea, then I wish for coffee.

Punch. 1902

2000 DRINKS

2001 LEMON CORDIAL
juice and finely grated rind
   of 6 lemons
1½-2kg [4 lb] sugar

30g [1 oz] tartaric acid
60g [2 oz] citric acid
8 cups boiling water

Put all dry ingredients and lemon juice in basin and add boiling water slowly. Mix to dissolve, cool, then bottle and seal. Serve diluted with water or soda water, according to taste.

2002 LEMON AND ORANGE CORDIAL
1kg [2 lb] sugar
5 cups water
grated rind of 1 lemon

2½ cups lemon and/or
   orange juice
2 teaspoons lemon essence

Simmer water, sugar and rind for 5 mins, stirring to dissolve sugar. Cool, then add juice and essence. Bottle and keep in refrigerator. Serve diluted according to taste.

2003 CITRUS CORDIAL
(Blender method)
2 oranges ⎤
2 lemons ⎦ more if desired
7 cups water

1.5kg [3 lb] sugar
30g [1 oz] Epsom salts
30g [1 oz] tartaric acid

Puree fruit and water in blender. Add sugar, Epsom salts and acid. Leave to stand 24 hours. Strain and bottle. Dilute to taste.

2004 PASSIONFRUIT CORDIAL
May be used as topping for ice cream.
3 cups water
3 cups sugar

12 passionfruit, pulped
½ teaspoon tartaric acid

Boil sugar and water to make thick syrup. Add pulp and acid. Cool and bottle. As a cordial, dilute with milk or water; one part of cordial to five parts liquid.

*To make extra ice-cubes for a party remove ice-blocks from trays and place in a plastic bag in the freezer, leaving the ice-cube tray free for another batch.

2005 ROSE HIP SYRUP

1kg [2 lb] rose hips
250g [8 oz] sugar
juice of 1 lemon

10 cups water
bottles

Wash bottles well and place in low oven for 30 mins. Bring water to boil. Mince rose hips and add immediately to water. Bring quickly back to boil, then remove from heat and stand 20 mins. Strain contents through jelly bag or muslin. Pour juice into saucepan with lemon juice and sugar. Stir to dissolve and boil 5 mins. Pour into bottles and seal well. Dilute according to taste.

2006 BARLEY WATER

A delicious, thirst-quenching drink in hot water, and for the sick child.

3 tablespoons pearl barley
  and enough water to cover
9 cups water

juice and peel of 2 oranges
juice and peel of 2 lemons
4 tablespoons sugar

Cover barley with water, bring to boil, strain and discard water. Cover barley with 9 cups water, bring to boil again and simmer 15 mins. Thinly peel rind from fruit and place with juice in bowl. Add sugar, then pour in barley water using sieve to strain out barley. Remove rind, cool and keep in refrigerator. If wished, you can add 4 cups freshly boiling water to the used barley to make a second weaker concoction, simmering only 10 mins, and adding to fresh bowl of juice and rinds and sugar.

2007 FRUIT EGG NOG

½ cup orange juice
1 cup grape juice
1 egg, separated

sugar or honey to taste
¼ teaspoon salt

Beat juices, yolk and sugar. Beat white stiffly with salt and fold into drink.

2008 BLACKCURRANT AND APPLE FIZZ

30ml [1 oz] blackcurrant syrup
1 cup apple juice

300ml [½ pint] lemonade
icecream

Chill fruit juices. Add lemonade just before serving and beat in icecream until frothy.

2009 PINEAPPLE DRINK

skin and core only of 1 large
  pineapple
8 cups water

¼ cup lemon juice
1 cup sugar
mint to garnish

Put skin and core of pineapple in pan and simmer covered 2 hours. Strain liquid into another saucepan. Add juice and sugar. Boil 5 mins, stirring to dissolve sugar. Cover and cool. Serve icy cold and garnish with mint.

2010 GINGER BEER (1)

4½ cups boiling water
2 cups sugar
9 cups cold water
15ml [½ oz] ginger essence
30g [1 oz] compressed yeast

] obtainable
from Health
Food shops

Pour boiling water over sugar and stir well until sugar dissolves. Add cold water and ginger essence. Mix yeast with a little of the mixture, then add to remaining mixture. Stir well. Bottle and cork as illustrated.

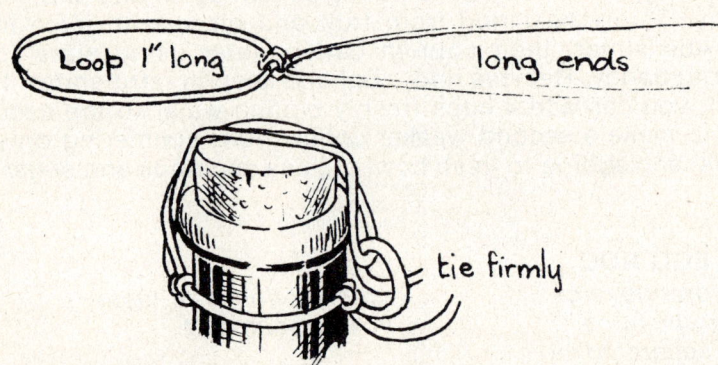

Loop 1" long   long ends

tie firmly

2011 GINGER BEER (2)

12 cups hot water
12 cups cold water
3 cups sugar
4 teaspoons powdered ginger

1 teaspoon tartaric acid
juice of 2 lemons
18 sultanas
6 bottles, with screw lids

Mix all ingredients except sultanas. Pour into bottles and place 3 sultanas in each bottle before capping. Leave 1-2 weeks before using.

2012 ADVOKAAT

6 eggs
1 can [420g] condensed milk
1⅓ cups brandy

1 teaspoon vanilla
1 tablespoon malt extract

Mix together thoroughly and bottle. Keep in refrigerator. Serve topped with lemonade.

2013 FRUIT CUP

Serves about 35.
8 lemons
8 oranges
3 litres [5 pints] canned
  pineapple juice
3 cups cold black tea
1½ cups sugar

3 litres [5 pints] soda water
3 litres [5 pints] dry ginger
3 tablespoons chopped mint
1 cup strawberries, fresh or
  canned
large chunks of ice

Squeeze oranges and lemons, combine juice with pineapple juice and cold tea. Add sugar, stir well to dissolve. Just prior to serving add soda, dry ginger, ice and lastly strawberries and mint.

Variation: Replace one or two litres of the soda and dry ginger with white wine, or for an attractive appearance try claret.

2014 SANGRIA

An easy and pleasant drink for summer parties.
1 bottle [780ml] dry red wine
1 bottle [780ml] lemonade
1 bottle [780ml] soda water
juice of 2 lemons and 2
  oranges

1 banana, thinly sliced
2 lemons, thinly sliced

Mix all ingredients together in large jug. Serve chilled. An extra bottle of wine can be added if a stronger drink is desired.

*To avoid diluting the punch too much use lemonade or fruit juice for ice blocks.

2015 MULLED RED WINE

2 bottles [780ml] red wine
250g [8 oz] castor sugar
orange and lemon rind
lemon slices

6 cloves
1 nutmeg
2 sticks cinnamon

tied together
in muslin
bag

Pour wine into saucepan, add sugar, rind and muslin bag containing spices. Stir well and heat until nearly boiling. Remove bag and rind and ladle into wine glasses. Add small slice lemon to each glass. Reheat if necessary but do not add spice bag again.

2016 CHAMPAGNE COCKTAIL

For each person:
1 cube lump sugar
lemon peel
dash of bitters

1 teaspoon brandy
1 glass champagne or any
    dry white sparkling wine,
    chilled

Rub sugar on lemon peel to absorb lemon oil. Place a lump in each champagne glass, add bitters and brandy. Fill glass with champagne and top with twist of lemon peel.

2017 CAFE BRULOT DIABOLIQUE

Marvellous end to a dinner party
6 cups strong black coffee
rind of ½ lemon or orange
12 cloves
15 cubes lump sugar
2" cinnamon stick

¾ cup cognac
¼ cup cointreau or grand
    marnier
6 tablespoons slightly whipped
    cream

Prepare coffee and keep hot. Stud rind with cloves. Place sugar, cinnamon and clove studded rind in an ovenproof bowl. Heat liqueurs and pour over sugar. Ignite and stir until sugar is dissolved. While liqueurs are still flaming add hot coffee and stir. Serve in brulot cups, Irish coffee glasses or coffee cups with cream floating on the top.

IRISH COFFEE (R 2421)

*To make a pretty ice-ring for the punch bowl place decoratively cut pieces of fruit in the bottom of a ring-tin. Pour a small amount of lemonade on to the fruit and freeze until firm. Now pour more lemonade over the first layer (the fruit has been "set" and cannot float around). Freeze and unmould to float in the punch bowl. For an adult party, white wine can be used instead of lemonade.

Milk Drinks

The following are good high protein drinks.
Place all ingredients in blender or beat well with a rotary beater.

2018 EGG NOG
1 cup milk
½ teaspoon vanilla
1 tablespoon honey
1 teaspoon brandy

2 teaspoons skim milk
   powder
1 egg yolk

2019 BUTTERMILK
1 cup commercial butter-
   milk
2 teaspoons powdered skim
   milk

2 teaspoons honey
¼ teaspoon grated nutmeg

2020 ORANGE MILK
1 cup orange juice
2 teaspoons skim milk
   powder

1 teaspoon honey
1 tablespoon ice-cream

2021 BANANA MILK
1 cup milk
2 teaspoons brown sugar
1 banana
2 teaspoons skim milk
   powder

1 teaspoon brewers yeast
   [optional]
nutmeg to sprinkle on top

2022 PINEAPPLE MILK PUNCH
1 cup chilled milk
¾ cup chilled pineapple juice
¼ cup evaporated milk

¼ teaspoon peppermint
   flavoring [optional]
mint to garnish

Blend thoroughly until foamy. Garnish with sprigs of mint and serve immediately.

2023 MARSHMALLOW CHOCOLATE
1 cup milk, hot or cold
1-2 teaspoons drinking
   chocolate

2 teaspoons ice-cream
   [optional]
1 marshmallow to float on top

Ten pounds of flour, ten pounds of beef, some sugar and some tea,
That's all they give to a hungry man, until the Seventh Day.
If you don't be moighty sparing, you'll go with a hungry gut—
For that's one of the great misfortunes in an old bark hut.

The bucket you boil your beef in has to carry water, too,
And they'll say you're getting mighty flash if you should ask for two.
I've a billy, and a pint pot, and a broken-handled cup,
And they all adorn the table in the old bark hut.

The rain comes down the chimney, and your meat is black with soot—
That's a substitute for pepper in an old bark hut.

The Old Bark Hut. Anon.

310

Candles Cakes & Candy

Candles, Cakes and Candy

2100 CHILDREN'S PARTIES

Parties are special occasions, so mother can afford to turn a "blind-eye" to the sweet treats handed out.

The age group of the children determines the type of party given and the amount and the variety of food offered. Preparation and involvement are the keys to success, and to this end, consultation with the birthday child is essential. Decide on a theme (for 5 years and upwards) and prepare well in advance. Even post the invitations—give each guest the rare thrill of getting a letter. Involvement of older children is half the fun and of inestimable help to mother, so suggest that the children make the invitations, decorations, prizes for games and containers for sweets.

Children of three years and over seem to like savoury food as well as jelly and cakes. They love tiny pies and pasties as well as sausage rolls and cocktail sausages. These are very easy to make using your usual recipe and just cutting the pastry into very small pieces. Make sandwiches in shapes by using a biscuit cutter on the bread and butter—tiny round ones are popular with small children. Open sandwiches—also small—are an attention getter too. If making jelly, use a ring mould and fill the centre with fruit salad, flavoured coloured custard, or ice cream. For the table setting, perhaps use the paper cloths now available in nursery or cartoon prints. They often have matching plates, drinking cups, napkins, etc. and although expensive make a table gay, and save much cleaning up afterwards. If the weather is fine, move the table outside. Be sure that the birthday cake is one that young children can eat. Don't be too elaborate—children don't really mind, as long as it is colourful and gay. Make servings of everything really small, they can always come back for more. Don't forget too, that any drink tastes better with a straw in it!

Ask older children, for whom sweet party food is 'out', to suggest a dinner menu, and you will be delighted or amazed at the sophistication of their palate; hot legs of roast chicken, quiches, savoury pies, crayfish, cheese sticks, celery, tomato wedges and tossed green salad. Serve a variety of dried fruits and fun fresh fruit in season, e.g. water melon, cherries, coconuts, grapes, almonds and walnuts.

312

Children of school-age enjoy an outing away from home. Have you thought of going blackberrying, mushrooming, cherry-picking, bike riding, bushwalking or having a barbecue with billy tea and damper? One way of catering for this type of party is to write each child's name on a cardboard box or similar container, and fill it with paper napkin, cup, cocktail frankfurts, potato chips and other goodies, to be eaten outdoors. This can lead to a good deal of swapping, as a child who doesn't like cocktail frankfurts will swap them for potato chips and so on, but it makes for minimum preparation of the decorative kind and no cleaning up is involved.

Children love to take something home but this need not be sweets. However, should you decide to send sweets with each child wrap them in bundles of coloured cellophane or try some of these ideas:

2101 PARTY BAGS

1. Umbrellas
Cut crepe paper in triangles and stitch sides together. Use a candy walking stick with a curve for handle, and after filling with sweets, tie around handle with ribbon.

2. Carrots
Make triangles of orange crepe paper, stitch sides together, and stick a green piece to top. When dry, cut green ends finely, fill with sweets and tie at junction of green and orange paper.

3. Fish lolly bags
You will need cylinders of cardboard (4" long approx), crepe paper, curtain rings.
Roll cylinders in crepe paper to form a bon-bon shape. Tie one end, fill with lollies then tie other end. Paste an eye on either side, and scraps of crepe paper for fins. Staple curtain ring to nose. Have a few fishing rods handy so children *catch* their fish before going home.

Fish lolly-bag

4. Paper Bags

Cover brown paper bag with wrapping paper. Punch holes at top and use string to make handles. Write child's name in conspicuous place.

5. Popcorn Flowers

You will need clear cellophane, coloured crepe paper, wooden skewers, obtainable from butcher, or coloured pencils, popcorn, approximately 1 handful for each child. Place popcorn in a circle of clear cellophane—8" in diameter. Place skewer in middle and secure at base with elastic band. Cut crepe paper into strips 2" wide tapering at one end. Arrange these at base of cellophane popcorn ball, and wind down end of bare skewer.

2102 EGG FACES

1. Savoury

Allow half a hard boiled egg for each child. Cut eggs in half lengthwise and place on individual plates—yolk down or up. Use grated cheese, grated carrot or shredded lettuce to make hair around 'egg face'. Use sultanas, pieces of tomato, beetroot, etc to make eyes, nose and mouth and beetroot for bow tie. Stick pieces on with salad dressing or cheese spread. Sometimes a child who doesn't eat salad will eat 'lettuce hair' quite happily.

2. Clown

6 hard boiled eggs
½ cup tuna
1 tablespoon soft butter

1 tablespoon lemon juice
1 red pepper or tomato

Cut top off eggs and carefully scoop out yolks. Mix yolks, tuna, butter and lemon juice together. Pile filling into eggs leaving some protruding and place tops back to form hats. Cut tiny eyes, nose and mouth from red pepper or tomato and place on the protruding filling to form a face. Serve on lettuce leaves.

2103 CHEESE BALLS

125g [4 oz] very soft butter
1 cup grated cheese
¼ teaspoon cayenne pepper

1 cup wholemeal S.R. flour
coconut

Cream butter and cheese. Add pepper and flour. Make into small balls, roll in coconut. Bake in moderate oven for 15 mins.

314

2104 TRAFFIC LIGHT SANDWICHES

24 slices of brown bread
butter
12 cheese slices

4 small tomatoes
3 lettuce leaves
salt and pepper

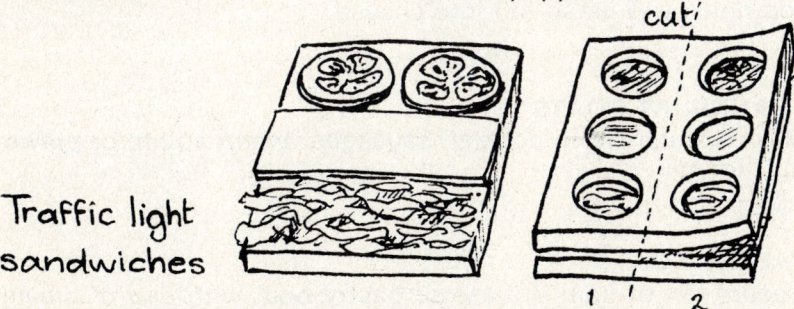

Traffic light sandwiches

Spread bread lightly with butter. Trim crusts. Using round ¾"
cutter, press 6 holes into each of the 12 slices. Slice tomatoes
and shred lettuce. On plain slices, arrange alternately tomato,
cheese and lettuce. Season with salt and pepper. Top with cut
out slices and cut each sandwich in half. Cover with plastic
wrap and leave in refrigerator until ready to serve. The cut out
slices of bread and butter can be used for a crumble topping
for fruit (R 1105.4).

2105 SALAD YACHT

Butter halved bread roll or sliced bread stick, top with lettuce,
tomato, and ham and secure cheese triangle with toothpicks
for sail.

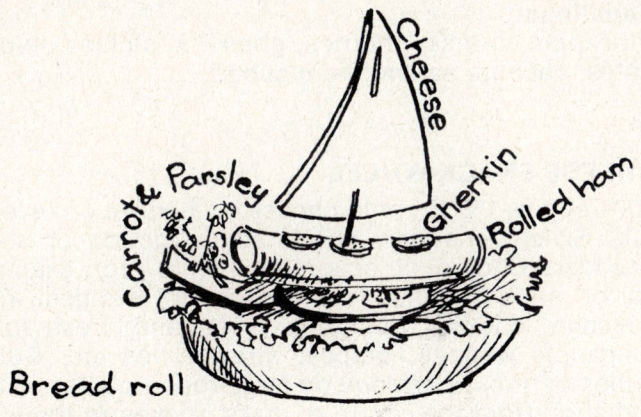

Cheese

Carrot & Parsley

Gherkin

Rolled ham

Bread roll

SANDWICH FILLINGS (R 1801)
SAVOURY SNACKS (R 401)

315

2106 CELERY BOATS
Cut inner stalks of celery into lengths. Cut cheese sticks into smaller lengths and place on celery. Cut small sails from coloured paper. Write children's names on paper, secure to a toothpick and press sail into cheese.

2107 FRANKFURT BOATS
Make a small slit in cocktail sausages. Insert a chip or prawn puff for sail.

2108 PASTRY BOATS
Secure roll of ham in base of pastry boat with dab of cream cheese. Use cheese triangles for sail and attach with toothpick.

2109 MELON CHEESE BITS
mild cheddar cheese   fresh mint sprigs to garnish
watermelon

Cut cheese into bite sized cubes. Using a melon baller, hollow out the watermelon into balls. Thread cheese, watermelon ball and a fresh sprig of mint on to a toothpick, which can be stuck into an orange, apple or grapefruit.

Variations:
Pineapple chunks, cherries, gherkins, pickled onions, prunes, dates, cabana, salami, ham cubes.

2110 CHEESE SNACK WHEEL
500-750g (1-1½ lb) mild cheese or mixture of several varieties e.g. Swiss, cheddar, taffel, edam, gouda or semi-matured cheddar. Choice of accompaniments, for example: celery, carrot sticks, radish roses, tomato wedges, nuts, sliced sausage, cocktail frankfurts or cabana, fresh fruit such as pineapple wedges, grapes, strawberries etc. Cut cheese in cubes or sticks. Arrange on large round platter or tray in rows radiating from the centre to make spokes to the wheel. Fill in the spaces between 'spokes' with your choice of accompaniments keeping each type separate.

2111 CABANA CATERPILLAR

Cut cabana or frankfurts into 1" pieces—secure one piece to the other with toothpicks. Use small triangles of cheese and gherkin (or green cherries) for eyes (attach with toothpicks). Use fine strips of licorice for feelers. Depending on length made, this can be used as the centre piece or part of table decorations.

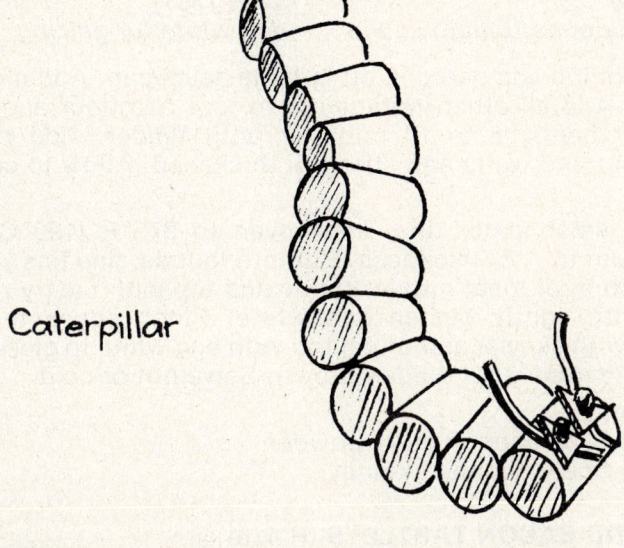

Caterpillar

2112 PRUNE MICE

Use large dessert prunes, replacing stones if desired with jelly beans or almonds. Make licorice tails and use pieces of almonds or rice bubbles for eyes and ears.

Prune mice

2113 MEAT PIES

1 medium onion, chopped	2 teaspoons soya sauce
1 clove garlic, crushed	1½ cups beef stock
1 tablespoon oil	salt and pepper
250g [8 oz] sausage meat	2½ tablespoons cornflour
500g [1 lb] finely minced steak	3 tablespoons water
1 tablespoon worcestershire sauce	500g [1 lb] short crust pastry [R 1301]
4 tablespoons tomato sauce	egg white for glazing

Brown onion and garlic in oil in large saucepan. Add meat and brown. Add all other ingredients except cornflour and water. Simmer gently 5 to 10 mins or until tender. Add blended cornflour and water and stir until thickened. Allow to cool.

Pastry:
Grease small patty tins. Heat oven to 375°F (190°C). Roll pastry out to 1/8" thickness. Cut into rounds, line tins. Place a tablespoon of meat into each one and top with pastry rounds. Seal with lightly beaten egg white. Pinch edges together. Pierce with skewer and brush top with egg white to glaze. Bake for 30-35 mins until golden brown. Serve hot or cold.

Variations:
1. Add 1 tablespoon curry powder.
2. Add finely chopped kidney.

EGG AND BACON TARTLETS (R 416)

2114 JELLY WHIP
Chill one can of evaporated milk overnight. Drain juice from a can of fruit e.g. strawberries, and heat. Add jelly crystals (same colour as fruit), stir until dissolved, then cool. Beat evaporated milk until stiff, slowly add jelly mixture, then fruit. Place in individual serving dishes or icecream cones and refrigerate until set.

2115 RAINBOW JELLIES
Make up 1 packet lime jelly and 1 packet raspberry jelly, set in trays 1" deep. Meantime make up 1 packet lemon jelly, cool but do not allow to set.
To assemble: turn red and green jellies out and cut into ½" dice. Pile roughly into tumblers. Spoon cold yellow jelly over and allow to set. Decorate with whipped cream.

PEANUT BUTTER WHIP (R 1157)

2116 JELLIED ORANGES

Halve oranges lengthwise and scoop out flesh. Use 450ml (¾ pint) juice or water for each packet of jelly. Allow to cool then fill orange halves (on tray). Allow to set then using a warm, sharp knife carefully cut in half again. Alternatively, leave in halves and pipe whipped cream around edge for decoration.

2117 PINEAPPLE CANDLES

Place ring of pineapple on plate. Stand ½ peeled banana in centre. Top with a cherry or dip in orange splinters.

Variation: Instead of pineapple use a round piece of jelly.

2118 PINEAPPLE SCOOP

Cut a whole unskinned pineapple down the centre leaving green top. Remove core, dice flesh, add to other fruit and return all to pineapple case.

2119 LUSCIOUS ICE BLOCKS

1. Cut bananas in half across. Poke pop stick in cut end, then freeze. When frozen, dip ends in melted chocolate for a special treat.
2. Cut oranges into quarters and freeze.
3. Fruit salad ice blocks. Chop up an assortment of summer fruits. Pack into ice block containers. Add a little orange juice or pineapple juice. Freeze.

2120 CHOCOLATE FROG POND

1 tablespoon gelatine
150ml [¼ pint] cold water
2 tablespoons sugar
1 tablespoon cocoa

rum essence
450ml [¾ pint] milk
cream, coffee, sugar,
chocolate, chocolate frogs

Soften gelatine in cold water, stir over gentle heat until dissolved. Add sugar and cocoa and stir. When cool add rum essence and stir into milk. Pour into a shallow dish—bearing some resemblance to a pond. Leave 4-5 hours to set in refrigerator. Immediately before serving, spread with cream, sprinkle with either coffee, sugar, drinking or grated chocolate and place a frog on top for each child.

Quick variation: Make up lime jelly in shallow bowls and when just setting, place chocolate frogs strategically in jelly.

2121 CANDLE CAKES
Use any plain cake mixture cooked in hot greased gem irons. Cool. Make up three quarters of a packet of jelly, cool, and brush cakes with the jelly. Then toss cakes in remaining jelly crystals. Refrigerate until set. Insert candle. Place in front of each child, as young children love to blow out their own candle. Good to send to kindergarten.

2122 PEACH CAKES
Follow R 2121 to stage of tossing cake in jelly crystals (use orange or red jelly). Scoop out top with teaspoon and fill with whipped cream. Replace cake top and insert thin piece of angelica for stalk.

2123 BOAT CAKES
plain cake [R 1401]	drinking straws, cut in
icing	quarters
smarties	cut out paper flag

Cut oblong shape cakes, ice and place 3 smarties along each side (portholes). Attach paper flag to straw, stick on top of cake.

2124 BISCUIT HATS
(No bake)

Marie biscuits	silver cachous
coloured icing	packet of white marsh-
popcorn	mallows

Ice complete one side of biscuit (brim of hat). Place 1 marshmallow on top (crown of hat). Place small pieces of popcorn and silver cachous around base of hat crown.

PATTY CAKES (R 1402)
After icing, let the children decorate with sprinkles, smarties, hundreds and thousands, cherries etc.

ECLAIRS (R 1404)

CREAM PUFFS (R 1405)

320

2125 JAM TARTS (Mushrooms)

Pastry:
90g [3 oz] butter
60g [2 oz] castor sugar
1 egg
185g [6 oz] flour
½ teaspoon baking powder

Filling:
125g [4 oz] butter
125g [4 oz] sugar
vanilla essence
raspberry jam
drinking chocolate

Pastry: Cream butter and sugar. Beat in egg. Sift flour and baking powder and stir into mixture. Knead into smooth ball, wrap and chill for at least an hour. Keep aside some pastry for stalks. Roll remaining pastry out thinly on floured board. Cut into rounds to fit greased patty tins with rounded bases. Prick with a fork. Chill while preparing stalks. Roll reserved pastry between palm of hands to make a narrow roll. Cut at ¾" intervals. Bake with the shells in hot oven 400°F (200°C) for 5-7 mins. Cool.

Filling: Cream butter and sugar well, until sugar is dissolved. Flavour with essence. Spoon some jam into each pastry case. Top with butter mixture and smooth over. Mark with a fork to resemble mushrooms and dust lightly with drinking chocolate. Place stalks in centre of tarts. Makes about 30.

2126 MERINGUE MOONMEN

1½ cups castor sugar
2 egg whites
1 teaspoon vinegar

1 teaspoon cornflour
½ teaspoon vanilla
4 tablespoons water

Place all ingredients in a bowl and beat until shiny (10-15 mins). Use large piping bag with plain ½" nozzle. Pipe into greased oven trays in shape shown using currants or sultanas for features and bake in slow oven until dry and crisp (about 1½ hours). For plain meringues place teaspoonfuls of mixture on greased oven trays and bake as above.

PAVLOVA (R 1161)

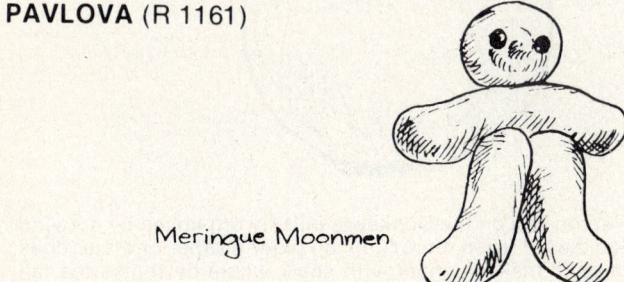

Meringue Moonmen

Birthday Cakes

A round cake can be decorated as a basket, clock, bicycle, sun, wishing well, pussy cat, face or maypole.

A square cake can be a book, field with animals, house, treasure chest, truck or train.

If time is short, make a Simplicity Chocolate Cake (R 1409), ice, and decorate with a border of smarties, which can also be used to "write" the first letter of the birthday child's name in the centre of the cake.

2127 SNOWMAN BIRTHDAY CAKE

1 quantity basic plain cake [R 1401]
2 egg whites
juice of 1 lemon

2 tablespoons gelatine
125g [4 oz] icing sugar
½ cup water

Make cake according to directions. Bake most of mixture in a pudding mould 6"-7" across and remainder in a cup or small mould for 40 mins. Allow to cool. Secure head to body with icing, then dissolve gelatine in water and allow to set partially. Beat egg whites until stiff, add lemon juice, gelatine and icing sugar. Beat well. Pour over cake. Decorate, add bow and scarf.

*The ever-popular Pin the Tail on the Donkey is quickly organised by drawing the donkey on a blackboard (even more fun if an older brother or sister does the art work). Each child makes a mark with chalk where he thinks the tail should be and his name is written beside it.

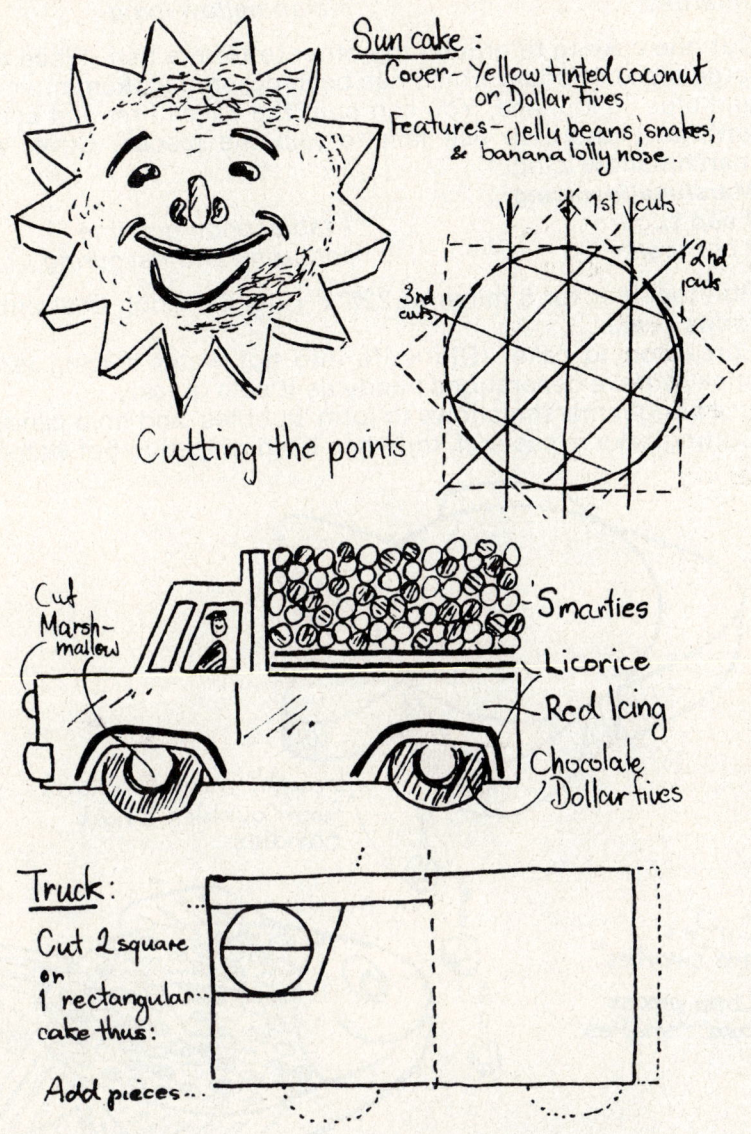

Sun cake :
Cover — Yellow tinted coconut
　　　　or Dollar Fives
Features — Jelly beans, snakes,
　　　　& banana lolly nose.

1st cuts
2nd cuts
3rd cuts

Cutting the points

Cut
Marsh-
mallow

'Smarties
'Licorice
'Red Icing
Chocolate
Dollar fives

Truck :
Cut 2 square
or
1 rectangular
cake thus :

Add pieces...

2128 FISH BIRTHDAY CAKE

two 7" sponge cakes　　　　　*snake lollies*
smarties　　　　　　　　　　*marshmallow icing*

Cut one cake to fit around the other to form a fish. Place on a large piece of board which has been covered in aluminium foil and blue cellophane. You can split the cakes first and spread with jam, and also use jam to join the pieces. Cover with marshmallow icing.

Marshmallow icing:

1 cup sugar　　　　　　　*1 tablespoon gelatine*
1 cup water　　　　　　　*colouring and flavouring*

Boil together for 5 mins, at 225°F (110°C). Cool, beat until it forms peaks.

Spread on to cake. (Dip knife into hot water if icing is too sticky.) Have decorations handy as it sets quickly.

Use bought marshmallows to form 'bubbles' and hold candles.

Cutting cake is easier if knife has been dipped in hot water.

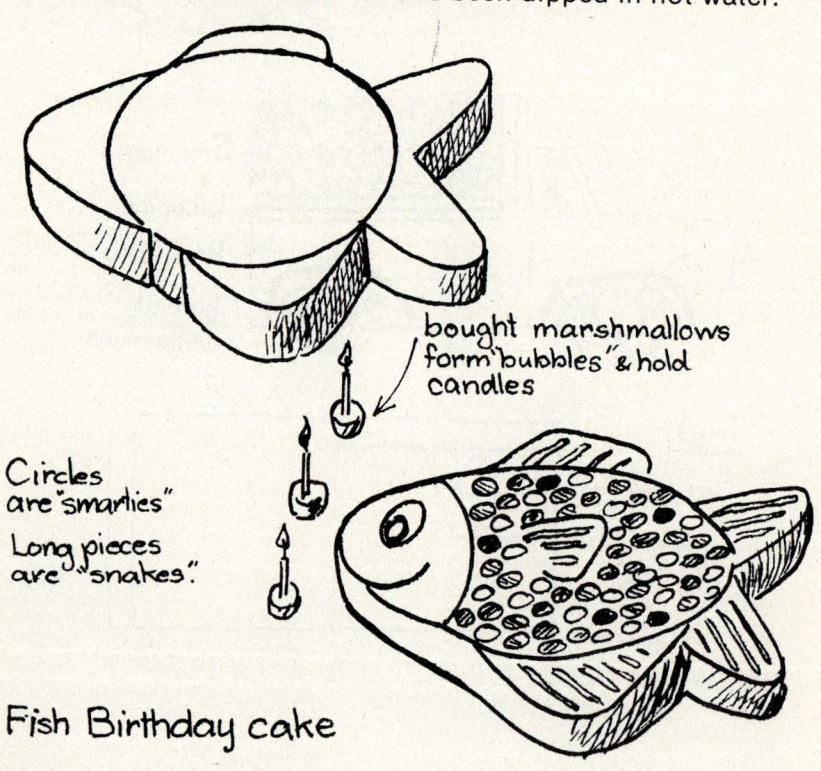

bought marshmallows
form "bubbles" & hold
candles

Circles
are "smarties"

Long pieces
are "snakes".

Fish Birthday cake

324

2129 HANSEL AND GRETEL BIRTHDAY CAKE

750g [1½ lb] flour
2 tablespoons ground ginger
2 tablespoons cinnamon
2 teaspoons baking powder
250g [8 oz] brown sugar

4 tablespoons golden syrup
250g [8 oz] butter
4 eggs, beaten
¼ teaspoon salt

Sift dry ingredients. Melt butter and blend in sugar and syrup. Add eggs, then dry ingredients and mix to a smooth dough. Leave until cold, then knead and roll on a lightly floured board (roll to generous ¼").

Make house as follows: cut
Roof—2 pieces 10" by 5".
Side walls—2 pieces 9" by 5".
End walls—2 pieces 8¾" by 5". Start slope of roof at 5".
Chimney—4 pieces 3½" by 1½".
Bake at 400°F (200°C) for 12 to 15 mins. Leave on trays until cold. Pipe doors and windows. Use royal icing (R 1442) to join walls. If necessary prop until dry.

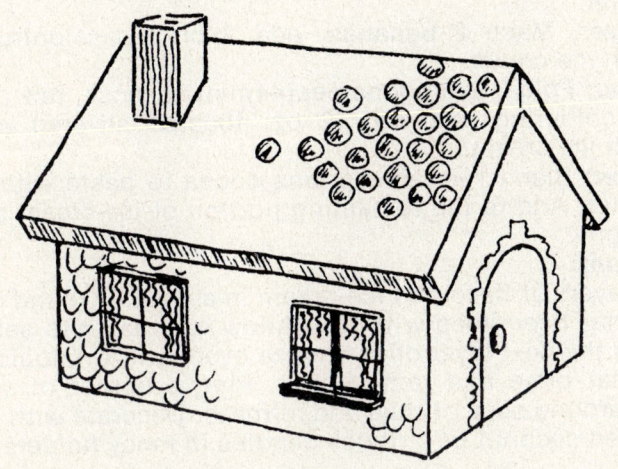

Hansel and Gretel House

2130 ICE-CREAM BIRTHDAY CAKE

1 litre ice-cream
whipped cream
1 tablespoon sugar

1 teaspoon vanilla
decorations—smarties,
grated chocolate, etc.

Make sure ice-cream is frozen firmly. Remove from container (dip into hot water quickly, run knife around edge), cover with whipped cream, which has been flavoured with sugar and vanilla. Decorate as desired e.g. smother in smarties and candles or use small plastic doll or car as a feature. Best to do it the day before and place in freezer to make sure it is firmly frozen. Serve small portions in wafer ice-block containers to save washing up.

2131 RAINBOW ICE-CREAM BIRTHDAY CAKE

Divide 2 litres of vanilla ice-cream into four equal portions and mix each one as follows:

1st layer: Mash 250g (8 oz) packet frozen strawberries or one punnet of fresh strawberries, fold through ice-cream. Colour pale pink.

2nd layer: Mash 2 bananas, add 2 or 3 passionfruit, fold through ice-cream.

3rd layer: Fold 3 teaspoons peppermint essence, few drops of green colouring and 60g (2 oz) toasted slivered almonds through ice-cream.

4th layer: Blend 1½ tablespoons cocoa to paste with a little hot water. Add to the remaining portion of ice-cream and mix thoroughly.

Ice-cream:

Place layers of flavoured ice-cream in a deep 8" round cake tin which has been lined with foil. Allow each layer to set before placing the next layer on it. Freeze overnight. Unmould onto a large flat plate and remove foil. Pipe a border of whipped cream around base of cake and refreeze. Decorate with toasted shredded coconut or birthday candles in fancy holders.

---

*A brightly coloured or striped single bedsheet makes a sturdy and attractive cloth for a party table and easily camouflages two tables pushed together for extra length. Afterwards it can be easily washed in the washing machine.

2132 BOMBE ALASKA

box of sponge fingers, Swiss
   jam roll, broken biscuits
   or stale cake
4-5 tablespoons orange juice
5 egg whites [at room
   temperature]
155g [5 oz] castor sugar

4-5 tablespoons orange juice
¼ teaspoon salt
1 litre block vanilla ice-cream
60g [2 oz] flaked toasted
   almonds
pure icing sugar to dust meringue

Cover ovenproof serving dish with sponge fingers, broken biscuits, or sliced cake. Drizzle with orange juice. Beat egg
whites until stiff, add 1 tablespoon sugar and salt. Whisk
remaining sugar into egg whites. Place ice-cream on biscuits
then flaked almonds to protect the ice-cream from heat. Using
a force bag with large star, cover all of ice-cream with egg
white mixture. Dust with pure icing sugar. Bake for 3-4 mins in
very hot oven 475°F. (250°C). Serve immediately.

Can be prepared 1½ hours before serving and kept in the
freezer. Dust again with icing sugar before baking.

Confectionery

2133 TOFFEE APPLES

500g [1 lb] sugar
½ pint cold water

2 tablespoons vinegar
12 red eating apples

Boil sugar, water and vinegar to 310°F (154°C) or until a
spoonful of mixture cracks when placed in cold water. Stand
saucepan in basin of hot water. Dip skewered apples in syrup.
Place to dry on greased trays.

2134 CREAMY TOFFEE

90-125g [3-4 oz] butter
1 cup sugar
2 tablespoons golden syrup
1 can [400g] sweetened
   condensed milk

90g [3 oz] almonds, chopped
vanilla

Melt butter, add sugar, syrup and condensed milk. Boil slowly,
constantly creaming with wooden spoon for 20-25 mins. Add
nuts and vanilla, and cook another min. Pour into greased tins
to set.

HONEY SLICE (R 1537)

RUM TRUFFLES (R 1539)

2135 MARSHMALLOW FLOWERPOTS

1 tablespoon gelatine
¼ cup cold water
2 cups sugar
1½ cups boiling water

2 teaspoons vanilla or
1 tablespoon lemon juice
or few drops peppermint
flavouring and green colouring

Soak gelatine in cold water, then heat gently until dissolved. Dissolve sugar in boiling water, add gelatine, flavouring, and colouring if used. Beat for about 10 mins on high speed until it stands in peaks and is very thick and creamy. Spoon into flat-bottomed ice-cream cones. Decorate tops with hundreds and thousands or coloured coconut. Refrigerate until set. Put a lollypop into each top to represent a flower. Use angelica for leaves at base.

Variations:

1. Pour in tins sprinkled with coconut if desired, refrigerate until set. Cut into squares and roll in coconut.
2. Marshmallow Hedgehogs: Allow mixture to stand for 10 mins. Toss tablespoonfuls into toasted shredded coconut. Refrigerate until set. Use currants or chocolate drops for eyes, a piece of licorice for nose.

Marshmallow Hedgehogs

Marshmallow Flowerpots

2136 MARSHMALLOW POPS

125g [4 oz] marshmallows
2 tablespoons oil

45g [1½ oz] popping corn
drinking straws

Place marshmallows in large basin over saucepan of boiling water. Stir until melted. Heat oil in medium-sized saucepan. Add corn, cover tightly with lid, and cook over medium heat, shaking occasionally until popping stops. Remove from heat, stir into melted marshmallows until well coated. With slightly wet hands, form mixture into balls about the size of small apples, place on greaseproof paper. Press a drinking straw into each, and leave until set. Makes about 9.

Join two marshmallows with a toothpick to make the head and body of a snowman. Use licorice to make features and a hat.

2137 FRENCH JELLIES

450ml [¾ pint] cold water
1kg [2 lb] sugar
60g [2 oz] gelatine

1 teaspoon tartaric acid
colouring and flavouring
icing sugar

Place gelatine, water and sugar in saucepan and stir over gentle heat until dissolved. Simmer gently for 20 mins, stirring occasionally. Add tartaric acid. Divide mixture into 3 parts. Leave first white (or colour it yellow with lemon or pineapple colouring). Colour second red and flavour with raspberry essence. Colour third green and flavour with lime. Set jellies in separate tins then press together when set, cut into squares and roll in icing sugar.

2138 HONEYCOMB

3 teaspoons bicarbonate of
  soda

1 cup sugar
4 tablespoons golden syrup

Mix sugar and golden syrup in a large saucepan, simmer on low heat for 7 mins. Remove from heat and quickly add bicarbonate of soda. This will foam up. Quickly pour into a greased 8" square tin. Leave to set.

2139 COCONUT ICE

2 egg whites
2 cups icing sugar
1 cup coconut
½ teaspoon vanilla

250g [8 oz] copha
few drops red food
  colouring

Beat egg whites slightly, mix with sugar, coconut and vanilla. Melt copha over gentle heat and stir into mixture. Press half into ice-cream tray. Colour remainder pink and press firmly on top. When cool, cut into bars.

2140 LOLLIPOPS

Place 1 cup of sugar and ⅔ cup of water in heavy based saucepan over low heat and stir with wooden spoon until sugar dissolves (before coming to the boil). Then bring to the boil (do not stir), reduce heat and simmer until hard-ball stage (P 330) is reached (250°F, 120°C). Add colouring. Arrange rows of small sticks on oiled trays. Drop one teaspoonful of toffee on to pointed end of each stick (hold spoon upright to ensure a good round circle). Allow to set firmly. Best made on day of the party.

2141 APRICOT BALLS

250g [½ lb] dried apricots,
minced or cut finely
2 cups coconut
1 cup icing sugar

⅔ cup sweetened condensed
milk
almond essence to taste
nuts or coconut or icing sugar

Mix all ingredients together and form into small balls or one long roll. Toss in finely chopped minced nuts, desiccated coconut or icing sugar. Set in refrigerator. If making roll, wrap in paper and when set cut in small circles. In hot weather it is advisable to keep them in refrigerator.

2142 FRUITY TRUFFLES

Delicious, loved by children. Any diced fruit or nuts may be used, the more different kinds of fruit the better, e.g. apricots, pears, dates, apples, raisins, sultanas.

1kg [2 lb] mixed diced fruit
250g [8 oz] ground almonds

250g [8 oz] mixed nuts
desiccated coconut

Put fruit and nuts through mincer, add enough ground almonds to make mixture dry enough to handle, but not crumbly. Form into small balls and roll in coconut, or make into sausage shapes. Wrap in polythene and chill before slicing.

2143 BUMBLE BEES

1 cup dates
1½ cups sultanas and raisins
[mixed]
1 cup dried apricots
1 cup dried figs
4 or 5 pieces preserved ginger

1 cup sunflower seeds [or
chopped walnuts]
1 cup desiccated coconut
and extra coconut
400g [14 oz] can sweetened
condensed milk

Chop dates, sultanas, raisins, apricots, figs and ginger and mix thoroughly. Add sunflower seeds and mix in coconut and condensed milk. Form into shapes and roll in extra coconut. Place in slow oven for 20-25 mins (until bottom becomes slightly browned).

Variation: Instead of sunflower seeds and preserved ginger, substitute ½ cup prunes and ½ cup currants.

*Soft-and hard-ball stage—terms used in making candy. Drop a little of the boiling mixture into a saucer of cold water. Soft-ball stage is when the mixture can be gathered into a soft "mass" or ball. When boiled for a longer period the mixture will harden in the cold water. This is the hard-ball stage.

Rainy Day Play

Rainy Day Play

2201 FINGER PAINT

Fills 3 ice-cream containers

12 tablespoons cornflour 1 cup soap flakes
8 cups water 1 teaspoon disinfectant
Edicol dye

Set aside 1 cup water, pour rest into a pan and put on to boil. Meanwhile, measure cornflour into basin and mix in cup of water very gradually, to make a smooth paste. While water is boiling on stove, add cornflour mixture gradually. Add soap flakes and disinfectant while stirring. Place 1 teaspoon of dye (use different colours) into separate containers mixing each with one teaspoon cold water until dissolved. Then add 3 teaspoons hot water, stirring while doing so. Add cornflour and water mixture to container and stir until dye is evenly distributed. Place in refrigerator, use when cool.

2202 PAPIER MACHE PULP

newspaper cold water
paste [R 2204] 2 large basins

Tear newspaper into small pieces and soak overnight. The following day, place layer of soaked newspaper pieces and layer of paste (or amount as required) in second basin, then thoroughly mix with hands to make pliable.

2203 PLAYDOUGH

Mix: then add:
½ cup salt 1 cup water
1 cup flour 1 tablespoon oil
2 tablespoons cream of tartar food colouring

Stir, cook on medium heat 3-5 mins until dough is pliable. Store in ice-cream container or plastic bag.

2204 PASTE

12 tablespoons cornflour   4 cups [approx] boiling water
1 cup cold water   1 tablespoon disinfectant

Blend cornflour and cold water. Add boiling water to make 5 cups. Boil for 1 min until clear, then add disinfectant. If too thick, add a little more water.

2205 BUBBLE PIPE MIXTURE

(For children old enough not to drink it)
¼ cup glycerine   1 tablespoon liquid detergent
½ cup water

*Potter's clay, usually obtainable in large quantities from the art department of a technical college, remains usable indefinitely if kept sealed in a plastic bag or container.

Fathers in the Kitchen

Father's in the Kitchen

2300

Any moron can cook a steak, I kept saying to myself, as I went about my work in the kitchen early Thursday evening. I was not only going to give them someting to get their teeth into, but I was going to serve it to them all by myself.

Elaine Dundy, *"The Dud Avocado"*

At some time or other most families face the situation when mother is not around and more often than not father has to fill the temporary gap made by her absence. When a new baby is expected mother has 9 months to prepare the family and the kitchen for her departure! But the occasion does arise when there is no warning and father finds himself in the kitchen. Of course many fathers are gourmet cooks. If you are, then stop reading, this is not for you! However, if you have difficulty boiling an egg, read on, we have written this with you in mind—perhaps we can help!

Assuming mother's absence is only for a short time, don't be too concerned if you find yourself being more relaxed than she is over what the children eat. It is far better to maintain harmony and let mother cope with the problem later. You can use the excuse "You are only having this because Mummy's in hospital!"

If you are unable to take time off from work, preparation time for meals is all important. Therefore eliminate any dish which isn't simple to prepare and quick to cook. Take a trip to the supermarket and fill your pantry shelves with canned fruit, vegetables, prepared salads, soups, baked beans, spaghetti sauce and anything else which you know your family will eat. Don't forget tomato sauce—most children will eat anything provided it is smothered with tomato sauce! It is worth a close look at the freezer section of the supermarket for vegetables, fish fingers, hamburgers and similar items which take a minimum of effort to cook. If you are going to use mainly processed food items, make sure that the family also has some fresh food such as fruit. For example, you can always add a chopped fresh tomato to a can of baked beans.

Take away food is also a boon in emergency situations, but few of us can afford to make it a habit. Nevertheless, don't forget it is available.

Accept every invitation from friends to eat at their house, and if the next door neighbour offers a casserole, don't be a hero, accept gratefully!

Now here are our suggestions to ensure that you and the family survive with the minimum of fuss!

Breakfast
Fruit juice, canned or bottled or fruit, fresh or canned.
Cereal, with milk and sugar—let the children choose their own favourite to eliminate any disagreements.
Eggs—if the family expects a cooked breakfast, we suggest you start with fried eggs. At least you can see when they are cooked!
Toast—now is maybe the time to buy a pop-up toaster. Children are not keen on charcoal! Have a supply of peanut butter, honey, marmite or vegemite. Most children seem to like one or the other.
Milk.

Lunch:
If you have to pack school lunches, ask each child what filling he prefers in his sandwiches, but keep it simple. Include a piece of fruit, perhaps some cheese and if you want to, a biscuit or cake (bought ones will do). Don't forget most schools have a tuck shop—make use of it!
If the children are not at school, and at weekends and holidays, you may prefer to give them their main meal in the middle of the day and a light tea at night. However if you don't, what about:
Sandwiches: for ideas refer to R 1801 in this book.
Salad: a quickly prepared salad with bought cold meat. Just cut up any fresh salad vegetables or fruit that happen to be around, e.g. tomato, cucumber, carrot, celery, lettuce, apple, banana and perhaps add cheese and sultanas. If the children are old enough, put it all on one large plate and let them help themselves (it saves washing up).
Soup: from the packet or can, simply read the directions.
Biscuits and cheese: perhaps toss in some celery or fruit.
Open a can: things like baked beans, spaghetti, sweetcorn can be regarded as a treat by children.
Scrambled eggs: filling and easy to make, see Peter's Scrambled Egg Variations (R 1707) or if you're feeling creative Special Scrambled Eggs (R 409).

Dinner:
Grilled chops, steak or sausages are probably the easiest. No preparation is involved, but they do need watching while

337

cooking. If cooking for only 1 or 2 people try a one-pan fried dinner. Slice 1-2 potatoes thinly, heat a little oil in a large frying pan and fry potatoes, turning frequently until nearly cooked. Push them to one side and fry steak or chops on both sides until nearly cooked. Push aside and heat halved tomatoes, turning once. By this time meat and potatoes will be cooked and you have only one pan to wash.

Hamburgers: for a change buy 500g (1 lb) minced steak from the butcher and add a packet of hamburger mix from the super-market—just read the packet for directions.

Cold meat: seek the guidance of the man in the delicatessen.

Chicken: buy chicken pieces. It's easier than working out how to cut it up. Brush with a little oil and a squeeze of lemon juice and grill (or they can be cooked in the frying pan)—the children will marvel at Father's cooking ability.

Vegetables: using frozen vegetables eliminates preparation; if using fresh, buy whatever is in season, cut them roughly the same size and fling them all into one saucepan or use a steamer—don't forget you are probably going to have to wash up.

Roast dinner: Don't be put off—it's really easy. Buy a leg of lamb, or a piece of beef. Peel and cut vegetables so that all are about the same size—we suggest you use potatoes, pumpkin, parsnip, carrots and whole onions. Pre-heat the oven to about 350°-400°F (180°-200°C), put meat in pan with 1 tablespoon of fat or oil and place in oven. Add vegetables after about 10 minutes and cook for about 1-1½ hours. Turn the vegetables once. When they are cooked (i.e. soft), the meat will be ready to eat—pork must be well cooked but lamb and beef are nicer if slightly under-cooked. For chicken allow about 25 mins per pound, for beef about 30 mins, for lamb 30-35 mins and pork and veal about 45 mins. If possible remove meat and keep warm on a serving dish for 15 mins before carving. Using tongs or an egg slice, drain vegetables on brown paper or kitchen paper and keep them warm in the oven, leaving the door ajar. To make gravy, pour off all but 1 tablespoon fat from roasting tin and place it on stove. Stir in about one tablespoon of flour and when well mixed, gradually add about one cup of water from vegetables or stock or wine or water. Stir until it boils and thickens. A roast is very nice served with a green vegetable.

Dessert: the very best you can serve is fresh or canned fruit, topped with cream, ice-cream or plain or flavoured yoghurt.

What about just putting a bowl of fresh fruit on the table? For a change have dry biscuits and cheese.

For ideas for fruit salads refer R 1108.
For quick and easy banana dishes refer R 1124.
For yoghurt desserts refer R 1155.

If you browse through this book it is likely you will come across recipes you could make with little or no fuss.
Why not try them and then make a note of the number below for future reference?

When mother is ready to take back the reins you will probably wonder what all the fuss was about, but we suggest you don't keep telling her how easy it was—you may find yourself in the kitchen permanently!

Notes from Mother for Father

Better is a mess of pottage with love, than a fat ox with evil will.
Proverbs (from a 1535 version)

*Freezer Meals for Emergencies
Cut a 2 litre plastic ice-cream container down to a depth of 2", and use as a freezer tray for pre-cooked foods such as sweet and sour pork, chicken and meat stews. Wrap each frozen meal in plastic and store in freezer stacked inside whole lidded containers (about 3 to each container).

Let's Entertain!

Let's Entertain

2400 DINNER PARTIES

Celebration Dinner

The kitchen has developed into the focal point of our home, for the weekend family lunch, the after-school re-fuelling and news of the day, and, I am loath to admit, the pre-dinner drinks, even when we have guests. As I spend some of my most satisfying hours there, it was with a feeling of challenge and pleasure that I compiled the following menu for a 'Celebration Dinner', for NMAA's 10th Birthday.

I have tried to select and adapt recipes that could be served either to guests, or the whole family, but open to alteration to suit the children's special tastes. The courses can be prepared hours, and some even days, ahead, and there is minimum time spent in meal supervision to enable you to enjoy this special dinner with your guests and family.

APPETIZERS

1. Prunes, stoned, then filled with either cashews, cheese or gherkin.
2. Mini-meat balls, simmered in chicken stock for 10 mins, served hot on toothpicks with lemon flavoured mayonnaise dip.
3. Asparagus spears on a bed of whipped cream, flavoured with salt and pepper in pastry boat cases.

2401 PRAWN-FILLED ARTICHOKE HEARTS

Use canned artichokes (1 can holds approx 10). Allow 2 for each person. Drain well, make a depression in each artichoke with a teaspoon, turn upside down and leave to drain on a dish.

Prawns—Beat ¼ pint cream until thick but not stiff, fold in ¼ cup tomato sauce, 1 dessertspoon worcestershire sauce, a squeeze of lemon juice, salt and pepper. Add 1 small can of prawns, well drained, to sauce.

Fill each artichoke with prawn mixture, spoon any extra sauce over, and serve on a lettuce leaf decorated with a sprig of parsley.

Note: Children may prefer a small serve of fruit cocktail, made with pineapple pieces, mandarin and grapefruit segments.

342

2402 CITRUS VEAL

Boned leg of veal or fillet of veal.
Rub meat over with salt, pepper and lemon juice, tie with string if necessary, and place on rack in baking dish. Pre-heat oven to 325°F (160°C). Mix together the juice of 3 oranges and 2 lemons, add ½ cup of water and 2 tablespoons of melted butter. Pour over veal and bake. It is most important that the meat is cooked slowly and basted often with the juices. Cooking time is approx 2½ hours.
The meat and fruit juices will form a thick gravy. Remove meat and keep warm. Add ¼ cup sour cream to gravy, and a small can of champignons, using liquid if the gravy is too thick. Blend well and re-heat for serving.

Suggested vegetables
1. Potatoes, baked in jackets in oven. Split top, add dob of butter or spot of cream and a sprinkle of nutmeg.
2. Broccoli, or sliced buttered zucchini and parsley.

2403 CHOCOLATE ICE-CREAM

2 eggs	*250g [4 oz] dark chocolate*
½ cup castor sugar	*300ml [½ pint] cream*

Whisk together eggs and castor sugar in a pan. Place on gentle heat, stirring for several minutes to cook slightly, remove from the stove. Stir again to prevent bottom of mixture setting. Soften chocolate in a basin over hot water, blend into egg mixture and mix in well.
Whip ½ pint cream in a large basin until thick, add chocolate mixture, blend thoroughly. Pour into wet mould or trays. Freeze. To turn out, dip container in hot water for several seconds, then invert on to serving plate. Ice-cream can be served plain or decorated with whipped cream and trimmed with cherries or grated chocolate. These finishing touches can be completed in the morning and the dish re-frozen until serving.

Hospitality is a wonderful thing. If people really want you, they'll have you even if the cook has just died in the house of small-pox.
F. Scott Fitzgerald

2404 HAZELNUT GATEAU

Make the cake 2-3 days before it is needed and fill 24 hours prior to serving.

Cake:

5 eggs, separated
1 cup castor sugar
125g [4 oz] ground hazelnuts

1 tablespoon fresh bread-
    crumbs
grated rind of 1 lemon

Separate yolks and whites into two basins, beat yolks with sugar until thick and creamy, beat the egg whites stiffly and gently fold the yolks into them. Mix together the hazelnuts, breadcrumbs and lemon rind, sprinkle into the egg mixture, fold through until well blended.

Pour into two buttered and papered springform tins. Bake 15-20 mins in moderate oven, until firm to touch. Loosen sides with knife, leave in tin until cold, turn out and store in air-tight tin with paper between the two cakes.

Filling:

1 cup cream, whipped
1 tablespoon castor sugar
1 tablespoon brandy

1 teaspoon vanilla
1 can loganberries or similar
    berry fruit

Divide the whipped cream into two basins, flavour one with sugar, brandy and vanilla. Drain the berries and keep aside 8 berries for decoration. Mix berries into flavoured cream and fill the cake.

Spread remaining half of the cream over the top and sides of the cake, pipe or spoon swirls of cream to decorate on the top of the cake, and finish with the reserved berries.

The cake will now keep for 24 hours in the refrigerator. Remove one hour before serving.

—Jan Barry

It's in Bolton Hall, and the clock strikes one,
And the roast meat's brown and the boil'd meat's done,
And the barbecu'd sucking-pig's crisped to a turn,
And the pancakes are fried, and beginning to burn;
The fat stubble-goose Swims in gravy and juice,
With the mustard and apple-sauce ready for use;
Fish, flesh, and fowl, and all of the best,
Want nothing but eating—they're all ready drest,
But where is the Host, and where is the Guest?
R. H. Barham, The Lay of St. Cuthbert. 1840

"A Day Before" Dinner Party

In selecting this menu I have chosen recipes which can be prepared well ahead of time, as I can then cope with any emergency on the day of the dinner party and really enjoy the evening instead of being exhausted after a last minute panic.
Many of our friends have conventional tastes so I usually stick to fairly simple ingredients but try to prepare and serve them in an interesting way. Dessert seems to be the highlight of many of our dinner parties and so I often serve a choice of two.

APPETIZERS

Devilled Party Nibbles (R 111).
Pumpernickel or rye bread with smoked oysters or smoked salmon or creamed cheese and sliced gherkin.
Chunks of pineapple and cheese and halved glace cherries on toothpicks, stuck into a grapefruit. (Children will enjoy making these.)

2405 GRAPES IN ASPIC

Grapes in Aspic

500g [1 lb] grapes
2 tablespoons gelatine
4 tablespoons sugar
1¼ cups water

⅓ cup lemon juice
2 tablespoons finely chopped mint
little green colouring

Wash grapes well, remove skins and large pips. Dissolve gelatine and sugar in water, add lemon juice, and green colouring. Allow to cool. When on the point of setting, add grapes and mint and pour into small individual glasses or dishes. Serve with hot herb bread.

2406 GARLIC HERB BREAD

1 French stick
90g [3 oz] butter, softened
1 clove garlic, crushed with
    ½ teaspoon salt

1-2 tablespoons chopped fresh herbs, e.g. parsley, oregano, thyme, chives or 1 teaspoon dried herbs

Mix butter, garlic crushed with salt, and herbs. Slice French stick and spread butter on each slice. Reassemble loaf, wrap in foil and bake in moderate oven for 15 mins.
The garlic butter can be made the day before using, or alternatively the whole loaf can be prepared, wrapped in foil and frozen until required.

2407 VEAL AND CHEESE ROLLS

1.5kg [3 lb] thin veal slices
250g [½ lb] bacon, chopped
125g [4 oz] tasty cheese, grated
1 clove garlic, crushed

2 tablespoons flour
2 cups chicken stock
¼ cup sherry or 1 tablespoon lemon juice
salt and pepper

Pound veal as thinly as possible. Cut into pieces about 2" x 4". In a large pan fry bacon gently until crisp. Remove and drain well. Sprinkle bacon and cheese over veal pieces, roll up neatly and tie with firm cotton or string. Heat bacon fat and add veal rolls and garlic. When rolls are brown on all sides place in casserole dish. Blend flour with remaining bacon fat. add stock and stir until smooth and thick. Add sherry, salt and pepper and pour over rolls. Cover and bake at 325°F (160°C) for 1½-2 hours. This can be prepared in advance and gently reheated when required. Serve with baby carrots tossed in butter and parsley, broccoli, or mixed butter and green beans and scalloped potatoes or buttered rice.
A French salad (R 914) also makes a tasty accompaniment.

2408 CHOCOLATE PEPPERMINT PIE
Pie Shell

220g [7 oz] chocolate biscuits, crushed

90g [3 oz] butter, melted

Combine and press into base and sides of buttered 8" spring-form tin. Refrigerate while preparing filling.

Filling

250g [8 oz] white marshmallows
½ cup top of milk
2 tablespoons creme de menthe
1 tablespoon brandy

300ml [½ pint] cream, lightly whipped
2 egg whites, stiffly beaten
extra cream and peppermint crisps for decoration

Melt marshmallows and top of milk over very low heat, stirring constantly until marshmallows have melted. Cool, then add creme de menthe and brandy. Fold lightly whipped cream and beaten egg whites and put in pie shell. Decorate with extra cream and grated peppermint crisps or chocolate.

2409 APRICOT ALMOND SOUFFLE

250g [8 oz] dried apricots,
    soaked overnight in water
    to cover
2 lemons
3 teaspoons gelatine
2 eggs, separated
1 cup sugar
1 large can [1¾ cups approx]
    evaporated milk, chilled

1 teaspoon vanilla
¼ teaspoon almond essence
½ cup finely chopped
    almonds [optional]
whole almonds and whipped
    cream for garnishing

If desired, prepare a 2 pint souffle bowl by placing a 3" strip of wetted greaseproof paper around the top and fix firmly with string.
Put combined apricots and water, juice of two lemons and rind of one in saucepan, cover and cook until soft, about 5-10 mins. Drain and reserve ½ cup syrup. Dissolve gelatine in this. Remove lemon rind and puree apricots in blender. Beat in egg yolks and sugar. Allow to cool slightly then stir in dissolved gelatine. Beat evaporated milk until stiff, add vanilla and almond essence and then apricot mixture. Beat egg whites stiffly and fold in. Pour into prepared souffle case or into individual dishes. Chill until set. Remove paper carefully and press finely chopped almonds into side. Decorate top with whipped cream and whole almonds.

Well, there is one sin for which a lot of cooks and hostesses are some day going to have to atone,
Which is that they can't bear to cook anything and leave it alone.
                                        Ogden Nash, Parsley for Vice-President

Russian Dinner Party

My husband and I enjoy entertaining with an international theme and as we met in Russia we frequently choose to cook Russian food for a dinner party.

This particular menu is very good for midwinter entertaining when appetites are keen. The food is hearty, filling and warming.

Russian folk music provides background as we welcome our guests into the warm and cosy lounge for a pre-dinner drink of—what else—vodka! Preferably neat but for the faint hearted perhaps diluted with orange juice or tomato juice.

With the drinks I serve Blini—tiny yeast pancakes, which I have made earlier and reheated in a covered dish.

Besides the Blini we have Pirozhki—small turnover pastries—the filling can be meat, chicken or fish (these are also made ahead and reheated). And finally smoked salmon slices—not quite so extravagent if you buy salmon "lax" (the end bits) which can be made into dainty little rolls secured with a toothpick.

We start our meal with soup—a hearty Russian peasant soup called Rassolnik, made with kidneys and dill cucumbers, served with sour cream and accompanied by dark pumpernickel or sour rye bread.

Our main course is Hussars Roast—topside with stuffing of mushroom, bacon and onions braised in wine, which has been simmering all afternoon. This is served with Buckwheat Kasha which can be cooked ahead and reheated, and zucchini sauteed in butter. The cooking time for the zucchini is so brief that I do it while I am placing the meat and buckwheat in their serving dishes. As an alternative to the vegetables suggested here, I sometimes serve foil baked potatoes with a sour cream and chive topping (R 2418) and any green vegetables in season. Select a good robust red wine to accompany the main course. Dessert is Chestnut Duvshenka—uniquely different and delicious despite its simplicity—light, yet rich enough in the Russian tradition to provide a fitting climax to the meal. Champagne is a good accompaniment to any dessert.

Then we have lots of fresh brewed coffee with liqueurs of our choice or more vodka, so that guests can linger around the table for as long as they wish, and finally roll home replete in the early hours of the morning.

2410 BLINI (tiny yeast pancakes)

30g [1 oz] compressed yeast
1 teaspoon sugar
¼ cup warm water
1½ cups lukewarm milk
1 teaspoon salt
3 eggs, separated

3 cups flour, sifted
6 tablespoons melted butter
  or margarine
melted butter, caviar and sour
  cream for serving

Cream yeast and sugar and add ¼ cup warm water. Add milk, salt, beaten egg yolks and 1½ cups flour. Mix well, cover and stand in warm place for 1 hour. Add the melted butter or margarine and remaining flour. Mix well and allow to stand again for 1 hour. Fold in the stiffly beaten egg whites and bake on a hot griddle. If you allow the batter to drop from the point of the spoon the blini will be perfectly round. Make them about 2" in diameter. Cover the cooked blini with a cloth and reheat in a covered dish just before serving. This quantity, used as appetizers, would serve 10-15 people.

To serve, prepare small bowls of melted butter, caviar and sour cream. Each person pours a teaspoonful of the melted butter on his blini, then a spoonful of caviar and tops the lot off with sour cream.

2411 PIROZHKI (sour cream pastries with filling)

Pastry

½ cup butter
½ cup sour cream
2 eggs

½ teaspoon salt
470g [15 oz] flour
1 egg for glaze

Filling

Mix together:
250g [8 oz] cooked, finely
  minced meat or chicken or
  fish
1 small onion, finely chopped

salt and pepper
grated nutmeg
1 tablespoon chopped parsley

Cream together butter, sour cream, eggs and salt. Add flour and knead for 5 mins to a workable dough. Roll out 1/8" thick. Cut into squares or rounds and put 1 teaspoon of filling on to each portion. Moisten edges and fold over to seal. If preferred, use thinner circles of pastry. Place filling on one and cover with another. Crimp edges decoratively. Brush tops with beaten egg and bake for 15 minutes at 375°F (190°C) until golden brown. Serve hot. Can be made earlier and reheated.

2412 RASSOLNIK (kidney and dill cucumber soup)

375g [12 oz] ox kidney
7½ cups beef stock
250g [8 oz] potatoes, peeled
    and diced
1 large onion, finely chopped
1 carrot, cut in julienne strips

2 dill cucumbers, cut in strips
1 bay leaf
salt and pepper
sour cream
parsley to garnish

Clean kidney, remove skin and dice. Cook in stock 30 mins, then add vegetables and bay leaf and simmer 40 mins. Add salt and pepper. Serve with 1 tablespoon sour cream in each plate and garnish with parsley.

2413 HUSSARS ROAST

1.5kg [3 lb] topside,
    cut in an oblong piece
2 onions
125g [4 oz] mushrooms
60g [2 oz] lean bacon

nutmeg, salt and pepper
1 cup breadcrumbs
150ml [¼ pint] cream
yolk of 1 egg
2 cups [approx] stock and wine

Chop onions, mushrooms, and bacon and cook until soft (add a little oil if bacon is very lean). Soak the breadcrumbs with the nutmeg, salt and pepper in the cream.
To prepare the meat: cut in slices ¼" thick to within ½" of the base of the meat so that the slices are like the pages of a book. Add the breadcrumbs to the bacon, mushrooms and onion mixture. Cook for a few minutes, mixing well. Cool and add the beaten egg yolk. Place stuffing between slices of meat. Press together gently and tie with string (not too tightly or stuffing will be forced out as it swells).
Braise gently for 3-4 hours in a heavy closed pan in a little well seasoned stock to which you have added dry wine or sherry. Serve with the sauce in which it has cooked.
To serve, cut right through the base of the meat every second or third slice.

*Use a melon-ball cutter to remove olives and cherries from bottles and to make party butter balls.

414 KASHA (buckweat with mushrooms and onions)

2 stock cubes
2-3 cups boiling water
185g [6 oz] buckwheat [obtainable from larger supermarkets]
1 egg, beaten

1 teaspoon salt
125g [4 oz] butter
250g [8 oz] onions, finely chopped
250g [8 oz] fresh mushrooms, finely chopped

Add stock cubes to boiling water. Toss the buckwheat in the beaten egg until the grains are well coated. Toss in a large frying pan (preferably non-stick) over medium heat until lightly toasted and dry. Do not allow to burn. Add salt, 45g (1½ oz) butter and 2 cups of hot stock. Stir thoroughly, cover the pan tightly and simmer for about 20 mins, stirring occasionally. If the Kasha is not tender, and seems dry, add additional stock and cook for 10 minutes more. The water should be absorbed and the buckwheat grains separate and fluffy. Remove from heat and allow to stand uncovered for 10 minutes.
Melt 45g (1½ oz) butter in a frying pan, add onions and fry 3-4 minutes until soft. Add onions to Kasha.
Melt remaining 30g (1 oz) butter and saute the finely chopped mushrooms for 2-3 mins. Cook briskly over high heat to evaporate liquid and stir into Kasha. Check seasoning.
Reheat covered in a slow oven 200°-250°F (100°-120°C) for 20 mins.

415 CHESTNUT DUVSHENKA

360g [12 oz] can sweetened chestnut puree
150ml [¼ pint] cream, whipped
2 tablespoons rum

60g [2 oz] toasted slivered almonds
1 tablespoon chopped, preserved ginger

Mix the almonds, ginger, rum and chestnut puree very well. Fold in whipped cream and chill thoroughly.

—Myra Sawyer

Let's Entertain — in a hurry

When we have friends or acquaintances to dinner at our home, the invitation is often a last minute one, and thus preparation time is all important to me.

Although I enjoy cooking and entertaining, I prefer to avoid, except for very special occasions, dishes which are time consuming to prepare. I also avoid dishes which need last minute attention, as when my guests arrive I like to be able to enjoy their company, rather than keep disappearing into the kitchen!

APPETIZERS
Green and black olives
Polish sausage, sliced
Nuts, assorted, or cashew or macadamia
Dill cucumber, sliced
Smoked mackerel (available from most delicatessens)—leave whole and serve with dry or salted biscuits. The skin is peeled back as each guest serves himself.
These appetizers take little preparation.

2416 FISH PATE

1 medium [210g] can tuna or salmon
2 eggs, hard boiled
60g [2 oz] softened butter
1 teaspoon minced onion
salt and pepper
cream [optional]

1 tablespoon fresh mixed herbs [parsley, chives, tarragon]
1 lemon, quartered
3 sprigs parsley
1 small [120g] can shrimps
hot toast

Drain tuna, discarding oil, and place with eggs, butter, onion, salt and pepper in blender. Blend thoroughly, adding a little cream if mixture is very thick. Finely chop herbs and stir through mixture. Heap on to serving dish and garnish with shrimps and parsley. Serve with lemon and plenty of thin, hot toast.

417 BEEF CASSEROLE

1.5kg [3 lb] bladebone steak
1 packet mushroom soup
2 teaspoons ground mixed
  spice
½ teaspoon curry powder
2 onions, chopped
1 tablespoon tomato sauce

1 tablespoon worcestershire
  sauce
2 tablespoons vinegar
1 cup dry sherry
14 prunes, stoned
14-20 pineapple pieces, fresh
  or canned

Dice meat into 2" pieces. Combine soup, spice and curry. Roll meat in it, coating well. Place meat and onions in casserole, add sauces, vinegar and sherry. Cover and cook in moderate oven for about 2 hours. Add pineapple and prunes during last hour of cooking. Add more liquid if necessary to prevent drying out.

418 *Accompaniments*

1. OVEN BAKED POTATOES WITH SOUR CREAM SAUCE
Select medium to large potatoes. Scrub skins well. Cut aluminium foil to wrap around each potato. Brush foil with a little cooking oil to prevent sticking. Dust potatoes with salt and pepper. Seal them well in foil and bake in moderate oven 1 hour—longer if potatoes are large. Serve in foil with a bowl of sour cream sauce.
Sauce: 1 cup thick sour cream mixed with 3 tablespoons finely chopped chives, salt and pepper.

2. TOMATO SALAD
4-6 tomatoes, peeled
Slice thickly, arrange in bowl and sprinkle with salt, freshly ground black pepper and a little basil.

3. FRENCH SALAD
Any variety of lettuce, washed, well dried and torn into pieces. Place in salad bowl. Just before serving, pour over French Dressing (R 1004) and toss.

2419 CITRUS CREAM

4 oranges
2 lemons
½ cup boiling water
4 egg yolks
For decoration:
1 cup whipping cream
¾ cup castor sugar
¼ teaspoon vanilla

1 cup castor sugar
3 teaspoons gelatine
¼ cup cold water
2 cups whipping cream

1 can [300g] mandarin
  segments

Grate the rind from 2 oranges and 1 lemon and soak in boiling water for 15 mins. Beat yolks with sugar until mixture is light and creamy. Add the juice of 4 oranges and 2 lemons and mix well. Then add rind and water in which it has soaked. Place mixture into double saucepan and cook over hot water, stirring constantly until custard is thick. Cool. Soak gelatine in cold water for 5 mins then dissolve over hot water. Add gelatine to custard and blend well. Whip 2 cups cream and fold gently in to custard mixture. Place in a ring mould and chill in refrigerator 2 hours. Whip 1 cup cream with sugar and vanilla. Drain mandarin segments well. Unmould dessert on to plate and fill centre with whipped cream and decorate with mandarin segments.

2420 GLAMOROUS FRUIT SALAD

If I am really short of time, I serve this fruit salad which takes almost no preparation, and is delicious. I always keep a few dried apricots covered with brandy in the refrigerator for this purpose, and I ensure I have one or two cans of "exotic" fruit in the pantry.

Vary the fruit according to what you like and have available. The following is our favourite:

   dried apricots soaked in brandy and left whole
   peaches, sliced, preserved or canned
   paw paw, chunks, fresh or canned
   lychees (available in cans)
   pineapple chunks (fresh or canned)
   strawberries, raspberries or loganberries, fresh, frozen or
     canned
   cherries, stoned, fresh or canned
   pears, cut into large pieces, fresh or canned
   Chinese gooseberries, sliced

Drain fruit and reserve a small quantity of the juice to pour over the top of the mixture. Be careful not to break up fruit as it is very soft. Serve with masses of whipped cream.

354

CHEESEBOARD

I like to serve a variety of cheeses on a wooden platter surrounded by a choice of dry biscuits, and decorated with celery curls and red radishes. I usually include a blue cheese such as Danish castello, a milder one such as gouda or emmentaler, a smoked type and either grape seed, walnut or a very good ripe camembert.

I find my guests usually linger over the dining table so I serve them there with the cheese and Irish coffee.

2421 IRISH COFFEE

May be served in Irish coffee glasses, heat proof glasses, or large coffee cups.

For each serve:

30ml [1 oz] Irish whisky—
    Australian can be used if
    necessary
1 teaspoon raw sugar

hot, black coffee—percolated
    is nice
1 tablespoon whipped or
    thick cream

Percolate coffee and keep hot. Warm glasses. Place sugar and whisky in glasses and fill with coffee to within ½ inch of top. Stir well to dissolve sugar, then float cream on top. To ensure the drink is very hot I sometimes make a syrup of the sugar and pour it hot into the glasses before the whisky.

—Judith Laird

Summer Entertaining

This can be an easier and more interesting time of the year to invite friends and family to your home. The warm weather draws you outside and the barbecue or pool gives you an excuse to entertain informally.

Here is a menu which can be prepared in advance, using fruits, vegetables, and fish all available over the summer period. Have fun!

2422 MUSHROOMS A LA GRECQUE

500g [1 lb] button mush-
   rooms, well washed but
   not skinned and with
   stems intact
4 tablespoons olive oil
90g [3 oz] white onions
60g [2 oz] carrots, roughly
   chopped
thyme, bay leaf and stem
   of parsley

2 teaspoons coriander
salt and pepper
1 teaspoon lemon juice
1 teaspoon tomato paste
¾ cup white wine
¾ cup water
lettuce leaves

In blender place oil, onions, carrots, herbs, spice, seasoning, lemon juice and tomato paste. Combine wine and water in jug and pour enough fluid into blender to just cover the contents. Blend for 20 seconds until the raw vegetables are of an even texture. Add rest of fluid and transfer to a saucepan. Bring to boil and simmer for 5 mins. Add mushrooms and simmer for 8 mins. Remove mushrooms and allow mixture to simmer a further 5-10 mins until it has been reduced by half.

When cold, arrange mushrooms on lettuce leaf and pour dressing over them.

Variation: Instead of mushrooms, try leeks, artichokes or zucchini.

Do not despise cook books and recipes, for whether it be music, painting or cooking, there is much to be learned from the experienced masters.
                              Royal Hostess Cookbook, South Africa

2423 CRAYFISH CREOLE

1.5kg [3 lb] crayfish or
    Moreton Bay crab, cooked
60g [2 oz] butter
1 tablespoon brandy
2 tablespoons flour

150ml [¼ pint] crayfish stock
¼ teaspoon paprika
½ teaspoon curry powder
salt and pepper
150ml [¼ pint] cream

Remove flesh from fish by carefully cutting body and tail in half. Remove legs and extra flesh from them. Put flesh to one side. To make crayfish stock, place shell and legs gently in saucepan, barely cover with water. Bring to boil and simmer for 5-6 mins. Carefully reserve and drain shells in which to serve crayfish.

Melt 30g (1 oz) butter in frypan and warm through the large pieces of seafood first. Remove. Add further 30g (1 oz) butter to pan and warm smaller pieces. Remove. Remove pan from stove, add flour to butter left in pan and blend well, scraping brown pieces from base. Blend in stock, bring to boil and allow to simmer 5 mins. While boiling add cream and stir until well incorporated. Simmer further 3 mins, then add curry powder, paprika, salt and pepper. Warm brandy, ignite and add to sauce. Before serving heat sauce, add crayfish and reheat. Serve in crayfish shells with rice and tossed green salad (R 914).

2424 "GIANT STRAWBERRIES"

Can be prepared the day before.

4 packham pears
185g [6 oz] sugar
1½ cups water
cinnamon stick tied in muslin
1 punnet [250g] strawberries
    [reserve a few to decorate]

1 tablespoon lemon juice
slivered toasted almonds
150ml [¼ pint] whipped,
    sweetened cream

In a shallow, wide pan combine sugar, water and cinnamon stick, bring to boil and simmer 4-5 mins. Peel, halve and core pears and place round side down in syrup. Simmer for 4 mins then turn to other side and simmer for 2 mins. Remove pears with slotted spoon and drain. Reduce syrup by boiling quickly. In blender, place washed and hulled strawberries and lemon juice and blend for 15 seconds. Add the strawberry puree to syrup and boil for 1 min. Allow to cool.

Arrange pears attractively on round plate and pour strawberry syrup over pears. Decorate with almonds and a few whole strawberries and serve with cream. Keep any extra syrup for serving over vanilla ice-cream on another occasion.

—Jenny Jordan

Cooking Terms

Al dente—with a little "bite" left in it. The term is generally used for cooking pasta or rice.

Aspic—a savoury jelly.

Bake blind—to cook a pastry case without a filling. The pastry shell is lined with waxed paper and filled with dried beans or rice to prevent the pastry rising. Baking time is usually 15 mins.

Baste—to keep food moist while baking or roasting by spooning over the liquid in which it is being cooked.

Blanch—to pour boiling water over meat or vegetables to remove strong flavours and tenderise.

Bouquet garni—a bunch of mixed herbs used to give flavour to soups, sauces or casseroles. The most usual combination is parsley, bay leaves and thyme. These are tied up in a small muslin bag for easy removal after cooking. They can be bought ready-made.

Dice—to cut into small cubes.

Dredge—to sprinkle lightly.

Flour—in this book means plain flour unless specified S.R.

Garnish—to decorate or add flavour by adding chopped or sliced ingredients.

Glaze—to brush or coat the surface of the food with some preparation, e.g. egg, milk, sugar, syrup or a gelatine mixture.

Julienne—thin matchstick strips of meat, fish or vegetables.

Marinate—to soak meat, fish or vegetables in liquid for a period of time to season or tenderise.

Parboil—to partly boil—for about half the length of time normally required for cooking.

Poach—to cook gently in liquid below boiling point.

Puree—to make into a smooth pulp or liquid by forcing through a fine sieve or blending in a blender.

Roux—a mixture of melted butter and flour cooked together.

Saute—fry lightly and quickly in a small amount of hot butter or oil.

Scald—to heat a liquid to just under boiling point.

Seasoned flour—flour mixed with salt and pepper in the proportion of 1 level teaspoon of salt and a pinch of pepper to 30g (1 oz) of flour.

Setting point—1. For jams and preserves—to boil until enough liquid has evaporated to give you a mixture of fruit liquid and sugar which will set when cold.

2. For gelatine mixtures—when slight thickening of the liquid occurs.

To the following contributors, our thanks.

Jenny Ainsworth
Phillipa Andrew
Helen Bagley
Rosemary Balmford
Peter Balmford
Brenda Barber
Karen Barrett
Jill Barnett
Jan Barry
Beverley Batt
Elaine Beddie
Beth Berridge
Kay Berry
Heather Borland
Vivianne Brain
Julia Breen
Vivienne Brennan
Terry Bruce
Nan Buchanan
Elizabeth Burman
Marita Bushell
Georgina Cattley
Rae Carter
N. Casey
Sandra Champion
L. Christie
Marilyn Cobain
Marlene Corby
Jan Culka
Sarie Culka
Ariadna Culpan
Joyce Culpan
Ursula Cummins
Lesley Anne Curtis
Maria Cutts
Rosemary Darby
Roberta Davies
Maree Delbridge
M. Denize
Roslyn Devine
Jillian Drury
Janice Dudley
Aileen Dunipace
Trisha Edwards
W. Ellis
Dorothy Fairbrother
Paquita Farmer
Karys Fearon
Noelene Forbes
Marilyn Frood
Margaret George
Judy Gifford

Jennifer Gold
Margaret Graetz
Elizabeth Grant
Josie Gregory
Barbara Griffiths
Kay Hall
Carol Hancock
Anne Hapke
Sue Heidel
Carole Hester
Jasmine Hewson
Jan Hunter
J. Hyden
Dorothy Hyslop
Beryl Jackson
Dorothy James
Gabrielle Jarvis
Lauris Jephcott
Eril Jolly
Lois Jones
Loris Jones
Muriel Jones
Jenny Jordan
Margaret Justice
Cheryl Kemp
Carolyn Kerr
A. Kriegler
Margaret Kinton
Carolyn Klug
Ann Lacey
Judith Laird
Marion Latham
Heather Leverington
Leslie Anne Lewis
Judith Lumb
Betty Lynch
Anne McDonald
Judith McDonald
Margaret McCredie
Hilary McKelvie
Kerril Maloney
Beverley Martin
Diana Martin
Margaret Mason
Moya Masters
Jennie Meares
Rosemary Mitchelhill
Denise Needle
Helen Nelson
Mary Nichols
Joan North
Marie Oakes

Margaret O'Callaghan
Carolyn Ockley
Brenda O'Donnell
Val O'Regan
Jenny Pandey
Mary Paton
Pam Petschack
Virginia Phillips
Dorothy Potter
Fay Presland
Nancy Price
Beverley Rae
Margaret Rae
Mary Raftery
Mazi Rani
Beryl Rasmussen
Lyn Rasmussen
Val Rentsch
Chris Roberts
Helen Roberts
Jan Roberts
Margaret Rolfe
Myra Sawyer
Rosemary Scarborough
Di Schmied
Constance Schofield
Ellen Scott
Lesley Singleton
Glenda Smith
Jan Smith
Marjory Spicer
Mary Stanley
Christine Sturrock
Bridget Sutherland
Pam Taylor
Bessie Thompson
Anthea Tonkin
F. L. Van Laar
Audrey Villiers
Leigh Wigglesworth

360

Introducing NMAA

In 1963, when NMAA's founder Mary Paton was breastfeeding her first baby, she found little information or encouragement to help the nursing mother. Early the next year she invited five other young mothers to a meeting at her home in Melbourne. From that meeting evolved the idea and aims of the Nursing Mothers' Association of Australia, namely to help, encourage, educate and support mothers who wish to breastfeed their babies, thus creating a basis for skilled and loving mothering and close, happy family relationships.

Branches throughout Australia

Since then, NMAA has spread Australia-wide. Its National Headquarters is at 5 Glendale St., Nunawading, Vic. 3131 (telephone 878 3304) and there are Local Groups in every State—consult telephone directory for addresses.
By February 1984, more than 70,000 members had been enrolled.

Work of NMAA Counsellors

Group Leaders and Counsellors of the Association are mothers who have breastfed their babies and have undergone a period of training before qualifying. All NMAA Counsellors work in a voluntary capacity and are bound by a Code of Ethics. Their help and encouragement is only offered when sought and suggestions given are on a mother-to-mother basis. If a mother has a medical problem, she is referred to her doctor or Infant Welfare Sister.

Advisers

The Association is supported by a distinguished panel of advisers who include general and specialist medical practitioners, nutritionists and members of the legal profession.

SOME OF NMAA'S SERVICES

Discussion Groups—conducted by Group Leaders—are held regularly in members' homes. These particularly help expectant and new mothers by providing the confidence and moral support which is so important to the nursing relationship. Topics include many aspects of breastfeeding, child care and family management.
Mothers are encouraged to contribute to the discussion and to bring forward their problems. Besides the sharing of ideas and experiences, discussion groups also help to overcome the

feelings of isolation and loneliness which many new mothers have. All mothers are welcome at meetings—it is not necessary to be a member to go along.

Counselling by telephone and letter is always available—both to members and non-members. Each month, the Association receives thousands of requests for information and help with breastfeeding problems.

Literature—booklets and leaflets are produced on many aspects of breastfeeding and child care. All material is approved by the appropriate members of NMAA's advisory panel before publication.

Newsletter—Members receive issues of the NMAA Newsletter regularly which contains articles on breastfeeding and related subjects, personal experience letters, research information, meeting notices, book reviews, hints, recipes and other items of interest to mothers.

Library books on breastfeeding and child care may be borrowed from local Groups. Films and slides on breastfeeding are available for hire from National Headquarters.

NMAA's **Information Service** collects and files the latest information on breastfeeding from world-wide sources. This material is available on request to interested persons.

Community Education—Specially trained members of the Association give ante and post natal talks to mothers at hospitals and at childbirth education classes. With the approval of State Education Departments, they take part in education-for-living programmes from pre-school to tertiary level.

Counsellors speak regularly to community groups such as Young Wives, Mothers' Clubs, kindergarten committees, etc. The Association also receives numerous requests to speak to such professional groups as medical students, obstetrical physiotherapists, trainee midwives, mothercraft nurses, trainee dietitians and home economists.

Index

Please note that numbers in this index refer to recipe numbers, not to page numbers.

365

panettone, 1622

Ricotta cheese and spinach filling, ravioli
  with, 503
   pancakes, 1205
   pie filling, 1102
Rigatoni with meat sauce, 508
Rieska, 1609
Roast dinner, page 338
   duck with cherry sauce, 725
   Hussars, 2413
   loin of lamb, 649
   seasoned flaps, 648
Rock cakes, 1408
Rockmelon jam, 1902
Rolled oat cookies, 1512
Rolls, asparagus ham, 428
   beef, 614, 615
   cabbage, 699L
   cloverleaf, 1627
   fancy, 1627
   French, 1604
   onion, 1612
   parkerhouse, 1627
   sesame and poppy seed, 1627
   veal and cheese, 2407
Rolypoly, jam, 1148
Rose hip syrup, 2005
Royal icing, 1442
Rum Baba, 1618
   balls, 1538
   cream sauce, 1027
   souffle, 1159
   truffles, 1539
Rummy pears, 1139
Russian pashka, 1164
Rye biscuits, 1544
   bread, sour, 1608

Sage and onion stuffing, 1040
Sago plum pudding, 1195
Salad yacht, 2105
SALADS, 900
   avocado cheese salad, 921
   bacon ratatouille, 434
   bean salad, 902
   carrot balls, 904
      raisin surprise, 905
      rice casserole, 433
   Chinese vegetables, 912
   coleslaw, 908
   cucumber and green pepper salad, 906
      in sour cream, 907
   curried rice salad, 924
   French salad, 914, 2418
   fruit cheese salad for one, 922
   grapes in aspic, 2406
   hot potato salad, 816
   jellied beetroot, 903
   macaroni salad, 925
   marinated vegetable salad, 913
   mushrooms a la Grecque, 2422

Neiman Marcus salad, 917
   peach or pear appetiser, 919
   peach salad, 918
   piquant fruit cream salad, 920
   potato salad, 909
   ratatouille, 826
   rice salad, 923
   salad ideas, 901
   sauerkraut salad, 910
   spinach salad, 916
   tomato salad, 2418
   tomatoes in mint jelly, 911
   tossed salad almondine, 915
Salami "pizzas", 108
Salmon bake, 322
   mousse, 330
   stuffed avocados or aubergine, 321
   whiting fillets with, 315
Sandwich fillings, 1801-1804
"Sandwiches", ham, 107
Sandwiches, open, 402
   traffic light, 2104
Sangria, 2014
Satay, beef, 613
SAUCES, Savoury, 1000; see also Dressings
   barbecue, 675
   barbecue dip, 117
   bechamel, 1018
   bernaise, 1016
   bolognese, 507
   caper, 1010
   cheese, 1010
   cheese, poached eggs in, 408
   cheese, tomatoes in, 431
   cherry, 725
   chocolate wine, 623
   curry, 675
   fish, 1010
   green almond, 511
   hollandaise, 1017
   horseradish, 1015
   lemon, 711
   marinara, 513
   mint, 1011
   mushroom, 1010
   mushroom/anchovy, 512
   mushroom and tomato, 656
   mustard, 730, 1010
   orange, 727
   oyster, 619
   parsley, 1010
   pesta, 509
   plum, 1917
   prawn, 308
   satay, 613
   seafood, 1014
   spicy, 681, 710
   sour cream, 1008, 2418
   soya, lamb in, 645
   sweet and sour, 1012
   tartare, 1009

steak, 621
veal, 665
Swedish limpa bread, 1610
Sweet and sour chicken, 718
  gravy, pot roast with, 626
  sauce, 1012
  tuna, 326
  veal, 664
Sweet apple tart, 1111
Sweetcorn and ham flan, 419
  casserole, 809
  fritters, 412
Sweet potatoes, 821, 822
Sweet short crust pastry, 1303, 1304
Swiss style beef and rice, 604
  chicken breasts, 713
Syllabub, lemon, 1130
Syrup, rosehip, 2005

Tagliarini, 699E
Tahitian fish, 331
Tart; *see also* Flan and Pie
  apple crumb, 1118
  Dutch, 1412
  egg and bacon, 416
  mince, 1111
  onion, 418
  orange, 1132
  sweet apple, 1111
Tartare sauce, 1009
Tartlets, egg and bacon, 416
Tarts, fruit, 1102
  jam, 2125
Teacake, apple, 1411
Tea ring, Continental, 1625
Thousand Island dressing, 1001
Tipsy cake, 1150
Toad in the hole, 674
Toddy sauce, hot, 1028
Toffee apples, 2133
  creamy, 2134
Tomato and frankfurt casserole, 673
  and mushroom sauce, 656
  and sour cream sauce, 510
  and tuna bisque, 221
  baskets, 1054
  chutney, 1918
  flowers, 1053
  macaroni cheese, 424
  omelette, 407
  rarebit, 405
  salad, 2418
  sauce, 1013, 1916
    beef in, 606
    octopus in, 303
    pork chops with, 651
  soup, 208
Tomatoes and mushrooms, kidneys with, 679
  and zucchini, 828
  beef and mushroom, 611

in cheese sauce, 431
in mint jelly, 911
provencale, 825
Tongue, 600
  braised, 680
  cold, 683
  in soya sauce, 682
  in spicy sauce, 681
Toppings for fruit, 1103, 1105
Tossed salad almondine, 915
Traffic light sandwiches, 2104
Trifle, 1151
Tripe Catalane, 688
Tropical dip, 102
  freeze, 1174
Trout in cream, 301
Truffles, fruity, 2142
  rum, 1539
Tuna and cashews, 327
  and pineapple, 325
  and tomato bisque, 221
  cauliflower cheese, 328
  curried, 329
  sweet and sour, 326
Turkish style carrots, 807

Upside-down cake, pineapple, 1414

VEAL, 600
  veal and cheese rolls, 2407
    and ham, 667
    and mushrooms, 662
    bacon and pineapple, 661
    bake, 668
    citrus, 2402
    Cordon Bleu, 670
    paprika, 666
    supreme, 665
    sweet and sour, 664
    with capers, 663
    with herbs and cream, 669
  Wiener Schnitzel, 671

Vegetable cups, 1049
  salad, marinated, 913
  soup, cream of, 207
  whip, 1806
VEGETABLES, 800
  bacon ratatouille, 434
  barbecued beans, 432
  beetroot in hot relish, 802
  broccoli savoury, 430
  cabbage baked with sour cream, 803
  candied carrots, 805
  candied sweet potatoes, 821
  carried away spinach or sprouts, 824
  carrots delicious, 806
    rice casserole, 433
    Turkish style, 807
  celery spears almondine, 808